HELL HATH NO FURY

True Profiles of Women at War from Antiquity to Iraq

Rosalind Miles and Robin Cross

Three Rivers Press
New York

This book is for our mothers,
Lucy Simpson and Betty Cross,
who lived through two world wars

Library of Congress Cataloging-in-Publication Data

Miles, Rosalind.
Hell hath no fury : true stories of women at war from antiquity to Iraq /
by Rosalind Miles and Robin Cross. —1st ed.
Includes bibliographical references and index.
1. Women and war—History. 2. Women in war—History. I. Cross, Robin.
II. Title.
JZ6405.W66M55 2008
355.0082—dc22   ③ Soldiers – Women
2007027905

ISBN 978-0-307-34637-7

Printed in the United States of America

Design by Philip Mazzone

10 9 8 7 6 5 4 3 2 1

First Edition

Let the generations know that women in uniform also guaranteed their freedom.

—Mary Edwards Walker, Civil War doctor and only female holder of the Congressional Medal of Honor

CONTENTS

4 REBELS AND REVOLUTIONARIES
Women Taking Up Arms for a Cause

5 CREATURE COMFORTS
Courtesans, Consorts, and
Camp Followers: Women Drawn
into War to Minister to Men

6 INTO UNIFORM
Women Mobilized to Support the War Effort

7 AT THE SHARP END

Modern Soldiers, Sailors, and Airwomen

Cochran, Jacqueline | Duckworth, Tammy | Hester, Leigh Ann | Holm, Jeanne | Hopper, "Amazing" Grace | Litvak, Lily | Lynch, Jessica | McGrath, Kathleen | McSally, Martha | Mixed Antiaircraft Batteries | Night Witches | Raskova, Marina | Reitsch, Hanna | Rossi, Marie T. | Warsaw Ghetto Uprising |

8 HEALING HANDS

Doctors, Nurses, Medics, and
Health Workers

Ang, Swee Chai | Army Nurse Corps | Barton, Clara | Bickerdyke, Mary Ann | Bullwinkel, Vivian | Chisholm, Mairi, and Elsie Knocker | Dix, Dorothea | Etheridge, Anna | Inglis, Elsie | Keil, Lillian Kinkela | Nightingale, Florence | Seacole, Mary "Mother" | US Military Nurses and Doctors | Walker, Mary Edwards

9 RECORDING ANGELS

Singers, Entertainers, Artists,
Propagandists, and Chroniclers of War,
the Good and the Bad

Al Haideri, Sahar Hussein | Amanpour, Christiane | Bourke-White, Margaret | Deuell, Peggy Hull | Frank, Anne | Gellhorn, Martha | Gillars, Mildred Elizabeth | Kirkpatrick, Helen | K'tut Tantri | Lynn, Vera | Politkovskaya, Anna | Toguri, Ikuko

10 VALKYRIES, FURIES, AND FIENDS

Ruthless Opportunists, Sadists, and
Psychopaths Unleashed and Empowered by War

Ammash, Dr. Huda Salih Mahdi | Braunsteiner, Hermine | England, Lynndie | Grese, Irma | Khaled, Leila | Lakwena, Alice | Mbandi, Jinga | Mukakibibi, Sister Theophister | Plavsic, Biljana | Suicide Bombers | Tribal Revenge

11 ARMIES OF THE SHADOWS

Spies, Agents, and Underground Workers   *333*

American Civil War | Atkins, Vera | Bentov, Cheryl | Brousse, Amy
Elizabeth | Cohen, Lona | de Jongh, Andrée | Hall, Virginia |
Khan, Noor Inayat | Manningham-Buller, Eliza | Office of Strate-
gic Services | Rimington, Stella | Sansom, Odette | Sendlerowa,
Irena | Skarbek, Krystyna | Special Operations Executive | Szabo,
Violette | Vertefeuille, Jeanne | Werner, Ruth | Witherington, Pearl

INTRODUCTION

T HEY FOUGHT LIKE DEVILS, far better than the men."

So Georges Clemenceau, then mayor of Montmartre, recalled the women of the Paris Commune who manned the barricades at France's republican uprising of 1871. Fighting to the last under a relentless bombardment as government troops stormed the city with a loss of 25,000 lives, they died like men, too. As Clemenceau somberly testified, "I had the pain of seeing fifty of them shot down, even when they had been surrounded by troops and disarmed."

History has seen many such acts of courage, daring, and self-sacrifice by women like these. These traits are to be found today, in the opening years of the twenty-first century, in such women as former US Army helicopter pilot Major **Tammy Duckworth** (see p. 221), who lost both her legs when her Black Hawk was shot down in Iraq in 2004; and Colonel **Martha McSally** (see p. 232), who flew A-10 ground-attack missions in Afghanistan and in 2004 became the first woman to command a United States Air Force combat squadron.

No comprehensive record exists of the many roles played by women in the countless wars, both hot and cold, that have marked human history. This book is written to bridge the gap in the way we look at history, women, and war, pulling together in a single volume the many strands of this continuing historical drama. Women have taken a vital part in ancient and medieval warfare; in the world wars of the twentieth century; in armed insurrections; in religious, ethnic, and tribal conflicts; and in the Cold War that lasted from 1945 to the early 1990s.

Today they are caught up in the so-called clash of civilizations between Islam and the West and in the violent politics of the Middle East and Africa. In the modern, mixed-gender armed forces deployed in these trouble spots, often under the banner of the United Nations (UN) or the **North Atlantic Treaty Organization** (NATO) (see p. 171), women play increasingly significant and sometimes controversial roles both in making war and in keeping the peace.

Naturally, women have not always served on the side of right. No account of women and war can be complete without coverage of its dark side, like the part played in the death camps of World War II by the women of the SS, or the career of Saddam Hussein's biological warfare expert, **Dr. Huda Salih Mahdi Ammash** (see p. 312), infamous as "Dr. Germ." Nor can we overlook the intelligence careers of master spies such as **Ruth Werner** (see p. 372), or the grim exploits in the more recent past of female **Tamil Tigers** (see p. 115), or Palestinian **Suicide Bombers** (see p. 327). These pages contain characters as diverse and complex as "General" **Harriet Tubman** (see p. 117), the former slave who became the only woman to command a military mission in the American Civil War; **Margaret Thatcher** (see p. 58), a modern **Boudicca** (see p. 12); and the Cuban revolutionary and cultural tsar **Haydée Santamaría** (see p. 114).

This rich history is crammed with other characters and events crying out for a wider audience. Readers will find here most of the names they know, or think they know: **Boudicca, Joan of Arc** (see p. 75), **Elizabeth I** (see p. 34), **Florence Nightingale** (see p. 264), and **Golda Meir** (see p. 48). But they appear here as they have not always done in the past. Florence Nightingale, for instance, was not known to the troops in the Crimea as "the Lady with the Lamp," an invention of the war correspondent of *The Times* of London, but as "the Lady with the Hammer." This nickname arose from one of her fearless exploits, when she defied a military commander to smash her way into a locked storeroom and released much-needed medical supplies, to the great delight of the wounded men.

Like Nightingale's story, most accounts of women at war offer an unsatisfying and often mythologized pop-up history of a few outstandingly courageous and sometimes eccentric women, which invites the reader to do little more than mutter, "What a gal!" So the courage in World War II of the British agent **Odette Hallowes** (see p. 351) is solemnly celebrated, but not the complaint by her French Resistance colleagues that she spent too much of her time in bed with fellow agent Peter Churchill.

And these women did not operate alone. The story of Hallowes and other British women agents can only be understood in the context of the **Special Operations Executive** (SOE, see p. 366), which directed their work. Many fascinating questions about women at war are raised by considering the aims and methods of the SOE, its policy on the recruitment of women, and the legal problems this brought in its train. The same is also true for the American equivalent of the SOE, the **Office of Strategic Services** (OSS, see p. 355).

In *Hell Hath No Fury,* these women—both the good and the bad—rub shoulders with one another, and challenge conventional notions of womanhood. Yet many of their stories are not widely known and have not been incorporated into an overview of women's experience and achievement in thousands of years of warfare. Encyclopedias or general accounts of war give little or no attention to the contribution of women, and "the fair sex" finds itself consistently written out of the records. Female war leaders of the past regularly found their victories attributed to their generals, while some women were not acknowledged at all: the Muslim chroniclers of Africa, a continent whose tradition of warrior queens reaches back into prehistory, regularly omitted queens regnant from their lists of rulers, because women holding power did not accord with their theology of Islam.

As this suggests, the careful massaging of the record to ignore or minimize the contribution of women is as old as history itself. Resisting the Roman invasion of Britain while contending with the infighting of rival Celts, the first-century British queen **Cartimandua** (see p. 18) displayed outstanding qualities as a war leader, defending her considerable territories for many years. But her success has proved far less interesting to historians than the spectacular downfall of her contemporary, the warrior queen Boudicca, who serves as an Awful Warning to women not to embark on the path of war. When Cartimandua's career is discussed, her marital status and her sex life receive greater coverage than her military prowess, just as any tabloid newspaper would treat her today.

Boudicca herself illustrates another derogatory historical technique that turns war-fighting women into monsters, unnatural creatures more masculine than feminine. In his account of Boudicca, whom he never saw, the Roman historian Tacitus stresses her huge size, deep, rasping voice, and terrifying plume of flame-red hair. Later historians repeat this description without question and also follow the Roman dismissal of her followers as "fanatics," on the lazy assumption that they must have been crazy to follow a madwoman. In contrast, all the local tribes rallied to her banner because they believed she was divine, the incarnation of the Great Goddess on earth.

Where information about women at war exists, it is often sparse, and many warlike women blaze all too briefly into view. One such was the rambunctious Irish war leader Dearbhfhorgaill, daughter of the chief Magnus O'Connor, who held command of her own army in 1315. Given the strenuous oppression of fighting women by the early Christian church, it is understandable that Dearbhfhorgaill "with all the gallowglassses and men of Clan Murtagh that she could obtain, marched against the churches of Drumcliffe and plundered many of its clergy." But we know nothing more of her than this.

Inevitably, those who figure in these pages represent only a fraction of the millions who served, fought, and died. There are far more heroines, and more victims, than can be contained in a single volume. Some candidates did not make the final cut because of their undeniably contemporary but tenuous connection with a military event, like the sixteenth-century Cornish sea captain Lady Killigrew, who fell on a wrecked Spanish warship during the expedition against England by the Spanish Armada, looted it, and drowned all the surviving Spaniards.

Of those who are featured, each exemplifies a reality we thought important to emphasize. Many more women deserve to be included, and we would be glad to hear from anyone who has a candidate to propose for the next edition. Nevertheless, *Hell Hath No Fury* presents a comprehensive picture of women as front-line combatants and as war leaders; as civilians swept along by titanic events in global conflicts; as diplomats, spies, and spy mistresses; and as chroniclers, propagandists, politicians, and cheerleaders in conflicts large and small: a cast of characters that includes women of every stripe from the **FLN bombers** (see p. 94) to **Anne Frank** (see p. 291).

All have been accommodated within a structure that we hope will highlight a number of overarching and abiding themes. Like every creature at the dawn of human history, the earliest females had to learn to fight in order to survive, neither expecting nor receiving any quarter for their sex. Those who failed would die, and the survival of the human race is the living proof that most of them succeeded. Initially fighting for themselves, our primitive foremothers naturally progressed to defending their homes, families, and countries as Boudicca did, in a campaign that made her one of the most famous women warriors of all time. That meant learning to organize themselves in bands like the **Amazons** (see p. 5), and, as society evolved, gaining entry to the ranks of captains and kings.

For some women, however, warfare in succeeding ages offered the chance not to rise within the masculine hierarchy but to escape it. Trapped in unbearably stultifying lives as females, they embraced the chance of war to live and fight like men, as the brief and strange story of Joan of Arc illustrates. In contrast, many thousands of other women were only drawn into conflict by their menfolk, and shared with them the fortunes of war, like the Mexican *soldadera* (see p. 140) mother of the film star Anthony Quinn, who followed her husband into the army of Pancho Villa, where the life was very hard. For these women, however, war was not always a tragedy. In eras when women were not allowed full employment or any significant occupation, warfare could give them a function, a family, and a home.

In the modern era, warfare has demanded increasing efforts of women behind the lines, when like **Rosie the Riveter** (see p. 180), they threw their weight into the war effort along with their men. Some sought and found more active roles, including leadership, both in the oldest services, the army and the navy, and in the newest, the air force. Others fought not for their society but against it, challenging the established order as rebels and revolutionaries, often meeting an early end on the scaffold or facing a firing squad.

But whatever and wherever the war, doctors and nurses like the Civil War doctor **Mary Edwards Walker** (see p. 278) are always needed to care for the troops. In World War II, women also gained access to this masculine and increasingly technologized world as war correspondents; **Martha Gellhorn** (see p. 293) was one of the many dedicated female writers, interpreters, and propagandists of war. There have also been countless women whose innate violence and cruelty are unleashed by war. The stories of such SS women as **Hermine Braunsteiner** (see p. 314) and **Irma Grese** (see p. 316) are less easy to understand than those of other fighting women, since the depths of female sadism are so hard to confront.

Our final chapter contains the largest number of women in the book, since historically the areas of espionage and resistance have offered women the greatest opportunity to contribute. In World War II, numbers of them chose to work as spies or members of the underground, a particularly dangerous and demanding branch of war service, and one in which they enjoyed much success. Inevitably this arena entailed great risk, and the penalty for capture was often torture and death. In this field, however, women were most able to fight on the front line and to use to the full their imagination, intelligence, and initiative. Their valor, heroism, endurance, and native wit helped to make the free world we live in today.

Modern female soldiers, sailors, and airwomen carry the standard for mixed-gender warfare, in particular the much-debated introduction of women to front-line combat. Some see this as an unmitigated tale of triumph, charting women's progress toward present-day equality. Yet questions remain. Has warfare speeded up women's progress to freedom? Is aggression as natural for a woman as for a man, or are women who go to war deranged in some way, "fighting mad"? Do women leaders make war to establish their authority as men do? And today, when men and women fight side by side in modern mixed-gender units, do the men always feel they have to protect their female counterparts? All these questions and more are dealt with in this book. We do not have all the answers, but we hope to provide the material for readers to make up their own minds.

Many still ask if women have any place in war as combatants. The reality of women at war challenges a profoundly held fantasy in both women and men, that men make war to protect and defend women; that women are too weak to fight and unsuited to warfare; and that all women have to do in wartime is to keep the home fires burning. This has led to a widespread denial of the reality of women's engagement in war. It says much about the wider societal attitude to women in World War II that while SOE was absolutely committed to the recruitment and employment of women in the field, it was also careful to conceal the fact from the public for much of the war, fearing popular disapproval of the use of females in what was one of the most hazardous of all the theaters of operations.

Yet from 1942 onward, by the time SOE was leaving a footprint in Nazi-occupied Europe, the British and the Americans had adopted the wide-scale employment of women in war industry and the armed services as part of their war-winning strategy, an essential element in the waging of a Total War. American and British women could be nurses in field hospitals, fitters and welders in shipyards, and workers on aircraft and tank production lines. They could load submarines with torpedoes and serve as code breakers and air-raid wardens, but the governments of the Western Allies shrank from allowing them to bear arms. Even in

Britain's antiaircraft defenses, the women of the **Auxiliary Territorial Service** (ATS, see p. 153), who served in mixed anti-aircraft (AA) batteries, could do everything but fire the guns.

In trials conducted during the war, the Americans discovered that the women serving in their equivalent anti-aircraft batteries were as good as the men when it came to dealing with a potential enemy raider. But the acquisition of this skill was deemed "unladylike." Male commanders could not countenance the idea of British and American women in the front line. In the case of the Special Operations Executive, where the number of women in harm's way was small, it was easier to turn a blind eye.

In the Soviet Union, however, where the fight for national survival against a ruthless enemy was at its most savage, the Red Army had no qualms about employing women to fight on the ground and in the air. Even on the Eastern Front, however, male resentment at the presence of women surfaced with some regularity: "Why are you bringing those girls here?" demanded one Red Army officer faced with a detachment of some of the 800,000 Russian women who served in the armed forces during World War II, 70 percent of them at the front.

In the years following the end of World War II, the women who had kept the war production lines rolling from Los Angeles to Leningrad were encouraged by their governments to melt back into domestic life. Nevertheless, in postwar struggles for independence in countries like Algeria, Vietnam, and Eritrea, they continued to play an important role. In contrast, in the developed world the role of women in the military was largely confined to fields in which women had traditionally played an accepted part. In the Vietnam War, for example, the majority of the female US service personnel in the theater were nurses.

Still the belief persists that men go to war, and if women are involved at all, they simply trail behind, "following the flag." Military experts are particularly insistent that women only enter the annals of warfare as hapless bystanders or as the spoils of war. This could not be more at odds with the true story of the range of women's involvement in the past and with today's vibrant and ever-changing reality of mixed-gender combat units and asymmetric warfare. In the years following World War II, women have made steady advances in gaining entry to armed forces throughout the world. But progress has not been consistent everywhere, and many still feel that allowing women to fight is not progress at all, either for women or for the forces of the country they serve. A survey of a number of different countries reveals differing attitudes toward women fighters and highlights problems that are often ignored but refuse to go away.

Should the military have become a battlefield at all? Identified as a bastion of male dominance—one of the oldest on the earth, along with religion—the military assumed a symbolic importance in the quest for female equality far greater than it deserved: most women, whether feminists or not, have no desire to join up and serve. Nevertheless, female penetration of the armed forces—and the resistance to it—has been a struggle of huge significance, which has led to distortions on both sides. A key tenet of feminism is that equality for women must not mean trying to do things in the same way as men. This has been forgotten or obliterated in the drive to be fair to women and to be seen to be fair. This laudable aim cannot, however, disguise some real problems of integrating women into armies, navies, and air forces worldwide.

Many would argue that women's newfound equality in the armed forces of some Western societies merely reflects the chronic shortage of men. As with stenography in the United States of the nineteenth century, women only gain entry to certain professions when men are leaving them. The oldest professions of the military and the church, both of which offer the chance of considerable power and influence, retained their attraction for men longer than most. But it is significant that the conclusion of the Vietnam War coincided with the end of the draft in the United States, causing a recruiting crisis within the US military and the introduction of volunteer professional armed forces. Subsequently the number of American women serving in the military began to rise and continues to do so to this day. So the suspicion remains: Have women only been acknowledged as members of the US armed forces because men no longer wish to sign up?

The question can be asked of other armed forces in the First

World, although the pattern varies from country to country. This phenomenon has sparked a heated debate between those who have championed the integration of women into mixed-gender units and those who remain deeply skeptical about the development. The latter argue that far from being an advance, the arrival of women in the armed forces is only a symptom of a wider malaise pervading military life. They contend that, as with other professions, when a growing male reluctance to serve is offset by the introduction of women, the policy has to be forced through at the expense of physical standards and unit cohesion.

It is doubtful that this argument against women at war would impress the redoubtable British SOE veteran **Pearl Witherington** (see p. 375), who during the closing stages of World War II commanded an army Resistance of some two thousand. She sufficiently impressed her German enemies for them to place a million-franc reward on her head. Witherington's British bosses were less impressed, and after the war, she was offered a civil, not a military, decoration to reward her work. Spirited as ever, Witherington declined it on the grounds that she had never done a civil thing in her life.

Witherington resisted the official attempt to confine her to a footnote in history. But her career illustrates another abiding truth about women at war. Wherever they serve, they have always had to fight a double battle, and the easier of the two has been the straightforward engagement with the enemy. On the home front they still battle against suspicion and prejudice when they first join the ranks, and often have to live with ingrained resentment afterward.

Powerful women may be the subject of myth and legend, but the fascination they exert is tempered by a fear that demands they must be tamed. So the term "battle axe" is applied to bullying and loud-voiced women, sundered from its original connection with the Great Goddess, whose double-headed labrys was once invoked to bring victory but now serves as a perennial gibe at any woman of character and drive.

The reasons for this are not hard to understand. It deeply offends many men to think that they need the help of women in an essentially masculine affair. They query the women's motives—although no one ever questions why a man would want to fight—and insist that women fighters can never be as good as men.

By a painful paradox, male leaders are often very glad to have women's help at the beginning, particularly in a revolutionary war, or one where the struggle is likely to be hard, long, or extreme. But once it is won, the women's contribution is diminished and dismissed and they themselves often downgraded and vilified. This process can be seen in the seventh century after women's involvement in the early battles of Islam and was still vigorously at work in the twentieth, in Africa, in Algeria, and in Mexico, where *soldaderas* were stigmatized as no more than a rabble of whores.

Yet there remain thousands of women ready to go to war, following the millions through the ages who have gone before. In January 2007, the first all-female United Nations peacekeeping force was dispatched to the West African state of Liberia, which from 1989 to 2003 was wracked by a civil war in which some 200,000 people died and 1.5 million people—half the country's population—were displaced. The female force consisted of 105 Indian policewomen, veterans of insurgencies in such trouble spots as Kashmir, where they battled Islamic militants, and central India, where Maoists were active. Their principal tasks included training Liberia's national police, maintaining prison security, and supervising elections. Their unit commander, Seema Dhundia, explained: "Women police are seen to be much less threatening, although they can be just as tough as men. But in a conflict situation they are more approachable, and it makes women and children feel safer."

It remains to be seen whether the introduction of women to the Gurkha Regiment, one of the British Army's most feared and formidable formations, will have a similarly calming effect. In the summer of 2007, hundreds of Nepalese women—many of them former Maoist rebels—began high-altitude training in the Himalayas in the hope of joining the Gurkhas, previously an all-male preserve numbering some 3,500 men. One of the women's instructors, retired Gurkha Yam Bahadur Gurung, observed, "More and more women are joining the private training program. We are happy for women to be allowed the same opportunity as men. Many of them aren't being taken seriously by the men, who see them as weak, but I disagree. The women work as porters climbing the Himalayas. They are incredibly fit. There is no reason why they cannot take their place alongside men." Eventually, around fifty women will qualify for a pilot entry scheme to the regiment. The women Gurkhas will have a proud tradition to live up to. In two world wars the Gurkhas suffered 43,000 casualties and won twenty-six Victoria Crosses—more than any other regiment.

Our story of women at war reaches a positive conclusion with these individuals, each one affirming women's courage, loyalty, and strength, often to the point of extreme suffering and death. For each of us, there is a responsibility to see that their story is better known. We have therefore included a range of references in the hope of encouraging further reading and stimulating a wider interest in these women and their experiences. Women who served, fought, and died must be given their due. They fought for us, and we must fight for them.

This story will never end. Women have always gone to war, knowing that in this arena they could make a real difference. And as long as war goes on, they will, too. As you read this, some woman somewhere is cleaning her rifle, checking her ammunition, and preparing for action. We hope we have done her justice. We have certainly tried.

We would like to thank the Wiener Library, the Imperial War Museum, and the librarian of the Reform Club in London for their help in the preparation of this book. To all those who have had faith in the project and given us their support, we extend our warmest gratitude.

—Rosalind Miles and Robin Cross

1

IN THE BEGINNING

⟨≈≈⟩

Women Warriors of Myth
and Early History

When war comes, even women have to fight.
—Vietnamese proverb dating back to the Trung sisters, who drove the
Chinese from their homeland, Vietnam, in 40 CE

WHAT MAKES WOMEN FIGHT? A better question would be, why shouldn't they? At the dawn of time, as our primate ancestors evolved into human beings, aggression and speed of response to sudden threat would have been as important to the female of the species as to the male, bred into both genders by natural selection, since those who could not fight would die. We are all the descendants of those females who won, and the living proof that they did. Their genes are to be seen in women of all ages, races, and nations, from the female gladiators of the ancient world to the most decorated women fighters in US Army history today.

As they matured, our primitive foremothers would have borne children. The defensive instinct of a mother is arguably the most powerful trigger for aggression in the world, and this overriding maternal drive to protect and defend has drawn many women into war who might otherwise never have lifted a sword, spear, or gun. Many of those who proved the fiercest and bravest fighters of all were only impelled to fight when their country was invaded or their homes attacked, like the Celtic warrior queen of the first century, Boudicca (see p. 12). A goddess in the eyes of her people, she led a fighting force estimated at seventy thousand men against the Romans in 61 CE, with terrifying consequences.

With the advent of social organization, females no longer faced a daily struggle to stay alive, but the instinct to fight lived on. Yet the reality of the woman fighter, taking up her weapons for war and staking her life on her strength and skill, has proved hard to accept. Images of female catfights, or women wrestling in mud, are served up for erotic delight in popular fiction like Ian Fleming's James Bond novels and as a staple of modern pornography, but society remains deeply resistant to the true story of women's history of combat. The pervasive image of women in early societies remains that of a wilting sexual stereotype, huddled in fear inside the cave or castle, waiting for the men to come home.

In reality, women have always fought, and accounts of their activities are to be found in the earliest annals of history. Women warriors were everywhere in the ancient world, with a surprising continuity over a long period. Roman accounts of battles record finding numbers of bodies of female warriors on the battlefield. Thirty captive Gothic warrior women were paraded in front of Emperor Aurelian in a triumph at Rome in 273 CE. There are centuries of records like these.

And like men, the women of the classical period fought for sport and recreation, too. During the Roman Empire, women fought in the public arenas, both as free women and as slaves, and competed at the opening of the Colosseum in 80 CE. Around the year 100 CE, the Roman satirist Juvenal recorded that it became fashionable for women of the nobility to fight in the arenas, and so many signed up for training that they were finally banned in 200 CE.

Individual warriors such as the seventh-century Arab princess **Khawlah bint al-Azwar al-Kind'yya** (see p. 9) often sprang from royalty or nobility, and their family or tribal pride drove them on. As high-born women, too, they would have access to weapons, horses, and armor, which were normally available only to the rich. But the lack of all these never deterred those women who wanted to fight from finding the means.

A striking number of these early women warriors rose to become commanders-in-chief. From the days of the Great Goddess of prehistory, also known as Magna Mater, the Great Mother, and Mother Earth, women held power in their tribes and communities based on their connection with the land. As the human representatives of the sovereignty and spirit of the land, women were the land's logical defenders. Despite their tribal differences, the Celts living and fighting throughout continental Europe and the British Isles made no distinction between men and women in choosing a leader, and women also held sway in Egypt, China, and elsewhere in the East.

Traditional historians often dismiss the earliest female commanders as mythical, but many of them have been shown to exist. *Women Intelligent and Courageous in Warfare,* a treatise attributed to the Greek intellectual Pamphile of Epidaurus writing in the first century CE, features a number of bold and successful female war leaders whose military exploits are well documented and generally agreed upon.

Women warriors mostly saw full combat in preindustrial times, when hand-to-hand fighting was the order of the day. Undoubtedly some fighting women were taller or stronger than the average: Khawlah bint al-Azwar al-Kind'yya was at first taken to be a man because of her height, and she revealed herself as a woman only reluctantly, when the battle was won. But more important than size for any fighter, female or male, is a fighting spirit, which Khawlah and all women warriors have in abundance. Muhammad himself paid tribute to the prowess of the most famous female warrior of the period, **Nusaybah bint Ka'b,** also known as Umm 'Umara (see p. 10), recalling, "On the day of [the battle of] Uhud, I never looked to the right nor to the left without seeing Umm 'Umara fighting to defend me."

As with men, a deficiency in size or strength could be made up by swiftness, confidence, and skill. There are many records of women receiving martial training. Perhaps the greatest tribute to its success can be seen in the career of the semilegendary female samurai **Tomoe Gozen,** in twelfth-century Japan (see p. 22). A consummate fighter, she is described as skilled with many different weapons, an outstanding swordswoman, a remarkably strong archer, and a superb horsewoman. In battle, her commander always sent her out at the head of the host, "equipped with strong armour, an oversized sword, and a mighty bow, [with which] she performed more deeds of valour than any of his other warriors."

There is a compelling poignancy in the image of this tiny Japanese woman leading troops into battle and laying about her with her massive sword. But even for a small woman, handling a sword, shield, spear, or bow would not have presented an insuperable problem in these early times, since the size difference between male and female was far less marked, an effect still observed in the great apes today. In addition, as each item of warfare had to be handmade, women could always have the tools of war adapted to their personal needs, as smaller or less able-bodied males had to do.

Fighting women flourished in an age of single combat and had no place in the organized military formations that began to emerge. The Macedonian battle phalanx, a key military innovation of the ancient world, consisted of a densely packed mass of fighting men, each wielding a *sarissa* or spear up to twenty-three feet long and weighing thirteen to fifteen pounds; not surprisingly, this was an all-male affair. Similarly, women, excluded from the Roman army, took no part in warfare involving the *testudo,* or tortoise, a Roman infantry maneuver that required the shields of the attackers being held above their heads in time of siege to shelter them from bombardment from above.

The decline of the fighting woman continued into the early modern period, when military experts argue that the first military firearms, such as the musket, were too heavy for women to bear. However, at ten pounds, a French musket of 1777 represents less than the weight any normal woman puts on in pregnancy and less than that of a one-year-old child, which in the days before contraception, a woman would carry everywhere, very probably along with a newborn infant or an older child as well.

Modern weapons such as the automatic rifle are considerably lighter than the weapons of the past. But weight is not the real issue. Through the ages, the decline of the fighting woman has gone hand in hand with the progress of "civilization," which in every age has insisted on women's weakness and inferiority through a battery of religious, biological, social, and cultural constraints that have kept women out of public life and in the home. In particular, anything that smacked of "mannish" or "masculine" behavior was severely discouraged and even punished by law: wearing men's clothing remained a capital offense in Europe until the eighteenth century. How were women to fight when they were not allowed to wear pants or any form of masculine attire, the offense for which **Joan of Arc** (see p. 75) was burned to death in 1431?

But even in the depths of the Dark Ages and up to the present day, some women were still active in the front line, battling it out, unfazed by any supposed weakness of their sex. History has consistently refused to grant the dignity and status of warrior to the female of the species. The women we have chosen to write about seized it for themselves.

AMAZONS
Female Fighting Bands of the Classical World

"Golden-shielded, silver-sworded, man-loving, male-child-killing Amazons": so the Greek historian Hellanicus described Amazons in the fifth century BCE.

Stories of women who organized themselves to fight in bands are found in history, literature, and legend from the dawn of time. They are most persistent in the Mediterranean region and the Near East, where written and oral accounts record the existence of a tribe of women warriors who lived and fought together, taking men to sire children but destroying any boy babies who resulted, rearing only the girls. Amazons were also famous for their skill in horse taming and were among the first people in history to be recorded fighting on horseback. Their association with horses is evident from the recurrence of the Greek *hippos* (horse) in their names: three Amazons known by name were Hippolyta (stamping horse), Melanippe (black mare), and Alcippe (powerful mare).

Most famous of all the Amazons was the queen Hippolyta, who

became the target of the great hero Heracles around 1250 BCE, when he demanded her girdle, the symbol of her sacred and sexual power. The whole tribe of Amazons rose against him in anger, and Hippolyta met him in pitched battle, where she was thrown from her horse and lay helpless at Heracles' feet. He offered to spare her life if she would submit to him, and she chose to die rather than yield. Heracles killed her, stripped her of her girdle, seized her battle-axe, and slaughtered all the other Amazon champions, one by one. Only when the tribe had been savagely reduced did the Amazon commander Melanippe seek a truce. Heracles granted it on condition that she, too, give up her girdle, symbolically handing all her power as queen and woman over to him. Heracles then raped her and let her go, knowing the humiliation would be worse than death.

Heracles gave another of the surviving Amazons, Antiope, to his friend Theseus, who bore her off to Athens as his concubine. The remaining Amazons mounted a war party to rescue her and in the succeeding battle, Antiope was killed and the Amazon force was heavily defeated and driven off.

The Amazons suffered many such assaults at the hands of the Greeks, who were bent on imposing their patriarchal rule on tribes who followed the older earth religion of the Great Goddess, a belief system honoring womankind and led by queens. Driven to revenge, the Amazon queen Penthesilea traveled to Troy around 1250 BCE to fight on behalf of the Trojans, who were also at war with the invading Greeks. She fought with great distinction on the Trojan side and more than once drove the greatest champion of the Greeks, Achilles, from the field.

But in their final encounter, Achilles ran her through. Stripping the dying body of its armor, Achilles realized for the first time that his enemy was a woman and, falling in love or lust with her as she died, had sex with her body while it was still warm. Another Greek, the troublemaker Thersites, taunted Achilles for his sexual perversion and boasted that he had gouged out Penthesilea's eyes with his spear while she was still alive. Achilles promptly killed him, and in revenge one of Thersites' kinsmen dragged Penthesilea's body around the battlefield by the heels and threw it into the River Scamander (the modern-day Menderes), before it was finally rescued and buried with great honor. Penthesilea was the last true Amazon, and the tribe died with her.

Astonishing stories—but are they truth or myth? Later historians, writing in more strait-laced times, puzzled over the anomaly of women who chose to fight. The word "Amazon" was taken apart and interpreted as deriving from the Greek *a* (without) and *mazos* (breast). This paved the way for the explanation that these fighting women cut off their right breasts to improve their skill at arms.

This fanciful derivation of the Amazons' name is now known to be linguistically spurious as well as anatomically ridiculous: how many women have a right breast so unmanageable that they cannot swing a sword or draw a bow? It also implies that women who want to fight must be so perverted and unnatural that they would mutilate themselves. This detail adds a thrill of violence and horror to the eternal fascination of male-dominated societies with women's breasts. Perhaps this explains why this piece of nonsense has passed into common currency and remains the only "fact" many people know about the Amazons.

Faced with this fiction, traditional historians have been able to dismiss the Amazons as pure myth. Feminist historians, too, have been uncomfortable with the Amazon story, finding it an all-too-convenient reinforcement of the inevitability of male domination, since the Amazons are always finally defeated, raped, and enslaved by or married to victorious men.

But the written accounts, ranging from the gossip of travelers and storytellers to the work of otherwise reliable historians, are too numerous and coherent to ignore. There is far more evidence, both literary and archaeological, for the existence of the Amazons than survives for other tribes such as the Hittites or the Massagetae of Iran, whose existence is unquestioned. The Amazons are described by classical writers as diverse as Pliny, Strabo, Herodotus, Aeschylus, Diodorus, and Plutarch, all of whom treat their existence as fact. In one of many such accounts, the Greek historian Herodotus reported on the aftermath of a battle of the fifth century BCE when the Greeks were taking several boatloads of Amazons away as slaves. Raising a mutiny on the Black Sea, the "slaves" overthrew their captors, took command of the ships, and made their escape.

Narratives like these receive historical support from the numerous rituals, sacrifices, mock battles, and ceremonials of later ages, which were confidently ascribed to Amazon origins by those who practiced them. Amazons were seen in action, too. The Romans, who never admitted women into their own armies, frequently record encountering women in the ranks of their enemies, especially those to the north of Italy, while the Scythians included women fighters in military campaigns as a matter of course. Numerous Iron Age Scythian burial sites from around 600 BCE contain women who have been buried with their swords, spears, armor, and other trappings of war, along with more typical female items such as mirrors and spindles (essential for spinning wool into yarn, which was always women's work). At one site, the body of a girl aged between ten and twelve was found buried in full-body chain mail, which suggests that she was already trained for combat and considered fit to fight.

The original Amazons appear to have lived in Libya, where rock drawings have been discovered dating from around 2000 BCE showing women armed with bows. During the Heroic Age of Greek civilization, around 1600 BCE, they emerged in mainland Greece, where relief carvings and vase decorations invariably show them sporting (and cheerfully exposing) both breasts. Their heyday came around 1250 BCE in the time of the great Greek heroes Heracles and Theseus, the latter the founding father of Athens, and just before the Trojan War of around 1200 BCE.

The internal wars of the Greek city-states have left records of a number of real-life Amazons such as the war leader and poet Telesilla of the fifth century BCE. Telesilla took command of her city-state of Argos after its defeat by the Spartan leader Cleomenes and used her verses to rouse the female occupants to such fury that they attacked and drove out the enemy. She later composed a battle hymn in honor of the event, and her grateful fellow citizens raised a statue to her in the temple of Aphrodite.

The first literary reference to the Amazons is found in the *Iliad,* the ancient Greek poet Homer's account of the Trojan War, written around 750 BCE; he describes them as "women the equal of men." But the Greece of the classical era from about 500 BCE onward was not interested in women's equality. When Athenians evolved the world's first "democracy," women were specifically excluded, along with slaves, criminals, foreigners, and the insane. The gradual subjection of women throughout Greece, and indeed the rest of the civilized world, is mirrored in the story of the Amazons, whose fortunes fell as those of the heroes rose. Powerful, deadly, glamorous, gifted, and free, they represented a type of woman who had no place in the new world of father gods and men of might, and one who still has to fight for her right to exist.

Reference: Lynn Webster Wilde, *On the Trail of the Women Warriors: Amazons in Myth and History,* 1999.

ARAB WOMEN WARRIORS
Seventh Century

During a fierce fight against the Byzantines in the early struggles of Muhammad, the chronicles report that the wavering forces of Islam were rallied by a tall knight muffled in black and fighting with ferocious courage. After the victory, the "knight" reluctantly revealed herself as the Arab princess Khawlah bint al-Azwar al-Kind'yya.

Even losing in battle could not break Khawlah's spirit. Captured at the battle of Sabhura, near Damascus, she rallied the other female captives with the challenge, "Do you accept these men as your masters? Are you willing for your children to become their slaves? Where is your famed courage and skill that has become the talk of the Arab tribes as well as of the cities?" Ordering each to arm herself with a tent pole, she formed them into a phalanx and led them to victory. "And why not," the narrator of their story concluded, "if a lost battle meant their enslavement?"

This question betrays the mixed feelings of Arab and Islamic commentators about the women warriors who were an established feature of pre-Islamic culture in the Middle East. For centuries, Muslim women in different struggles and communities joined men on the front lines of war, fighting and dying at their side. Another honored battle heroine and war leader of the early Islamic era was Salaym bint Malhan, who fought in the ranks of Muhammad and his followers with an armory of swords and daggers strapped around her pregnant belly.

The list goes on. A warrior called Safiyya bint 'Abd al-Muttalib is reported on the battlefield at Uhud, one of Muhammad's early engagements, lashing about her with her weapon in her hand. The most famous female warrior of the period is the Ansari woman Nusaybah bint Ka'b, also known as Umm 'Umara. Armed with sword and bow and arrow, she fought at the battles of Uhud and Mecca in 630 CE with her husband and two sons, and was still active at Khayber, Hunayn, and al-Yamama in 633–34 CE.

At Uhud, fighting alongside her mother according to some accounts, she valiantly defended Muhammad when the tide began to turn against the Muslims, sustaining severe injuries in the process and later losing a hand. Muhammad himself is recorded as saying, "On the day of Uhud, I never looked to the right nor to the left without seeing Umm 'Umara fighting to defend me."

The Prophet's own female relatives were also active in Islam's wars; his young wife, 'A'ishah, threw off her veil to take command at the Battle of the Camel, and his granddaughter Zaynab bint Ali fought in the Battle of Karbala. Another woman, Umm Al Dhouda bint Mas'ud, fought so magnificently at the Battle of Khayber that the Prophet allotted her a share of the spoils equal to a man's.

Not all women accepted Muhammad's cause. Many fought against Islam as it set out to replace the existing faith in the Great Goddess with the insistence on one father God. Countless women who worshipped "the Queen of Heaven," "the Lady," and "the Mother of Life and Death" took up arms to resist. Foremost among them was the Arab leader Hind al-Hunnud, who led the opposition of her tribe, the wealthy and powerful Qu'raish, to the forced imposition of Islam.

The climax of her campaign came at the terrible Battle of Badr in 624, where she succeeded in exchanging blows with Muhammad himself, but her father, uncle, and brother were killed. For a time she directed a guerrilla war of vengeance, but she was eventually outnumbered, surrounded, and forced to submit and to convert to Islam. In her heyday, al-Hunnud had been not only a warrior and a leader in battle but also a priestess of the Great Goddess in the incarnation of "the Lady of Victory." After she submitted to the will of Allah, nothing more was heard of this brilliant and unusual woman.

Despite defeats like this, the tradition of women fighters in the Arab world was slow to die out. The twelfth-century memoirs of the Syrian notable Usama bin Munqidh describe the women combatants of his own day, including his mother. In fifteenth-century Yemen, the Zaydi chieftain Sharifa Fatima, daughter of an imam, conquered the city of San'a, and as late as the eighteenth century, Ghaliyya al-Wahhabiyya led a military resistance movement in Saudi Arabia to defend Mecca against foreign incursions.

But the tide of repression had long been turning against women warriors. Islamic authorities began to question the martial activities of their own women warriors who had helped Muhammad to victory, and later chroniclers made much of the case of an obscure woman companion of the Prophet by the name of Umm Kabsha, who is said to have been refused permission to accompany Muhammad in battle. This was taken to mean that the earlier permission given to women to participate in battles had been withdrawn.

As the oppression of women under Islam gathered strength, male religious authorities concluded that women could take no part in jihad. For centuries, albeit with a few rare exceptions, the women in the East were denied basic physical freedoms and autonomy and subordinated to the control of men, destroying the heritage of women fighters at its source.

With the encouragement of generations of misogynists and fundamentalists, the insistence that only men could fight or participate in a holy war hardened into dogmatic certainty. This view was revised as soon as the male war makers of the late twentieth and early twenty-first centuries realized the potential of the burqa-clad female body to carry explosives undetected, and thereby to advance their cause (see **Suicide Bombers**, p. 327).

Reference: Azizah al-Hibri, *Women and Islam,* 1982.

BOUDICCA
British Queen, d. 61 CE

Dubbed by the Romans "the Killer Queen," Boudicca became the ultimate symbol of the fighting Amazon, despite having only the briefest of military careers to her name. She leaps into history for one short campaign, blazing like a comet across the sky with her enduring cry of "Death before slavery!" before falling into oblivion. But in the space of a few months, she succeeded in giving the Romans one of the greatest shocks their vast empire ever faced, driven to make war by a series of insults and cruelties so savage that all the tribes of East Anglia rose in rebellion and flocked to her side.

Boudicca was queen of the Iceni, one of the most powerful tribes in Europe, based in the modern English counties of Norfolk and Suffolk. Women fighters were a continuous element of Celtic culture, and the Celts had many war goddesses, two of which—Boudiga and Andraste—Boudicca invoked for victory.

Boudicca's tragedy was to face the invading Romans as a female ruler in a society whose women enjoyed exceptionally high status and whose queens often ruled in their own right (see **Cartimandua,** p. 18). Celtic queens were seen as embodying the spirit and sovereignty of the land, and as women, their royalty was only a step away from the divinity of the Great Goddess, who was worshipped everywhere.

Boudicca's link with the Great Goddess is evident in her name, which derives from *bouda,* or victory, investing her with all the force of the goddess in her warlike incarnation as Boudiga, "the Lady of Victory" (see **Arab Women Warriors,** p. 9). The Romans by contrast denied their women almost all legal or civil rights. Faced with Celtic queens, they insisted on imposing their own rules. When Boudicca's husband, Prasutagus, died in 61 CE, leaving her with two young daughters, Roman law did not permit royal inheritance to be passed down in the female line. In addition, the Celtic royal households were stocked with cattle, grain, jewelry, and gold; the chance was too good to miss. Looting and pillaging, the Romans attacked the palace and hauled Boudicca out to be stripped and flogged. Next she was forced to watch while her two young daughters were raped by the soldiery.

This was more than simple physical abuse. As females, Boudicca's daughters shared the divinity that attached to women of royal birth. Rape destroyed their virginity and thereby robbed them of their special powers, making it impossible that they could ever claim priestess status or inherit their mother's semidivine role.

To the Celts, the insult was intolerable. All the tribes exploded in revolt. "The whole island [of Britain] now rose up under the leadership of Boudicca, a queen, for Britons make no distinction of sex in their appointment of commanders," recorded the Roman historian Tacitus, whose father-in-law, Agricola, as a senior officer, encountered Boudicca on the battlefield.

Boudicca's perceived divinity may explain the passion and courage of her followers. Her appearance in battle seems to have struck fear in friend and foe alike, as the Roman historian Dio Cassius described her, writing a century later:

> [She was] tall, terrifying to look at, with a fierce gaze and a harsh, powerful voice. A flood of bright red hair fell down to her knees; she wore a golden necklet made up of ornate pieces, a multi-coloured robe and over it a thick cloak held together by a brooch. She grasped a long spear to strike dread in all those who set eyes on her.

Dio Cassius also recorded with true Roman superiority that she was "possessed of greater intelligence than is usually found in the female sex."

Boudicca rapidly moved her army south, where she sacked the city of Camulodunum (modern Colchester) and routed the Roman relief force. Londinium (London) and Verulanium (St. Albans) were next. Racing south from crushing another outbreak, the Roman governor in Britain, Gaius Suetonius Paulinus, reached London before the rebels but then decided that the city was indefensible. Ignoring what Tacitus calls "the lamentations and appeals" of the Roman merchants, he withdrew his forces and left the settlers to their fate.

The sacking of London was particularly savage, with most of the Celts' fury falling on the Roman women. The male inhabitants were given no quarter as the Celts swept through the city, looting and killing the settlers indiscriminately, and Tacitus estimates that seventy thousand died. But for the women, the victors reserved a special fate. They were rounded up, taken out of the city to a wooded grove sacred to the Celtic war goddess Andraste, and sacrificed to her there in an elaborate ritual of startling cruelty. Boudicca and her warriors impaled them on outsize skewers, suspended them from trees, then cut off their breasts and stuffed them into their mouths or stitched them to their lips in a ghastly parody of mothers giving suck.

To the patriarchal Romans, the worst of this disaster was that it was led by a woman, "which caused them the greatest shame." With a force of about ten thousand, Suetonius brought Boudicca's considerably more numerous army to battle somewhere in the English Midlands, cheering his soldiers by telling them that they had little to fear from Boudicca, as her army consisted of more women than men.

Tacitus describes Boudicca on the opposing side, driving around all the tribes in her chariot, with her daughters in front, to deliver a fiery speech:

> We British are used to women commanders in war . . . but I am not fighting for my kingdom or my wealth. I am fighting for my lost freedom, my battered body and my violated daughters. . . . Consider what you are fighting for, and why. Then you will win this battle, or perish. That is what I, as a woman, plan to do. Let the men live in shame and slavery if they will!

In a symbolic gesture, she released a live hare, an animal sacred to the Great Goddess, between the two armies and dedicated it to Andraste, for victory.

On a more practical level, her army labored under the signal disadvantage of having no battle plan. Though a charismatic commander, Boudicca displayed scant generalship, meeting Suetonius and his force on open ground where Celtic fervor proved no match for Roman organization and discipline. Suetonius, a veteran of mountain warfare, fought with a forest at his back, forcing the Britons to charge headlong up a slope onto Roman javelins. The Britons' women, confident of victory, watched from a laager of wagons on the edge of the battlefield.

When the Britons had exhausted themselves, the Romans counterattacked in wedge formation, driving them back onto their wagons, where they were routed. In the bloody mêlée of defeated warriors, women, children, pack animals, and baggage, the Romans slaughtered everything that moved. Tacitus estimated the Roman dead at four hundred, compared with eighty thousand Britons. In Tacitus' account, Boudicca took poison, although others assert that she was taken prisoner after the battle and died in captivity. What became of her daughters is unknown.

Reference: Anne Ross, *Druids,* 1999; and Graham Webster, *Boudicca: The British Revolt Against Rome,* 1978.

BRUNHILDE AND FREDEGUND
Frankish Empresses, fl. 567–613 and 549–597, respectively

Chiefly remembered for her hideous death, Brunhilde deserves more credit for her long and power-packed life. As warrior queen and stateswoman, she displayed indomitable courage and formidable skill through forty years of continuous war. Thrown into the bear pit of Frankish politics as a young bride, she ruled until she was regent for her great-grandchildren, and was almost eighty years of age when she died.

Her lifelong rival and mortal enemy, Fredegund, the Lady Macbeth of the Dark Ages, achieved power through her husband and used it to keep his kingdom in a state of war for more than forty years. One of the most bloodthirsty and sadistic women in history, she spent a lifetime stirring up old conflicts and creating new ones throughout the vast empire of the Franks, a territory covering most of modern Europe. Always ready for open aggression, Fredegund was also an early exponent of dirty warfare and relied heavily on poison and other covert operations to dispatch her foes.

Fredegund's career as a psychopath began humbly enough, as a slave girl at the court of the depraved and vicious Frankish emperor Chilperic, whose kingdom comprised most of northern France. Fredegund caught Chilperic's eye, became his mistress, and persuaded him to set his wife aside and later to have her killed. The oldest of four brothers who had carved up the vast empire of their father, the powerful Chlotar I, at his death in 561, Chilperic was always at odds with his siblings, above all his youngest brother Sigebert, who held the kingdom next to his.

Brunhilde's tragedy lay in her entanglement with these warring brothers as soon as she was old enough to marry. A Spanish princess christened Bruna, the daughter of the king of the Visigoths, she was noted for her intelligence and beauty from an early age, and in 568 she was married to Sigebert, ruler of the eastern Frankish kingdom that covered most of modern Germany.

Her father the king then sought another union with the Franks. Chilperic had already murdered one queen at the instigation of his slave mistress, Fredegund, but despite his vicious reputation, Brunhilde's sister Galswintha was forced into marriage with him.

The marriage did not last. Brunhilde soon learned that her sister was dead. Fredegund had persuaded Chilperic to have Galswintha strangled in her bed, only to marry the less-than-grief-stricken widower herself a few days later.

With her husband's help, Brunhilde made war upon the murderous couple. In early engagements, Chilperic was defeated by Sigebert, but Fredegund turned the tables in 575 when she hired assassins to stab Sigebert to death. Brunhilde was captured but set free by Chilperic's son Meroveus, who fell in love with her. In revenge, Fredegund hounded Meroveus to his death.

Returning to her own kingdom, Brunhilde found herself at war again. Her young son was now established on Sigebert's throne, and Brunhilde took up the reins of power on his behalf. The rule of a woman was anathema to a strong political party of noblemen, who raised an army against her. Brunhilde appealed for peace, but in a grim foreshadowing of her eventual fate, she was warned, "Depart from us, lest our horses' hooves trample you underfoot." Undeterred, Brunhilde led her forces into battle and won the day. Confirmed in power, she was able to rule openly on behalf of her still-youthful son, Childebert.

At Childebert's majority, Brunhilde stepped down. Meanwhile the war with Fredegund dragged on, and Brunhilde's son and his wife were poisoned, most probably on the orders of the wicked queen. Brunhilde took up arms again to govern on her grandsons' behalf, making them and herself once again the target of Fredegund's uncontrollable rage. Fredegund's lust for power only deepened in 584 when she had her own husband murdered and began to rule in her own right, posing as regent for her young son, Chlotar II.

Brunhilde and her grandsons were now in constant danger of assassination, as Fredegund made more than one attempt to have them poisoned. She was still directing both open and dirty warfare, involving her favorite weapons of knife and poison, when she died unexpectedly in 597, leaving her kingdom to her equally cruel and murderous son, Chlotar II.

The threat from Fredegund had ceased. But Brunhilde's wars were not over. Her former enemies among the Frankish nobles now persuaded the older of her two grandsons to seize power and to banish her. With the aid of the younger brother, Brunhilde fought back, mounting a successful military operation in which her opponent was defeated and killed. But her success was short-lived. Her victorious grandson died suddenly at the age of twenty-six, leaving four young sons.

Approaching seventy years of age, Brunhilde found herself regent again, this time for her great-grandchildren, but was no longer able to contain the rapacious ambition of her noblemen. Her enemies turned in secret to Fredegund's son, Chlotar II, and offered him the kingdom if he would remove the queen.

Chlotar accepted. Betrayed by the leader of her own party,

Brunhilde was handed over to her former rival's equally depraved and cruel son. Accounts of her death vary, but all agree that she was subjected to three days of appalling humiliation and torture before Chlotar and all his army, and finally torn to pieces by wild horses.

Reference: Gregory of Tours and Lewis Thorpe, *A History of the Franks,* 1976.

CARTIMANDUA
British Queen, First Century CE

Faced with war and invasion, Cartimandua was a ruler who chose to negotiate rather than to fight. Unlike her contemporary **Boudicca** (see p. 12), she came to a working accommodation with the Romans in Britain, thereby preserving the peace of her people and her own throne.

Cartimandua was the ruler in her own right of the Brigantes, the largest tribe in Britain, whose lands stretched from Stoke-on-Trent in the English Midlands to Newcastle in the north, and ran from coast to coast. Like a number of Celtic queens in the pre-Christian era, Cartimandua enjoyed full sovereignty as the incarnation of the Great Goddess and the spirit of the land. The early relations of the Brigantes with the Roman conquerors were friendly, since Cartimandua was a ruler of considerable diplomacy and skill. "Sleek Pony," the meaning of Cartimandua, described a horse far above the rough-coated native breeds, and the queen lived up to her name. She negotiated a treaty relationship with the Romans and the invaders allowed her to continue her rule as an independent ally.

In 51 CE, Cartimandua divorced her consort, Venutius, and replaced him with a younger man, fulfilling the Goddess tradition of refreshing herself with a more vigorous lover, since the sexual power of the ruler was vital to the health of the tribe. But in the world of the Romans, men held sway, and the cast-off consort refused to go quietly. Venutius may also have been infuriated by Cartimandua's choice of his replacement, a youth called Vellocatus, who had served as his armor bearer. He decided to usurp Cartimandua and seize her throne. Her supporters rose in outrage against him, and a full-scale civil war broke out. Cartimandua appealed to the Romans for support, and their commander declared the whole of the vast Brigantine territory a Roman protectorate.

But she was powerless to contain the intertribal war. A skilled commander, she scored many victories but was finally forced to flee. With Vellocatus in tow, she sought refuge with the Romans, who took her into the safety of their massive fort at Camulodunum, modern Colchester, where they spent the rest of their days. She had held power for twelve turbulent years, and, unlike many of her fellow Celtic rulers, lived to die in her own bed.

Nevertheless, the impulse to turn Cartimandua's story of survival against the odds into one of disaster has been strong. Accounts of her rule found their way back to Rome, and Roman mothers used Cartimandua as an example to their daughters of the fate that attended women who descended into adultery and lust, unaware that adultery did not exist in the British world: unlike Roman and Christian wives, Celtic women did not become the possessions of the men they married. Cartimandua was strong, she was successful, sexual, powerful, and free, and in the end she lived to enjoy all that. It is not hard to imagine why later historians found this difficult to admire.

Cartimandua's career shows that in the first century CE, British women held supreme authority, made treaties with foreign powers, led their own armies into battle, and disposed of unwanted husbands at will, rights denied to her Roman sisters at the time and to most women worldwide for the next two thousand years.

Reference: John King, *Kingdoms of the Celts,* 2000.

CLEOPATRA VII
Egyptian Queen, b. 690 BCE, d. 30 BCE

Cleopatra, wrote the French poet Théophile Gautier in 1845, "is a person . . . whom dreamers find always at the end of their dreams." She was born in Alexandria, the third daughter of King Ptolemy XII, a descendant of one of Alexander the Great's generals, whose family had ruled Egypt since 323 BCE and whose empire, at its greatest extent, had extended as far as Syria and Palestine.

By the time of her birth, however, Ptolemy was a puppet of Rome. Cleopatra had no Egyptian blood, and although she may have spoken Egyptian, she was to all intents and purposes Greek. Her father's singularly undistinguished reign ended with his death in 51 BCE, and he was succeeded by the eighteen-year-old Cleopatra and her twelve-year-old brother-husband, Ptolemy XIII. Their roles as sister-wife and brother-husband underlined their divine origin as lawgivers.

Within three months, relations between the siblings broke down. Cleopatra's attempts to govern alone defied the Ptolemaic tradition of the subordination of female rulers to males. She was removed from power by a cabal of courtiers and, after failing to raise a rebellion, was forced to flee Egypt with her surviving sister, Arsinoë.

In the subsequent Egyptian civil war, Ptolemy XIII sought the aid of Julius Caesar, one of Rome's ruling Triumvirate. Caesar's response was to seize Alexandria and impose himself as arbiter of the rival claims of the young king and his sister. Cleopatra played a finely judged hand, allegedly having herself smuggled to meet Caesar inside a carpet. Caesar abandoned his plans to annex Egypt and backed Cleopatra's claims to the throne. Ptolemy XIII drowned in the Nile, and Cleopatra was restored to the throne with a younger brother, Ptolemy XIV, as co-regent. Cleopatra bore Caesar a son, dubbed Caesarion, who in 47 BCE accompanied his mother to Rome, where she lived in one of Caesar's villas. After Caesar's assassination in 44 BCE, she returned to Egypt, where in all probability she was responsible for the death by poisoning of Ptolemy XIV. With another brother successfully dispatched, she resumed her position as co-sovereign with her son Caesarion (Ptolemy XV).

Two years after Caesar's death, Cleopatra was summoned to a meeting in Tarsus to confirm her loyalty. Her inquisitor was

Marcus Antonius (Shakespeare's Mark Antony), another triumvir. Through Cleopatra's Eastern techniques of seduction, Antony was expertly reeled in and persuaded to live with her in sybaritic idleness in Alexandria. There she bore him three children and, according to the Roman historian and gossip Suetonius, married him in an Egyptian rite, despite the fact that he was already married to the sister of one of his fellow triumvirs.

As Anthony's credit ran out in Rome, where he was believed to have lost his Roman integrity and sunk into Eastern excess, Cleopatra financed his disastrous campaign against the Parthians, in which he lost the greater part of his army. This did not prevent Antony and Cleopatra from celebrating with a triumph (a formal victory parade) in Alexandria, where she and her children were declared rightful rulers of both the Roman and Egyptian Empires. Mark Antony now planned to found a new imperial dynasty whose power base was to be Alexandria rather than Rome. Cleopatra would be Isis to Antony's Osiris, a notion that did not endear him to his enemies in Rome.

In 32 BCE the Senate was persuaded to declare war on Cleopatra—in effect a move against Antony, who would not desert her. The Roman poet Horace gloated that Cleopatra would be dispatched "as swiftly as the hawk follows the feeble dove." The conflict was decided by the Battle of Actium, fought at sea off the west coast of Greece while land-based hosts looked on. Of the four hundred warships under Antony's command, Cleopatra had provided two hundred.

Caesar's great-nephew and adopted son and heir, Octavian, another triumvir, prudently delegated operational command of the Roman fleet to his competent lieutenant Vipsanius Agrippa. Mark Antony was able to break through Agrippa's battle line but lost the day and fled to Egypt with Cleopatra, who had been present at the battle to inspire her own fighting men.

As Octavian's armies closed on Alexandria, they both committed suicide. The ancient sources assert that Cleopatra killed herself with two asps that she applied to her arm, although it is possible that she ended her life with a poisoned hairpin. Her son Caesarion was captured shortly afterward and put to death. Thus ended the line of the Hellenistic rulers of Egypt, and with it the line of the pharaohs. Cleopatra's children by Mark Antony were spared, reared in Rome by his wife Octavia.

As Caesar Augustus, Octavian remodeled the constitution and carried Rome into a new age. Cleopatra was demonized by Horace as "the wild queen" who had plotted the ruin of the Roman Empire. In spite of the destruction of all her plans, Cleopatra nevertheless became a legend, reworked in countless paintings, poems, plays, and, since 1908, movies. She lives again as the baleful silent diva Theda Bara's kohl-stained temptress of 1917; as Claudette Colbert's Art Deco sex kitten in 1934; and in the well-upholstered Elizabeth Taylor, dripping with diamonds and diaphanous nightwear, as she conspicuously consumes Richard Burton's Mark Antony in the 1963 *Cleopatra*.

Reference: Lucy Hughes-Hallett, *Cleopatra*, 1990.

TOMOE GOZEN
Japanese Samurai, b. ca. 1161, d. ca. 1184

An example of the consummate woman warrior, Tomoe Gozen was a legendary fighter at the time of the Genpei War (1180–85), a period that saw the birth of the samurai tradition in Japan. Gozen is not a surname but an honorific applied principally to women.

The sources differ on the details of her life. She was either the wife, concubine, or female attendant of the Japanese commander Minamoto no Yoshinaka. Skilled in the martial arts and fearless in battle, she was one of Yoshinaka's senior officers in the struggle for the control of Japan between the Taira and Minamoto clans.

Tomoe Gozen's beauty and prowess are described in the *Heike Monogatari* (Tales of the Monogatari):

> Tomoe was especially beautiful, with white skin, long hair and charming features. She was also a remarkably strong archer, and as a swordswoman she was a warrior worth a thousand, ready to confront a demon or a god, mounted or on foot. She handled

unbroken horses with superb skill; she rode unscathed down perilous descents. Whenever a battle was imminent, Yoshinaka sent her out as his first captain, equipped with strong armour, an oversized sword, and a mighty bow; and she performed more deeds of valour than any of his other warriors.

Minamoto no Yoshinaka's ambition to head the Minamoto clan eventually led to his downfall. The clan chieftain, Minamoto no Yoritomo, decided to nip his cousin's designs in the bud and dispatched his brothers to kill him. Yoshinaka did battle with Yoritomo's forces at Awazu in February 1184, where it was said that Tomeo Gozen decapitated at least one of the enemy. With only a few of his soldiers left standing, Yoshinaka ordered Tomoe Gozen to quit the field. One account has her remaining and meeting death at Yoshinaka's side. Another has her surviving to become a member of a religious order. In yet another she casts herself into the sea, clutching Yoshinaka's severed head.

    Reference: Helen Craig McCullough, trans., *The Tale of the Heike*, 1988.

WOMEN WARRIORS IN ANCIENT GREECE AND ROME
Pre-Christian Era

Like the tribes of women warriors, fearless individual female fighters crop up so often in the poetry and history of the ancient Greek and Roman world that their existence cannot be dismissed simply as myth (see **Amazons**, p. 5). In the early classical period, young girls led a free, open-air life and were given athletic and gymnastic training to promote both fitness and beauty. In Crete, chosen young women trained as *toreras* to take part in the Minoan ritual of bull leaping, while Ionian women joined in boar hunts, nets and spears at the ready.

    The freedom of the young, unmarried women in the military city-state of Sparta was so marked that it scandalized others, as the Athenian playwright Euripides records:

The daughters of Sparta are never at home!
They mingle with the young men in wrestling matches,
Their clothes cast off, their hips all naked,
It's shameful!

The hardening of these young women's bodies by sport and the regular practice of nudity had a deliberate aim: to foster their strength, physical ability, and endurance for military service. Both the Spartans and Athenians trained their girls in the art of war and encouraged their participation in competitive war games. Plato stated in his *Republic* that women should become soldiers if they wished, though he later modified that in his *Laws*.

Rome followed Greece in this, as it so often did. Musonius Rufus (30–101 CE) advocated that women and men should receive the same education and training and that any differences should be based on ability and strength, not gender. The Roman heroine Cloelia, taken hostage by the Etruscan king Lars Porsena during an attack on Rome in the sixth century BCE, escaped, stole a horse, and swam the Tiber River to get back to Rome to fight.

The Romans promptly handed her back as proof of *Romana fides* (the unwavering truth of a Roman pledge). But Lars Porsena was more impressed by Cloelia's valor than he was by her compatriots' rigid view of honor, and he freed her and all her fellow hostages. Throughout the ancient world there is scattered but abundant evidence of women like Cloelia under arms, fighting in the front-line engagements traditionally believed to be reserved for men. Another was the Roman fighter Camilla, whose story is told by the poet Virgil in his account of the founding of Rome, the *Aeneid*, written between 26 and 19 BCE.

A daughter of the royal house of the Volscian tribe, Camilla was dedicated by her father at an early age to Diana, the Roman goddess of hunting, and given an early training in the use of weapons and the mastery of horses and dogs. She joined the forces of Turnus, king of the Rutulian tribe in central Italy. Turnus was at war with the neighboring kingdom of the Etruscans over the mastery of this crucial area, and Camilla died in the fighting, killed by the Etruscan warrior Arruns.

In creating his portrait of Camilla around 20 BCE, Virgil drew on some aspects of the life and character of another famous woman fighter, Harpalyce, daughter of Harpalycus, king of the Amymonei in Thrace (an area of northern Greece that extended into modern Turkey and Bulgaria). Her father brought her up as a warrior after her mother died. She fought at his side and on one occasion saved his life. After his death and the loss of his kingdom, she became a brigand and was finally captured and killed. Despite the lawless ending of her life, Harpalyce was given civic honors after her death. Her tomb became a shrine, and the rituals celebrated at her graveside included a mock fight.

In the Roman Empire, individual women warriors fought in public arenas both as free women and as slaves. They competed at the opening of the Colosseum in 80 CE. According to the Roman satirist Juvenal, it became fashionable for women of the nobility to train and fight in the arenas until 200 CE, when the emperor Septimius Severus issued an edict banning all women from gladiatorial combat.

Reference: *The Oxford Classical Dictionary.*

ZENOBIA
Znwbya Bat Zabbai, Syrian Warrior Queen, b. ca. 240, d. after 274 CE

Zenobia enters history as the military partner of her husband, Odenathus, a client king of the Romans who had colonized their city-state of Palmyra in modern Syria, a rule Zenobia, like **Boudicca** (see p. 12), never accepted. Always described as beautiful, intelligent, and virtuous, she chose a life of action from an early age. Odenathus was a renowned and fearless fighter, and they made many conquests together. But the historians of her era record that Zenobia was as daring and effective as her husband in combat and more reckless in war, able to walk three or four miles with her foot soldiers and drink with them without getting drunk, dubbing her "the better man of the two." Zenobia rode with Odenathus on many campaigns against the Persians and the Goths until he was assassinated, when she took up the reins of government on behalf of herself and her infant son, Vaballathus.

Riding into battle was an important element of Zenobia's success. Appearing on horseback before a battle makes a warrior woman a powerful inspiration to her troops (see **Isabella I of Spain,** p. 44 and **Elizabeth I,** p. 34). By presenting herself as a goddess, Zenobia tapped into an ancient Arab tradition, the pre-Islamic belief in the Great Goddess in her incarnation as the Lady of Victory. Boudicca, too, claimed kinship with the Great Goddess in her martial aspect, stirring up women's valor as well as men's passion, and uniting both sexes in the desire to resist.

Zenobia always claimed to be descended from the ruling house of Ptolemy in Egypt, specifically from **Cleopatra** (see p. 19), and spoke Egyptian as well as Greek, Latin, and Aramaic. She soon laid claim to Roman territory there, marching her armies into upper Egypt in 269 CE after Odenathus' death.

Zenobia also moved into Roman territories in Arabia and Asia Minor to expand Palmyra's trade. By the end of 269 CE, she had secured most of Egypt and annexed vast swathes of Syria. Within a few years of taking control, she had forged a vast empire out of tiny Palmyra, from Egypt in the south to the Bosporus in the north. She defeated one Roman expedition sent against her, proclaimed her son Vaballathus "Augustus" (emperor), and declared herself independent of Rome by minting her own coinage with her image on it. To the Roman emperor Aurelian, this was a rebellion so grave that he personally took command of the campaign when he sent the Roman army into Syria to crush Zenobia and her son.

Commanding a large army with a heavily armored cavalry, Zenobia confronted Aurelian near Antioch. She was seen in the forefront of the battle, galloping alongside her troops shouting orders. Aurelian instructed his cavalry to flee, luring the Palmyrenes to give chase until the weight of their armor exhausted both horses and men. Then the Roman horsemen turned on their opponents and cut them down.

The battle lost amid horrible slaughter, Zenobia fell back into Antioch, keeping the city loyal by leading through the streets in chains a man who resembled Aurelian, as if she had defeated and captured him. But at the next engagement, the seasoned Roman legions prevailed once more, and Zenobia was forced to flee, losing her treasury to Aurelian in the abandoned city. Setting out by camel to seek help from the Persians, she was overtaken by Aurelian's horsemen and captured on the banks of the Euphrates.

Aurelian executed most of Zenobia's supporters, but displayed a Roman magnanimity toward the vanquished citizens of Palmyra, sparing their lives and contenting himself with seizing all the city's wealth. Facing Aurelian as a woman of beauty, intellect, and sexual allure, Zenobia demanded immunity on the grounds of her sex. One tradition claims that she then committed suicide like her ancestor, Cleopatra, rather than face the humiliation of captivity. But Latin sources state that she was brought to Rome in safety and led through the streets in 274 CE, shackled in golden chains, to celebrate Aurelian's triumph. Disdaining her royal right to ride in a chariot, she walked defiantly with Aurelian's other conquests, defeated Goths and Vandals and a band of Scythian fighting women the Romans called **Amazons** (see p. 5).

After a triumph, Roman captives were normally killed or sold into slavery. Zenobia succeeded in building a new life. Granted a pension and a villa outside Rome, she married a Roman senator and settled down to country life, fading into history like her son Vaballathus, whose end is not known.

Reference: Antonia Fraser, *The Warrior Queens,* 1988.

2

THE CAPTAINS AND THE QUEENS

~~~

Women Leaders and Commanders,
Directing War and Conflict

*Though I have the body of a weak and feeble woman,
I have the heart and stomach of a king.*
—Queen Elizabeth I of England, defying the might of the Spanish
Armada in 1588

EARLY HISTORY ABOUNDS in records of women on the battle-field assuming a wide range of roles, including that of commander-in-chief. The rise of patriarchy changed all that. Whether expressed as a religion like Judaism, Christianity, or Islam, as a social and military system like the Roman or Chinese Empires, or as a philosophy like Confucianism, the message to warrior women everywhere was plain: in the words of St. Paul, "I permit no woman to usurp authority over a man."

This drastic reversal of women's right to equal status put power firmly in the hands of men for thousands of years. Only toward the end of the twentieth century, and then principally in the West, have women such as **Golda Meir** (see p. 48) and **Condoleezza Rice** (see p. 51) regained the place in councils of war that their sisters enjoyed from the dawn of recorded time.

Their careers, like that of **Margaret Thatcher** (see p. 58) lay to rest the sentimental and belittling myth that if the world were ruled by women, they would handle their power in a more kindly and maternal way. Like **Boudicca** (see p. 12), who encouraged her troops to commit appalling atrocities against the hated Roman occupiers, especially their women, Condoleezza Rice implemented a US foreign policy that had disastrous consequences for the civilians of Iraq.

As the modern era evolved, and as organized religion drove out older beliefs, especially in Europe, women tended to lose access to military command based on their semidivine status, which had derived from their connection with the Great Goddess and hence the sovereignty of the land. However, they could still gain entry by being born into the sovereign elite, especially if male offspring were in short supply. In the early Middle Ages, the power of the hereditary monarchy often enabled female rulers to act independently, like the tenth-century Saxon queen **Ethelfleda** (see p. 37), a sharp strategist and rough handler of Viking raiders.

Equally tenacious was **Matilda of Tuscany,** "the Pope's handmaid" (see p. 46), who appeared on the battlefield "armed like a warrior" and later presided over the spectacular humiliation of the Holy Roman Emperor Henry IV at the hands of Pope Gregory VII. In a reign of almost ceaseless campaigning, the twelfth-century **Tamara** of Georgia (see p. 56) increased the size of her realm to the greatest extent in its history, while simultaneously crushing a series of internal rebellions and presiding over a golden age of Georgian culture.

Less cultured and even more brutal was **Caterina Sforza** (see p. 54), the illegitimate daughter of Duke Francesco Sforza of Milan. But her career of ruthless leadership, savage feuding, and murderous reprisals was interrupted in 1500 when she was forced to surrender her stronghold to Cesare Borgia, who consolidated his victory by raping her.

Almost all these women had husbands, but they were creatures of such overriding will that they were capable of acting as leaders on their own account with all the ruthlessness required. **Isabella I** (see p. 44) proved a notable exception when she achieved the reconquest of Islamic Spain at the end of the fifteenth century by working hand in glove with her husband, Ferdinand of Aragon. In

Antonia Fraser's memorable phrase, the two monarchs "came to resemble two great oaks whose roots were inextricably entwined somewhere below the surface."

Perhaps the most famous of all female ruler–commanders was **Elizabeth I** (see p. 34), an implacable opponent of the overmighty Spain created by Ferdinand and Isabella's success. Like many women rulers, Elizabeth only came to power in the absence of any male heir, and all her advisers assumed that she would swiftly marry and put that right. But with an assurance beyond her twenty-five years, she deftly avoided marriage and remained sole ruler for the rest of her life, using her single status to powerful political effect by offering herself around as a potential bride.

Elizabeth constantly presented herself as one entitled by God and the people to act with all the powers of a man, but who still remained a woman at heart. This technique was later used with similar success by Margaret Thatcher, who gloried in her reputation for masculine strength and dominance, but who was equally at home posing as a housewife managing the family budget and trumpeting the infallibility of "a woman's instinct" to force through some particularly unpopular piece of legislation.

This assumption of the role and prerogative of men in order to achieve the status of an honorary male is shared by many commander queens. Just as Elizabeth I positioned herself as the daughter of Henry VIII, her near contemporary, the African queen **Jinga Mbandi** (see p. 322) always donned male attire for ritual sacrifices. Even the austere and devout Spanish Catholic wife Isabella I of Spain would appear at sieges wearing armor, a sight that invariably drove the troops into a frenzy of excitement. In the same spirit, **Catherine II of Russia** (see p. 32) wore a borrowed uniform from a crack regiment to seize power in a 1762 coup d'etat.

But as with male supreme commanders in wartime, the presence of women war leaders on the battlefield gradually became symbolic rather than real, and fewer and fewer thrust themselves into the thick of the fighting. Like **Tamara of Georgia** (see p. 56), they would retire to a secure vantage point to protect themselves before battle began. Tamara was known throughout Georgia as "King of Kings and Queen of Queens." But high birth was never a prerequisite of leadership. In the twentieth century, women in most Western countries gained the vote, and with it access to political power, enabling some women to rise to supreme power by sheer force of ability and outstanding drive.

As a result, a small number of women politicians, such as **Indira Gandhi** (see p. 39), Golda Meir, and Margaret Thatcher, found themselves at the helm, holding crucial decision-making positions in time of war. They seldom had any direct military experience—indeed, Margaret Thatcher had remained inactive in her hometown of Grantham during World War II when she could easily have joined one of Britain's auxiliary services (see **Conscription,** p. 159).

Like Catherine the Great, these women relied heavily on the advice of their male military commanders. Golda Meir confessed at the time of the Yom Kippur War that she had only the haziest notion of the strength of a division. However, they more than compensated for this deficiency with their resilience and willingness to "bite the bullet." Margaret Thatcher in particular relished the task, and during the Falklands War was famously described as "the only man in the [British] cabinet."

Never a feminist, Thatcher undoubtedly relished the chance to live up to this characterization in the manner of her wartime hero, Winston Churchill. In a striking example of deliberate image-making, she was photographed riding triumphantly in a main battle tank like a modern-day Boudicca, giving her own unspoken V-sign to the generations of men who had deemed women unfit for combat or command. She and other twentieth-century women war leaders have seen women in both the West and the East once more directing military campaigns and leading their countries in war, as their sisters in command did thousands of years ago.

Meanwhile, far from the sheltered calm of cabinet rooms and the luxury of democratic decision making, women in war-torn regions are still leading their troops into battle all over the globe.

CATHERINE II
"Catherine the Great," Empress of Russia, b. 1729, d. 1796

Known as an enlightened absolutist, Catherine was a clever and calculating ruler, the ultimate small-town girl made good. The wars she waged took up only six years of her twenty-five-year reign but nearly doubled the population of Russia. She once cannily observed, "We need population, not devastation. Peace is necessary to this vast empire."

She was born Princess Sophia Augusta Frederika of Anhalt-Zerbst, in Stettin, now Szczecin in modern Poland. At the age of fifteen she visited Russia to meet the heir to the throne, sixteen-year-old Grand Duke Peter, whom she married in 1745. The marriage was unsuccessful and was not consummated for nine years because of Peter's impotence and mental immaturity.

At the beginning of 1762, Peter succeeded to the throne as Peter III, but his eccentricities and the great unpopularity of his pro-German policies led to his overthrow six months later by his own guardsmen, who then proclaimed Catherine their empress. Peter was imprisoned and later killed—supposedly accidentally—by Aleksei Orlov, younger brother of Gregory Orlov, one of Catherine's many lovers.

The short, stout Catherine was gallantly but inaccurately characterized by William Richardson, the tutor to the children of the British ambassador, as "taller than middle-sized, gracefully formed, but inclined to corpulence." To the deeply conservative Russian nobility, she was seen as an egregious example of the monstrous regiment of women and a threat to the traditional morals of "Mother Russia."

Presenting herself as an enlightened ruler, a "philosopher on the throne," Catherine corresponded with French writers and thinkers such as the philosopher Voltaire, who dubbed her "the Star of the North." With considerable drive she initiated an ambitious program to reform the laws, education, and administration of Russia. By the end of her reign, however, the Russian nobility were even more entrenched than when she had taken power. And in spite of the establishment of her capital, St. Petersburg, as a vibrant cultural center, all intellectual protest was stifled.

In foreign policy, Catherine was an ambitious expansionist. She extended the borders of the Russian Empire westward and southward at the expense of two rival powers, the Polish-Lithuanian Commonwealth and the Ottoman Empire. Voltaire was a great supporter of her wars against the Turks, principally on the grounds that Catherine's adversaries did not speak French. In November 1768, a month after she had gone to war against the Ottoman Empire, Voltaire wrote to Catherine, "Clearly, people who neglect all the fine arts and who lock up women deserve to be exterminated."

Victory in the first Russo-Turkish War (1768–74) gave Russia access to the Black Sea and to vast tracts of land in what is now southern Ukraine, where the new city of Odessa was founded. In 1783 Catherine annexed the Crimea, which nine years earlier had gained independence from the Ottoman Empire. She attended the twice-weekly war councils that planned the campaign and in all probability was the originator of the daring indirect strategy in which the Russian Baltic fleet sailed five thousand miles around the coasts of Europe to engage the Ottoman enemy. In 1787 the Ottomans launched a catastrophic second war, which was ended by the Treaty of Jassy (1791) and the legitimization of the Russian claim to the Crimea. However, the ambition she nursed to seize Constantinople was unrealized.

Catherine also established herself as a formidable power broker with the nations of western Europe and acted as a mediator in the War of the Bavarian Succession (1778–79) between Prussia and Austria. In 1780, mindful of her enlightened image, she refused to intervene in the American Revolution in support of the British. In the Russo-Swedish War of 1788–90, she thwarted Swedish designs on St. Petersburg. The grounds around the imperial palaces at Tsarskoe Selo were littered with columns and obelisks marking her military victories—all seventy-eight of them.

During her long reign, Catherine hugely enjoyed recreational sex and took many lovers, the last of whom, Prince Zubov, was forty years her junior. She was controlling but notably generous with her lovers, although she was a harsh mother to her son, Paul, who was kept in a state of house arrest and denied any independent authority. To the end of her life, she remained supremely aware of her image. When she consolidated the coup d'etat of 1762 in which her husband was overthrown, she borrowed the green and red uniform of a suitably short lieutenant in the Semeonovsky regiment to create an iconic symbol, and throughout her life attended carefully to every nuance of her appearance as a public figure. Sometimes military and masculine, she was once noted as greeting a delegation of French diplomats like "a charming lady on her country estate," an effect that was minutely choreographed to linger in her visitors' memories. Her own memoirs were written in different versions for different readers and allies.

Catherine suffered a stroke while taking a bath on November 5, 1796, and died the following day. She was buried at the Peter and Paul Cathedral in St. Petersburg. Palace intrigue ensured that a scurrilous fiction about the details of her death quickly gained circulation and has survived to this day. She is supposed to have expired in the throes of being serviced by a stallion, a cautionary myth that clearly reveals the depth of fear, loathing, and incomprehension that attend any woman of power and voracious sexual appetite.

Reference: Virginia Rounding, *Catherine the Great: Love, Sex and Power*, 2006. Catherine was memorably played by Marlene Dietrich in the 1934 movie *The Scarlet Empress*.

ELIZABETH I
Queen of England, b. 1533, d. 1603

Queen Elizabeth I became the most famous woman in the world in 1588, when she led England to a stunning victory over the Spanish Armada, the most fearsome foe her sceptered isle had ever faced. When still in the womb, she had earned the undying hatred of the Most Holy Catholic Majesty of Spain, and when the mighty Armada finally put to sea, it bore down on the fifty-five-year-old Queen with all the force of an Islamic jihad.

Elizabeth's notoriety was due to the desperation of her father, King Henry VIII, for a son, after his twenty-four-year marriage to the Spanish princess Catherine of Aragon had failed to produce a live male heir. Frantic to secure his Tudor dynasty, Henry cast Catherine off in order to remarry, and tried to get his marriage declared null and void by the Church.

Spain's fury at Henry's cruel treatment of Catherine only increased when the king broke with Rome and set up his own Protestant church, in order to marry his pregnant mistress, Anne Boleyn. Anne was confidently expected to produce a boy, but the child was a girl. Elizabeth's conception had triggered Henry's break with Rome in vain. Worse, it fueled the vicious European wars of religion that created the three-hundred-year agony of Ireland, and that still reverberate today.

From her earliest years, the threat of Spain's hostility hung over Elizabeth, but as queen, she did everything she could to keep the foe at bay. For a woman who is revered as one of the greatest war leaders Britain has ever known, Elizabeth was an extremely reluctant belligerent and never willingly went on the attack. She hated the chaos of war, the loss of life, and above all the drain on the Exchequer with the massive costs involved. This natural aversion hardened into a settled policy early in her reign, after a costly and futile expedition against the French.

But indirect operations were a different game. Elizabeth had no scruples about encouraging her privateers such as Francis Drake and John Hawkins to wage a maritime guerrilla war. Secretly funding their expeditions to raid the great galleons of the Spanish main, she greedily pocketed the lion's share of their stupendous loot. Pieces of eight, silver bullion, ingots of gold, sapphires, rubies, and emeralds as big as pigeon's eggs all found their way into the queen's hands. But in public she was always swift to disown and condemn her sailors when the Spanish ambassador came to rage about the "English pirates" and their attacks on the Spanish treasure fleet.

For Elizabeth, these buccaneering raids made strategic sense. Convinced of its religious rightness and driven by a moral crusade, Catholic Spain dominated Europe and bestrode the world, imposing her will and trampling lesser nations in her path. Little England had to take every chance to tip the balance against such an overwhelming enemy.

By 1588 the king of Spain, Philip II, was ready to embrace war against England as a religious crusade. Some 130 mighty ships, including massive galleons of war standing seven stories above the water and thirty lesser warships equipped with 2,360 cannons, set sail with 19,295 handpicked fighting men, 8,460 sailors, and 2,088 galley slaves. It was the greatest force ever assembled against England until Hitler laid his plans for Operation Sealion in the summer of 1940.

Through the superb intelligence of her spymaster, Francis Walsingham, Elizabeth was only too well aware of the situation. But her unwavering courage won the admiration of all, even her ancient enemy, the Pope. As a war leader, Elizabeth rose to the crisis, chose her commanders brilliantly, and reined in her instinct to micromanage. Above all she remained at the helm, fearlessly refusing to leave London despite the entreaties of her ministers, just as the royal family stayed in Buckingham Palace throughout the Blitz of World War II. "Yet David beat Goliath," she averred.

And Elizabeth's faith in her tiny English fleet was fully justified. Although numerically outclassed by the massive Spanish galleons and only a fraction of their size, the little English warships were far easier to maneuver, nipping in and out of close combat like dogs baiting a bear. Among the English captains, Drake, Hawkins, and others also had the advantage of their previous successful attacks against the galleons on the Spanish main.

The result was devastation. One by one the galleons were blown up, boarded and sunk, or harried up the length of the English Channel in a desperate flight to find a way back to Spain around Scotland and Ireland, where many more were wrecked on those inhospitable shores. Only 54 of the proud 130 ever returned to Spain, and those in such bad shape that they never went to sea again.

The scale of the Spanish disaster was not known at the time. In the following days, England prepared for a land invasion from the Low Countries, where the Duke of Parma had assembled a fleet of 1,500 barges to ferry thousands of Spanish pikemen across the

Channel. Elizabeth rode out to hearten her army clad in armor previously made for her late brother Edward VI, who had died at sixteen, as his silver breastplate was the only piece in the royal treasury small enough to fit her slender frame (see **Isabella of Spain,** p. 44, for the identical tactic).

At Tilbury on the Thames outside London, she delivered the speech that has become world-famous, declaring, "Though I have the body of a weak and feeble woman, I have the heart and stomach of a king, yea and a king of England too." She went on to heap insults on the enemy, in the long tradition of commanders pumping up the aggression of the troops: "I think foul scorn that Parma or Spain or any prince of Europe should dare invade the borders of our realm!" she proclaimed, promising her soldiers cash rewards and "a famous victory over the enemies of God, my kingdom and my people."

So the battle of the Armada was won by tactics, but also by fate. That summer the Channel saw violent winds and unseasonable storms, which ravaged the top-heavy galleons while the English fleet escaped damage. But to an Elizabethan, there was no such thing as random good luck, only the working of the hand of God. Once victory was certain, Elizabeth, image-conscious to the last, seized the opportunity for a worldwide anti-Spanish and anti-Catholic propaganda coup. She ordered a medal to be struck and widely distributed with the Latin slogan *Deus flavit, et dissipati sunt* (God blew, and they were scattered). God was a Protestant, and he'd shown his true colors: he'd fought on England's side. With a little help from England's rightful if not Holy Roman Majesty, Elizabeth herself, of course.

Reference: Rosalind Miles, *I, Elizabeth,* 1994.

ETHELFLEDA

Aethelflaed, "The Lady of the Mercians," Saxon Queen and War Leader, d. 918 CE

Ethelfleda was the daughter of England's founding king, Alfred the Great, born into war as her father fought to free his emerging country from the invasions of the Danes. A bold tactician and an outstanding commander, she played a major part in driving out the warriors, raiders, and thugs of various races grouped together under the name of the Vikings, who regularly fell on the eastern coast of England from the plague-ridden and famine-prone German and Scandinavian countries across the North Sea.

As king, Alfred insisted on the establishment of the English language and the importance of education, and maintained a lifelong interest in philosophy. It is therefore highly likely that Ethelfleda was taught to read, write, and think, in an age when almost all were illiterate. As a Saxon woman, Ethelfleda also enjoyed more freedom in choosing a husband than the females of the other tribes and cultures of her day. She married Ethelred, *ealdorman* (lord) of the kingdom of West Mercia, and governed with him, though she was the controlling force from early on.

West Mercia, the country at the heart of the English Midlands, formed a first-rate strategic base where Ethelfleda created a military household that she dominated totally. After Ethelred's death in 911, Ethelfleda ruled alone, using her military might to defend the throne. When her father died, she threw her forces into the battle against the Vikings to ensure that her brother Edward succeeded as king of Wessex.

Ethelfleda's sense of strategy went beyond defensive campaigns. Marching the length of England, she fortified key strongholds such as Chester in the northwest and created new fortresses in the Midlands, boosting both peace and local commerce as they became important centers of trade.

By 917, still battling for her brother Edward, she was ready to launch a major attack on the Vikings who continued to harry England's eastern shores. She was also intent on pushing forward the boundaries of her brother's kingdom by conquest, and led her army to major victories over the towns of Derby and Leicester. In 918 she was in the Midlands, planning campaigns farther north. She had already achieved the capitulation of the Viking stronghold in the northern capital city of York when she unexpectedly died.

Ethelfleda followed in a long line of ruling Saxon queens like

Bertha, who died in 616, and Eadburga and Cynethryth, who flourished in the eighth century. She paved the way for the imperious Saxon warrior princess Aelgifu (b. 1010), who as mistress of King Cnut of Denmark, regent of Norway, and mother of King Harold "Harefoot" of England, held supreme power in three countries in the eleventh century.

Reference: Antonia Fraser, *The Warrior Queens,* 1988.

GANDHI, INDIRA
Indian Politician, b. 1917, d. 1984

The only child of Jawaharlal and Kamala Nehru, Gandhi was born into India's political aristocracy and led her country to a decisive victory over Pakistan in the 1971 war that followed the declaration of the independent state of Bangladesh. Although she was only the second woman elected to lead a democracy after Sirimavo Bandaranaike of Sri Lanka in 1960, Gandhi often displayed a ruthless and autocratic approach. She remains, nevertheless, one of her country's most charismatic leaders. Significantly, she once told a friend that **Joan of Arc** (see p. 75) was an early heroine of her childhood. She also declared that she was "in no sense a feminist" but nevertheless believed that "women are able to do everything."

She was born in Allahabad into a family in the vanguard of Indian nationalism—her father had been president of the Congress Party since 1929—and politics was the pulse that regulated her adolescence. By the time she was thirteen, she headed the so-called Monkey Brigade, consisting of children who were used to run messages for the Congress Party, which led the fight for independence from British rule. Nevertheless, her parents sent her to England to be educated, at the elite private Badminton School for Girls and Somerville College, Oxford.

On returning to India in 1938, she joined the Congress Party and four years later was married to the journalist Feroze Gandhi (no relation to Mahatma). As a patriarch with no sons, Nehru planned to make Feroze his political heir, and it is doubtful that

Indira would have had any political career if the hapless Feroze had proved up to the task. But the marriage was brief, and the couple were soon separated by events. Between September 1942 and May 1943, both were imprisoned by the British in Allahabad on charges of subversion.

India won its independence from Britain in 1947, and in the same year her father became the country's first prime minister. Nehru was now a widower, and Indira became his hostess and intimate, a role she played until his death in 1964. She proved an adept political trainee, and after the death of her father, she was elected to Parliament in his place and appointed minister of information and broadcasting by Prime Minister Lal Bahadur Shastri.

In 1966 Shastri died of a heart attack, and after only two years in Parliament Indira Gandhi emerged as the compromise candidate to succeed him. She went on to win the general election of 1967, and in her first year in office she was described as "the only man in a cabinet of old women" (see also **Meir, Golda** [p. 48], and **Thatcher, Margaret,** p. 58). In the 1971 election, she swept to a landslide victory under the slogan "Abolish poverty."

In 1947 Hindu India and the smaller Muslim nation of Pakistan had both gained their independence from the British in a welter of blood. The major war that had been threatening to erupt between the two nations ever since independence finally broke out after Indira Gandhi's 1971 election triumph. East Pakistan had declared itself the independent state of Bangladesh. West Pakistan attempted to suppress the independence movement, and the ensuing civil strife cost hundreds of thousands of lives. Up to ten million Bengalis took refuge in India, where initial support for a guerrilla response gave way to preparations for a full-scale military intervention.

Gandhi laid the ground with great skill. In August she signed a twenty-year treaty of friendship with the Soviet Union, which ensured that China, an ally of Pakistan, would stay out of the conflict. In the autumn of 1971 she launched a diplomatic offensive, touring Europe and ensuring that Britain and France would join with the United States, which she visited in early November, in blocking any pro-Pakistan resolutions in the United Nations Security Council.

However, US President Richard M. Nixon, whose sympathies lay with Pakistan, was not a soft touch. In conversation with his national security adviser, Henry Kissinger, Nixon referred to Gandhi as "the old witch." Nevertheless, after the outbreak of war in December 1971, Nixon's attempts to persuade the Chinese to come to the aid of Pakistan by mobilizing its forces against India, with the pledge of American support if the Soviet Union became involved, fell on deaf ears. The old witch had the last laugh.

At the beginning of December 1971, Pakistan attempted to forestall the growing threat of an Indian invasion of Bangladesh by launching a preemptive invasion of Kashmir and the Punjab. The Indian Air Force survived attacks on its airfields, and the next day the Indian invasion of East Pakistan began. Within thirteen days the Pakistani commander in Bangladesh had surrendered, while in West Pakistan the Indian Army halted the Pakistani advance. By December 17 the war was over and Pakistan had lost Bangladesh.

The 1971 war was unique in that the Indian political leadership exhibited a proper understanding of the use of military power to achieve a clear national aim. Vital to this success, and a tribute to Indira Gandhi's accomplished handling of the crisis, was the use of the Indian Navy. As East and West Pakistan were two separate geographical entities separated by over more than sixteen hundred miles, the only way Pakistani forces in East Pakistan could be sustained was by sea. Indira Gandhi decided that the Indian Navy was to be given the strategic task of denying East and West Pakistan access to war supplies by mounting a comprehensive naval blockade, a mission that it carried out with complete success. Not for nothing was Gandhi sometimes compared to the Indian goddess Durga, who rode on a tiger.

In 1971 India had carried the day, but victory was followed by a period of acute economic instability. In 1975, after a series of massive demonstrations, Gandhi declared a state of emergency, imprisoned thousands of political opponents, and imposed harsh censorship of the Indian press. Her growing unpopularity was exacerbated by the ambitious commercial plans of her younger son, Sanjay, and his project to control the spiraling Indian population by the enforced sterilization of men, for which each was to be compensated by a free transistor radio. She was defeated in the general election of 1977, and a coalition of parties, the Bharatiya Janata (BJP), came to power.

In 1980 factional fighting among her political opponents enabled Indira Gandhi to regain power. But it could never be glad, confident morning again. That same year Sanjay died in a plane crash. His mother was now preoccupied with mounting political problems in the Punjab. In June 1984, seeking to crush the secessionist Sikh movement led by the militant Jarnail Singh Bhindranwale, she ordered the storming of the holiest Sikh shrine in Amritsar, the Golden Temple (Operation Blue Star), in which Bhindranwale died and the temple was badly damaged. In October 1984, Gandhi was assassinated at her home by two of her Sikh bodyguards. Her elder son, Rajiv, became prime minister in December 1984, and in 1991 he was assassinated by a **Tamil Tiger** suicide bomber (see p. 115).

Reference: Katherine Frank, *Indira: The Life of Indira Nehru Gandhi*, 1998.

ISABELLA OF FRANCE
"The She-Wolf of France," Queen of England, b. 1292, d. 1358

Isabella, a French princess given in marriage to King Edward II of England, earned her wolfish nickname for raising the war that cost her husband his throne and his life. Her military prowess owed much to her lover, Roger de Mortimer, Earl of March, but her skill in winning the propaganda war against the king was all her own.

The marriage in 1308 had been ill-starred from the first. Although a beauty, the fifteen-year-old Isabella held no charms for the openly homosexual Edward, who treated her with neglect, if not contempt. Although he performed his dynastic duty and fathered a son on her, the king centered his life on his male lovers, which provided Isabella with an opportunity she was not slow to take.

In the religious Roman Catholic temper of the time, homo-sexuality was regarded as a mortal sin, and it was also a capital of-fense under the law of the land. Not for a king, however, who was above the law. Edward's behavior thus alienated many of his sub-jects, who could not have said which they hated most, Edward's gay lifestyle or his blunders in running the country, squandering money on his favorites while England's overseas territories were being reannexed by the French. Playing upon this, Isabella secretly won to her side most of the powerful men of England, including the dashing Mortimer, later Earl of March, who became her lover.

Isabella then traveled to France to raise an army, trading her teenage son in marriage in return for an army of mercenaries, and returned in 1326 to invade England, with Mortimer at the head of her troops. Drawing near London, she bombarded the city with slogans claiming she had come to end the tyranny of her husband the king, and, although a Frenchwoman born and bred, to cham-pion the good old English freedoms of ancient days.

Isabella played the battered-woman card to great effect in her campaign, declaring Edward had sworn "that if he had no other weapon, he would crush her to death with his teeth." But, she loudly complained, "the King carried a knife in his hose to kill the Queen." Reference to what Edward carried in his hose (i.e., in his pants) was a crude attempt to stir up hatred for him on the grounds of his homosexuality, and it helped to turn public opinion against the king, who fled for his life. Edward was captured and forced to abdicate in favor of his young son, Edward III, and Isabella de-clared herself and Mortimer regents for the boy.

The next year, 1327, she saw to it that the king was killed in captivity. Conscious as ever of public opinion, she ordered the king's body to be displayed to show that there was no mark of violence upon it, claiming that he died from natural causes. This did nothing to allay the widespread belief that he had been mur-dered, since Edward was a man of famously good health, with a strong constitution and a lineage of outstanding longevity. The display of the unblemished body merely gave rise to the rumor sniggered over by every English schoolboy from then on, that

Edward had met his end through a red-hot poker inserted up his anus, which, in the temper of the time, would have been considered poetic justice for his sins.

Edward's death secured Isabella and Mortimer from further plots on his behalf, but the stench of adultery and murder created a strong backlash against them. Isabella made a final attempt to deflect criticism by planning a war against the Scots, but her power was ebbing. And the "She-wolf" was not the only plotter in the family. In 1330, her eighteen-year-old son, Edward, copied her tactic of using the nobility to turn the tables on a hated ruler and had Mortimer arrested. Mortimer was hauled out to be hanged, drawn, and quartered, while Isabella was imprisoned in Castle Riding in Norfolk. But Edward bore no long-term grudge against his mother, restoring her to court and giving her an honored place before she died—unlike her enemies, her husband, or her lover—in her old age, at peace, and in her own bed.

Reference: Michael Prestwich, *Plantagenet England,* **2005.**

ISABELLA I OF SPAIN
Queen of Spain, b. 1451, d. 1504

Isabella was a warrior monarch who, during the reconquest of Spain, often appeared on the battlefield "superbly mounted and dressed in complete armour." This tactic to inspire the soldiers with both loyalty and chivalry was employed by a number of queens in time of war (see **Elizabeth I,** p. 34).

The daughter of Juan II of Castile and Isabella of Portugal, she was three years old when her father died. She was brought up by her mother until the age of thirteen, when she was taken to the court of her ineffectual half-brother, Henry IV, king of Castile. Although Isabella became the focus of opposition in the corrupt and febrile court, she avoided entanglement in conspiracy and in September 1468 was eventually recognized as the heir to the throne of Castile.

She married Ferdinand of Aragon, her own choice, in 1469. In 1474, on the death of Henry IV, Isabella swiftly arranged to be crowned "Queen Proprietress" of Castile instead of Juana, Henry's illegitimate daughter and his final choice as heir. The king of Portugal invaded Spain in support of Juana but was defeated in 1479. Juana retired to a convent, and in the same year Ferdinand succeeded to the throne of Aragon as Ferdinand II.

In 1480 the intensely austere and pious Isabella allowed the establishment of the Inquisition in Andalusia, principally as a measure to deal with Jews and Muslims who had been forcibly converted to Christianity but whose loyalties she did not trust. Both Ferdinand and Isabella were later given the title "the Catholic" by the Pope in recognition of their "purification" of the Catholic faith.

Although Isabella and Ferdinand governed independently, they came together in the wars to expel the Moors (Muslims) from the territories in Spain that they had occupied for centuries. The *Reconquista* lasted ten years and was completed in 1492 with the conquest of the kingdom of Granada. Isabella played a prominent part in the campaign, traveling with her five children and involving herself in every detail of the military establishment. She founded the Queen's Hospitals, consisting of six large hospital tents staffed with physicians and surgeons, which trundled across the landscape from siege to siege.

The *Reconquista* was primarily a war of sieges, during which the arrival of Isabella in her chain mail was counted on to stimulate such enthusiasm in her troops that the beleaguered citadels quickly fell. Her qualities as a quartermaster-general were invaluable. She oversaw the recruitment of thousands of pioneers to build roads that eased the passage of the cannon in her siege train and also engaged Don Francisco Ramirez, dubbed "El Artillero," to deploy them at their destination under the direction of her husband.

With her final victory over the Moors, 1492 was a busy year for Isabella, which also saw the expulsion from Spain of all Jews who refused to convert to Christianity and the voyage of discovery undertaken by Christopher Columbus, a venture she supported after much procrastination. In addition to sponsoring exploration, Isabella supported many scholars and artists, founded educational establishments, and amassed a huge art collection. She left the throne of Castile to her daughter Joan, as she had been predeceased by her eldest son, Juan, and daughter Isabella. Another daughter, Catherine of Aragon, became the first wife of Henry VIII of England.

A portrait of Isabella shows her with a long nose and a glum expression. The surviving armor of the husband-and-wife architects of the *Reconquista* indicates that Isabella was taller than Ferdinand by as much as an inch.

Reference: William Thomas Walsh, *Isabella of Spain: The Last Crusader (1451–1504)*, 1987.

MATILDA
Countess of Tuscany, b. 1046, d. 1115

Matilda was the right-hand woman of Pope Gregory VII in the struggle between the papacy and the Holy Roman Empire. Her spiritual adviser, Anselm of Lucca, later Pope Alexander II, observed that she combined the will and energy of a soldier with the mystic and solitary spirit of a hermit. Fighting for the Supreme Head of the Church of Rome provided Matilda with the opportunity to fulfill both the spiritual and martial sides of her indomitable nature.

She was born in northern Italy, the daughter of the Margrave Boniface, whose citadel was the impregnable Apennine fortress of Canossa, and Beatrice, the daughter of the duke of Upper Lorraine. Her father was assassinated in 1052, and the death of her siblings left her to inherit some of the richest lands in Italy.

As a child, Matilda was taught to ride like a lancer, spear in hand, and to wield a battle-axe and sword. She was strong and tall and was said to be accustomed to the weight of armor. She also liked needlework, and sent an embroidered war pennant to William the Conqueror. Her mother supervised her education, and she was unusually well schooled for the time, fluent in German, French, Italian, and Latin.

Matilda's introduction to the turbulent power politics of the eleventh century came in 1059, when she accompanied Beatrice and her stepfather, Godfrey of Lorraine, to the Council of Sutri, at which noble families maneuvered and bickered over the papal succession following the death of Pope Stephen IX.

It is likely that Matilda's first appearance on the battlefield came two years later, at her mother's side, as Alexander II battled against the schismatics who challenged his succession to the papacy. A contemporary account describes the young Matilda, "armed like a warrior" and carrying herself with "such bravery that she made known to the world that courage and valor in mankind is not indeed a matter of sex but of heart and spirit." It is also possible that she was present at the Battle of Aquino (1066) in which Godfrey of Lorraine defeated the Roman and Norman supporters of a rival pope.

The death of Godfrey in 1069 marked a turning point in Matilda's life. Aided at first by her mother, who died in 1076, she began to exercise her own authority in Italy in the absence of her husband, her stepbrother Godfrey the Hunchback, whom she had married in 1069. Matilda controlled Tuscany, parts of Umbria, and Emilia-Romagna and encouraged the economic power of the Florentine guilds.

In February 1076, Godfrey the Hunchback was killed campaigning in the Low Countries, and Matilda's mother died the following April. Marriage to Godfrey had left her with no heir— their children had died at birth—and she was free to take up arms for the papacy of Gregory VII in his struggle with the Holy Roman Emperor Henry IV. In 1077 Henry was received by Gregory as a penitent at Matilda's stronghold at Canossa. The emperor was obliged to stand for three days in the bitter winter cold outside the castle, barefoot and clad only in a woolen penitential robe, before he was allowed in to beg forgiveness from the Pope.

This spectacular triumph was short-lived. Gregory was driven from Rome into exile, dying in 1085. The emperor's allies preyed upon Matilda's possessions, and their efforts, although grievously undermining her strength, provoked the occasional stinging riposte. Her castle at Sorbara, near Modena and a softer target than Canossa, was besieged in 1084, only for the attackers to be driven off by an audacious sortie launched under the cover of darkness, and personally led by Matilda wielding her father's sword.

The election of Pope Urban II in 1088 saw an improvement in Matilda's fortunes. However, papal politics required her, at forty-three, to marry the seventeen-year-old Welf V of Bavaria and thus bring the callow teenager into an alliance with the See of Rome. It was a marriage of convenience that lasted six years and gave no pleasure to either partner, but it enraged Matilda's old enemy Henry IV.

At the end of her life she made peace of a kind with Henry's successor, his son Henry V, who came to visit her at Canossa on happier terms than his father and swore that "in the whole earth there could not be found a Princess her equal." She died in her seventieth year, having willed her lands to Henry V, a generous gesture that conveniently ignored the fact that in 1102 she had made them over to the papacy. Much confusion ensued, and ironically, the jostling between emperor and pope was renewed. In the seventeenth century the body of the "Pope's handmaid " was reinterred in St. Peter's Cathedral in Rome.

Reference: Antonia Fraser, *The Warrior Queens,* 1988.

MEIR, GOLDA
Israeli Politician, b. 1898, d. 1978

The trajectory of Golda Meir's career carried her from Kiev to the Knesset, the Israeli parliament, and to the position of prime minister in the Yom Kippur War of October 1972. In the highly masculine world of Israeli politics, Meir was an "Iron Lady" long before the term was coined for **Margaret Thatcher** (see p. 58).

She was born Goldie Mabovich in the Jewish quarter of Kiev, in Ukraine, and later emigrated with her family to join her father in the United States. In 1917 she married a sign painter, Morris Myerson, with whom she emigrated in 1921 to Palestine, where they worked for three years on a kibbutz (collective farm). The couple later moved to Tel Aviv, where Golda worked as a clerk and took in washing to support her two children and ailing husband.

By 1928, Meir had become secretary of the Women's Labor Council and was a rising force in the Histadrut, the Jewish labor federation, representing it at international conferences. She was elected as a delegate to the World Zionist Congress and in the 1930s accompanied missions to the United States and Britain.

After 1946, under the British mandate in Palestine, Meir was in the forefront of the Jewish Agency, the Jewish self-government organization. She succeeded Moshe Sharett as head of its political department, which liaised with the British. As a member of the agency's executive, she played a significant role in raising money in the United States for the nascent state of Israel.

In May 1948, on the eve of the British withdrawal and with armed conflict looming between the emerging Jewish state and its Arab neighbors, Meir was sent by the Jewish leader David Ben-Gurion on a secret mission. Disguised as an Arab woman and accompanied by Ezra Danin, a conduit between the Jewish Agency and Arab leaders, Meir crossed into Jordan to meet King Abdullah and attempt to persuade him to join an Anglo-Jordanian pact. King Abdullah, however, was already committed to an invasion of Palestine, and Meir returned to Tel Aviv to report the failure of her mission and the imminence of war. On May 14, 1948, she was one of the twenty-five signatories of the declaration establishing the state of Israel.

In January 1949, after the Israeli War of Independence, Meir was elected to the Knesset as a Labor candidate and was appointed Minister of Labour and Social Security, the only woman in the Ben-Gurion administration. In 1956 she became Israel's foreign minister and was closely involved in the secret negotiations, this time with the French, that preceded the Israeli campaign in the Sinai Peninsula, itself timed to coincide with the Anglo-French occupation of the Suez Canal Zone.

Subsequently, Meir was instrumental in restoring relations with the United States following the Suez debacle and providing assistance to emerging nations in Africa. Now a widow, she was asked by David Ben-Gurion to take a Hebrew name, and she chose Meir, which means "to burn brightly." She always stood out from the "suits," the male politicians all around her, an imposing but warm figure whose heavily lined features were in later years strongly reminiscent of US president Lyndon Baines Johnson.

Meir became Israel's prime minister in 1969 after the sudden death of Levi Eshkol. She was the world's third female premier, after Sirimavo Bandaranaike of Sri Lanka and **Indira Gandhi** of India (see p. 39), and governed through a select band of advisers known as her "kitchen cabinet." In 1972 she authorized the relentless international pursuit by a secret service unit of the terrorists responsible for the deaths of eleven Israeli athletes at the Munich Olympics.

But her administration came to be dominated and defined by the Yom Kippur War, which burst upon Israel on October 6, 1972, when the Egyptians crossed the Suez Canal. In the months leading up to the operation, Israeli military intelligence had failed to interpret correctly the many danger signals it had received during the deliberate Egyptian buildup. Indeed, on September 26, Israel's ambassador in the United States, Yitzhak Rabin, had declared that "there never was a period in which Israel's security situation seemed as good as now."

However, early on the morning of October 6, when it was clear that an attack on Israel was about to be launched, Meir overruled a proposal by the chief of staff of the Israeli Defense Forces (IDF), General David Elazar, to make a preemptive air strike on Egypt's ally, Syria. Meir knew that Israel had to be seen by the world as the victim of aggression and could not risk the withdrawal of US military and political support, without which Israel might have been forced to launch a nuclear response to the Egyptian and Syrian assault.

Throughout the October War, Meir remained a firm hand at the helm while those about her faltered and panicked in the crisis. In three weeks of bitter fighting, Israel secured victory over Egypt and Syria but at a heavy cost in men and matériel. The spring of 1974 saw the publication of a report by the Agranat Commission, which had been appointed to draw lessons from the debacle. It was highly critical of all aspects of Israel's political and military leadership. The two most notable victims of the commission's findings were General Moshe Dayan, Israel's minister of defense and a leading member of the kitchen cabinet, and Golda Meir herself. Following the commission's findings, they both resigned.

Reference: Golda Meir, *My Life,* 1975.

RICE, CONDOLEEZZA
US Diplomat, b. 1954

Her unusual name is derived from an Italian musical expression, *con dolcezza* (with sweetness); Rice's mother is a music teacher. Equally formidable as a high-flying academic, the first African-American and female US national security adviser, and latterly the United States' second female secretary of state, Condoleezza Rice presented the acceptable face of the George W. Bush presidency to America's allies during a turbulent era of foreign relations. However, while forging an exceptionally close relationship with her commander-in-chief—a complex transaction of deference and sweet talk—she proved unable or unwilling to change significantly the thrust of White House foreign policy during the Bush years.

Rice was born to middle-class parents in Birmingham, Alabama, heartland of American racism in the 1950s and 1960s, and was encouraged by her parents to use the opportunities opened up by the civil rights struggle to follow an academic career. Rice has often observed that to get ahead she had to be "twice as good," and her belief in education and self-improvement is one of the keys to her character.

Rice graduated with a degree in political science from Denver University in 1974, and went on to earn a master's degree and a PhD in international studies. In 1981 she was appointed professor of political science at Stanford University and became a member of the Center for International Security and Arms Control (now the Center for International Security and Cooperation).

Fluent in Russian, Rice served on the National Security

Council as a senior director of Soviet and East European affairs between 1989 and 1991, the years that saw the fall of the Berlin Wall and the collapse of the Soviet Union. She so impressed President George H. W. Bush that he introduced her to the Soviet leader Mikhail Gorbachev with the observation that Rice was the one "who tells me everything I know about the Soviet Union."

In 2000, during the presidential campaign of George W. Bush, a novice in international affairs, Rice rarely left the candidate's side. Her reward came in 2001 when Bush appointed her national security adviser, a post famously filled in the early 1970s by Henry Kissinger during the Nixon presidency. Rice's influence over the new administration's policy was equally important, and she helped to set the unilateralist mood music for the initial phase of the Bush presidency. The former Soviet-watcher saw US foreign policy in terms of *realpolitik*, the safeguarding of the national and strategic interest. Rice's uncompromising positions on missile defense, the environment, and the 2003 invasion of Iraq won grudging respect but hardened the intransigent, go-it-alone image of the Bush administration.

In April 2004, after a lengthy delaying action, Rice became the first sitting national security adviser to testify before the National Commission on Terrorism Attacks Upon the United States (the 9/11 Commission). While admitting that Saddam Hussein had not possessed nuclear weapons—a climb-down from her prewar position—Rice insisted that the very existence of Saddam's Iraq was a destabilizing influence in the Middle East and "part of the problem that created the problem on September 11," a reference to the al-Qaeda attacks on New York and Washington. Significantly, however, she was silent on a postwar stabilization plan for Iraq.

In January 2006, the US Senate confirmed Rice's nomination to succeed Colin Powell as secretary of state. Unlike the hapless and inert Powell, Rice had the ear of the president. On the surface at least, she seemed ready to adopt a more measured approach to such intractable problems as relations with Syria, Iran, and North Korea.

However, a halfhearted attempt at shuttle diplomacy in the

summer of 2006, in the wake of Israel's abortive attempt to destroy the power of the extremist Islamic organization Hezbollah (Party of God) in Lebanon, produced little or nothing, which was unsurprising considering that President Bush gave Israel the green light for the offensive. Rice, it seems, did not caution against the possibility of Israeli failure, largely because she was party to the decision to lend full war supplies and intelligence support to an Israeli effort to smash Hezbollah in the "war on terror."

In turn this stoked the uneasiness expressed by the United States' NATO allies over US policy on the "special rendition" of terrorist suspects to countries where, in all probability, torture might be used to extract information. Rice had long stonewalled on this issue, but her public declaration, in December 2005, of the United States' adherence to the UN convention against torture helped to clear the way for the White House's subsequent reluctant embrace of legislation banning cruel, inhumane, and degrading treatment. In September 2006, however, Bush's frank admission of the reality of rendition coupled with the denial that the process involved torture—to which the president ascribed a very narrow definition—left Rice further exposed and embarrassed such allies as the British prime minister Tony Blair, who had denied the existence of rendition.

Perhaps the greatest constraint on Rice was her intense loyalty to President Bush—in a Freudian slip she once started to refer to him as "my husband," before biting her tongue—and her reluctance to push him out of the comfort zone created by his circle of cronies. Her attempts to define a "transformational diplomacy" for the Bush years had foundered by the autumn of 2006, as the situation in Iraq grew steadily worse, and Rice took to comparing the war on terror to the American Civil War, declaring, "I am sure that there are people who thought it was a mistake to fight the Civil War to its end and to insist that the emancipation of slaves would hold." Meanwhile, President Bush continued to promise "complete victory."

In the latter part of 2005 there was growing talk of drafting Rice as the Republican presidential candidate in 2008, possibly to run against Hillary Clinton. Rice ignored the groundswell, and it remained to be seen whether, if nominated, she could successfully reach out to a black constituency that casts a mere 10 percent of its votes for the Republican Party. However, she once tellingly remarked, "My parents had me absolutely convinced that, well, you may not be able to have a hamburger at Woolworth's, but you can be president of the United States." However, by the summer of 2007, the train wreck of the Bush presidency had dented her dream.

Reference: Condoleezza Rice and Philip Zelikov, *Germany Unified and Europe Transformed,* 1995; and Antonia Felix, *Condi: The Condoleezza Rice Story,* 2005.

SFORZA, CATERINA
Countess of Forlì, b. 1462, d. 1509

In one papal bull, Caterina Sforza was castigated as "the daughter of iniquity" and in another, equally bluntly, she was labeled "the daughter of perdition." War and strife were her natural element. In her early twenties she threw herself into soldiering, and when in command she maintained an iron discipline with the aid of blood-chilling punishments.

Born the illegitimate daughter of Galeazza Maria Sforza, later Duke of Milan, she was married in 1477 to Girolamo Riario, the nephew of Pope Sixtus IV. Well educated by the standards of the day, she was also athletic and a passionate huntress. She was a handsome woman, but her beauty regime left little to chance. Lotions of nettle seed, cinnabar, ivy leaves, saffron, and sulfur kept her golden locks in perfect condition. Her shining teeth received daily applications of charcoaled rosemary stems, pulverized marble, and coral cuttlebone. Her blue eyes were bathed daily in rose water, and unguents smoothed her breasts.

Her approach to war was equally stylish. In August 1484, on the death of Sixtus IV, Caterina was dispatched to Rome to hold the ancient castle of Saint Angelo, a papal property, until it could be handed over to Sixtus's legal successor. Seven months pregnant, she cut a striking figure in a gold satin gown, plumed hat, and belt from which dangled a bag bulging with golden ducats. The only martial touches to the ensemble were a curved sword and the ripe language she employed to curse and cajole the soldiers under her command. Caterina held the castle until October 1484, when she surrendered it by her husband's order to the Sacred College of Cardinals.

In 1488 Riario was murdered by members of the rival Orsi family. His palace in Forlì was sacked and his children held as hostages. Caterina, who remained in control of the citadel at Forlì, is said to have shouted to her enemies, "Do you think, you fools, that I don't have the stuff to make more?" and with those defiant words hoisted her skirt to expose her genitals. More polite historians have pointed out that she was pregnant when the threat to her children was made and, in a more decorous gesture, merely indicated her swelling belly. History does record, however, that with the assistance of her uncle Ludovico "il Moro" Sforza, she was able to defeat her enemies, wrest back possession of her dominions, and exact revenge on the murderers of her husband.

There were public executions and secret stranglings, but the most hideous fate was reserved for the eighty-year-old patriarch Andrea Orsi. Dressed in a vest, shirt, and one sock, and with his hands bound, Orsi watched helpless as his house was razed to the ground; he was then dragged around a square by a horse before being disemboweled and dismembered while still alive. His limbs and organs were tossed to a baying crowd.

Caterina was not a woman to cross. The man who had mutilated and murdered Giacomo Feo, one of her many lovers, was done to death as an entrée before his wife and sons were flung down a deep well and left to die. She contrived to establish more friendly relations with the new pope, Alexander VI, and with the Venetians, whose ambassador, Giovanni de' Medici, she secretly married in 1496. When he died two years later, the resourceful Caterina deterred the Venetians from seizing her lands by negotiating an alliance with the Florentines.

However, she eventually managed to fall out with Alexander VI by refusing to allow his daughter Lucrezia Borgia to marry her son Ottaviano. The Pope also had his eye on her fiercely guarded lands, which he had earmarked for his son Cesare. On March 9, 1499, he issued a bull declaring that the house of Riario had forfeited the lordship of Imola and Forlì, which he conferred on his son.

Cesare moved against Sforza with an army reinforced by fourteen thousand French troops. The castle at Imola held out until December 1499. Caterina clung on grimly at Forlì, sending Alexander VI letters impregnated with poison in the forlorn hope that dispatching the pontiff would save her. But she would have needed a very long spoon to poison a Borgia, and her plan came to nothing.

In a desperate throw, she ordered the magazines in her stronghold to be blown up, but the order was disobeyed and the citadel taken in January 1500 after Cesare Borgia had demanded *"la bellicosa signora"* be brought to him dead or alive. On receiving her alive, he raped her and subjected her to the same humiliations that had befallen the women of Forlì, later boasting to his officers that Caterina had defended her fortress with greater determination than her virtue.

Caterina was imprisoned for a year in the castle of St. Angelo. Thereafter she fled to Florence to escape persecution by the Borgias. When their baleful power collapsed with the death of Alexander VI in 1503, she attempted to regain control of her lands but was thwarted by her Medici brothers-in-law. In her final years, she found refuge in a convent and consolation in training her son by Giovanni de' Medici in the art of war.

Reference: Antonia Fraser, *The Warrior Queens*, 1988.

TAMARA
Queen of Georgia, b. 1160, d. 1213

Dubbed "King of Kings and Queen of Queens" by her subjects, Tamara presided over an all-too-brief "golden age" in the history of Georgia, a trans-Caucasian kingdom on the very edge of the medieval Christian world. Canonized by the Orthodox Church and, with scant regard for history, characterized by the nineteenth-century Russian writer Mikhail Lermontov as a "sprite from hell," she extended Georgia's boundaries to their greatest extent in its history while mounting numerous military expeditions and quashing a series of rebellions in a reign of perpetual campaigning.

Georgia first emerged as a regional power during the reign of Tamara's great-grandfather, David Aghmashenebeli (1089–1125)—sometimes known as "David the Builder"—who drove the Seljuk Turks from his kingdom and established the capital city of Georgia in Tbilisi. By the time of his death, his empire stretched from the Black Sea in the west to the Caspian Sea in the east.

In 1178, David's grandson, George III, declared his nineteen-year-old daughter, Tamara, his co-ruler and heir apparent. Proclaiming her "the bright light of his eyes," he hailed her as queen with the assent of Georgia's patriarchs, bishops, nobles, viziers, and generals. Seated on George's right hand and wearing purple robes trimmed with gold and silver, she was given her official title, "Mountain of God," while a crown encrusted with rubies and diamonds was placed on her head.

On George's death in 1184, Tamara became sole ruler, although she was placed under the guardianship of her paternal aunt Rusudani. The Georgian nobility, anxious for her to produce a male heir, rushed Tamara into a marriage with George Bogolyubski, a debauched Russian prince. He lasted two years before Tamara sent him into exile. Her second husband, David Sosland, an Ossetian prince, fathered a son and a daughter, both of whom would later ascend the Georgian throne.

With the succession secure, Tamara was now free to embark on a policy of military expansion, which also had the advantageous by-product of distracting the Georgian nobility from their favorite sports, limiting the power of the monarch and increasing their own. However, she had first to deal with Bogolyubski, who in 1191 attempted to wrest the kingdom from her. She defeated her former husband twice in the field, took him prisoner, and exiled him for a second time.

She then turned her attentions to the Seljuk Turks, fulfilling the roles of queenly figurehead and active strategist in her campaigns. In the field, she always addressed her troops before they went into battle. At Cambetch in 1196, she urged them on with the words "God be with you!" to which the army responded with cheers of "To our king Tamara!" Eight years later, Tamara marched barefoot at the head of the army to make camp on the eve of the Battle of Basiani. The next day she gave the order to mount before taking up a position to watch the Georgian victory from a safe vantage point.

The campaign of 1204 took her troops to Trebizond, on the southern shore of the Black Sea, which became a Georgian protectorate. Tamara exercised a loose sway over Muslim semi-protectorates on her southern marches, while on her northern borders the people of southern Russia paid her tribute. In 1210, she launched a furious response to an incursion by the Sultan of Ardabil, who in the previous year had crossed the Arak mountains, slaughtering and pillaging as he went. Ardabil was seized in a surprise attack, and on Tamara's orders, the emir and thousands of his subjects were put to the sword. The rampage surged deep into northern Persia, and her army returned laden with booty.

During Tamara's reign, Georgian culture flourished alongside martial glory. Shota Rustaveli's epic poem *The Knight in Panther's Skin* was dedicated to her, and she sponsored the building of many churches. Tbilisi, situated athwart busy trade routes, prospered. When Tamara died, a chronicler wrote, "Ploughmen sang verses to her while they tilled. . . . Franks and Greeks hummed her praises as they sailed the seas in fair weather."

Sadly, her achievements could not stand the test of time. Twenty-five years after Tamara was laid to rest in the tomb of her ancestors, her daughter Rusudani was driven from Georgia by the Mongols, and Georgia descended into chaos.

Reference: W. E. D. Allen, *A History of the Georgian People,* 1932.

THATCHER, MARGARET
British Politician, b. 1925

Thatcher's reputation as "the Iron Lady" was earned during the Cold War and strengthened by her steadfast conduct of the

Falklands War, a rare example in the post-1945 era of a female politician's standing being enhanced by the ready adoption of a military solution to international problems.

Born Margaret Roberts, the daughter of a Lincolnshire grocer and local politician, she was not conscripted for military service in World War II and later studied chemistry at Oxford University. While at Oxford, she became president of the university's Conservative Association, the first woman to hold the post.

From 1947 she worked as a research chemist in industry, developing new ice cream products among other things, and pursuing her political ambitions. In 1950 and 1951 she stood unsuccessfully as the Conservative candidate for the Dartford constituency and during this period met and married Denis Thatcher, a successful industrialist and millionaire. She studied law, qualifying as a barrister in 1953, the year in which she gave birth to twins, an early indication of her immense capacity for sustained hard work. It was not until 1959, however, after many attempts, that she obtained a seat in Parliament as the successful Conservative candidate for the north London constituency of Finchley.

When the Conservatives returned to power in 1970, she was appointed secretary of state for education and science. In 1975, following the Conservative defeat in the general election of 1974, she defeated the incumbent Edward Heath to become the first female party leader in British politics.

In May 1979 Thatcher became Britain's first woman prime minister, quickly earning the nickname "Iron Lady" for her robust attitude toward the Soviet Union's invasion of Afghanistan. It was typical of her that she embraced the sobriquet, originally intended by the Soviets as an insult.

In 1979 she agreed in principle with a Foreign Office proposal that the sovereignty of the disputed Falkland Islands, in the South Atlantic, should be handed to Argentina, which also claimed sovereignty, provided that the views of the islanders were taken into account. However, the ruling Argentine military junta was already committed to the occupation of the Falklands, irrespective of the subsequent British negotiating positions. Their resolve had been hardened by Thatcher's backing for the 1981 decision by her defense secretary, John Nott, to withdraw the patrol ship *Endurance* from the South Atlantic. In March 1982 an Argentine force occupied the whaling station at South Georgia, a British dependency some one thousand miles south of the Falklands. At the beginning of April an Argentine task force landed in Port Stanley (the Falklands' main port) and swiftly secured the lightly garrisoned islands.

On Saturday, April 3, in an emergency session of the House of Commons, Thatcher announced that "a large task force will sail as soon as all preparations are complete. HMS *Invincible* will be in the lead and will leave port on Monday." She was able successfully to negotiate the opening phase of the Falklands War for a number of crucial reasons: her own unbending determination to expel the Argentines; support from the Royal Navy's high command, who assured her that an opposed landing in the Falklands, if it came, was feasible although fraught with danger; and the incompetence of the Argentine junta, whose intransigence enabled the British to seize and retain the moral high ground in the United Nations. Later, Britain's ability to sustain the operations to retake South Georgia and the Falklands was ensured by the considerable active logistical and diplomatic help of the Americans. Although Thatcher was determined to fight if she had to, she also recognized the importance of seeming to pursue every diplomatic channel offered by her US ally.

In the following ten weeks, Thatcher assumed an almost Churchillian mantle, imperiously rounding on querulous journalists after announcing the recapture of South Georgia and commanding them, "Just rejoice at the news . . . rejoice!" She displayed immense stamina and a voracious appetite for detail and did not shrink from tough decisions, notably when on May 2, 1982, the elderly Argentine cruiser *Belgrano* was torpedoed and sunk by the submarine *Conqueror* outside the maritime exclusion zone established by the British around the Falklands.

On June 14, Thatcher told the House of Commons that "the Argentine forces are reported to be flying white flags over Stanley." The prime minister herself and the Conservative Party drew immense benefit from the British victory. Margaret Thatcher had risked all and won. Her handling of the Falklands conflict was a classic example of the fundamental military principle of maintenance of aim.

Her role in the run-up to the conflict was less clear. That she and her government had unwittingly played a part in encouraging the Argentine military junta to invade the Falklands was apparent in the circumspect words of the Franks report on the war in the South Atlantic, published in January 1983. However, Lord Franks and his colleagues shrank from attaching personal blame to Mrs. Thatcher and her cabinet. Thereafter she reveled in her warrior image, captured in one iconographic photograph as she rode in the turret of a Challenger tank, resplendent in a white anti-flash suit, a modern **Boudicca** in a twentieth-century chariot (see p. 12).

In 1987 Margaret Thatcher became the first British prime minister to win a third term in office, and the word "Thatcherism" entered the language. But she drifted out of touch with the British electorate and fell to fighting with her partners in the European Union. Her cabinet came to the reluctant but inevitable conclusion that Margaret Thatcher was now an electoral handicap to her party, and confronted her with the bitter truth—she had to go. On the night she left No. 10 Downing Street for the last time, the pitiless cameras caught bitter tears in the eyes of the Iron Lady. She was later created Baroness Thatcher.

Reference: Margaret Thatcher, *The Downing Street Years 1979–1990,* **1993; and Denys Blakeway,** *The Falklands War,* **1991.**

TZ'U-HSI
Hsiao-ch'in, Empress of China, b. 1835, d. 1908

The empress dowager of China was one of the most formidable women in modern history. Famously beautiful, she was a good friend and a fearsome enemy, who never shrank from war and sought ways to profit from it. She was greedy, ruthless, and an immensely skilled manipulator of the tortuous court politics of the moribund Manchu Empire.

Her father was a minor bureaucrat, a government clerk and

later a provincial administrator. In 1852 she was selected as a low-ranking concubine of the young but degenerate Emperor Hsien-feng. She rapidly rose in status, working as his secretary, gaining insights into the administration of the state, and bearing his only son, T'ung-ch'un, in 1856.

When Hsien-feng died in 1861, Tz'u-hsi was still in her twenties and the mother of the new six-year-old emperor. T'ung-ch'un was advised by a council of eight elders, but none of his decrees could be passed without the approval of his grandmother the empress dowager, who became the effective ruler of China together with the late emperor's chief wife, Tz'u-an, who became co-regent. Together with Hsien-feng's brother, Prince Kung, they rode out a succession of crises, including the Taiping Rebellion (1850–64), which was triggered by famine and only finally put down with the help of Western military leadership, notably that of Britain's General Gordon.

The precarious maintenance of order was accompanied by the cautious Westernization of China, with the establishing of foreign-language schools, the creation of modern customs services, and the reform of the army and navy. Simultaneously, Tz'u-hsi gathered more power into her own hands, since the official wife, Tz'u-an, was not interested in affairs of state. In 1873, when her son came of age, Tz'u-hsi refused to give up the regency. She declined a second time when he died in 1875 (he had begun to resent her, and there was a strong suspicion that his mother arranged his death). Instead, she flouted all precedents for the succession, adopted her three-year-old nephew as her son, and made him the new emperor Kuang-hsu. In 1881 Tz'u-an died, possibly from poisoning, and the late emperor's brother Prince Kung was removed in 1884.

In her fifties, Tz'u-hsi ostensibly retired to her sumptuous Summer Palace outside Peking (now Beijing), the rebuilding of which was funded by siphoning off revenue intended for the Chinese navy. The palace boasted a huge room filled with ingenious mechanical toys and dolls, an entire wing stocked with fabulous dresses, and another stuffed with jewels—she was obsessed with pearls and jade. She officially handed over power in 1889 but kept herself exceptionally well informed while making a fortune peddling influence.

In the 1890s, China was faced with a new regional military power in the form of Japan, which in 1894–95 expelled the Chinese from Korea. The blow to Chinese morale led Emperor Kuang-hsu to implement a new series of reforms designed to deal with the stifling corruption of China's bureaucracy. He also determined to confine Tz'u-hsi to the Summer Palace. His adoptive mother reacted swiftly. She rallied the support of conservative mandarins by moving reliable army units to Peking to replace guards loyal to Kuang-hsu. She then descended on the Forbidden City, with a train of eunuchs scurrying in her wake, to confront the quaking Son of Heaven and strike him full in the face with her fan, the only physical blow delivered in this remarkable coup. After compelling the emperor to issue an edict proclaiming her regent, she confined him to a palace where he could do no harm. The most dangerous reformers were beheaded or strangled, and Tz'u-hsi once again gathered up the reins of power.

That power, and the remnants of China's integrity, were now increasingly compromised by the encroachment of European powers seeking to divide the spoils of the decaying Manchu dynasty. Tz'u-hsi sent an imperial message to all the Chinese provinces: "The present situation is becoming daily more difficult. The various Powers cast upon us looks of tiger-like voracity, jostling each other to be first to seize our innermost territories. . . . Let us not think about making peace."

The result was the Boxer Uprising, in which Chinese nationalists, encouraged by the empress, rose up against the foreigners. When the Boxers marched on Peking, the empress assured nervous diplomats that the Chinese army would crush the "rebels." When they entered the capital, she did nothing. While the foreigners were besieged in their compounds outside the walls of Peking, the empress slipped away disguised as a peasant.

By the time she returned in 1901, the power of the Manchu dynasty had been destroyed utterly. The empress came back on terms dictated by the foreign powers, whose punitive expeditionary force had relieved a two-month siege and had crushed the

Boxers. Measures reluctantly introduced by the empress included the ending of foot binding and the opening of state schools to girls. Railways were constructed, opium growing was suppressed, and the centuries-old civil service exams ended; work began on writing a constitution. The modern world that she had kept at bay for so long had finally broken in.

Nevertheless, she retained her ruthlessness to the end. When she was dying, she ensured that her adoptive son, Emperor Kuang-hsu, was poisoned. Tz'u-hsi had wielded greater direct power than Queen Victoria (whom she greatly admired) but in so doing had destroyed any lingering hope for a modernized imperial China. In a life largely spent shut away in Peking's Forbidden City, where the emperors of China lived among a colossal retinue of officials, eunuchs, concubines, and servants, she was unable to gain any insight into the workings of the modern world, something that historians have usually described as a disadvantage. However, when combined with her steely will and force of character, these were probably the factors that enabled the Dragon Lady, as she became known, to function as the virtual ruler of a vast and chaotic empire for almost fifty years.

Reference: Fascinating glimpses of life in Tz'u-hsi's court can be found in *Two Years in the Forbidden City* (1911), written by one of her ladies-in-waiting, Princess Der-ling.

3

RUNAWAYS AND ROARING GIRLS

~∞∞~

Mavericks, Misfits, Malcontents, and
Wild Ones—Women Seizing the Chance of War to Live and
Fight as Men

You, young woman, only you can comprehend my rapture, only you can
value my happiness! You, who must account for every step, who cannot go
fifteen feet without supervision and correction . . . only you can
comprehend the joyous sensations that filled my heart.
—Nadezhda Durova, who disguised herself as a man and became a
Polish cavalry officer between about 1793 and 1816

From Zenobia to Margaret Thatcher, the captains and
the queens who held command in time of war were either born
into power and wealth or else made their way up the social scale
by turning the ruling system to their account. For others, war has
always offered a unique opportunity to break out of the existing
structures and make a new life elsewhere. Far from shunning warfare, for centuries some women ran toward it, fleeing their homes
and families in their determination to escape their fate as females,
whatever the cost, because the discomfort and danger of war was
preferable to what they faced at home.

From earliest times, folklore and legend abound with stories of
female runaways who took flight to avoid an enforced marriage,
seclusion in a nunnery, or some other predetermined but unwelcome fate. Denied freedom and autonomy, they took their lives

into their hands to avoid male control. Disguising themselves as
men and losing themselves and any pursuers in the chaos of war
was an obvious escape route. As the Middle Ages lurched toward a
recognizably modern world, an unparalleled chance of freedom
was offered to any woman who chafed against domesticity when
the urge for adventure was beating in her heart. We will never
know how many young women of the past saw the redcoats
marching through their town, heard the irresistible call of the fife
and drum, and ran after them, dazzled by brass and scarlet.

Men, too, could be easily seduced by the glamour of a martial
life. A strong narrative thread in the stories of the women dubbed
"she-soldiers" in the seventeenth century involves their search for
husbands who had unwisely enlisted in a fit of enthusiasm, or had
been forcibly press-ganged.

But countless men suffered this fate without wifely intervention. The women who chose to follow their men in disguise
wanted the freedom of passing as a man, taking the risks of life as
an adventurous man, and actively seeking conflict in an all-too-
corseted women's world. From the seventeenth century onward,
as the modern era dawned, their struggles mirrored the convul-
sions of the wider society, when women were beginning to reach
for the personal freedoms denied them for thousands of years.

In their day, almost all these women, like **Deborah Sampson**
(see p. 80), could not fit into their world as it was. Outsize per-
sonalities, they were women of action, aggression, physical resource, and fighting skill. Today they could be athletes, astronauts,
or entrepreneurs, but in centuries past, warfare was the only opening they had. Accordingly, like the captains and the queens, they
pushed the boundaries of their female roles to the limits of tolerance. Too fiery and volatile for conventional society, they had to
find a wider arena for their verve and drive.

Undoubtedly some were mavericks and oddballs, a category
into which many cross-dressing military women of all nationalities
fell. In the fifteenth century, **Joan of Arc** (see p. 75) made her
place in history as the quintessential woman fighter, the virgin
warrior clad in fine armor and mounted on a horse. But the

peasant Jeanne had no connection with war before she heard her voices from God telling her to dress and act as a man in order to drive the English out of France. Jeanne chose to die rather than to give up wearing men's clothes, a capital offense at the time. Without the cloak of patriotism and "divine inspiration," her teenage rejection of her lot, her identity crisis, her hallucinations and delusions, can clearly be seen for what they were.

There are many reasons why women chose to dress and live as men. The longing to impress a father or to work off the stigma of being born a girl surfaces clearly in the story of **Nadezhda Durova** (see p. 73), a well-born runaway who served in the Russian army in the Napoleonic Wars, and who wistfully described herself as "wanting to be a son to my father."

Another little-discussed motivation for female runaways is the desire to avoid not only marriage and domesticity but also childbirth. In an era before contraception, when married women had no right to refuse sex, giving birth often meant death. In these circumstances, the decision to adopt a man's lifestyle looks less like craziness than like simple common sense.

Yet anger is almost a prerequisite for a life apart, and the stories of these runaways and roaring girls carry recurrent themes of madness and women on the edge. Many of their careers were propelled by dreadful childhoods, by loss and bereavement in adulthood, or by both. Losing her husband and all three of her children drove the Civil War soldier **Loreta Janeta Velazquez** into action (see p. 83). War provided a vast and forgiving arena for such unconventional, disturbed, and alienated women to give some shape and purpose to their lives, or else to lose themselves in action when life itself became too much to bear.

And it is not all tragedy. Many of the more remarkable individuals who trod this path have found their lives commemorated in the literature of warfare. Some, like Nadezhda Durova and Deborah Sampson, enjoyed a measure of celebrity in their own lifetimes. Others, like **Flora Sandes** (see p. 82), carved out a life of action and fulfillment beyond their wildest dreams.

Whatever their individual reasons, women through the ages

have taken this path. As the first standing armies were created from the seventeenth century onward, numbers of women donned uniforms and served in the ranks as men, establishing a tradition that lasted well into the nineteenth century.

With the advent of written records, their stories become easier to trace. Between 1550 and 1840, 119 women are known to have enlisted in the Dutch armed forces. The women represented a range of nationalities, and most were between sixteen and twenty-five years old. About half of them were sailors, who spent at least part of their service in disguise before being discovered.

The information we have about them comes from the military proceedings that followed their exposure. As they spent most of their lives masquerading as men, they must have been haunted by the fear of discovery every day. How did they handle the problems of urination, defecation, or menstruation under the rough-and-ready conditions of former times, especially within the confines of a ship? Inevitably very few were flamboyant, preferring to keep their heads down and maintain a low profile, like Miranda Stuart, better known as **James Barry** (see p. 69). As a military doctor, Barry was unusual in maintaining a professional career for an entire lifetime without her true identity coming to light.

Discovery did not always mean automatic discharge from the service. Durova's secret was revealed after she incautiously contacted her father, telling him of her new life. Significantly, perhaps, the Russians seemed to be more relaxed than other nations about the presence of women in the ranks. This led to the formation in World War I of the women's Battalion of Death, a unique female fighting formation (see **Bochkareva, Maria,** p. 88). In World War II, the Soviet Union was the only nation to commit women to air combat (see **Night Witches,** p. 235).

Exposure often came when the women were wounded, obliging them to treat their own injuries rather than submit to the ministrations of army doctors. Whatever their war history, the time came when all these women could no longer fight. Most of them finally settled down to a quiet life and, like all old soldiers (see **Michel, Louise,** p. 78), simply faded away.

BARRY, JAMES
Miranda Stuart, British Army Doctor, b. 1795, d. 1865

"James Barry" had a distinguished but turbulent career as a military doctor in the British colonies, rising to the position of Inspector-General of Military Hospitals in Canada. He would certainly have remained a footnote to medical history but for the fact that after his death, it was discovered that the eminent army surgeon was a woman.

Barry's origins are obscure—she was an orphan—but it has been suggested that she was related to the distinguished artist James Barry. At the age of fifteen she enrolled at the University of Edinburgh as James Barry, a "frail-looking young man" with the "form, manners and voice of a woman," to study literature and medicine. This may have been the reason for her masquerade, since all forms of higher education were barred to women in the British Isles at the time, and she would never have been admitted to study as a woman. She took her medical degree in 1812 and, following a period of study in London, joined the army in 1813 as a medical assistant.

In 1816 she was posted to the garrison at Cape Town in South Africa as an assistant surgeon. Here Barry assumed a wide range of responsibilities, including the regulation of the sale of drugs and the inspection of jails, and acquired a reputation for decisiveness and great speed in difficult operations, an essential skill in the days before anesthesia. However, the speedy surgeon was also a peppery and disputatious character, and she lost her civil role in the Cape Colony in 1825.

Barry later served as a staff surgeon in Mauritius and Jamaica before becoming principal medical officer on the island of St. Helena, a posting that saw more disputes with her colleagues and superiors, and from which she was returned to England under arrest. The maintenance of a male mask must have imposed an acute strain—Barry is known to have fought at least one duel and sought many more. Nevertheless, she survived these setbacks, possibly through the influence of friends in high places, and went on to serve as principal medical officer in Trinidad, Malta, and Corfu, where she provided medical facilities for servicemen wounded in the Crimean War.

In her medical career she is known to have performed at least one caesarean section and never to have shrunk from making controversial decisions about sanitation and the diet and accommodation of her patients. She clashed with **Florence Nightingale** (see p. 264) over the treatment of the Crimean wounded and wrote a report on the treatment of syphilis and gonorrhea with a plant from the Cape of Good Hope.

In 1857 Barry was posted to Canada as inspector general of military hospitals. She fell ill with influenza in the spring of 1859 and, after being treated by Dr. George William Campbell, later dean of the medical faculty at McGill University, returned to England on half pay. During her life it is thought that her gender was known to the high command of the British Army and at least one fellow physician. After her death, rumors about her identity rapidly spread and the registrar general ordered an autopsy on Barry. When it was concluded that she was female, her military funeral was canceled. However, recent research has indicated that Barry might have been a male hermaphrodite who had feminine breast development and external genitalia.

Reference: Rachel Holmes, *The Secret Life of Dr. James Barry: Victorian England's Most Eminent Surgeon,* 2000.

DAHOMEY, WARRIOR WOMEN OF
1600–1900

The warrior women of Dahomey, an ancient kingdom in West Africa and present-day Benin, first came to the attention of European travelers in the latter half of the sixteenth century. A German book published in 1598, *Vera Descriptio Regni Africani,* describes an African royal court whose palace guard consisted of women, and similar royal formations occurred elsewhere in the world from ancient times, particularly in the East. The kings of ancient Persia had female bodyguards, as did a prince of Java.

As late as the nineteenth century, the king of Siam, now Thailand, was guarded by a battalion of four hundred women armed with spears. They were said to perform drills better than male soldiers and were crack spear-throwers. Women in general were regarded as more loyal and trustworthy bodyguards than men, because they were less likely to be bribed or suborned; many rulers chose female bodyguards for this reason.

But the women of Dahomey outclassed them all. More than 250 years after the first reference, we catch sight of them again in the high summer of the British Empire when the British general Sir Garnet Wolseley, in a report on his successful campaign against the Ashanti (1873–74), compared his energetic and disciplined Fanti female porters to the king of Dahomey's "corps of Amazons."

Eighteenth-century accounts of Dahomey by European merchants and slave traders—slavery was the basis of the kingdom's wealth—paint a picture of a colorful feudal world whose kings were surrounded by hundreds of serving girls and guarded by armed women. One of Dahomey's kings, Bossa Ahadee, would march in ceremonial procession accompanied by several hundred wives, surrounded by female messengers and slaves, and escorted by a guard of 120 men armed with blunderbusses and 90 armed women.

The presence of the armed women was, at this stage in Dahomey's history, more a symbol than a real threat to Dahomey's neighbors. The tables were turned, however, when one of them, the king of Oyo, took to the field against the Dahomeans with a raiding party of eight hundred women to enforce a claim of female tribute he had leveled against King Adahoonzou. It was left to the all-male Dahomean army to defeat the Oyan Amazons.

By the time of King Ghezo (1818–58), Dahomey's royal court consisted of some eight thousand people, the majority of them women, many of whom existed in a minutely graded pyramid of concubinage, at the top of which were the so-called Wives of the Leopard, the women who bore the ruler's children. One of the functions of the armed female element of the court, all of whom were recruited in their early teenage years, seems to have been the capture and execution of women from rival tribes. All the

"Amazons" carried giant folding razors, with blades over two feet long, which were apparently used to decapitate female enemies and castrate male foes.

From the late 1830s Ghezo seems to have used members of his predominantly female court in battle against neighboring tribes. It is possible that he deployed four thousand female warriors in an army totaling sixteen thousand. When in 1851 he laid siege to the city of Abeokuta, the siege was repulsed with losses of some three thousand, of whom two thirds were women. A French account of the engagement describes their officers standing in the front line, "recognisable by the riches of their dress" and carrying themselves with "a proud and resolute air." Nevertheless, these women warriors occupied an inferior and ambivalent position in the hierarchy of the Dahomean court and, significantly, referred to themselves as men in their war cries and battle chants.

Far from discouraging Ghezo, this setback spurred him on to include more women in his army. They seem to have been divided into a regular corps of well-trained and highly disciplined "Amazons" armed with muskets and machete-like swords, who also formed an elite personal bodyguard, and a rather less satisfactory reserve, armed with cutlasses, clubs, and bows and arrows, who were more interested in rum than rigorous military discipline. In peacetime the "Amazon" corps was wholly segregated from men, and outside the confines of the royal palace its approach was signaled by the ringing of bells, upon which civilians had to turn their backs and males had to move away.

There were several practical reasons for Ghezo's use of women in battle. Dahomey was exceptionally warlike, and lost many men on campaign, while simultaneously depending for its wealth on a slave trade that favored the disposal to slavers of a large proportion of its able-bodied male population. At its peak strength in the early 1860s, the Dahomean army was approximately fifty thousand strong—one-fifth the total population—of which the female element numbered ten thousand, a quarter of their number consisting of the "Amazons."

It has been suggested that many of the women, as well as some of the men in the Dahomean army, went to war as camp followers, much in the manner of the *soldaderas* who marched with Mexican armies in the nineteenth and early twentieth centuries (see p. 140). The Victorian explorer Sir Richard Burton, who saw them in 1863, likewise poured derision on "the fighting Amazons." "Mostly elderly and all of them hideous," he ruminated with all the authority of the European white male, "the officers decidedly chosen for the size of their bottoms . . . they manoeuvre with the precision of a flock of sheep." But he also noted that this army, then some 2,500 strong, was well armed and effective in battle. Nor could all of them have been old and hideous, since all 2,500 were official wives of the king.

In spite of the dread in which they were held, the "Amazons" were no match for small but well-armed colonial armies. In a series of engagements in 1892, the male and female Dahomean warriors were defeated by a French army, and the kingdom became a colony of France. The victorious French commander commended the women warriors on their speed and boldness and installed a puppet ruler who was permitted a few token women in his bodyguard. A troupe of so-called Amazons from Dahomey formed part of a display at the recently erected Eiffel Tower, under which they danced and drilled.

Reference: Stanley B. Alpern, *Amazons of Black Sparta: The Women Warriors of Dahomey,* 1998.

DUROVA, NADEZHDA
Russian Cavalry Officer, b. 1783, d. 1866

Very few of the women who disguised themselves as men to become soldiers in the past have told their own life stories. Perhaps the best known of those who have given us an insight into this secret world is Nadezhda Durova, a member of the minor Russian aristocracy who fought in the Napoleonic Wars.

Her father, a captain in a regiment of Hussars, brought her up to a military life, as her mother was neglectful and hostile to her little girl. In her early childhood Nadezhda became familiar with drilling, marching, and the world of military encampments. She declined to take up girlish pursuits, taught herself to ride, and subjected imaginary formations to punishing drill exercises and blood-curdling battlefield maneuvers.

At the age of eighteen she submitted to an unhappy marriage and bore her husband a child. But she chafed at her dependent status and yearned to become "a warrior and a son to my father and to part company forever from the sex whose sad lot . . . had begun to terrify me." She ran away, cut her hair short and, assuming the name of Alexander Vasilevich Sokolov, enlisted in a Polish cavalry regiment. There she found that she enjoyed training and reveled in the new feeling of independence. Later she wrote: "You, young woman, only you can comprehend my rapture, only you can value my happiness! You, who must account for every step, who cannot go 15 feet without supervision and correction . . . only you can comprehend the joyous sensations that filled my heart."

For the next seven years, Durova fought in the wars against the emperor Napoleon's Grande Armée. She underwent her baptism of fire near Guttstadt in Germany, where her conduct later won her a silver St. George's Cross for saving a wounded officer, and fought at Friedland (1807) and Borodino (1812), two of the bloodiest battles of the era of Napoleonic warfare. Paradoxically she was happiest when in battle; when the bullets were not flying, she was forced to remain aloof from her fellow soldiers to avoid exposure. She seems to have been fearless in combat but otherwise was timid, frightened of the dark, fretful about her inability to grow a mustache, and, on one occasion, alarmed by the innocent advances of her colonel's amorous daughter. In her memoirs she claimed never to have killed anyone.

Eventually she made the mistake of writing a letter to her father in an attempt to reassure him. He immediately took the matter up with the Russian minister of war, whom he urged to find his daughter. In 1807 Durova was summoned to St. Petersburg to be interviewed by Tsar Alexander I, who proposed to send her home with honor, a prospect that horrified her.

She succeeded in being returned to her regiment with a commission but thereafter was treated more like a military mascot than a serving soldier. In 1812 she was introduced to Marshal Kutuzov, the Russian commander-in-chief and hero of Borodino, who told her archly that he knew exactly who she was and was delighted to meet her. She finally left the army as a captain in 1816 to tend to her ailing father.

Reference: Durova, Nadezhda, *The Cavalry Maiden: Journals of a Russian Officer in the Napoleonic Wars,* trans. Mary Fleming Zirin, 1989.

JOAN OF ARC
Jeanne d'Arc, Medieval French Soldier, b. 1412, d. 1431

The legendary heroine of the bitter wars of the Middle Ages between England and France, Joan of Arc has inspired generations of schoolgirls as the embodiment of female courage and patriotism, going into battle in shining armor at the head of her troops. In reality, her value to the French rested more on her usefulness for propaganda purposes than on any military prowess (see **Lynch, Jessica,** p. 229), and her war career ended without her dispatching even one of the enemy.

Almost all the concrete details we possess of the real-life Jeanne d'Arc come from the records of the two trials she underwent—one at the end of her life and the other after her death. In the first, orchestrated by the English but presided over by French judges, the aim was to prove the English claim that she was a witch, the most hated form of female life at the time (between the ninth century and the nineteenth, many thousands of women were hanged or burned as witches, with the persecution reaching its peak in the early fifteenth century). During the second, posthumous process, which was held for the benefit of the king of France, the judges were under a different kind of pressure, to rehabilitate her as a divinely inspired national savior and embryo saint.

Jeanne was born to a prosperous peasant family of Domremy

in Lorraine and led an apparently unremarkable life until she was thirteen. In that year, which may have coincided with the onset of puberty, she claimed that she had had visions of St. Michael, St. Catherine, and St. Margaret, all of whom told her that she had been chosen to free France from the English and ensure the coronation of the dauphin (heir apparent), Charles, later Charles VII. However, it was not until four years later, in 1429, that she succeeded in persuading the commander of the local castle in the neighboring town of Vaucouleurs to escort her to Charles at Chinon.

Dressed in male attire—she later explained that "for a virgin, male and female clothes are equally suitable"—she was able to pick Charles out of the crowd at Chinon (he had made a deliberate attempt to disguise himself), and after careful inspection, her virginity was confirmed. Charles decided that the striking young woman might prove useful and had a suit of armor made for her, complete with lance and shield. An excellent horsewoman, she quickly mastered the basics of combat.

Under the watchful eyes of two marshals of France, she was assigned to the French army as it struggled to lift the English siege of Orléans, the key to Charles's continuing hold on territory south of the Loire River. Jeanne's role was to dispatch threatening letters to the city's English besiegers, to participate in councils of war, and to play a part in skirmishing, where her powerful voice could be heard over the din of fighting in which she was twice wounded. Although she had no official standing with the French troops, her bravery and coolness—remarkable for an uneducated peasant girl—earned her instant respect. The siege was lifted after nine days of fighting, and Jeanne was present at Charles's coronation at Rheims.

When the French launched an unsuccessful bid to regain Paris in August and September of 1429, Jeanne was wounded a third time. By the time she joined the attempt to relieve Compiègne, which had been besieged by the Burgundians, she was famous throughout France and rode into battle in a sumptuous cloak of red and gold. But this proved her last moment of glory. She was captured in a skirmish by the Burgundians and treacherously ransomed to the English. Her captors imprisoned her in Bouvreuil castle and subjected her to a lengthy interrogation, after which she was tried for witchcraft and fraud by an ecclesiastical court whose task was to show that her mission was inspired not by God but by the Devil himself.

Jeanne bore her captivity with equanimity, remained calm when threatened with torture, made a bold, physically grueling, but unsuccessful attempt to escape, and declined parole on the condition that she would not try to escape again. She also refused to promise her captors that she would not wear men's clothes or take up arms again. She was eventually convicted only of wearing men's clothes, an offense against the Church.

Jeanne then signed an "abjuration" but recanted two days later, which meant she could be convicted as a relapsed heretic of having fallen into "various errors and crimes of heresy, idolatry [and] invocation of demons." She was burned at the stake in Rouen marketplace on May 30, 1431. She died of smoke inhalation, and her body was burned a second time. A third fire was required to reduce her organs to ash, which was reportedly thrown into the Seine. Her active career had lasted barely eighteen months, and although she had seen action, she confessed before she died that she had never killed anyone.

In 1456 the judgment was reversed by an ecclesiastical court, and her legend began to grow. She was dubbed "d'Arc" in the sixteenth century and became a French national heroine in the nineteenth century. In 1920 she was canonized. During World War II, both Vichy France and the French Resistance (see **Special Operations Executive,** p. 366) claimed her as a symbol of their cause. In the spring of 2007, scientific tests on the supposed remains of Jeanne, rescued from the ashes and later housed in a Chinon museum, revealed that the "holy relics" were part of an Egyptian mummy at least 2,000 years old. Their age was confirmed by carbon dating.

Reference: Marina Warner, *Joan of Arc: The Image of Female Heroism,* 1981. There have been many movies about Joan of Arc, the most memorable being the 1928 silent classic *The Passion of Joan of Arc,* starring Maria Falconetti in the title role and directed by the Danish master Carl Dreyer. George Bernard Shaw's play *Saint Joan* is a superb examination of the complexities and contradictions inherent in the legend of Joan of Arc.

MICHEL, LOUISE
"The Red Virgin," Heroine of the Paris Commune, b. 1830,
d. 1905

One of the most tempestuous and celebrated female Communards, Michel was dubbed "the Red Virgin" for her fiery temperament, not for any aversion to men. Her funeral in Paris brought traffic to a standstill and produced crowds to rival the tribute paid to Victor Hugo when he was laid to rest in 1885.

She was born in a castle in the region of Haute-Marne, the illegitimate daughter of the son of the house and a housemaid, and was brought up by her grandfather. In 1856 she moved to Paris, where she rapidly acquired a reputation as a radical opponent of the emperor Napoléon III and a fanatical member of republican clubs.

In the summer of 1870, France stumbled into a war with Prussia in which the French army suffered a rapid succession of humiliating defeats. At the beginning of September the 120,000-strong Army of Chalon was forced by the Prussian Third Army to capitulate at Sedan, and in Paris the Second Empire was replaced by the Government of National Defense. In March the French capital fell to the Prussians after a long siege. During the siege, Michel had become a member of the Committee of Vigilance for the Eighteenth District (Montmartre) and, under the influence of her lover, Théophile Ferré, had grown increasingly militant.

At the end of March 1871, with the Prussian army encamped outside Paris while the French government negotiated a humiliating peace treaty, a Paris mob went on the rampage, burning the palace of the Tuileries and the Hotel de Ville and torching the Faubourg Saint-Honoré. Michel was everywhere, a baleful sight lit by flames, stalking the streets in a man's uniform and armed with a rifle and fixed bayonet. The Paris Commune, which was declared on March 28 amid the ruins of defeat, was inspired by France's revolutionary past, but its leaders lacked any coherent political program.

With the loyalty of the National Guard militia in Paris wavering, regular troops were dispatched to Paris from Versailles, where the government had taken refuge. A bombardment of the capital began on May 1 and at the end of the month the city was stormed, resulting in the loss of some 25,000 lives. Georges Clemenceau, a future French premier and then the mayor of Montmartre, said of the women of the Commune, "They fought like devils, far better than the men; I had the pain of seeing fifty of them shot down, even when they had been surrounded by troops and disarmed."

Michel had been in charge of the Commune's social and educational policies and had fought on the barricades. She had been one of the last defenders of the cemetery in Montmartre, the Communards' final redoubt, but escaped the debacle in Paris only to give herself up when she learned that her mother was being held as a hostage. The government, reluctant to confer instant martyrdom on her as they had with many Communards, including her lover Ferré, imprisoned Michel in Versailles and placed her on trial.

She appeared in court wearing black, a token of mourning for the thousands of Communards who had been summarily executed. Justifying her part in the burning of Paris, she declared, "I wanted to oppose the Versailles invaders with a barrier of flames. . . . Since it appears that every heart that beats for freedom has no right to anything but a slug of lead, I demand my share. If you let me live, I shall never cease to cry for vengeance. If you are not cowards, kill me." The judiciary of the Third Republic refused to oblige and dispatched Michel to a penal colony in New Caledonia in the South Pacific, where she insisted that she receive the same treatment as male prisoners.

Imprisonment did not dull Michel's ardor, and on her return to France after the amnesty of 1881 she resumed her career as radical agitator, with the police in constant attendance. A six-year jail sentence, for inciting a mob to break into bakeries during a food riot, failed to silence her. In 1890, shortly after her release from prison, she led strikes in the district of Vienne and survived an assassination attempt in which she was shot in the head by a Breton.

This did nothing to calm her increasing turbulence. Plans were now afoot to certify Michel as insane, and she fled to London, where she befriended the young painter Augustus John, wrote about the Paris Commune, raised funds for revolutionary groups in Europe, and met the American revolutionary and anarchist Emma Goldman ("Red Emma"). In 1896 she returned to France and, still working at a frantic pace for the revolution, died on a trip to Marseilles. Of the Communards, the painter Auguste Renoir said, "They were madmen, but they had a flame within them that will not die!"

Reference: Bullitt Lowry and Elizabeth Ellington Gunter, eds., *Red Virgin: Memoirs of Louise Michel,* 1981.

RED VIRGIN, SEE **MICHEL, LOUISE,** p. 78.

SAMPSON, DEBORAH
American Soldier, b. 1760, d. 1827

A soldier of the American Revolution, Sampson was wounded several times, met George Washington, and in 1792 was awarded the sum of thirty-four pounds by the Massachusetts General Court for service in the Continental Army where she "did actually perform the duty of a soldier . . . and exhibited an extraordinary instance of female heroism, by discharging the duties of a faithful, gallant soldier, and at the same time preserving the virtue and chastity of her sex unsuspected and unblemished, and was discharged from the service with a fair and honorable character."

Sampson was born in Plympton, Massachusetts, and was brought up in some hardship after her father abandoned his family and went to sea. On her mother's side, her ancestral line stretched back to William Bradford, governor of Plymouth Colony, and her spirited grandmother, Bathsheba Bradford, regaled the young

Deborah with tales of **Joan of Arc** (see p. 75). One of her father's cousins, Captain Simeon Sampson, had been held hostage during the French and Indian Wars, and had escaped by dressing as a woman. The captain, however, laughingly rejected the four-year-old Deborah's pleas to allow her to be his cabin boy.

Between the ages of ten and eighteen Sampson worked as an indentured servant, and the hard labor toughened her physically. In her teens she became an expert shot, hunting with her employer's sons, and later worked as a teacher in a public school. After the American War of Independence broke out in April 1775, Sampson enlisted. She signed up for three years in the Fourth Massachusetts Regiment of the Continental Army as "Robert Shirtleff" (the name of her mother's son, Robert Shirtleff Sampson, who had died at the age of eight).

Firm-jawed, physically robust, and five feet seven inches tall, she passed for a man, binding her breasts to approximate a male physique. Over the next eighteen months she took part in several battles and was wounded at least three times, tending herself to avoid detection. However, Sampson's sex was discovered in 1783 when, after developing a fever, she was examined in a Philadelphia hospital. The physician said nothing, but when Sampson had recovered, he arranged with her commanding officer that she should deliver a letter in person to George Washington. With some tact, Washington discharged Sampson from the Continental Army, which she left in October 1783. A year later she married Benjamin Gannett, with whom she had three children.

Sampson resumed her career as a teacher and later, dressed in military regalia, embarked on lecture tours of New England and New York State, talking about her experiences in the War of Independence. A somewhat fanciful biography of Sampson, written by Herbert Mann, was published in 1786. From 1804, after an intercession by Paul Revere, Sampson received a pension of four dollars a month and a land grant from the US Congress in acknowledgment of her service as a Revolutionary soldier.

Reference: Lucy Freeman and Alma Bond, *America's First Woman Warrior: The Courage of Deborah Sampson,* 1992.

SANDES, FLORA
World War I Nurse and Soldier, b. 1876, d. 1956

The daughter of a Suffolk clergyman, Sandes worked as a secretary in London before 1914 and received elementary medical training in the **First Aid Nursing Yeomanry** (FANY, see p. 161) and the St. John's Ambulance Brigade. In August 1914, along with thirty-six other nurses, she sailed from London, bound for Serbia, then at war with Austria-Hungary.

Initially attached to the Serbian Red Cross and then to the Second Infantry Regiment, she soon exchanged a nurse's uniform for the khaki and puttees of a front-line soldier in a war in which the Serbs were now fighting Austro-German forces and their Bulgarian ally. In November 1915, Sandes, now enlisted in the Serbian army, joined the "Great Retreat" across the mountains of Albania to the island of Corfu in the Adriatic.

Buxom, open-faced, and immensely tough, Sandes relished the military life and was idolized by her Serbian comrades. She quickly adapted to trench warfare, explaining that she derived particular satisfaction from the fighting in which the explosion of her grenades was followed by "a few groans, then silence," since a "tremendous hullabaloo" indicated that she had inflicted "only a few scratches, or the top of someone's finger . . . taken off." Like **Nadezhda Durova** (see p. 73) she always insisted that her wartime experience—with its mixture of discomfort and boredom, interspersed with moments of terrible savagery—gave her a freedom that had been previously unimaginable for a woman.

In 1916 she was badly wounded in hand-to-hand fighting and reluctantly returned to nursing and, briefly, to England. She noted that it was like "losing everything at one fell swoop and trying to find bearings again in another life and in an entirely different world."

At the end of World War I, Sandes decided to throw in her lot with the Serbian army. In June 1919, the Serbian parliament passed legislation enabling her to become the first woman to be commissioned in the Serbian army. She rose to the rank of captain and retired with her adopted country's highest decoration, the

King George Star. In 1927 she married Russian émigré Yurie Yudenich and lived in France and Belgrade, where she was interned by the Germans during World War II. Her husband died in 1941, and at the end of the war Sandes returned to Suffolk, where her remarkable journey had begun.

Reference: Alan Burgess, *The Lovely Sergeant,* 1963.

STUART, MIRANDA, SEE BARRY, JAMES, p. 69.

VELAZQUEZ, LORETA JANETA
Civil War Soldier of the Confederacy, b. 1842, d. 1897?

The Cuban-born widow of a Confederate soldier who died of accidental gunshot wounds, Loreta Janeta Velazquez also lost her three children to a fever and, utterly bereft, left her home in New Orleans with the intention of becoming "a second **Joan of Arc**" (see p. 75).

At her own expense, she raised and equipped an infantry unit in Arkansas, thus avoiding the risk of being recognized by any of her New Orleans acquaintances, and adopted the name of Harry T. Buford, donning a complicated metal corset to hide her curves and sporting a false mustache and roguish swagger.

As Buford, she commanded her Arkansas Grays at the First Battle of Bull Run (1861) and later campaigned in Kentucky and Tennessee, where she was badly wounded and cited for gallantry. However, her extraordinary demeanor led to her being arrested in Richmond, Virginia, as a suspected Union spy. According to her own account, Velazquez turned the situation to her advantage by convincing the Confederate authorities of her loyalty and persuading them to employ her as a secret agent. One of the exploits to which she laid claim was the theft of electrotype impressions of Union bond and note plates to enable the Confederates to make forgeries.

During the war, she married Captain De Caulp, a Scot serving in the Confederate Army, and lost her second husband when he was killed in action. Her third husband was Major Wesson, an explorer who had the misfortune to die of "the black vomit" at the start of an expedition the couple had launched into the jungles of Venezuela. Bereft again, Velazquez soon acquired a fourth husband, a gold prospector, with whom she met Brigham Young, finding the Mormon leader to be "a pleasant, genial gentleman, with an excellent fund of humour and a captivating style of conversation."

Velazquez's story has long been treated with skepticism by historians of the period, and the facts behind many aspects of her colorful career remain unproven. But her war service, her courage, her misfortunes, and her gallantry are beyond dispute. In her memoirs, published in 1876, Velazquez observed, "Notwithstanding the fact that I was a woman, I was as good a soldier as any man around me, and as willing as any to fight valiantly and to the bitter end before yielding."

Reference: David G. Martin, *The Vicksburg Campaign: April 1862–July 1863* (Great Campaigns), 1994.

4

REBELS AND REVOLUTIONARIES

⟨∞⟩

Women Taking Up Arms for a Cause

In any revolution, the women are more revolutionary than the men.
—Fidel Castro

Castro's pronouncement holds true for generations of human history. While some women have always sought to join the male power establishment in times of war or social upheaval and to work their way up through its ranks, others were natural rebels. Their wars lay outside the system and inevitably outside any protection of law or chivalry that might otherwise have been afforded to their sex.

Women rebels are an unusual breed. Whether the revolution is against the monarchy, the church, the local despot, or the state, women in general tend to be more conservative and religious than men, as modern voting patterns and church attendance demonstrate, and therefore more inclined to protect the status quo. This may be because both as women and as mothers, they have more to lose than men by putting themselves outside the protection of society. This was particularly true in the past, when without contraceptives they could not control their fertility, and without access to jobs they could not readily support themselves.

What makes a woman choose the rocky road of rebellion? For some, it chose itself through griefs and afflictions too great to be

borne. The devastation inflicted on **Lakshmi Bai, Rani of Jhansi**
(see p. 98) left her no other avenue but armed reprisal, a fate she
embraced, determined to return her injuries with interest.

But most revolutionary women were driven not by personal
injury but by deep, burning conviction, their ideologies sharpened
by years of debate with fellow revolutionaries in smoky back
rooms. Often highly educated and intelligent, especially from the
nineteenth century onward, they concerned themselves with the
intellectual and cultural struggle as strongly as with the armed conflict. For them, the works of Marx and Mao were weapons as vital
as any bomb or gun, and they were equally at home in the lecture
room or on the attack.

And as with the runaways and roaring girls of chapter 3, revolutionary war offered unparalleled opportunities to female idealists,
zealots, and true believers, as well as to the disaffected and dispos-
sessed who were ready to die for their cause. The women of
America were active as early as Bacon's Rebellion in 1676, when
one woman acting as Bacon's lieutenant was the first to gather his
followers together, riding up and down the back country as his
personal emissary, while a second, Sarah Grendon, was personally
exempted from the subsequent free pardon because she had been
such a "great encourager and assister in the late horrid Rebellion."
Another Sarah, Mistress Drummond of Jamestown, showed the
spirit that united them all when she responded to the governor's
threats of death by snapping a stick in two under his nose, shouting, "I fear the power of England no more than a broken straw!"

A century later when the American Revolution broke out,
American women were again well to the fore, both in active engagement and in the courage of independent thought that created
it (see also **American Civil War,** p. 336). An eyewitness account of
the first battle at Lexington in 1774 describes "at every house,
women and children making cartridges, running bullets, making
wallets, baking biscuits . . . and at the same time animating their
husbands and sons to fight for their liberties, though not knowing
whether they should see them again." Some women were unable
or unwilling to leave the fighting to their men. A number of accounts tell of women putting on uniform and arming themselves,

forming military-style companies like the Russian women's Battalion of Death (see **Bochkareva, Maria** p. 88), and performing dauntless acts of "masculine valour" in times of crisis.

With the harsh struggles of colonial life and the early death rate of women everywhere in the seventeenth century, most of these American women would still have been young and therefore trapped in the eternal cycle of reproduction, always pregnant, newly delivered, or about to be pregnant again. As they also lived under the early Puritan leaders' fundamentalist Bible-based belief in women's sinfulness and inferiority, it is remarkable how much they were able to do, and how little they were held back either by physical weakness or notions of mental incapacity. The same is true of every revolt and rebellion in recorded history. No revolution has taken place without some female freedom fighters, and the harsher the struggle, the more women have flocked to the cause.

Many of them paid a terrible price. But the risk has never deterred the true revolutionary, whatever the cost. The Russian anti-tsarist **Vera Figner** was imprisoned for twenty years in the dreaded Schlüsselburg island fortress in the Neva River where, as she later bleakly recorded, "the clock of life stopped" (see p. 93). Alone in her cell, the Cuban **Haydée Santamaría** was confronted with her brother's eye—or in some accounts, both eyes and testicles—in an attempt to make her talk (see p. 114). Santamaría held out and survived, when many male revolutionaries did not. All the women revolutionaries knew what they could expect if they were caught. It proved no deterrent. Their courage, sacrifice, and in some cases dreadful deaths are discussed below.

Not all revolutionaries fought with weapons of war. Many **Vietnam Women Fighters** in the 1970s worked on the Ho Chi Minh Trail, wielding picks and shovels, heaving baskets of soil, and filling bomb craters by day so that trucks could roll by night (see p. 118). Although numbers of them were university students or graduates, they had to learn new skills to operate heavy machinery and raise rice yields as they replaced the men. In the same spirit, the women on the **Long March** (see p. 101) were ready to rise to every demand the revolution made on them.

Whatever their roles, most of the women revolutionaries who

took up arms slipped back into obscurity afterward, welcoming the chance to live a quiet life. Those who could not found that revolution cast a long shadow down the years. For them, it became the demon lover who demands and expects total allegiance, ruling out any normal existence such as most women knew. For the sake of "the revolution," they sacrificed a loving husband and a peaceful home, a brood of children and a regular path through life. For them the struggle became the path itself, the only way forward, their courage and conviction lighting every step until the end.

And when the end comes, for women the light goes out. Once the revolutionary war is over, just as with any war, women are expected to return meekly to the home and not to demand their share of the revolutionary spoils. All revolutions, all uprisings, all revolts, all demands for equality throughout history, have stopped short of sexual equality. So there is no revolution for women in any of these revolutions we describe.

Indeed, the oppression of women in traditional societies can even increase, as the new political masters strive to return the country to some false notion of "the way it was before" (see **FLN Bombers,** p. 94). Sidelined and often stigmatized as unfeminine, aggressive, and part of the past, the women of most modern revolutions are left to ponder the summary of the eighteenth-century British politician Edmund Burke: "Every revolution contains in it something of evil."

BOCHKAREVA, MARIA
Russian Bolshevik Soldier, b. 1889, d. 1920

A self-styled "tigress" of World War I, Bochkareva had an appetite for combat that was not satisfied by fighting in the ranks of men. As Russia's soldiers faltered in the face of the German onslaught, Bochkareva created a formation composed entirely of women volunteers, initially some two thousand strong, under her command.

The twenty-eight-year-old Bochkareva had led a tumultuous life. Born in Tomsk in 1889, she was the daughter of a serf and in her teens had become a prostitute and the mistress of a succession of men. In 1914, after surviving an attempt on her life by her husband, she became an ultra-patriot, enlisting as a soldier, winning a chestful of medals, and rising to the rank of sergeant. Her bravery was extraordinary, and she was famous for rescuing wounded comrades in the face of enemy machine-gun fire.

In May 1917, a low point for Russia in World War I, Bochkareva persuaded Alexander Kerensky, head of Russia's newly installed provisional government, to agree to the formation of a women's battalion—the so-called Battalion of Death—a shock force with shaven heads that would challenge the prevailing mood of defeatism. In June 1917, at St. Isaac's Cathedral in St. Petersburg, where the battalion's banners were blessed, Bochkareva made this emotional appeal: "Come with us in the name of your fallen heroes! Come with us to dry the tears and heal the wounds of Russia. Protect her with your lives. We women are turning into tigresses to protect our children from a shameful yoke—to protect the freedom of our country."

Despite her own checkered past, Bochkareva set her standards of recruitment high. "Our mother [Russia] is perishing!" she declared. "I want help to save her. I want women whose hearts are pure crystal, whose souls are pure, whose impulses are lofty." Fifteen hundred women enlisted that night, and another five hundred the following day. Styling herself "Yashka" (note the male nom de guerre), she welcomed them all. Bochkareva's vision and enthusiasm proved contagious, and similar units were organized all over Russia. The formation of the Battalion of Death was much applauded by the English feminist and suffragette leader Emmeline Pankhurst, who was visiting Russia at the time and took the salute at the march-past.

Of the initial intake, several hundred members of the Battalion of Death—most of them peasants—were sent to the Kovno sector, in Lithuania, under the overall command of General Denikin, where they went into action supported by a male battalion. After three weeks of fighting, the Battalion of Death had suffered losses of 350 killed and 70 wounded, among the latter Bochkareva herself. In his memoirs, Denikin attested to the women's bravery but observed that they were "quite unfit to be soldiers"; he claimed that they had to be locked up at night to prevent them from being raped by the men under his command.

Some two hundred members of the Battalion of Death continued to serve at the front, but their position was undermined by Bochkareva's autocratic style of command, so unpredictable and tyrannical that she drove her remaining supporters away. The battalion also incurred the hostility of the Bolsheviks, who in October 1917 had swept away Kerensky's government. On November 21, 1917, the Bolshevik Revolutionary Committee disbanded Bochkareva's formation; subsequently it sentenced her to death. In 1918 she escaped to the United States via Vladivostok, disguised as a nurse, and dictated a colorful but unreliable book about her wartime experiences.

Bochkareva was subsequently introduced to President Woodrow Wilson and unsuccessfully attempted to persuade him to step up aid to the Russian White counterrevolutionaries, among whom her former commander Denikin was a leading figure. Then she turned up in England, where she unavailingly petitioned George V with a similar message. Undaunted, she was back in Archangel, the port on Russia's White Sea, in the autumn of 1918, attempting to raise another Battalion of Death to fight the Bolsheviks. She was sent packing by the commander of the British Expeditionary Force on the spot, General Ironside, who gave her five hundred rubles and a ticket back to Omsk, where she was arrested by the Bolsheviks and executed on May 16, 1920.

Reference: Maria Bochkareva and Isaac Don Levine, *Yashka: My Life as Peasant, Officer and Exile,* 1919.

ERITREA, WOMEN COMBATANTS
Late Twentieth Century

The war in Eritrea brought a landmark decision in the history of women and combat during the 1970s, when the Eritrean military became the only one in the world to conscript women into active front-line combat service. As many as 30 percent of the Popular

Front for the Liberation of Eritrea (EPLF) freedom fighters were women and girls.

In 1952 the former Italian colony of Eritrea, in the Horn of Africa, came under effective Ethiopian rule. After 1960, armed resistance in Eritrea grew when the region lost its autonomy and was reduced to the status of a province. To counter the guerrilla Eritrean movement, the Ethiopian emperor, Haile Selassie, was forced to reequip and modernize his army, a task made possible only by massive US aid. By the early 1970s, the United States was devoting more of its military aid budget to Ethiopia than to the rest of Africa combined.

After the overthrow of Haile Selassie by a military coup in 1974, Ethiopia's new leader, Mengistu Haile Mariam, turned to the Soviet Union for help in the war against the Eritrean separatists. However, in spite of an expanded and resupplied army and air force advised by some fifteen hundred Soviets and reinforced by a combat construction division of Cubans, the Ethiopian military government, the Derg, could make no headway in the war against Eritrea.

The women fighters were integral to the Eritrean war effort. Female volunteers came from all strata of Eritrean society, both Christian and Muslim. Most joined the EPLF against the will of their parents, and the majority described their background as "very traditional." In the EPLF they were plunged into a very different environment in which Marxist guerrilla leaders preached equality between men and women and challenged their basic beliefs. After 1977, the women fighters were allowed to marry their comrades in the trenches. After a brief honeymoon, husband and wife returned to the front, often not seeing each other again for several months.

Demography was the principal reason for this revolution in military affairs. Ethiopia had a population fifteen times greater than Eritrea's. However, although some Eritrean women rode in tanks, the overwhelming majority were used principally to hold fixed positions. Another potential problem, that of pregnancy, was obviated by the harsh reality of the war against Ethiopia, with its perpetual food shortages. Most women, if their body fat falls below a certain level, cannot conceive (see **Long March**, p. 101).

Eritrea gained its independence from Ethiopia in May 1993. In the months following the Eritrean victory, many women soldiers returned to their families, often after an absence of ten years. At the time they were seen as heroic freedom fighters and were instantly recognizable, with their cropped hair, military clothes, and plastic sandals. Many of them later handled the transition from soldier to working mother with some success, although the previously admired military style of dress was soon abandoned.

Nevertheless, the transition from war to peace was accompanied by social stress. Of twelve thousand women fighters demobilized on independence, more than half, according to UN figures, were reported to have divorced. Their marriages did not survive the arrival of peace. Male attitudes also underwent a change. One female EPLF fighter, Ruth Simon, observed: "The men have become traditional again . . . this traditional male thinking has deep roots that go back many generations. When they went to the front, men were forced to accept EPLF policy of equality between the sexes. When they came back to the towns after liberation, the government had other priorities and did not concern itself with the emancipation of women. Men fell back into the old way of thinking" (see **FLN Bombers,** p. 94, for the same postrevolutionary process at work).

In July 1995, on the urging of Miriam Muhammad, an EPLF veteran, a number of Eritrean women founded Bana (Dawn), the Eritrean Women War Veterans Association. Its aim was to help former women fighters become economically independent with the creation of a cooperative. Demobilized women were able to buy shares with the money they received when they left the EPLF.

In 1998, tensions between Ethiopia and Eritrea—principally ongoing economic and border disputes—boiled over into war between the two impoverished nations. Before a cease-fire was agreed upon in 2000, an estimated 100,000 people had lost their lives and 25 percent of the Eritrean population had been displaced.

In the late 1990s the Eritrean army contained the highest proportion of women fighters in the world, some 40,000 out of a total of 300,000, the latter figure representing approximately 10 percent of the population.

Reference: Olive Furley and Roy May, *Ending Africa's Wars: Progressing to Peace,* 2006.

FIGNER, VERA
Russian Revolutionary, b. 1852, d. 1942

One of the Narodnik terrorists who plotted the assassination of Tsar Alexander II, Vera Figner lived to a great age and died a heroine of the Soviet Union.

She was the eldest of six children in a prosperous Kazan family and had a happy childhood, in which she was educated at home. After attending the Rodionovsky Institute for Women in Kazan, she studied medicine in Switzerland, where she lived with her lawyer husband, Aleksey Filippov, and her sister Lidiya.

In 1873 Figner and her sister joined a student discussion club, members of which would later form the nucleus of the All-Russian Social Revolutionary Organization. In December 1875 she returned to Russia, and a year later she joined the revolutionary group Zemlya i Volya (Land and Liberty). She obtained a paramedic's license, divorced her husband, and went to work in the countryside, where she combined her medical duties with the distribution of revolutionary pamphlets. In 1879, after a split in Zemlya i Volya, Figner joined the terrorist branch of the movement Narodnaya Volya (the People's Will). She became the group's agent in Odessa, writing articles, establishing links with dissident members of the Russian military, and planning the assassination of Tsar Alexander II with, among others, Sofya Perovskaya and her lover, Andrei Zhelyabov.

In February 1881, Perovskaya directed the successful assassination of Alexander II in St. Petersburg. She was arrested in March, tried, sentenced to death, and hanged in April. Figner became the acting head of the remnants of the Narodnaya Volya, based in Kharkov, but was betrayed and arrested in February 1883 and sentenced to death the following year. The sentence was commuted to life imprisonment, initially in the Peter and Paul prison in St. Petersburg and then, for twenty years, in the dreaded Schlüsselburg island fortress on the Neva River, where, as she later wrote, "the clock of life stopped." These bleak words later became the title of her 1921 memoirs.

In 1904 she was released into exile in Archangel, on the White

Sea. Two years later she made her way abroad, living in Switzerland until her return to Russia in 1915. After the Russian Revolution, she chaired the Society of the Former Political Prisoners and Exiles. Between 1929 and 1932, her collected works were published in the Soviet Union in seven volumes.

Reference: Vera Figner, *Memoirs of a Revolutionist,* 1927.

FLN BOMBERS
Algerian War of Independence, 1954–62

In the early 1950s, Algerian demands for even limited political and civil rights had been repeatedly rebuffed by the French colonial regime and the nearly one million European settlers in the country. The National Liberation Front (FLN) was formed in October 1954 to fight for Algeria's independence, and women were integral to the campaign from the start.

Depending on where they lived, city or village, and their level of education, Algerian women participated in the struggle along with men in several capacities. Rural women either joined the National Liberation Front or provided food, provisions, and havens for the guerrillas; about 80 percent of the women who actively participated resided in the countryside. In cities, they joined the FLN. By the summer of 1956, the FLN could boast some twenty thousand active members organized on military lines and count on the passive support of most of the Muslim population of Algeria. FLN operations in the capital city of Algiers were controlled by Saadi Yacef, who had been ordered by his high command to prosecute a campaign of terror against "any Europeans between the ages of 18 and 54" but to avoid killing "women, children and old people."

Self-confident and ruthless, the twenty-nine-year-old Yacef had established a power base in Algiers's teeming Casbah and had built up a cadre of some fifteen hundred terrorists, a number of whom were attractive, well-educated young women who could pass as Europeans. At the beginning of what was later dubbed the Battle of Algiers, among the most significant of these women were

Djamila Bouhired, Yacef's chief recruiting officer of fighting women, and Samia Lakhdari and Zohra Drif, law students at Algiers University. The twenty-two-year-old Drif had decided to join the FLN after the 1956 execution by guillotine of two members, Ahmed Zabana and Abdelkader Ferradj, the latter disabled.

The women undertook their first mission on September 30, 1956, carrying three bombs into the heart of European Algiers. They had removed their veils, tinted their hair, and wore bright summer dresses. The bombs, carried at the bottom of beach bags filled with swimwear, weighed little more than a kilogram and were set to go off at one-minute intervals from 6:30 P.M. Drif and Lakhdari deposited their bombs in two fashionable cafeterias and left. The explosives detonated on time, killing three and injuring fifty, among them several children. Bouhired's bomb, placed in the hall of the Air France terminus, failed to detonate because of a faulty timer.

On January 25, 1957, two days before the FLN called a general strike in Algiers, Yacef launched another wave of bombings. Once again the bombs were carried by three women, whose operational value had been greatly increased by French body searches of every male leaving the Casbah, while women were allowed the cover of the all-enveloping traditional Muslim veil (see also **Suicide Bombers**, p. 327).

One of the bombers was a European, Daniele Minn, the stepdaughter of a Communist. Minn was among a number of French-educated women who had never worn the veil but adopted it as a military strategy in order to carry bombs, money, or messages from one zone of Algiers to another without being stopped and searched.

Another was Djamila Boupacha, who along with Bouhired would achieve international recognition for her suffering in the aftermath of the raid. Their targets were a student bar, a nearby cafeteria, and a popular brasserie. The bombs claimed sixty wounded and five killed, including an innocent young Muslim mechanic who was lynched on the spot in the backlash launched by the *pieds-noirs* ("black feet," the nickname of European settlers in Algeria). Two weeks later, two teenage girls placed bombs in two crowded sports stadiums, killing ten and injuring forty-five.

Freedom fighters to Algerians but loathed terrorists to the French, Bouhired and Boupacha were among a number of women soon captured by the French police or army, imprisoned, and subjected to severe torture. After considerable suffering, Bouhired was tried, convicted, and sentenced to death in July 1957. The execution was postponed after a national outcry, culminating in the publication of *Pour Djamila Bouhired* (For Djamila Bouhired), and Bouhired was sent to prison in France until the war was won in 1962.

Others also suffered grievously. Arrested in February 1960 for throwing a bomb into a café, Boupacha, a virgin, was subjected to a variety of tortures and sexual humiliation, culminating in rape with a broken bottle. Her case received widest publicity in France, a portrait of her by Picasso appearing in many magazines. A highly vocal "D B Committee" was founded by eminent philosophers and liberals such as François Mauriac, Simone de Beauvoir, and Germaine Tillion, which helped to foster antiwar sentiment and to ensure Boupacha's release.

The FLN's bombing campaign was just one part of an independence struggle that lasted until the spring of 1962 and was conducted with great savagery by the French military, the FLN, and the OAS (Organisation Armée Secrète, the backlash terrorist group that fought for a French Algeria in North Africa and metropolitan France). The war spread to the French mainland, brought down the French Fourth Republic, and led to the return to power of the war hero General Charles de Gaulle, who staved off a military coup d'etat, restored stability, and with great skill orchestrated the handing over of power to the Algerians.

This came at a heavy cost to both sides: in Algeria the French military suffered some 17,500 dead and 65,000 wounded. European civilian casualties ran to more than 10,000, including nearly 3,000 dead. It is estimated that the total number of Algerian casualties was somewhere between 300,000 and 1 million. At least 30,000 of them were FLN members who were the victims of internal FLN purges, or Muslims who died in the brutal reprisals that formed a key part of that organization's strategy of terror.

Zohra Drif, regarded as a heroine of the Battle of Algiers, spent five years of a twenty-year sentence in French prisons before completing her law studies and becoming secretary-general of the Algerian École Nationale d'Administration. Her fellow bomber Djamila Bouhired became a businesswoman and stood for election to the First National Assembly.

In the years following the struggle for independence, they remained among the very few examples of women liberated by the war. In the heat of the conflict, the French critic Frantz Fanon, the author of *A Dying Colonialism* and *The Wretched of the Earth* (both originally published in 1961), had predicted that a new social order would emerge from the dreadful carnage in Algeria, but he was wrong.

After the treaty of peace was signed with France in 1962, the independent Algerian government registered nearly eleven thousand women as war veterans, but this figure greatly undervalued the true number of women who actively contributed to the war effort. In an effort to assert political authority and cultural authenticity as well as to restore their masculinity so badly bruised by colonial rule, male nationalist leaders proved notoriously resistant to demands for female emancipation once they assumed power.

As in other liberation struggles (see **Partisans,** p. 107), the role of many FLN women had initially drawn them from a position of medieval subjection as passive complements to men to that of active participants in the fight for independence. After independence was achieved, the process was thrown into reverse gear.

Djamila Bouhired, now a grandmother, continued her militant activities after the war but shifted her battleground to feminist protest advocating immediate improvements in the legal, political, and social status of Algeria's women. Predictably, the horrors endured by these women and others did little or nothing to improve the status of Algerian women once the war was won. Despite heated opposition from women's groups, pressure from Islamists in the early 1980s resulted in the Family Code of 1984, which legally removed most of the rights given to women under the Charter of Algiers established after independence.

For the oppressed women of Algeria, there remains a bitter comparison with Tunisia, where women's rights are more firmly established and their roles less restricted. This demonstrates how closely women's lives in a postrevolutionary world are tied to levels of colonial violence and male definitions of nationalism. In Tunisia, independence was achieved in 1956 with relatively little upheaval, while unspeakable horror, bloodshed, and social chaos reigned for years in Algeria.

It is clear that the greater the institutionalized violence and the violation of basic rights under an imperial or colonial system of rule, the less likely it is that far-reaching, permanent changes in women's status, condition, and lives will occur. Indeed, women can lose precious hard-won rights that they had secured earlier due to invasion or imperial interventions—as events in United States–occupied Iraq have demonstrated.

Algeria remains an outstanding paradox of women's participation in colonial and nationalist struggles, whereby the new regime they have struggled to form with such suffering and sacrifice then makes them the first target of renewed oppression. The distinguished sociologist professor Marnia Lazreg comments: "Algeria is the only nation in the Middle East where women are killed as women because they are women. Women have lost their lives for not wearing the veil, as well as wearing it."

Reference: Marnia Lazreg, *The Eloquence of Silence: Algerian Women in Question,* 1994; and Alistair Horne, *A Savage War of Peace: Algeria 1954–1962,* 1996. The bombing mission of September 30, 1956, was re-created with chilling accuracy in Gillo Pontecorvo's 1966 movie *The Battle of Algiers,* in which Saadi Yacef played himself as well as acting as coproducer.

LAKSHMI BAI, RANI OF JHANSI
Indian Nationalist Fighter, b. 1835, d. 1857

Born a noblewoman in Benares (now Varanasi), the daughter of a Brahmin father and a cultivated mother who died when her little girl was only four, Lakshmi Bai practiced the arts of war from childhood. Later she enjoyed power and status as the wife of the raja of Jhansi, and as a reluctant but immensely able warrior queen she drew on her upbringing for the skills she needed as a military leader. She died fighting at the head of her troops.

Brought up in a predominantly male household, Lakshmi Bai received an equestrian and martial training. Her birthplace, on the holy river Ganges, was later to give the rani an important religious significance when she turned on the heathen British, prompting Sir Hugh Rose, the man who defeated her in battle, to dub her "a sort of Indian **Joan of Arc**" (see p. 75).

In 1842 she married the raja of Jhansi, a small, prosperous, independent, and pro-British state. In 1853, after the death of the raja, Lord Dalhousie, the governor-general of British India, refused to recognize the raja's declared heir, his adopted son Damodar Rao, and annexed the state. The decision was hotly contested in the British courts by the raja's widow but her petitions were rejected. Insult was added to injury when the British authorities took punitive action against the rani by confiscating the state jewels, deducting her husband's debts from her annual pension, and ordering her to quit the fort at Jhansi.

The rani remained in Jhansi and retired into private life. Jhansi was considered a backwater, and the British withdrew the greater part of the garrison there. This was shown to be a mistake in the Indian Mutiny of 1857, when native troops besieged Jhansi's Red Star Fort and then massacred the Europeans sheltering there after they had been promised safe conduct. The rani, who had succeeded up to this point in sitting out the mutiny, was not responsible for the act of treachery, but the British believed otherwise and later convinced themselves that she had been a prime mover in the mutiny itself.

For the next few months, however, the British were content to allow her to function as the effective ruler of Jhansi. She cut an impressive figure, dressing as a combination of warrior and queen in jodhpurs and silk blouse with a jeweled sword and two silver pistols in her belt. Her daily routine included riding and target practice with her pistols.

But time was running out for the rani. The British had now quelled the mutiny and were mopping up the last pockets of resistance. She had been tarred with the blame for the massacre of the defenders of the Red Fort, and her days in Jhansi were numbered. She decided that she had nothing to lose if she took up arms against the British.

She strengthened the defenses of the fort and assembled a volunteer army, fourteen thousand strong, including women who had been given military training. The siege of Jhansi began on March 20, 1858. The women who had been trained by the rani were seen by the British frantically working the batteries, hauling ammunition, and bringing food and water to the soldiers. The rani was everywhere. Men of the Fourteenth Light Dragoons, laying siege to the fort, recalled her as "a perfect Amazon in bravery . . . just the sort of daredevil woman soldiers admire."

The British captured the citadel after a two-week siege and took a terrible revenge. Thomas Lowe, an army doctor, witnessed the scene and recorded that the enemy dead lay in their "puffed-up thousands" in the blazing sun. "Such was the retribution meted out to this Jezebel Ranee and her people."

The rani escaped with four companions, including her father, and rode hard to Kalpi, more than a hundred miles away, to join the rulers still holding out against the British. On June 1 she participated in the capture of the fortress at Gwalior, which was held by Indian allies of the British, and was rewarded with a fabulous pearl necklace from the treasury there.

On June 16 the British counterattacked, and in the fierce fighting that followed, the rani was killed at the head of her troops, clubbed and shot by two British soldiers. Her dying words were to beg that the British should not touch her body, and her own men bore her corpse to a nearby haystack and set it alight. Her father was captured and shot a few days later. Her adopted son was granted a pension by the British but never recovered his inheritance.

In the Indian independence movement of the twentieth century, Rani Lakshmi Bai became a rallying figure for nationalists. Two statues have been raised to her, depicting her in dashing equestrian mode and with raised sword, in Gwalior and Jhansi. She is also remembered in many popular ballads, one of which hymns her courage:

How valiantly like a man fought she,
The Rhani of Jhansi
On every parapet a gun she set
Raining fire of hell,
How well like a man fought the Rhani of Jhansi
How valiantly and well!

Reference: Karl Meyer and Shareen Blair Brysac, *Tournament of Shadows: The Great Game and the Race for Empire in Asia,* 1999.

LONG MARCH
China, 1934–35

In the Long March, the Chinese Communist Party (CCP) and its armed forces made an eight-thousand-mile trek from their bases in southeast China, which had been encircled by the Nationalist forces of the Kuomintang, to a new stronghold in the northwest. As comrades in arms, lovers, and porters, women sustained the troops in the ordeal of this strategic retreat, during which Mao Tse-tung emerged as the party's supreme leader.

Mao's First Front Army, which set off from Jiangxi Province in October 1934, consisted of 86,000 men and some 30 women. The Fourth Front Army, which struck out from Sichuan in March 1935, had about 2,000 women in its ranks. The Second Front Army, formed by a merger of the Second and Sixth Army Groups and containing about 25 women, began its own march from a mountain base near the border of Hunan almost a year after the First Front Army set out.

Before the First Front Army began its march, the decision was taken to leave all the children behind. Mothers had to find local families willing to adopt their children. Children born on the march would also have to be placed among local populations. Few of these women ever saw their children again.

Most of the CCP leaders were with the First Front Army, and the women traveled with them. Women who had been peasants before the march and accustomed to heavy work in the fields carried supply and medicine boxes and undertook stretcher work. Educated women performed propaganda and recruitment roles, seeking out short-term transport workers who traveled with the army for several days before returning home (see also **Vietnam Women Fighters,** p. 118, for women fulfilling the same light and heavy work).

These workers were of crucial importance because the First Front Army had no motor vehicles and a severe shortage of pack animals. Kang Keqing (1912–1993), the wife of the Communist commander-in-chief, Chu Teh, marched with the military head-quarters as a political instructor. She was also armed and carried out the same tasks as the other women on the march. Liu Ying (later an assistant foreign minister for the People's Republic of China, 1954–59) worked with the First Front Army's logistics de-partment, dealing with everything from money and guns to uni-forms and printing presses.

Also traveling with the First Front Army was Mao's second wife, He Zizhen, who was pregnant when the march began and gave birth in the spring of 1935. She had to give the child away. This was the third time she had been forced to abandon a child. Her first child with Mao, a girl, was given to a peasant woman when she and Mao had to flee their guerrilla base. A second, a two-year-old boy, had been left in the care of her sister before the march began. He Zizhen later suffered a mental breakdown and spent many years in a sanatorium in the Soviet Union, an exile en-gineered by Mao's third wife, Jiang Qing, a former bit-part film actress who had not been on the Long March. He Zizhen died in Shanghai in 1984.

In June 1935, the First Front joined hands with the Fourth Front Army, whose two thousand female soldiers had been able to travel with their children and husbands. The older children were taken on as orderlies, messengers, and buglers. The Fourth Front fielded a women's factory battalion responsible for clothing, and an indepen-dent battalion, later a regiment. The principal factor in the larger role played by women in the Fourth Front Army was opium, a sta-ple crop in Sichuan. The high rate of male dependency on the drug meant that the Fourth Front had no choice but to recruit women.

In the Fourth Front Army, strict rules prohibited male soldiers from mixing with the female units. On the whole, discipline was maintained, but the Front's female troops suffered badly if they fell into the hands of hostile forces. Many were captured and raped by the private armies of the Muslim warlords of northwest China. The armies on the Long March also incorporated teenage recruits who were dubbed "the Little Red Devils." It is estimated that there were about 5,000 in the 100,000-strong Fourth Front Army, many of them young girls. Conditions on the Long March were grueling in the extreme. Moving at a punishing pace and often under both ground and air attack by the Nationalists, the columns crossed and recrossed freezing rivers, mountain ranges, and treacherous swampy grasslands. Battle casualties, disease, desertion, and political purges took a heavy toll. In October 1935, the First Front Army arrived in Yenan, its final destination, with its strength reduced to some 8,000.

Of the 30 women who began the march with the First Front Army, nineteen survived. The enormous privations suffered by the women of the First and Fourth Front Armies rendered many of the survivors infertile. One survivor observed of her sacrifice, "It was a small price to pay for the revolution." The observation reflects how Mao alchemized a seemingly wretched defeat into the founding myth of modern China.

In the 1980s, Kang Keqing became chairperson of the Chinese Communist Party. The vengeful Jiang Qing, who had seized power during Mao's dotage, was overthrown in 1976, imprisoned, and sentenced to death. "I was Chairman Mao's dog," she protested. "Whoever he told me to bite, I bit." Her sentence was later commuted to life imprisonment, and in 1991, diagnosed with throat cancer, she hanged herself in the hospital at the age of seventy-seven.

Reference: Sun Shuyun, *The Long March,* 2006.

MOLLY PITCHER
Thought to Be Mary Ludwig Hays McCauley, Iconic Figure in the US War of Independence, b. 1754, d. 1832

A water bearer to the troops in one of the hardest-fought battles of the American Revolution, a woman nicknamed Molly Pitcher became famous when she took the place of a fallen artillery gunner, her husband, and continued the fight. Her story abounds in vivid detail, including chatting with George Washington, but some historians question its authenticity and doubt that she existed as described.

The woman with whom Molly Pitcher is usually identified, Mary Ludwig, was born to German immigrants in Trenton, New Jersey, on October 13, 1754. She moved to the Pennsylvania town of Carlisle and began her connection with the army at the age of fifteen as a servant to Dr. William Irvine, later a brigadier general in the colonial army. Her first husband, John Hays, enlisted in the First Pennsylvania Artillery in 1775 at the outbreak of the Revolutionary War, and she soon joined him in the field with the permission of his regimental commander (for women accompanying their soldier husbands, see **Camp Followers,** p. 126, *Soldaderas,* p. 140, and **Vivandières,** p. 146).

During the Battle of Monmouth on June 28, 1778, according to contemporary accounts a broiling hot day, Mary is said to have earned her nickname by returning to the battle lines again and again with pitchers of water for her husband and his fellow artillery gunners, who were dying of heat and thirst. "Molly" was a common form of "Mary," and "Pitcher" commemorated the number of times the welcome water appeared at the front in her hands. As she watched, Hays, now an artillery sergeant, was knocked unconscious in the bombardment, and the order was given to remove his piece from the field. Without hesitation Molly came forward and seized the rammer staff from her fallen husband's hands. She kept the cannon firing for the remainder of the battle and continued to fight till the close of day.

Other legends grew up around Molly's service. While tending the wounded, she is supposed to have carried a crippled soldier "on her strong, young back" out of reach of a furious British charge. Another soldier, Joseph Plumb Martin of Connecticut, told this sexually tinted story of her coolness under fire:

While in the act of reaching for a cartridge, a cannon shot from the enemy passed directly between her legs without doing any

other damage than carrying away all the lower part of her petti-
coat. Looking at it with apparent unconcern, she observed that
it was lucky it did not pass a little higher, for in that case it
might have carried away something else.

Her bravery was rewarded by George Washington himself, who
issued a warrant making her a noncommissioned officer on the
spot, resulting in another set of nicknames, "Sergeant" or "Major"
Molly. This part of the story has seemingly endless variations, in
which Washington's cameo appearance also involves his presenting her with either a gold coin or, as befitting a magnanimous
leader, a hatful of gold.

After the war, Mary and John Hays returned to Carlisle,
where he died in 1789. Mary remarried one of her late husband's
comrades-in-arms, a John or George McCauley, but the marriage
was not a happy one. McCauley is said to have treated her like a
servant, a fate Mary, now known as Molly, had escaped years before. Perhaps it may have come as a relief to her that McCauley
also died before too long.

But without a male provider, Mary/Molly may well have
struggled financially, and she seems to have petitioned the government for relief. One undisputed fact is that later in life, in 1822,
her war service was officially recognized when the state legislators
of Pennsylvania awarded her a veteran's annuity of forty dollars,
which she claimed for the next ten years.

"Molly McKolly," as some sources call her, died in Carlisle on
January 22, 1832. Her son by her first husband, John Ludwig
Hays, became a soldier and was buried with full military honors
when he died in about 1853. At the age of eighty-one, John's
daughter, Polly McCleester of Papertown, Mount Holly Springs,
unveiled a monument to her grandmother, which boldly asserts
Mary/Molly's claim to fame:

MOLLY McCauley, Renowned in history as MOLLY
PITCHER, The Heroine of Monmouth, died Jan 1833, aged
79 years. Erected by the Citizens of Cumberland County,
July 4, 1876.

A wonderful story—but is it true? In Carlisle, the town Mary Ludwig Hays McCauley was born in, left, and returned to after the war, the place where she died among her descendants and where she is buried, there is no doubt. But however proud the local people were of their heroine, they mistook the date of her death. Molly died at least a year earlier than recorded on her monument, as shown by the fact that no application for her pension was made after January 1832.

There are other questions and inconsistencies. For many years it was believed that the real Molly Pitcher was born Mary Ludwig and that she had married John Hays in Carlisle. This identification with Mary Ludwig was later challenged in favor of another Mary, who married another Hays with another extremely common first name, William. Another woman known as Molly Pitcher, described as "the heroine of Fort Washington" and buried along the Hudson, is a different individual, frequently confused with the heroine of the Battle of Monmouth.

The confusion arose because Molly Pitcher was not unique. Mary Ludwig Hays was neither the first nor the only woman to take a gunner's place on an American battlefield and man a field gun. She was preceded by Margaret Corbin during the defense of Fort Washington in 1776—possibly the heroine of Fort Washington described earlier. Corbin was recorded as staying resolutely at her post in the face of heavy enemy fire, ably acting as a matross (gunner). Other women fought in numerous engagements in the Revolutionary War and Civil War (see **Sampson, Deborah,** p. 80, and **Tubman, Harriet,** p. 117). Historical sources confirm that at least two women fought in the Battle of Monmouth, one at an artillery position and the other in the infantry line. There is no evidence linking either of them to Mary Ludwig Hays. And when she died, there was no mention of a cannon or the Battle of Monmouth in her obituary.

"Molly Pitcher" may therefore be not one woman but a composite. But the legend refuses to die. She remains a cherished character of the American Revolution and since 1876 has been firmly identified with Mary Ludwig Hays McCauley. An unmarked grave believed to be hers was opened during the centenary events of that year, and the remains were reburied with honors under a plaque declaring her the real embodiment of the famous Molly Pitcher.

One fact remains. Whether or not Mary Ludwig Hays McCauley was the real Molly Pitcher, the forty-dollar-a-year payment she was awarded by the state of Pennsylvania was more than the usual war widow's pension granted to all soldiers' wives. The citation published in *The American Volunteer,* February 21, 1822, under the heading "Legislature of Pennsylvania," makes this plain:

> A bill has passed both Houses of the Assembly granting an annuity to Molly McCauley (of Carlisle) for services she rendered during the Revolutionary War. It appeared satisfactorily that this heroine had braved the hardships of the camp and dangers of the field with her husband, who was a soldier of the revolution, and the bill in her favor passed without a dissenting voice.

Note the date. In 1822, veterans of the Battle of Monmouth were still alive to dispute the facts, yet her award was unanimously passed. The "services rendered" by Mary/Molly Ludwig Hays McCauley undoubtedly amounted to something above and beyond the ordinary conditions of war. If only we knew what they were.

Reference: Rachel A. Koestler-Grack, *Molly Pitcher: Heroine of the War for Independence,* 2005.

PARTISANS
Yugoslavia, Italy, Greece, Soviet Union, in World War II

The term "partisans" historically denotes irregular troops who employed hit-and-run tactics. In World War II in the West, partisans attacked German rear areas, particularly in the Balkans and in the Soviet Union, which necessitated the diversion of large numbers of troops to secure lines of communications. Women have generally proved effective operators in this type of warfare, and their usefulness was widely exploited.

Yugoslavia

In Yugoslavia, women played a vital part in the effective and highly organized partisan movement led by Marshal Tito, the nom de guerre adopted by the Communist leader Josip Broz, who had seen active service in the Russian and Spanish civil wars..

Yugoslavia was invaded by the German army on April 6, 1941. Within two weeks it had been overrun and occupied, and thereafter the country was partitioned. The central portion, consisting of Croatia and Bosnia and Herzegovina, became the state of Croatia, under the leadership of a German-appointed puppet, Ante Pavelic. The remaining elements of Yugoslavia were absorbed by Germany, Bulgaria, Hungary, and Italy.

Two resistance movements emerged from the dismemberment of Yugoslavia, one led by the Communist Party under Tito and the other, the nationalist, right-wing "Chetniks" commanded by Draza Mihailovic. In Tito's partisan army, the Yugoslav antifascist Front of Women was a significant force. Some 2 million Yugoslav women, approximately 12 percent of the prewar population, played a part in resistance to the Axis occupiers; 100,000 of them fought as combatants, and the others worked as couriers and auxiliaries in handling supplies, communications, education, and hospital care.

More than 250,000 female Yugoslav partisans died in the war, at least 25,000 of them front-line fighters. Some 70 percent of the female partisans were under the age of twenty, and the majority of these women came from peasant backgrounds. Of great importance in the women's partisan movement was the tradition prized in Serbia, Montenegro, and Macedonia of the "cult of motherhood," which gave women a large amount of autonomy in the home and, in Montenegro, allowed them to don male attire and go to war.

In the field, relations between the male and female partisans were carefully policed. Sexual encounters were banned, and a man who ignored this prohibition was instantly transferred to another unit. Persistent offenders were reportedly shot. However, this stern discipline did not apply to Tito and several of his senior male aides, all of whom took partisan mistresses. Tito's mistress, the fiery Zdenka, apparently chafed at maintaining the fiction that she was his secretary. When she threw a spectacular tantrum, one of Tito's bodyguards, a grizzled veteran of the Spanish Civil War, offered the laconic advice to his unnerved chief that he should have her shot.

The partitioning of Yugoslavia and the number of Axis troops (forces allied to Germany) of different ethnic groups, including a high proportion of Balkan Muslims from Bosnia and Albania, ensured that the fighting assumed the character of a civil war rather than a conventional international conflict. In Yugoslavia, civil and guerrilla war accounted for the deaths of a million Yugoslavs. During this traumatic time, women's participation enabled them to achieve important legal and economic gains, but in the immediate postwar years they were not effectively consolidated.

Reference: Velimir Vuksic, *Tito's Partisans 1941–45,* 2003.

Italy

In Italy, the arrest on July 24, 1943, of the Italian dictator Benito Mussolini was swiftly followed by the opening of negotiations with the Allies by his successor, Marshal Pietro Badoglio. When the British Eighth Army established itself on the Italian mainland on September 3, the partisan war in Italy was about to begin. It was a struggle in which women were to play a central role.

Women had played a part in the series of strikes that preceded the overthrow of Mussolini. They came from all walks of life, and clothed and fed demobilized Italian troops, escaping Allied prisoners, and Jews seeking refuge. In war factories, women sabotaged materials destined for the Germans and turned the "go slow" into an art form. In providing practical help to the active partisan groups, they enjoyed considerable freedom of movement as, unlike men, they were not forbidden to ride bicycles and aroused less suspicion in the fascist security forces than Italian men (see also **SOE,** p. 366). Thus was born the *staffettas,* the army of messengers who became lynchpins of the Italian Resistance.

Staffettas were more than messengers. Some operated radios; others carried ammunition concealed in shopping bags and baby carriages. Posing as Red Cross nurses, they provided the partisans with medical supplies and the clandestine newspapers that kept civilians informed about the movement of Axis troops and Resistance operations.

In the latter years of the war, some 75,000 women joined defense groups that helped the partisan movement by organizing strikes and sabotage in Italian war industry. Approximately 35,000 fought with the partisans; of these, 5,000 were imprisoned, 3,000 deported to Germany, and 650 were executed.

Reference: Eric Newby, *Love and War in the Apennines,* 1998.

Greece

Greece was invaded by Axis forces on April 6, 1941. The British Expeditionary Force, which had arrived in Greece in March, was withdrawn from the mainland to the island of Crete at the end of April. The Greek government and royal family went into exile in the Middle East on April 27, and Greece was occupied by Germany, Italy, and Bulgaria in a tripartite arrangement in which the Germans held the whip hand.

In Greece the vacuum left behind by the flight of the royal family and political elite was eventually filled by two principal resistance organizations, the EAM–ELAS (National Liberation Front–National Popular Liberation Army) and the EDES (Greek Democratic National Army).

Women had already played a celebrated role in Albania, which had been annexed by Italy in April 1939 and used by the Italians as the springboard for an abortive invasion of Greece in October 1940. The women of the Pindus Mountains, in northeast Greece, carried supplies on their backs to the Greek forces in Albania. Women also served as auxiliaries during the heavy fighting in Crete that followed the German airborne invasion on May 20, 1941, and sheltered many British and Commonwealth troops as they retreated to the points on Crete's rocky southern coast from which they were evacuated.

The women of mainland Greece came to the fore in the terrible winter of 1941–42, when an estimated three hundred thousand Greeks starved to death as the result of the ruthless requisitioning of food supplies to feed their occupiers. To limit the suffering, women organized soup kitchens. Initially they had performed these roles in the absence of their men, but with the growth of organized resistance from the autumn of 1941, women and young girls undertook more radical activities.

In the towns this was particularly true of the youth organizations EPON and PEAN, whose participation in acts of sabotage was punishable by death. In the countryside, where the Communist-led EAM recruited entire populations of villages, married, widowed, and elderly women engaged in a wide range of activities, at risk of lengthy imprisonment or death. These included owning or using a radio, participating in a neighborhood soup kitchen, breaking the curfew, and knitting socks or providing any kind of food or shelter to victims of the occupation. It has been estimated that out of a wartime population of 7.5 million the final strength of EAM-ELAS was approximately 1.75 million, but it is difficult to state with certainty the proportion of women in the movement at any one time, as members drifted in and out of its formal structure according to the pressures of the moment.

Nevertheless, ELAS raised female fighting formations whose members took their responsibilities very seriously, and for whom their engagement with ELAS exposed them for the first time to the workings of political life. One woman who fought in the Peloponnese remembered, "Without the Resistance, I would have been a nobody. . . . The Resistance gave us wings."

The women of ELAS observed strict codes of conduct. One of them recalled:

We had a very beautiful girl in our platoon. And a lot of officers, the male officers, were attracted to her. In the end we were forced to vote her out of the group once it became clear

that she couldn't control herself, because we were not allowed
to have any kind of contact with each other beyond that which
was platonic and comradely. We couldn't form any other kind
of relationship. . . . We were all supposed to wait until after liberation to have our romances.

During the Axis occupation, the different organizations within the
Greek Resistance fought as much with one another as they did
with their occupiers. In the subsequent Greek Civil War, which
lasted from 1946 to 1949, Communist guerrillas opposed to the
restoration of the monarchy, the Democratic Army of Greece,
fought US-backed Greek government forces. Many of the women
who had fought with ELAS joined the Democratic Army. Many
of those who were captured were either executed or sent to prison
camps on the Greek islands. The mothers among them were often
accompanied by their children. Female relatives of former ELAS
fighters often suffered the same fate. Not until 1952, when a more
liberal Greek government took office, were the women of Greece
granted the vote.

   Reference: Janet Hart, *New Voices in the Nation: Women in the Greek
Resistance,* 1996.

Soviet Union

On July 3, 1941, barely two weeks after the Germans launched
Operation Barbarossa—the invasion of the Soviet Union—the
Soviet dictator Joseph Stalin made a radio broadcast in which he
called for a vast partisan movement to spring up in the enemy's
rear. However, it was not until after the defeat of the German
Sixth Army at Stalingrad in February 1943 that the partisans—
now supplied by air with food and medical supplies, and centrally
directed from Moscow—became a broad movement. Postwar Soviet sources estimated that in the winter of 1942–43 some 60 percent of Belorussia was under the effective control of partisans. The
"partisan regions" had their own airstrips into which supplies
could be flown and from which the wounded could be evacuated.

V. G. Grizodubova, a female pilot who commanded 101st Long Range Air Regiment, flew nearly two thousand missions into enemy-occupied territory, taking in ammunition and evacuating the wounded.

The partisan bands—or *otriads*—drew heavily on young men and women who fled from the threat of forced labor or escaped from German captivity. For the partisans, capture by the enemy had the most dire consequences, legendarily illustrated by the fate of Zoya Kosmodemyanskaya, an eighteen-year-old member of the Young Communist League who was taken prisoner by units of the German 197th Infantry Division in the village of Petrischevo, west of Moscow, in the winter of 1941, while attempting to set fire to some buildings. Kosmodemyanskaya was tortured and then hanged. Several of the German soldiers at the scene took photographs of her mutilated body, which remained on the scaffold for a month before being buried in a pit outside the village. When, shortly afterward, the village was recaptured by the Red Army, Kosmodemyanskaya's corpse was exhumed and, with the rope still around her neck, became one of the most powerful images of the war on the Eastern Front. When the 197th Division was overrun by the Red Army near Smolensk in October 1943, the body of one of its officers yielded up five photographs of Kosmodemyanskaya's execution, including one of her being marched to the gallows. A placard hung from her neck bears the legend "Incendiary."

In January 1944 there were some 288,000 active partisans in the Soviet Union, of whom approximately 27,000 were women. As the Red Army rumbled westward, the partisan war was wound up. Many partisans were incorporated in the Red Army. Others were rejected as physically unfit, and a substantial minority fell under suspicion by the NKVD (the Soviet secret police, forerunner of the KGB), which was responsible for restoring the loyalty of those regions that had been occupied by the Wehrmacht. Their fate, after they had survived Nazi occupation, was transportation to the gulags.

Reference: Ben Shepherd, *War in the Wild East: The German Army and Soviet Partisans,* 2004.

PITCHER, MOLLY, SEE **MOLLY PITCHER, p. 103)**

SANTAMARÍA, HAYDÉE
Cuban Revolutionary, b. 1922, d. 1980

Haydée Santamaría's career described an extraordinary arc from guerrilla freedom fighter to director of a world-famous literary institution and home for exiled Latin American artists and intellectuals.

She was born on a sugar plantation in central Cuba to parents who owned a small parcel of land. In Havana in 1952, Santamaría and her brother Abel joined Fidel Castro's insurgent movement against the Cuban dictator Fulgencio Batista.

On the evening of July 26, 1956, Santamaría and Melba Hernández became the only two women in the 120-strong force assembled by Castro to seize the Moncada Barracks in the city of Santiago de Cuba as the first step toward overthrowing the American-backed Batista regime. Among the male insurgents were Santamaría's boyfriend and her brother. The attack on the Moncada was a chaotic failure, and some three-quarters of those involved were either killed or taken prisoner. Santamaría, her boyfriend, her brother, and Hernández were among those captured.

In her cell Santamaría was confronted with terrible evidence in an effort to make her talk—an eye, or in some accounts both eyes and testicles—of her brother. Famously, she told her captors, "If you tore out his eye and he did not speak, neither will I." Her brother succumbed to torture, as did her boyfriend, but Santamaría did not crack, even when she and Hernández were burned with cigarettes.

Following an amnesty announced by Batista, Santamaría was released from prison and returned to the struggle. She worked as a gunrunner, international fund-raiser, coordinator of the urban underground, and combatant in the Cuban revolutionary movement. Later she fought alongside Che Guevara in the Sierra Maestra, the mountainous region in southern Cuba that became the redoubt for

Castro's forces and the battleground on which they defeated the numerically superior forces of Batista, who fled the country in January 1959.

After the revolution, Santamaría transformed herself from guerrilla to Cuban cultural emissary. Perhaps her greatest achievement was her work as founder and director of the Casa de las Américas, one of the foremost cultural institutions in Latin America, which over the years has hosted and published a pantheon of literary giants, including Gabriel García Márquez and Pablo Neruda. The Casa was responsible for bringing some of the world's greatest dancers, musicians, painters, and theater groups to Cuba, doing much to break down the isolation in which the Castro government found itself from the mid-1960s. Santamaría also fiercely defended young Cuban writers, artists, and performers from the dogmatism that muffled free speech in Cuba under Castro.

In the last year of her life Santamaría was badly injured in a car accident and left in constant pain. She was also deeply affected by the death of a close friend, Celia Sánchez, one of Castro's most trusted aides. Some have speculated that her decline was triggered by these events, combined with depression about Cuba's increasing material and ideological dependence on the Soviet Union. But it is more likely that she had reached the end of a long road that began during the horrifying aftermath of the attack on the Moncada Barracks. Perhaps Santamaría foresaw her own end in 1967 when she wrote after the death of Che Guevara in Bolivia, "Today I feel tired of living; I think I have lived too much already."

Reference: Betsy Maclean, ed., *Haydée Santamaría,* 2003.

TAMIL TIGERS
Sri Lankan Separatists, 1970–Present

From the early 1970s, the Liberation Tigers of Tamil Elam (LTTE) developed into a formidable fighting force dedicated to the establishment of a separate Tamil homeland on the island of Sri

Lanka. By January 2004, the Sri Lankan president, Chandrike Kumaratunga, estimated the strength of the LTTE guerrillas at approximately eighteen thousand, many of them women and small children.

The policy of recruiting women and children was initiated after the 1987 signing of the Indo–Sri Lankan peace agreement, when an Indian peacekeeping force was introduced to restore order in the Tamil-dominated regions of Sri Lanka's north and east. The LTTE soon faced a growing manpower shortage caused by the escalation in fighting, and within ten years almost one third of its strength consisted of women, who were assigned duties on the battlefield, in the medical corps, and in other support services.

All LTTE combatants undergo a physically rigorous four-month training program, during which they receive weapons training and are instructed in battle and field craft, intelligence gathering, and explosives. The Women's Front of the Liberation Tigers (Viduthalai Pulikal Makalir Munani) formed in 1983 and began combat training in 1985. October 1987 saw the establishment in Jaffna of the first training camp exclusively for women. The high recruitment of women during this period was matched by the figures for women killed while serving in LTTE formations, which between 1985 and 2002 were estimated at four thousand. More than one hundred belonged to the Black Tiger suicide squad (see **Suicide Bombers,** p. 327). In 1999, President Kumaratunga was blinded in the right eye in a suicide bombing.

The LTTE has been designated or banned as a terrorist organization by a number of countries, including the United States, the United Kingdom, Canada, Australia, India, and Malaysia—where it disseminates propaganda and raises funds and supplies for its campaign in Sri Lanka. But the writer Adele Ann, Australian-born wife of an LTTE theoretician, justified the decision by Tamil women to join the Tigers as one that sent a clear message to society at large: "They are not satisfied with the social status quo; it means they are young women capable of defying authority; it means they are women with independent thoughts; young women prepared to lift up their heads." (See **Eritrea,** p. 90).

In 1996 the leader of the LTTE, Velupillai Prabhakaran, described the liberation of Tamil women as "the fervent child" that had been born out of the Tamil nationalist movement. There is a price attached. Women in the LTTE are allegedly forced to suppress their femininity and sexuality. They are not allowed sexual relationships, as this is considered a crime that can sap their strength (see **Partisans,** p. 107). Marriage is not allowed for LTTE women up to the age of twenty-five and for men up to the age of twenty-eight.

Reference: Adele Ann, *Women Fighters of Liberation Tigers,* 1989.

TUBMAN, HARRIET "ARAMINTA"
"General," American Civil War Commander, and Leader of the Underground Railroad, b. 1820, d. 1913

Born into slavery in Maryland, Tubman worked as a field hand until 1849, when the death of her master and the threat of being sold into the Deep South prompted her to escape to Philadelphia. In December 1850 she slipped back to Baltimore to help her sister and two children to get away, returning in 1851 to fetch her brother's family. She also rescued her parents from the South. These qualities of leadership became evident in the years to come, when the former slave became the only woman to command a military mission in the American Civil War.

For the rest of the 1850s, Tubman took an active part in the Underground Railway, helping up to three hundred fugitive slaves to reach the northern states and Canada, and acting as an adviser to the abolitionist John Brown. In 1863 the Union army asked Tubman to organize a network of scouts—and spies—from the black population of South Carolina, where she had been working with slaves abandoned by owners who had fled the advancing Union army. Tubman established a sophisticated system to gather information and recruit men for the Union's black regiments, a task for which her work on the Underground Railway had provided an ideal training.

In July 1863, Tubman led troops commanded by Colonel James Montgomery in a mission to disrupt the South's interior lines by blowing bridges and cutting rail links. The mission also freed some eight hundred slaves, who benefited from Tubman's calm and reassuring presence while under Confederate fire. Her commanding general reported to the US secretary of war, "This is the only military command in American history wherein a woman, black or white, led the raid and under whose inspiration it was originated and conducted." Tubman's nickname, "General," arose from this.

In three years of service with the Union army, Tubman received only intermittent pay amounting to two hundred dollars and supported herself by selling beer and food, which she prepared in such spare time as she had. After the war she applied unsuccessfully for a pension in her own right but received one only as the widow of her soldier husband. Deeply religious, she devoted her later years to founding schools for freed slaves, teaching, and preaching. She also founded a home for elderly black people in Auburn, New York, where she had settled her parents, and financed it from the sale of her autobiography.

Reference: Sarah Bradford, *Harriet Tubman, The Moses of her People,* 1986.

VIETNAM WOMEN FIGHTERS
1945–75

"When war comes, even women have to fight." This ancient saying of the Vietnamese took on a new relevance in the thirty years that followed the end of World War II, during which the Vietnamese rid themselves of two more foreign interlopers, first the French and then the Americans.

By the summer of 1941, the French colony of Indochina had fallen under the effective control of the Japanese. In December 1944, the Vietnamese guerrilla commander Vo Nguyen Giap organized a group of thirty-five Viet Minh (Communist) guerrillas, of whom five were women. The women were particularly useful in explaining the party line to Vietnamese villagers, who were impressed by their skill in handling firearms.

In 1945, as the war came to a close, Vietnamese women seized Japanese food depots to stave off starvation, and in August and September they joined Ho Chi Minh, leader of the Viet Minh, in the seizure of power in Hanoi, in northern Vietnam. However, the French returned after the Japanese surrender and in 1946 reoccupied Hanoi, the prelude to an eight-year war.

At the outset, Ho Chi Minh's military commander, Vo Nguyen Giap, suffered a string of defeats before a vital victory at Dien Bien Phu, which led to the surrender of ten thousand French troops in May 1954. During the fifty-five-day siege, short and slight minority tribeswomen played a vital role, hauling heavy equipment, bicycles, artillery components, food, weapons, and ammunition on their backs to supply Giap's forces, and evacuating the Viet Minh wounded to the rear (see also **Long March,** p. 101 and **Greek Partisans**, p. 110).

In July 1954, Vietnam was partitioned into the Communist North and US-backed South, as the United States sought to stem Communist expansion in Southeast Asia. Approximately one million women had participated in the anti-French resistance, an experience that foreshadowed the twenty-year war for a reunited Vietnam. From its formation in 1961, women were active in the Communist National Front for the Liberation of Vietnam (NLF).

In 1965, US President Lyndon Johnson decided to commit combat troops to the war. For the North Vietnamese leadership, the struggle against the South and the Americans was seen as both military and political, including recruitment, the maintenance of morale, and the simultaneous undermining of the morale of the South Vietnamese forces and government. For these tasks, women were considered ideal, not least because by 1965 the NLF suffered a severe manpower shortage.

The Women's Liberation Organization, an arm of the NLF, also had a vital auxiliary military role to play, liaising between villages in the South and NLF units in the jungle, performing intelligence work, providing food and clothing for NLF fighters, concealing them from the enemy, and nursing the sick and wounded. They were also tasked with staging "face-to-face" confrontations with

US and South Vietnamese troops, the aim being to harass them at every turn.

Women were also responsible for placing propaganda leaflets for the enemy to find, and Nguyen Thi Dinh, who eventually became deputy commander of the armed forces of the NLF, launched her career in this way. These activities enabled some women to play a significant part in the NLF's political and administrative cadres. Ho Chi Minh honored them with the name "long-haired warriors."

Women mainly worked in support formations, carrying huge quantities of rice into the jungle to supply NLF units and returning with wounded fighters, often traversing the so-called Ho Chi Minh Trail, the infiltration route running through Laos to South Vietnam. The young women often had to negotiate the trail carrying burdens greater than their body weight, while suffering from malaria.

By the end of 1967, the numbers of women involved in NLF support and combat operations had risen steeply and they were a constant presence in the resistance to the Americans and their South Vietnamese allies, a factor that was badly underestimated by the US commander, General William Westmoreland, and his staff. While many of them did not bear weapons and few fought full-time, this did not prevent women from being imprisoned, tortured, and killed in Operation Phoenix, the CIA-sponsored attempt to eliminate the NLF.

Women also played a part in the 1968 Tet offensive, which, although a military catastrophe for the NLF, fatally undermined the claims made by the United States that it was making progress in the war. One of the combatant women in Saigon was Hoang Thi Khanh, who had been part of a sapper unit that liaised with NLF guerrillas in the surrounding countryside and smuggled arms into the city. In the buildup to the offensive, she had guided guerrillas—many of them women—into Saigon and coordinated them once the fighting started. After her unit had been roughly handled by South Vietnamese troops (ARVN), she organized a counterattack. She survived until November 1969, when she was captured by the ARVN.

Other women who took up arms during the Tet offensive included two sisters, Thieu Thi Tam and Thieu Thi Tao, who unsuccessfully tried to blow up the police headquarters in Saigon. They were captured, interrogated, tortured, and sent to the prison at Con Dao, notorious for its cramped "tiger cages," whose open ceilings enabled the jailers to drench the inmates with lime.

Fifteen miles west of Saigon lay the area of Cu Chi, which boasted a vast network of tunnels providing shelter for NLF fighters and containing underground hospitals and assembly points for major operations. The women of Cu Chi had helped to excavate the tunnels, claustrophobic work undertaken in the most dangerous and unhealthy conditions. Cu Chi also boasted a female fighting formation, C3 Company, which had been formed in 1965. All its members were trained in the use of small arms and grenades, the wiring and detonation of mines, and assassination. However, they were discouraged from taking on Americans in close-quarter combat because of their small stature.

The war also subjected the people of North Vietnam to a long strategic bombing campaign, undertaken from 1964 by fighter-bombers of the US Air Force, Navy, and Marine Corps. From the outset, female militias were raised for the defense of North Vietnam, guarding roads and bridges, engaging South Vietnamese Rangers around the 17th Parallel dividing the North and South, and serving in antiaircraft batteries, both artillery and surface-to-air missiles (SAMs). By the time US B-52s launched their own strategic bombing campaign, Linebacker II, in December 1972, Hanoi was the most heavily defended target in the world.

By then all young women in North Vietnam had long been required to join the local militias and self-defense units, making up some 40 percent of the total personnel. They also moved into roles that very few women had filled before 1965. Approximately 32 percent of North Vietnam's skilled and scientific workers were women. Women replaced men in the health sector and provided some 70 percent of the North's workforce, toiling in factories, fields, and offices. They taught in universities and worked for the government.

In the rural areas, women cared for and educated the children evacuated from urban centers to save them from the bombing. They worked on the Ho Chi Minh Trail, wielding picks and shovels, heaving baskets of soil, and filling bomb craters by day so that trucks could roll by night. Rural women were already inured to hard work. Now they had to learn new skills to operate heavy machinery and raise rice yields and a range of new crops.

The women defending North Vietnam provided ideal subjects for war photographers. Perhaps the most famous image of the home front in the North was that of a minute young peasant girl, Nguyen Thi Kim Lai, the seventeen-year-old commander of a female militia unit, escorting a US airman who had been shot down in December 1972 during Linebacker II. The sight of the hulking American, his head bowed and hands tied, dwarfing the tiny, alert woman wielding an elderly rifle, provides a metaphor for the humbling of the United States in Vietnam. In 1985 the airman in the photograph, William Robinson, returned to Vietnam to meet Nguyen Thi Kim Lai and to ask for her forgiveness, which she readily gave.

Reference: Sandra C. Taylor, *Vietnamese Women at War: Fighting for Ho Chi Minh and the Revolution,* 1999.

5

CREATURE COMFORTS

—∞∞—

Courtesans, Consorts, and Camp Followers: Women Drawn
into War to Minister to Men

We were just poor people fighting for our stomachs.
—*Soldadera* Manuela Quinn, mother of US movie star
Anthony Quinn, on her war service following the Mexican flag

THE RUNAWAYS, ROARING GIRLS, and revolutionaries all made
their own choices, striking out in search of war and adventure,
wherever that led. Countless more women through the ages have
been drawn into war by their men, either through the accidents of
love or marriage or as war followers, accepting both the risks and
rewards of the military life.

Like the women involved in other areas of warfare, they have
often been absent from the annals, strangely invisible when the
importance of their contribution is taken into account. But whoever contemplates any war, from the Roman invasion of Britain
(43 CE), to the battles of Hastings (1066), Waterloo (1815), or
Kursk (1943), invariably conjures up images of fighting men and
has no picture of the women who were also there in force, just
outside the frame.

And like the men they were following, the women who took
this route to war met different fates. Those who were tied to
one man, like Eva Braun or Clara Petacci, the mistresses of World
War II leaders Hitler and Mussolini, had little or no control over

their own destiny but stood or fell with the men they loved. Those who had a professional rather than an individual interest in military men tended to prosper, since men at war always demand more of women's traditional physical and sexual services, not less. During the Crusades, the laundry women were always the first to be ransomed by the victors, since in a pox-and-plague-ridden age, their skills could mean the difference between life and death, and the desert heat was intolerable without them.

The laundry women were only part of a larger whole. Before modern transport could move troops swiftly from place to place, armies of men on the march have been attended by armies of women performing a wide variety of functions, and the differences between them are often obscured by the general term **camp followers** (see p. 126). Throughout the history of warfare, these have come in all shapes and sizes, from the traders and prostitutes trailing in the wake of the Roman legions to the colorful **Vivandières** of the seventeenth to nineteenth centuries (see p. 146).

They were a sturdy breed. Military commanders striving to preserve troop cohesion or struggling to lash a rabble of untrained volunteers into a body of fighting men were often hostile to these female hangers-on. Without any understanding of the law of supply and demand, they made regular attempts to disperse or control the women, but no thought was given to the needs of the men. Camp followers performed vital functions. They provided food and other necessities when the military authorities often failed, and their sexual services also chimed with the age-old belief that a fighting force needs regular sexual relief if it is to fight at its best, a view still held today. What this sometimes means for women is shown in the sufferings of the **comfort women** (see p. 130).

Nevertheless, in keeping with the hallowed rule that women are required to supply sex and then are punished for it, camp followers of all kinds were subject to the rough discipline of the military. This could include stripping and flogging, a penalty inflicted by the Duke of Wellington, who had a particularly low opinion of the women who followed his army at every battle during the Napoleonic Wars, commenting, "It is well known that, in all armies, the women are at least as bad, if not worse, than the men." Other sanctions for women included having their heads shaved, being paraded naked, and worst of all, a savage punishment reserved for women alone, the "whirligig" (see **Leaguer Ladies,** p. 134).

Camp followers were prisoners of their place and time. However, some women saw a way to make their fortunes through war. The women **conquistadoras** (see p. 132) who accompanied the sixteenth-century Spanish adventurer Cortés on his conquest of Mexico were as hungry for gold and land as any of their men and were ready to fight to the death for rewards they could achieve no other way.

As late as World War II, some women following their men were able to strike out for adventure and parlay their given role into something more. The elegant and heroic **Susan Travers** (see p. 144) achieved the singular distinction in World War II of becoming the only female member of the French Foreign Legion at the time.

Manuela Quinn, the mother of movie star Anthony Quinn, had a very different war. As a *soldadera* who fought in the Mexican revolutionary wars of the early twentieth century (see p. 140), she grimly recalled, "We were just poor people fighting for our stomachs." But all these women were united by a bond that remained unchanged for centuries, following their men to war. And whatever survival for their families or small personal triumphs for themselves they may have carved out, their fate remained unchanged, a life dominated by men and by war.

Few women whose lives are bound up with men of war succeed in beating these odds. One exception was the Irish adventuress **Elisa Lynch** (see p. 135), who in the 1860s saw the chance to enrich herself at the expense of the impoverished Paraguayan people when her lover, Francisco Solano López, drove the country to collapse in an insane war.

Lynch escaped retribution by leaving Paraguay when both the victors and the losers had reason to take her life. In the closing days of World War II, the lovers of the twentieth-century dictators Adolf Hitler and Benito Mussolini met a far grimmer fate, Petacci fighting like a wildcat to protect Mussolini before she was gunned down by Italian partisans, and Braun, dubbed "the Angel of Death" by Hitler's entourage, acting as the mistress of the sinister revels in Hitler's bunker as the Third Reich spiraled down to destruction. Whatever the cost to their women, Il Duce and the Führer had their creature comforts to the last.

CAMP FOLLOWERS
Women Who Sustained the Soldiery with Food and
Sexual Services, BCE–Modern Times

From the earliest times, armies have been followed by women who sustained the soldiery with food and sexual services, in the process attracting the hostility of commanders who often regarded their presence as a threat both to discipline and to mobility. Women caught up in the movements of men at war could also be from the highest social caste. The wives and concubines of the kings of Persia often accompanied them on campaigns and were, from time to time, exposed to capture by the enemy. In 333 BCE, the wife and daughters of King Darius III were captured by Alexander the Great's Macedonian army after the Battle of Issus, fought on the border of Asia Minor and Syria in what is now modern Turkey.

The Greeks made much of the effete Persians' inability to leave their womenfolk behind when they went on campaign, but they were happy to take slave women to war, as the Greek poet Homer records in the *Iliad,* his epic account of the siege of Troy. The Romans sometimes took a sterner line on camp followers. The military leader Scipio Aemilianus, who had commanded the Roman forces in the siege of Carthage in 146 BCE, was a martinet of the old school. While campaigning in Spain in 134 BCE, he threw all the prostitutes and traders out of the Roman camp and introduced a regimen the legendarily tough and warlike Spartans would have approved of, including four-mile training runs in full armor.

In his account of the Jewish revolt against the Romans (66–70 CE), the Jewish historian Josephus gives an interesting account of the Roman army on the march, from the forward scouting patrols to the rearguard of light and heavy infantry and auxiliary cavalry. The military column was closely trailed by camp followers seeking the protection of the army, a motley crew including prostitutes, common-law wives, slave dealers on the lookout to purchase prisoners of war, and a gaggle of merchants.

From the days of Scipio Aemilianus to the reign of the emperor Septimius Severus at the end of the second century CE, both legionary and auxiliary troops in the Roman imperial army were not allowed to marry. Nevertheless, they often formed lasting partnerships that were treated as marriages by all concerned, and which the emperor recognized by granting citizenship to the children they brought into the world and to the auxiliaries themselves. Their sons were thus entitled to enlist in any of the legions, though they might prefer to join their fathers' regiment.

By the fourth century, the Roman army had become progressively less mobile, obliging the emperor Constantine (306–37 CE) to divide his army into mobile forces (*comitatenses*) and relatively static *limitanei,* who garrisoned forts and fortified towns along Rome's frontier. The enemies that the army faced, notably Celtic and German tribes, were themselves hampered in their mobility by their womenfolk, the warriors merely forming the cutting edge of the colossal tribal migrations that lapped against the increasingly leaky walls of the vast but now collapsing Roman Empire (see also **Boudicca,** p. 12).

But no army could do without women. Camp followers were also a feature of medieval warfare, providing many of the foraging, cooking, and washing services essential to the maintenance of European armies in the field (see also **Vivandières,** p. 146). Islamic observers of the Crusades were alternately fascinated and horrified by the women who accompanied Crusader armies.

One of them, Imad al-Din (1303–73), castigated some three hundred Frankish women who arrived at Acre as "licentious harlots, proud and scornful, who took and gave, foul-fleshed and sinful singers and coquettes, appearing proudly in public, ardent and inflamed, tinted and painted, desirable and appetising." The overheated and excitedly prurient tone of his address anticipates by seven centuries the outrage caused by the physical appearance of female US aircrew in the Persian Gulf after the defeat of Saddam

Hussein in 1991 and the initially pusillanimous efforts made by the
United States Air Force to placate their Islamic hosts (see **US
Army,** p. 188).

Thousands of women straggled after the European armies of
the sixteenth and seventeenth centuries, some in lumbering baggage trains, others working as unofficial sappers. Some commanders
attempted to make the best of a sometimes chaotic situation by ap-
pointing officials to provide them with basic rations, transport, and
shelter while on the march. From the latter part of the seventeenth
century, a limited number of soldiers were allowed to marry camp
followers and live with them in peacetime barracks; Prussian troops
were fortunate in that the ratio for them was fixed at one man in
three, while Bavarian troops were limited to one in twenty.

A similar arrangement was adopted in the British army of the
eighteenth century (see **Leaguer Ladies,** p. 134). In the early nineteenth century, the small number of British women who were allowed to marry soldiers did not live in married quarters but shared
with the men, living in a screened-off corner of the barracks room,
where they dressed, made love, and gave birth. Not surprisingly,
rape and sexual abuse were commonplace, and middle-aged soldiers lined up to marry the teenage daughters of their comrades.

In the American War of Independence (1775–82), George
Washington, the commander of the Continental Army, bridled at
the "pernicious" effect of female camp followers, while grudgingly
conceding that much of the work they did was entirely beneficial.
He attempted to bring the problem, as he saw it, under control by
ordering that there be no more than one woman for every fifteen
men, a measure that in practice he found impossible to enforce (see
also **Molly Pitcher,** p. 103). On the British side, Lady Harriet
Acland, the wife of a grenadier officer, sought out her husband
after he had been badly wounded and captured in 1777. Although
heavily pregnant, she commandeered a small boat, sailed down the
Hudson under cover of darkness, and slipped though the American
lines to recover her husband from the enemy. She kept him alive
on the hazardous return journey and nursed him back to health.

Some thirty years earlier, the Duke of Cumberland, the
hammer of the Scottish rebels at the Battle of Culloden (1746),

adopted a similar approach of weary resignation when he ordered the women accompanying the British army to "remain with the horses, between the general officers' luggage and the wheel baggage of the rest of the army." The Duke of Wellington, victor of the battle of Waterloo (1815), had a characteristically forthright approach to disciplining female camp followers, ordering some of them to be flogged. Wellington considered the rank and file of his army the "scum of the earth" and had an equally low opinion of their womenfolk, observing that it was "well known that, in all armies, the women are at least as bad, if not worse, than the men as plunderers." For Wellington, the exemption of such women from punishment would only have "encouraged plunder" (see also **Royal Navy,** p. 139).

Some female camp followers were extraordinarily courageous. In the Peninsular campaign during the Napoleonic Wars, Susanna Dalbiac rode beside her husband in the cavalry charge at the Battle of Salamanca (1812), clinging to the reins as bullets whistled through her riding habit. A less exhilarating ordeal was undergone by army wives during the retreat from Corunna (1808–9) as they staggered through snow and mud behind the baggage train, collapsing from exhaustion and sometimes stopping at the roadside for snatched minutes to give birth, as they were forbidden to ride in the baggage carts. In 1842, during the Afghan wars, the redoubtable Lady Florentia Sales endured an even more nightmarish journey through driving snowstorms, in which she lost a son-in-law, celebrated the birth of a grandchild, and survived numerous attacks by Afghan tribesman and ten months' captivity as a hostage of the ferocious warlord Akbar Khan. A happier time was had in the Crimean War by Fanny Duberley, a glamorous officer's wife, who cantered about on horseback wearing tight-fitting men's trousers beneath her riding habit and watched the charge of the Light Brigade at the Battle of Balaklava (1854) from a safe distance.

From the 1840s, the baggage trains that had accompanied the Roman legions, the Crusader armies, the hosts of the Thirty Years' War, and the men of the Continental Army were rendered obsolete by the advent of railway systems, and with them the detailed military planning that now made possible the mobilization of vast numbers of troops and their rapid delivery to the front.

This spelled the end of cumbersome baggage trains with their complement of female camp followers. They were now considered examples of military backwardness, and wherever the phenomenon lingered, as with the *Vivandières* of the American Civil War (see p. 146) and Mexican *Soldaderas* (see p. 140), they were considered an anachronism, out of step with the demand of modern, industrialized warfare.

Reference: Noel T. St. John Williams, *Judy O'Grady and the Colonel's Lady: The Army Wife and Camp Follower Since 1660,* 1989.

COMFORT WOMEN
Far East Theater, World War II

A self-serving male euphemism for the countless women who were forced to work in brothels as sex slaves to the Japanese military in countries occupied by Japan during World War II. After the war, their plight was swept under the carpet, but in 1990 the Korean Council for Women Drafted for Military Sexual Slavery filed suit in a Tokyo court, demanding apologies and compensation. This claim, other lawsuits, and a series of newspaper articles in Japan revived interest in this dark and disgusting footnote to World War II.

Initially, the Japanese had pandered to the first rule of war (sex for the troops) by establishing a system of military brothels. These were staffed by encouraging middlemen to advertise for Japanese prostitutes in newspapers circulating in the home islands and in the Japanese colonies of Korea, Manchuko, and mainland China. However, the military then became concerned that the use of Japanese prostitutes would tarnish the national image (in similar fashion Heinrich Himmler issued a directive that German prostitutes could not be employed in Nazi activities). This prompted them to employ local middlemen or community leaders to recruit women in Japanese-occupied territory, principally in Korea and China. Many women were tricked into sex slavery by offers of legitimate employment, or were forcibly impressed.

The aim of the brothels was both to improve the morale and military effectiveness of the Japanese soldier (military logic: the

Japanese squaddie became a better man and a better fighter every time he debauched or degraded a woman). By "regularizing the system," in effect controlling the women but not the men, the military authorities also sought to ensure effective management of sexually transmitted diseases (STDs).

It was also naïvely thought that the establishment of military brothels, most of them on Japanese bases but some of them close to the front line, would reduce the need to grant soldiers leave and lower the risk of random sexual violence for the women of occupied countries, as had happened in the Chinese city of Nanjing (Nanking) in 1937 when Japanese troops ran amok, raping an estimated 20,000 women and killing 300,000 of the city's inhabitants. Raping the "comfort women" in the comfort of their own brothels was supposed to diminish that risk. No one had yet made the simple calculation that sex and violence beget more sex and violence everywhere.

Life was nightmarish for the women made to work in the military brothels, where they were forced to endure sex with multiple men for hours on end. They were classified according to length of service, the highest category containing those least likely to suffer from STDs. When they were considered to be of no further use, they were abandoned. Many women reported that their uteruses rotted after multiple rapes and incessant disease over a period of years. As the tide of war turned against Japan and its armies retreated, many women were left behind to starve, often on remote islands in the Pacific. Only a few returned to their homes, the humiliation for themselves and their families proving impossible to bear.

It is estimated that at least 80,000 women of many nationalities were forced to work in these terrible places, including Japanese, Koreans, Chinese, Malays, Thais, Filipinas, Indonesians, Burmese, Vietnamese, Indians, Eurasians, Dutch, and natives of the Pacific Islands. In his 1978 autobiography, the former Japanese prime minister Yasuhiro Nakasone recounted how he had set up a "comfort house" for the troops under his command when he served as a naval lieutenant in World War II. He claimed that he was unaware that the women who worked there had been impressed, a state of innocence somewhat alarming in a man of his position.

When World War II ended, only one military tribunal was

convened, in Jakarta, to address the sexual abuse of the "comfort women." A number of Japanese officers were convicted of forcing thirty-five Dutch women into military brothels, but they were lucky enough to be white. No redress was sought for the many Indonesians or women from other ethnic backgrounds who had suffered a similar fate.

In 1965, a Treaty of Basic Relations and Agreement of Economic Cooperation and Property Claims between Japan and Korea (South and North) settled all claims that stemmed from World War II. But from 1990, the Japanese government, by now under increasing international pressure, denied any official connection with the military brothels. In 1992, however, the historian Yoshimi Yoshiaki uncovered incriminating documents in the archives of Japan's National Defense Agency indicating that the military was directly involved in running the brothels. Thereafter the Japanese government shifted its ground, admitting moral but not legal responsibility and, in 1995, set up an unofficial fund to compensate survivors of the brothels. Fifty years after the war had ended, these survivors were inevitably few and getting fewer as time went by.

In January 2005, the government of South Korea released documents relating to the 1965 Treaty of Basic Relations that suggested that it had been induced not to make further claims by an offer from Japan of $800 million in grants and soft loans in compensation for colonial rule stretching from 1910 to 1945. None of this cash reached the women themselves. As the handful of surviving "comfort women" die off day by day, it seems that time is on the side of the Japanese government.

Reference: Yuki Tanaka, *Japan's Comfort Women: Sexual Slavery and Prostitution During World War II and the US Occupation,* 2002.

CONQUISTADORAS
Spanish Women Accompanying Husbands and Fathers in Conquest of South America, Sixteenth Century

When the Spanish adventurer Hernán Cortés landed in the Yucatán in 1519 at the head of 550 men, his small command was accompanied by twelve Castilian women who were following their husbands and fathers. Eight were white and four were black, a reflection of the increasingly multiracial nature of Spanish society in the early sixteenth century, the result of the number of African slaves and free individuals living in Spain.

Cortés was at first reluctant to allow the women to join the march on the Aztec capital, Tenochtitlán. He planned to leave them all behind the lines at Tlaxcala, which he had captured after a hard fight. Only their husbands the conquistadors would follow him into the Mexican heartland to seize the native people's vast hoards of jewels and gold. But when he tried to billet the women in a safe town, they all refused, vehemently protesting that "Castilian wives, rather than abandon their husbands in danger, would die with them."

On the march, the women's duties were at first confined to domestic chores in the expeditionary force's camps, but inevitably they were exposed to battle. They were required to nurse the sick and wounded, to perform guard duties, and at times to join the fighting alongside the men. At least five of the twelve died in battle.

The conquistadoras had sacrificed comparative safety for the rigors of campaigning and the tangible but dangerous rewards it offered—prestige, land, slaves, and treasure. They fought hard to secure them. Two in particular, Beatriz Bermúdez and Maria de Estrada, distinguished themselves by ferocious courage in battle, and lived to reap the rewards. Both readily proved that they could fight as well as their men. During the battle of Tenochtitlán, Bermudez donned men's body armor and, brandishing a sword, rallied the flagging conquistadors with the words "For shame, Spaniards, turn upon these base people, or if you will not, I will kill every man who attempts to pass this way!" Fired with the same spirit, Estrada also armed herself like a man, with helmet, breast-plate, weapons, sword, and shield, and rode into battle, running many of the Indian fighters through with her lance.

Still campaigning years later, the Spanish women had not lost their appetite for a fight. Battling to take Morelos in 1522, Cortés announced that the soldier who led a charge against hostile Indians would be rewarded with a grant of land. This prompted Estrada to mount up with lance and shield and beg her commanding officer to allow her to charge the Indians as proof of her valor. Cortés granted her request and Estrada charged, shouting, "St. James, attack them!" and driving many of the Indians into a ravine. As a reward, she was granted the towns of Telala and Hueyapan.

In contrast, Isabel Rodrigo, who had some medical knowledge, devoted her time to caring for the wounded and, according to contemporary accounts, healed their injuries by the laying on of hands. The Spanish crown bestowed on her the title of "Doctor" and gave her permission to practice medicine in New Spain.

Reference: Antonio de Herrera y Tordesillas, *The General History of the Vast Continent and Islands of America,* 1740.

LEAGUER LADIES
United Kingdom, Eighteenth Century

"Leaguer ladies" was the name for prostitutes, usually drawn from the region in which the soldiers were encamped. They were encouraged not to flaunt their profession in dealing with both officers and men, and many of them gambled on the outside chance of finding a husband as an escape from poverty. Sometimes the leaguer lady was the widow of a soldier. Those fortunate enough to win a husband often remarried several times, usually having lost the current spouse in battle. This way of life often led to large families, and officers sometimes recorded in their diaries an anonymous delivery on the march, with the mother stopping to give birth, swaddling the baby, and then pressing on (see also **Soldaderas,** p. 140).

Sutlery cooks, who were responsible for feeding the troops, often employed women to help them with preparation and serving. Some of these women became sutleresses, scraping and saving enough money to survive the campaign and return home. Wives acquired abroad followed their husbands back to Britain, as a soldier would have to buy his way out of the army if he wished to remain in his wife's country. The wives were obliged to pay for their passage home by ship.

As camp followers, the leaguer ladies were in theory subject to the harsh discipline of the Articles of War and the Mutiny Act. However, punishment for an offender was generally limited to drumming a woman out of the regiment. One savage punishment reserved for women was the "whirligig," a pivoted cage whose rapid rotation reduced the inmate to violent vomiting and uncontrolled defecation and urination. Another form of rough justice was the shaving of women's heads or forcing them to parade naked.

Reference: Noel T. St. John Williams, *Judy O'Grady and the Colonel's Lady: The Army Wife and Camp Follower Since 1660*, 1989.

LYNCH, ELISA
Irish Adventuress, 1835–1886

In a cemetery in Asunción, the capital of Paraguay, a monument marks the last resting place of one of the most extraordinary adventuresses of the nineteenth century. It states simply, "Homage of the people, government and armed forces to Elisa Lynch."

Now neglected and little visited, it stands as a reminder of the remarkable career of one of the great anti-heroines of Latin America, a woman both reviled and respected, hailed as the faithful companion of Paraguay's General President López and damned as a malign enchantress, hell-bent on the single-minded acquisition of colossal wealth.

After an upbringing in Ireland that remains obscure, Elisa was taken by her mother to Paris, where in 1850 she met a soldier, Lieutenant Xavier de Quatrefages, on leave from the French colony of Algeria. She married him in Folkestone, Kent, in June of that year. The new wife accompanied her husband to Algeria but within three years had left him and gone to Paris, where she became a courtesan and met Francisco Solano López, the son of the dictator of Paraguay, Carlos Antonio López. When López returned to his native country in 1854, Elisa followed him.

The Paraguay of the 1850s was an exotic, impoverished backwater, but the tall, red-haired, self-styled "Madame" Lynch, now installed as López's principal mistress, was determined to transform Asunción, its flyblown capital, into an imperial city and herself into its empress. She launched a vainglorious building program, erecting opera houses and palaces, all of which went unfinished or remained uninhabited. She controlled access to López, who succeeded his father in 1862, and used the influence she gained thereby to amass a considerable fortune.

López, a psychopathic, lecherous, and ugly dwarf who modeled himself on Napoléon III, to whom he had been presented in 1854, began his rule by declaring a suicidal war on Argentina, Brazil, and Uruguay over access to the sea. This heaped misery on the wretched population of Paraguay and provided Lynch with greater opportunities to enrich herself. She acquired at scandalously low prices more than thirty-two million hectares of land, looted Paraguayan women of their jewels (ostensibly to fund the war effort), and stashed many thousand dollars' worth of Paraguayan gold in European bank accounts. While tens of thousands of her lover's soldiers, among them many women and children, starved and died in the meaningless conflict, Lynch toured their ramshackle camps resplendent in silk and velvet, grand piano in tow. While she dined off gold plate, the soldiers starved.

During López's disastrous war, over half the population of Paraguay died. At the Battle of Piribebuy (1868), after the ammunition had been exhausted, some six hundred Paraguayan women made their final stand hurling sand, stones, and bottles at the enemy before perishing under a hail of gunfire.

Having wrecked his country's economy and halved its population—it would take three generations for the population to recover—López launched a reign of terror. Convinced of a conspiracy to overthrow him, he ordered the torture and murder of those who had the questionable fortune to be left standing. He was, at least, egalitarian and included among his victims his brothers, sisters, and brothers-in-law. He even ordered the assassination of his own mother. He met his own death at Cerro Corá (1870), the last battle in the war and in effect little more than a glorified skirmish in which, having refused to surrender to the Brazilians, he was cut down and his body mutilated. Lynch was allowed to bury López and their eldest son, Panchito, who was also killed at Cerro Corá, with her own hands. But López's corpse was dug up during the night and subjected to more abuse. Lynch buried López for the second time the following morning.

With her assets frozen and a trial for war profiteering looming, Lynch left Paraguay in the summer of 1870 to live in London and Paris. But with her fortune dwindling, she returned to Paraguay in 1875 in a bold but fruitless attempt to recover some of her ill-gotten gains. She was sent packing and lived out her days in Jerusalem and Paris as a respectable widow of modest means. She died of stomach cancer and was buried in Père-Lachaise Cemetery.

Her life was subsequently mythologized, and Lynch was transformed from tyrant to martyr. A century after fleeing the ruined Paraguay, she was proclaimed a national heroine—"surpassed by none in her courage, her selflessness, and her loyalty"—and her remains returned to Asunción in a bronze urn wrapped in the tricolor.

Reference: Sian Rees, *The Shadows of Elisa Lynch,* 2003.

MATA HARI
Margaretha Geertruida MacLeod, Nee Zelle, Dutch Dancer, Courtesan, and Spy, b. 1876, d. 1917

In Mata Hari's heyday, her name was a byword for mystery and exotic glamour. At the end of her life she was stigmatized as a spy and executed by a French firing squad. In truth Mata Hari was an adventuress of striking imagination but limited intelligence, with a scant grasp of the dangerous game she was playing.

She was the daughter of a prosperous hatter and originally trained as a teacher in the Dutch city of Leiden. In 1895 she married a fellow countryman of Scottish descent, Rudolph MacLeod, a much older man and a soldier serving in the Dutch East Indies, where she lived for several years before returning to Europe and divorcing in 1906.

By then the former Mrs. MacLeod had moved to Paris and, after living for a while as "Lady MacLeod," had reinvented herself as "Mata Hari" (eye of the dawn), a Far Eastern erotic dancer descended from the British aristocracy. She made her debut in 1905 at the Museum of Oriental Art, performing a tasteful striptease before a small audience. Clad in a metal brassiere of her

own design and a fetching array of diaphanous veils, she was an instant sensation. Critics dismissed her, but she rapidly became an
early exemplar of modern celebrity, "famous for being famous,"
courted by rich and powerful men and capable of inducing a skeptical public to accept her on her own extravagant and fraudulent
terms. Even her now-bankrupt father attempted to get in on the
act by writing a kiss-and-tell biography of his celebrated daughter.

By 1914, however, the European public was beginning to tire
of Mata Hari. At thirty-eight, she was aging, thickening at the
waist, and had been supplanted by rivals such as Isadora Duncan.
The outbreak of war cast a shadow over her ambitions. In July
1915, while she was performing in Spain, British intelligence obtained information that Mata Hari was a German secret agent. Her
return sea journey, via neutral Holland, was interrupted at the
British port of Falmouth, where she was detained and taken to
London for questioning. In London she claimed that she was indeed a spy, but for Britain's allies, the French, who had suggested
that she seduce Crown Prince Wilhelm, son of Kaiser Wilhelm II.

Mata Hari was returned to Spain, where she is known to have
had an affair with the German military attaché in Madrid, Major
Kalle, who sent a signal, intercepted by the French, that Agent
H-21 (later supposed to be Mata Hari) had proved valuable. In
February 1917, shortly after her return to Paris, Mata Hari was arrested and put on trial for espionage before a closed tribunal. The
evidence she gave in her defense was contradictory and confusing,
as was the identity of Agent H-21, who might well have been a
figment of the French secret service's fertile imagination.

All sources agree, however, that the war was going badly for
France, and that the execution for spying of a now-notorious figure like Mata Hari would boost national morale. The corrupt
courtesan would be contrasted with Marianne, the incorruptible
symbol of France. A propaganda sacrifice, Mata Hari was found
guilty and executed by a twelve-man firing squad on October 15,
1917. She refused a blindfold and was gallantly blowing kisses at
her executioners when the shots rang out.

It seems likely that Mata Hari was the victim of her own fan-
tasies and the machinations of the French secret service, but the

image of the femme fatale that she called into being has long survived her and now has a life of its own.

   Reference: Sam Waagenaar, *The Murder of Mata Hari,* 1964. The
best of many cinematic evocations of the Mata Hari legend is
the 1931 *Mata Hari,* starring Greta Garbo.

ROYAL NAVY
Great Britain, Seventeenth to Nineteenth Centuries

In the heyday of sail, a few women went to sea with the Royal
Navy, either officially or unofficially. Some officers took their
mistresses with them. When a squadron touched at Newfoundland
in the summer of 1693, a settler bought one of "the officers'
misses" for one hundred pounds and married her.

   The marines aboard the navy's ships followed military practice
and allowed three men in every company to marry "on the
strength," and take their wives and children to sea. The practice continued throughout the eighteenth century, although
the presence of the women and children was not officially recognized and they had to make their own arrangements for food with
the ship's purser. It was thought that the wives of warrant and
petty officers older than the young men who made up the bulk of
the ship's company would exercise a steadying influence. They
supported themselves by washing, sewing, and looking after the
children.

   In port, a captain's wife and children might live aboard a guard
ship. If the men did not have leave to go ashore, they were also
permitted to have women on the ship. In the West Indies, slave
women often came aboard in search of a square meal. Admirals
were usually hostile to these practices but sometimes turned a
blind eye. The order book of HMS *Indefatigable* prescribed regulations for "the women belonging to the ship." Officially, however,
the only women on board were those "married on the strength"
of foot regiments serving as marines.

   At the Battle of the Nile (1798), a crushing victory over the
French secured by Admiral Horatio Nelson, one woman aboard

Indefatigable was killed, several were wounded, and a baby was born. Four of the nineteen men killed in the action left widows on the ship, which suggests that there may have been as many as one hundred women on board during the battle. After the battle, the four destitute widows were entered by Captain Foley in the ship's books as "dressers" (i.e., nurses), a device to provide them with some support. Some Frenchwomen captured during the battle were put ashore at the nearest port.

A few women disguised themselves and served in the Royal Navy as seamen. At an 1807 court-martial, in which an officer was sentenced to death for sodomy, one of the principal witnesses was a young woman who appeared in court dressed as a seaman. In another undisputed example, William Brown, the highly regarded black captain of the main top of the warship *Queen Charlotte,* served in the navy for eleven years before it was discovered in 1805 that she was a woman.

Reference: Dudley Pope, *Life in Nelson's Navy,* 1997.

SOLDADERAS
"The Women of the Soldier," Mexico, Nineteenth and Twentieth Centuries

The *soldaderas* reflected several significant aspects of warfare in Mexico from the days of the Spanish conquest to the twentieth century. Ostensibly at war to provide food and female services, they frequently proved themselves soldiers as valiant as their men.

Traditionally, armies in Mexico did not feed their soldiers but provided meager pay that could be used to forage, a function performed by the *soldaderas,* the large numbers of camp followers who accompanied an army on the march and who were often referred to as a *chusma* (mob). Mexican generals of the nineteenth century were often hostile to the *chusmas* and petitioned for their abolition. However, it was pointed out that without their presence, many Mexican soldiers would desert rather than face starvation (see **Camp Followers,** p. 126, and **Vivandières,** p. 146).

A vivid picture of the *chusma* that followed the army of General

Santa Anna in 1841 was painted by writer Frances Calderón de la Barca. She observed

> various masculine women with . . . large straw hats tied down with coloured handkerchiefs, mounted on mules or horses. . . . Various Indian women trotted on foot in the rear, carrying their husbands' boots or clothes. There was certainly no beauty amongst these feminine followers of the camp, especially among the mounted Amazons, who looked like very ugly men in a semi-female disguise.

At the start of the 1841 march, Santa Anna's army numbered some six thousand men while its accompanying *chusma,* consisting of "numerous children, women, herb healers and speculative merchants," was more than fifteen hundred strong. However, it was rapidly reduced by disease and starvation to no more than three hundred. Despite this, the populations who lived in the path of the *chusma* feared its depredations more than those of the soldiery, likening it to a swarm of locusts.

In the nineteenth century, Mexicans defeated the Spanish, clashed with the Americans, thwarted French colonial ambitions, and endured perpetual infighting among their own factions. All the armies involved in these conflicts, including those of the French and the Americans, made use of the *soldaderas,* who were by no means exclusively women of low status confined to menial tasks. Large numbers fought alongside their menfolk. Others, like Augustina Ramirez, worked on the battlefield as nurses. Ramirez, who served in the 1857–60 war between the liberal and conservative elements in Mexico, cared for the wounded. She lost her husband and several of her thirteen sons in this conflict. In recognition of her courage she received a small pension, which lasted only a few years. She died in poverty on February 14, 1879, days before she was about to be honored as a shining example of Mexican motherhood.

Pancho Villa had an ambivalent attitude toward the *soldaderas.* While respecting bravery in battle, whether shown by men or women, he regarded the camp followers as a hindrance to mobility. On occasions he visited harsh summary punishment on those *soldaderas* whose loyalty he considered questionable. Regular soldiers and military administrators, too, regarded *soldaderas* with deep suspicion. In 1925, *soldaderas* were banned from federal barracks by the minister of war, General Joaquín Amaro, who observed that they were "the chief cause of vice, illness and disorder." This did not stop women from following federal and rebel armies; nor did it prevent the formation, in 1926, of the Feminine Brigades of St. Joan of Arc, whose principal tasks were the manufacture and distribution of ammunition. The Feminine Brigades played an important role in the Cristero rebellion.

In the 1930s, *soldaderas* who had fought were eligible for small pensions; these benefits were not awarded to the camp followers. By the end of the 1930s, the term *soldaderas* had come to signify little more than the female relatives of a male soldier. Behind them lay a history of hardship and great courage, often borne with characteristic Mexican stoicism. Manuela Quinn, the mother of the movie actor Anthony Quinn, who had followed her lover into the army of Pancho Villa, recalled that while her menfolk believed that the revolution would usher in an earthly paradise, service as a *soldadera* meant for her "the smell of gunpowder and the crying of the wounded. I saw no romance in it. We were just poor people fighting for our stomachs; the talk of brotherhood and the flag-waving came later, from our suffering."

Reference: Elizabeth Salas, *Soldaderas in the Mexican Military: Myth and History,* 1990. The 1966 Mexican movie *La Soldadera,* directed by José Bolaños, paints a compelling picture of life as a *soldadera*. In contrast, Sam Peckinpah's *The Wild Bunch* (1969) conveys a wholly fanciful portrait of a Villaista junior officer called Si Si Chiquita.

TENEPAL, MALINALLI
"The Mexican Eve," Aide to Cortés, *b. 1498, d. 1529*

The most celebrated woman to have taken part in the Spanish conquest of Central America, Malinalli, known as *La Malinche,* was an Indian of noble birth who became the mistress of Spanish commander Hernán Cortés. Her contemporary fame as a native conquistadora was later obscured by the contempt in which she was held in nineteenth-century Mexico, which earned her the derisory nicknames of *La Vendida,* "she who sells out," *La Chingada,* "she who gets fucked," and "the Great Whore."

Malinalli was given away as a child, having been born under an ominous sign portending disaster. The merchants to whom she was handed over sold her into slavery with the Mayan Indians of Tabasco. After Cortés defeated the *cacique* (headman) of Tabasco in 1518, he was presented with twenty young women to serve his soldiers and cook for them. One of them was Malinalli, who was baptized and renamed Marina.

Marina advanced quickly in Cortés's service. She was a gifted linguist and soon became his interpreter, providing him with vital information about the mind-set and military tactics of the region's peoples. She was said to have been at Cortés's side in many battles but never to have taken an active part in the fighting, possibly an acknowledgment of the role of women in ancient Indian warfare, in which females often accompanied their menfolk into the thick of battle but only to advise and encourage them. Because Marina was invariably in the company of Cortés, and always spoke for him, the Indians dubbed Cortés "Marina's captain."

She also bore him a son, Martín, who was much loved by Cortés and became his legitimate heir by papal decree. Cortés never married any of his Indian lovers, but in Marina's case he made her substantial land grants, and around 1524 arranged for her to marry the captain of a merchant ship. Having deprived himself of his trusted military and diplomatic adviser, Cortés then embarked on a disastrous expedition to Honduras. In all probability Marina died in one of the epidemics that followed in the wake of the Spanish invaders and which, during the next century, killed some 98 percent of the native population. In 1542, in a dispute over the land granted to Marina, seven of Cortés's lieutenants testified to the governors of New Spain about the important role she had played in the Spanish conquest of Central America. However, that conquest had proved an unmitigated disaster for the region's native peoples, and in the nineteenth century the nationalist custodians of Mexico's past attempted either to vilify Marina or to write her out of history.

Reference: In her 2006 novel, *Malinche,* Laura Esquivel has made a spirited attempt to rehabilitate Tenepal, portraying her as a freedom fighter against the Aztecs and the architect of a rich, mixed heritage.

TRAVERS, SUSAN
*British Socialite, World War II Nurse, and French Foreign Legionary,
b. 1909, d. 2003*

A prewar member of Europe's gilded youth, Susan Travers became the only woman to have joined the French Foreign Legion in World War II and played an important role in the 1942 breakout from the fortress of Bir Hacheim in North Africa.

She was the daughter of a British naval officer who in 1921 had moved his family to Cannes, on the French Côte d'Azur. Small and striking, she excelled as a tennis player and spent the 1930s in a vapid whirl of travel, skiing, and tennis parties, where she was the object of much male attention. This was brought to an abrupt end by the outbreak of World War II. In 1939 Travers joined the French Red Cross. Blood made her queasy, a less-than-ideal qualification for a nurse, but she qualified as an ambulance driver and in 1940 accompanied the French expeditionary force dispatched to help the Finns in their "Winter War" against the Soviet Union (see **Lotta Svärd,** p. 169).

In May 1940, after the fall of France, Travers made her way to London to offer her services as a nurse to the Free French Brigade. She was attached to a unit of the Foreign Legion (about half of which had remained loyal to the Free French) and in September 1940 embarked on the abortive Franco-British expedition to capture the naval base at Dakar, in French West Africa, where the garrison had remained loyal to the pro-German Vichy government.

After serving as a driver in the Allied campaign in East Africa, where she was dubbed "La Miss" by the legionnaires, Travers was posted to Beirut as the driver of Colonel Marie-Pierre Koenig, who in November 1940 had captured Libreville, in French Equatorial Africa. Travers and the dashing Koenig became secret lovers.

In the spring of 1942 Koenig, now promoted to the rank of brigadier-general commanding the First Free French Brigade, was sent to hold Bir Hacheim, a fortified box in Libya at the southern end of the British Eighth Army's Gazala Line. Travers went with him and remained in Bir Hacheim after May 17 when it came under attack by German and Italian units of the Afrika Korps. They had assured their commander, General Erwin Rommel, that the fortress would fall in a matter of minutes. However, the Allied force at Bir Hacheim held out until the night of 10 June when, with water and ammunition exhausted, Koenig ordered a breakout.

Travers drove both her commanding officer and another Legion colleague, the White Russian prince Colonel Dmitri Amilakvari, who had been one of her lovers before her encounter with Koenig. Under heavy fire, Travers burst through the enemy lines, at one point careering through a laager of parked German armored vehicles. By the end of the night, some 2,500 of Bir Hacheim's 3,700 defenders, including 650 legionnaires, had reached the safety of the British lines. Travers was awarded the Croix de Guerre and the Ordre du Corps d'Armée for her gallantry in the breakout.

Her affair with Koenig ended shortly afterward, but she remained loyal to the Legion, serving in Italy and France until the end of the war. In May 1945 she applied to join the Legion officially, omitting her sex from the application form, and was appointed an officer in its logistics division, making her the only woman to serve in the Legion in World War II.

Travers later served in French Indochina but in 1947 resigned her commission to bring up her children by her husband, Nicholas Schegelmilch, a sergeant in the Legion. In 1956 she was awarded the Medaille Militaire. Poignantly, the medal was pinned on her by Koenig, who by then had become France's minister of defense. In 1996 she received the Légion d'Honneur in recognition of her unique role in the Legion's history. Four years later the French government decided as a matter of general policy to allow women to join the Foreign Legion.

Reference: Susan Travers, *Tomorrow to Be Brave: A Memoir of the Only Woman Ever to Serve in the French Foreign Legion,* 2000.

VIVANDIÈRES
Women Who Sold Food and Drink to the Troops,
Seventeenth-Century France–Early Modern Times

The term *vivandières* was originally associated with women, often the wives and daughters of soldiers, who sold food and drink to the troops. Its origins lie in the French army of the seventeenth century, possibly deriving from *viande,* the French word for "meat," or the Latin root *vivenda,* "food."

From the 1650s, the *vivandières* supplied the French troops with food and other necessities and were regulated by the army. Unlike the *cantinières,* who performed a similar function and went on campaign, they were usually confined to barracks or outposts and by the early nineteenth century had adopted a trademark wooden keg filled with brandy and frequently painted red, white, and blue.

In 1854 the term *vivandière* officially replaced the term *cantinière* in the French army. The clothing of the vivandières was standardized to echo the uniforms of the formations to which they were attached. The Zouaves of Napoléon III's day, in the 1860s, were followed by *vivandières,* who wore matching uniforms, often with a turban and a short sword. These women were wholly assimilated into the French army, received regular pay, and were entitled to decorations. A regulation of 1865 established the number of *vivandières* at one for every infantry battalion, two for a battalion of light infantry, two for each cavalry squadron, and four for engineer and artillery regiments. The *vivandières* were often exposed to danger. During the French intervention in Mexico (1862–67), some captured *vivandières* were shot and their bodies mutilated.

Until the humiliation of France in the Franco-Prussian War of 1870, the American armed forces were heavily influenced by French military doctrine, not least in the tradition of *vivandières.* During the Crimean War of 1853-56, General George B. McClellan had served as an observer with the British and French, and when the American Civil War broke out in 1861, the experience of the Crimea was still uppermost in the minds of many regular senior officers, both Union and Confederate.

Nowhere was this more evident than in the formation, at the

beginning of the war, of Union and Confederate volunteer regiments that adopted French nomenclature and resplendent uniforms, for example, Zouaves or chasseurs. These imitations of
French military tradition had their own *vivandière* (the term became interchangeable with *cantinière*), who were often known as
the "daughters of the regiment." Their outfits were reminiscent
of those worn in the Crimea. A photograph of Coppens's
Louisiana Zouaves, taken in May 1861, shows a *vivandière* wearing Zouave trousers, a short but full skirt, a short jacket, plumed
hat, and apron. However, many of these brightly caparisoned *vivandières* were more regimental mascot than any effective link in
the formation's logistical chain, and they played no part in the
campaigning.

There were exceptions. The Thirty-ninth New York Regiment, popularly known as the Garibaldi Guard, set off for war
with six *vivandières* wearing "feathered hats, jaunty red jackets
and blue gowns." One of the most notable *vivandières,* Marie
Tepe ("French Mary"), who served with Collis's Zouaves, the
114th Pennsylvania Regiment, was wounded at Fredericksburg
(1862) and decorated with the Kearny Cross after Chancellorsville
(1863). At the Battle of New Bern (1862), *vivandière* Kady Brownell,
of the Fifth Rhode Island Regiment, carried the regimental colors
into the thick of the battle to prevent the Rhode Islanders coming under fire from their own side. Some *vivandières,* however,
were not selfless heroines like Marie Tepe but little more than
prostitutes.

The activities of the *vivandières* were limited after September
1864, when General Ulysses S. Grant, the commander of the
Union forces, banned women from all military camps in his theater of operations. The number of *vivandières* who served in the
field in the American Civil War was relatively small and subsequently became the source of many myths about the role women
played. Nevertheless, the contributions of the *vivandières* in the
volunteer regiments of the period, which marked the beginning of
the era of modern warfare, was an early indication of what women
were capable of.

6

INTO UNIFORM

―∞∞∞―

Women Mobilized to Support the War Effort

I hate wars and violence, but if they come I don't see why we women should just wave our men a proud goodbye and then knit them balaclavas.
—Nancy Wake, New Zealand Resistance fighter, World War II

W HEN MEN MAKE WAR, women's lives are changed forever, though they may never see action or hear a shot fired. From the days of the **camp followers** (see p. 126), women's labor was vital to their countries' war efforts, and by the twentieth century it was no longer voluntary. "Without women, victory will tarry," declared the British prime minister David Lloyd George in 1915, addressing a rally organized by suffragette leader Emmeline Pankhurst on the theme of "Women's Right to Serve," "and the victory which tarries means a victory whose footprints are footprints of blood."

Less than thirty years later in Britain, America, and the Soviet Union, women volunteered or were conscripted and mobilized in their millions as part of a political program to win World War II. Whether they were "called up" into the armed forces or directed into civilian work, they saw years of service, which had a decisive effect on the outcome of the war. Meanwhile Nazi Germany, true to its ideology of keeping women pregnant and in the kitchen, paid a heavy price for fighting with only half its population. Only in 1943, when it became clear that Germany was facing defeat, did the Nazis attempt full mobilization of its females.

For the British, the Americans, and the Soviet Union, the contribution of women was a vital factor in securing victory over Germany and Japan. However, during World War II the Japanese, like the Germans, showed a notable reluctance to mobilize their female workforce or to put them into uniform. British and American military authorities also remained cautious about the appropriate deployment of women, insisting that their war effort consist of working in the fields and factories to replace the men who had joined the forces, or taking on previously male civilian jobs like servicing engines and driving trams. As women filled the gaps left by men in a wide variety of jobs, it was noted by Eleanor Roosevelt when she visited Britain on a fact-finding mission that they paid the women far less than the men for doing the same job.

But as women worked away behind the lines, all too often the war came to them. In twentieth-century warfare, the development of military aviation meant the extension of hostilities into a new dimension, and the populations of Europe's great cities found themselves propelled into the front line. With many of the men away fighting the war, women bridged the gap. During World War II, when the Luftwaffe arrived in force over London in September 1940 at the beginning of the Blitz on the United Kingdom's major cities, women played a major role in the nation's **civil defense** (see p. 157). At the height of the Blitz, one air-raid warden in every six was a woman. Women also worked in the previously all-male preserve of Britain's shipyards and built the bombers England needed to fight back in the strategic bombing offensive against the Third Reich.

The women of America had been spared their own Blitz, as the United States was too large and too far away from its Axis enemies to come under threat from the air. Nor had the female workforce of America been subject to conscription like its British counterpart. Nevertheless, American women played an equally important role in the wartime production of munitions, tanks, and aircraft. They also helped to build the so-called Liberty Ships, which were America's mass-production answer to the heavy loss of merchantmen in the

Battle of the Atlantic. Between 1941 and 1945, US shipyards built some 2,770 Liberty Ships, preserving Britain's Atlantic lifeline and giving birth to the enduring legend of **"Rosie the Riveter"** (see p. 180).

Life was immeasurably tougher for the **Soviet women in war industries** (see p. 183), and the female Soviet agricultural work-force endured grim conditions that were worlds away from the privations suffered on the British and American home fronts. On collective farms starved of machinery, Soviet women workers had to substitute their own muscle power for much-needed tractors, which were in desperately short supply. Punishments for being absent without leave from factory or farm were draconian, including heavy prison sentences.

In Britain the conscription of women was introduced in December 1941. The first conscripts, aged twenty to twenty-one, received their "call-up" papers in March 1942. They were given a choice between serving in the auxiliary services—the WRNS (**Women's Royal Naval Service,** see p. 214), the ATS (**Auxiliary Territorial Service,** see p. 153), and the WAAF (**Women's Auxiliary Air Force,** see p. 209)—civil defense or industry. By the summer of 1944 some 467,000 women had chosen the auxiliary services. Like their American equivalents, they became a crucial element in the war effort. By the end of 1943, for example, 80 percent of army driving in Britain was performed by the ATS. However, in common with their US sisters, who were not subject to conscription, they could not fire weapons, serve on warships, or fly aircraft in combat. No such prohibitions applied to Soviet women, who were to see action in the skies over their homeland; they also maintained and fired the guns in antiaircraft batteries and drove tanks all the way to Berlin.

The Western Allies did not use female aircrew in combat. But among their population were many women who had qualified as pilots, and they carved out a pioneering role in the British Air Transport Auxiliary and the American Women's Air Force Service Pilots (WASP, see **Cochran, Jacqueline,** p. 219). Inevitably there were obstacles for the pioneers. The 1,074 women of the WASP flew more than sixty million miles across the United States in every type of aircraft known to the US Air Force and also towed targets in gunnery schools. The daring WASPs were the first women to be trained to fly American military aircraft, and they paved the way for the United States Air Force of the twenty-first century, in which women now make up 19 percent of the force and work in 99 percent of all US Air Force career fields. But they were not acknowledged as military pilots until more than thirty years later, when Congress declared in 1977 that they were veterans of World War II.

Yet for a number of these women, war opened many doors. For American and British women in particular, wartime service in industry or in the forces introduced them to a range of possibilities that had been unthinkable in the 1930s. For the first time, they could enjoy the release from child care and domestic servitude that men took for granted, and experience the camaraderie of colleagues, the relaxation of a quick beer at the end of a shift, and above all, the sense of direct involvement in matters of importance to the world.

When the war was over, the great majority of women returned to domesticity on the urging of their governments. Women who had been building bombers, ships, and tanks found that almost overnight, bed-making and newfound domestic arts like "table-scaping" (designing a dining table to resemble a landscape) had become the order of the day. A similar fate awaited British women, too. The banked-down international resentment this caused came to a head in 1963, when the mother of modern feminism, Betty Friedan, cast a cold eye over women's restricted lives in *The Feminine Mystique* and demanded, "Is this all?" The subsequent explosion of feminist protest paved the way for the entry of women to the armed forces from the 1970s onward.

AIR TRANSPORT AUXILIARY
ATA, United Kingdom, World War II

In the summer of 1939, the Royal Air Force agreed to the formation of a unit, eventually administered by British Overseas Airways, to undertake noncombat flying duties. From the first, the decision was also made to widen the intake to include female personnel.

Initially the Air Transport Auxiliary's purview included flying mail and performing ambulance duties, and its pilots were qualified aviators ineligible for service in the Royal Air Force (RAF). From early 1940, the scope of the ATA's duties widened to include the ferrying of aircraft from manufacturer to air base or between air stations. A women's section was formed under the leadership of Pauline Gower, a pilot with some two thousand hours of flying experience. Eventually, 166 women served with the ATA, helping to deliver many of the 308,567 aircraft that passed through its hands during World War II. In addition to flying duties, nine hundred of the two thousand personnel employed by the ATA as office staff, trainers, and maintenance workers were women.

The female pilots were highly accomplished aviators. Issued only with "pilots' notes," a simple set of instructions, they had no radio on board and navigated by following the terrain below, often flying along railway lines. Using these methods, Lettice Curtis, who before joining the ATA had worked as a pilot for a survey company, delivered no fewer than four hundred four-engine bombers.

She also loved to ferry Spitfires, observing:

In the air the Spitfire was forgiving and without vice, and I never heard of anyone who did not enjoy flying it. It had a personality uniquely its own. The Hurricane [the RAF's most numerous fighter in the Battle of Britain] was dogged and masculine and its undercarriage folded upwards in a tidy, businesslike manner. The Spit, calling for more sensitive handling, was altogether more feminine, had more glamour and threw its wheels outward in an abandoned, extrovert way. From the ground there was a special beauty about it.

The pilots of the ATA never flew operationally and after D-Day were initially prevented from delivering aircraft to airfields in northwest Europe. However, as the Allied armies advanced, the ferry trips to forward airfields grew longer and, with the onset of winter, more hazardous. In the winter of 1944, ATA pilots, including women, flew through atrocious weather to deliver their aircraft to advanced airfields in northwest France. Navigation was immensely difficult, as snowfall blotted out all landmarks except forests, rivers were rendered invisible by ice and snow, roads and railways were indistinguishable, and airfields were often hidden beneath a treacherous haze. In all, 129 ATA pilots died in service, including the celebrated prewar aviatrix Amy Johnson.

In addition to flying to liberated Europe, the ATA operated an ambulance service, using specially converted Westland Rapides and Avro Ansons to ferry casualties from across the United Kingdom to the Canadian hospital at Taplow in Berkshire. Members of the ATA sometimes referred to themselves as "the Ancient and Tattered Airmen and Women." (See also **Jacqueline Cochran,** p. 219.)

Reference: Lettice Curtis, *Forgotten Pilots,* 1994.

AUXILIARY TERRITORIAL SERVICE
ATS, United Kingdom, United States, Commonwealth, and Worldwide, World War II

The origins of the British all-female Auxiliary Territorial Service can be traced back to the Women's Auxiliary Army Corps (WAAC) of World War I. The WAAC had been formed in 1917 to provide women for employment with the British army at home and on the Western Front. It had been divided into four sections: cooking, mechanical, clerical, and miscellaneous.

In September 1938, in the shadow of another war, the ATS came into being to meet the manpower demands that would inevitably flow from any future conflict. Its first director was Dame Helen Gwynne-Vaughan, who fought long and hard for the ATS to be accepted as part of the armed forces of the Crown. Initially, however, the ATS was placed under the umbrella of the all-male Territorial Army (volunteer reserve), and the women recruits received two-thirds of soldiers' pay. A number of ATS companies

were formed to serve with the Royal Air Force, but on the formation of the **Women's Auxiliary Air Force** (WAAF, see p. 209) in the
summer of 1939, the War Department washed its hands of them.

On September 4, 1939, seventeen thousand women enrolled
voluntarily in the ATS, undertaking to serve their country in
whatever place and capacity the authorities required, many clearly
making a break for freedom from the rigid confines of prewar
British life. In April 1941, with the introduction of the Defense
(Women's Forces) Regulations, the drive and determination of
Dame Helen Gwynne-Vaughan was rewarded when the ATS became an integral part of the armed forces of the Crown.

It was placed under the command of a chief controller with the
equivalent rank of a major general, a post held from June 26, 1941,
by Jean Knox. Female personnel from the age of seventeen to
forty-three could sign up, but women who had served in World
War I were accepted up to age fifty. Once enrolled, the "ATs," as
they were known, had three weeks' paid leave a year with free
travel warrants, free medical attention, and lodging, not a bad deal
in the days of wartime deprivation. Pay for the lower ranks was
two shillings a day, the same as that enjoyed by their male counterparts.

At the beginning of the war there were only five "trades" in
the ATS. **Conscription** (see p. 159), introduced in December
1941, was soon to change all that. By 1945, women had replaced
men in more than one hundred trades, seventy-seven of them
skilled. Secretarial, catering, and domestic work were all traditional areas of employment for women, but the demands of war
quickly demonstrated that they were more than capable of shoul-
dering responsibilities that would have been unthinkable in prewar
days. In 1942 approximately 50 percent of the new recruits in the
ATS were destined to serve in Britain's **mixed antiaircraft batteries**
(see p. 233).

Of the rest, 17 percent became drivers in an era when most
men could not drive, 10 percent telephone and teleprint operators,
9 percent cooks, 9 percent domestic workers, and 5 percent clerks.
By the summer of 1943, when there were 210,308 women in the

ATS, it was estimated that 80 percent of army driving in the United Kingdom was performed by women, who also maintained and repaired all types of vehicles, from staff cars to three-ton trucks and gun limbers. One of them was Princess Elizabeth, the future queen of England, who became a subaltern in the ATS in 1945. Women also became armorers, carpenters, coach trimmers, draftsmen, electricians, plotters, radiographers, sheet-metal workers, and welders, to mention only a few of the trades that became open to them. They undertook secret work, including gunnery and ammunition tests.

Life in the ATS was often tough for new recruits. One of them, Eileen Nolan, was called up in 1942 and posted to Halifax, in Yorkshire. The young women were housed in a Victorian barracks that Nolan later described as "cold, grim and demoralising for raw recruits thrust into a foreign environment where their lives were ordered from minute to minute." The recruits carried their eating implements wherever they went, fearful of theft, and never walked on the linoleum floors because they had to polish them.

Married women with children were exempt from the draft. What were the sexual implications of women serving with other women, almost all single, separated, or divorced? The number of cases of lesbianism reported in the ATS was small. Unlike homosexuality, lesbianism was not a criminal offense in Britain at the time, but the disciplinary aspect had to be considered, especially the vexed question of relations with other ranks. The ATS moved in this minefield with some circumspection, producing a memorandum entitled "A Special Problem," which was not issued generally but could be supplied to any senior ATS officer who was concerned about relationships that might have an undermining effect on the women under her command. The most frequent approach was a judicious posting. Only a few promiscuous lesbians had to be discharged from the service, in a surprisingly calm response to same-sex relationships for the time.

In the winter of 1939–40, three hundred women of the ATS were posted to France as part of the British Expeditionary Force. In May 1940 they were caught up in the Battle of France and in the evacuations from Dunkirk and other ports. The last ATS unit—some twenty-five women—set sail for England from St. Malo on June 22, the day France surrendered.

But as the tide of war turned, the ATS was back, active again in Normandy in 1944 and in the victorious Allied drive through northwest Europe and into Germany. The women in mixed anti-aircraft batteries had a particularly hectic time in the autumn of 1944, when the Belgian port of Antwerp, vital to Allied supply, came under heavy attack by V-1 flying bombs. By June 1945, there were some 9,550 ATs serving in northwest Europe.

During the course of the war, 375 members of the ATS lost their lives, 302 were wounded, 94 went missing, and 22 became prisoners of war. Among the honors and decorations awarded to members of the ATS were 238 Mentions in Dispatches, one French Croix de Guerre with silver star, four US Bronze Stars, and three US Bronze Stars with Mention in Dispatches.

Not all the women serving in the ATS were willing members, and the maintenance of discipline was made harder in these cases by the fact that miscreants were treated more lightly than their male counterparts. For some offenses, a soldier was liable to trial by court-martial and, if found guilty, could face a detention of up to three years, but an ATS woman could not even be brought before a court-martial unless she chose to appear of her own accord. Even if an offender opted for this, sentences for females were limited to confinement to camp or forfeiture of pay.

The usual tactic adopted by recalcitrant members of the ATS was to go absent without leave. Women who chose to remain in the ATs but to ignore any attempt to discipline them were often an even bigger headache for those in charge. Three unruly recruits left their mark when, among other outrages, they mobbed a regimental sergeant major on parade while wearing their pajamas. Contrary to standing orders, the women were placed under lock and key. Their response was to utterly destroy the cells in which they had been confined, a feat that had defied the efforts of generations of soldiers.

Nevertheless, for many women, wartime service in the ATS was a liberating experience. As one of them recalled: "It was an unexpected opportunity to do something different, something really good for the country, a chance to get away from all the dull jobs women had always had to do. It was a step thousands took to escape having to go into domestic service."

Reference: Dorothy Calvert, *Bull, Battledress, Lanyard and Lipstick,* 1978.

CIVIL DEFENSE
United Kingdom, World War II

Mainland Britain had come under aerial bombardment by German zeppelins for the first time in January 1915. On June 13, 1917, London was attacked when fourteen Gotha IV heavy bombers dropped seventy-two bombs near Liverpool Street station. In World War I, Germany mounted a total of 103 air raids against Britain, most of them on London, killing 1,413 people.

In 1924 the British Home Office drew on the experience of World War I by establishing a committee, under the chairmanship of Sir John Anderson, to examine the German bombing campaign and formulate future policy. This was the beginning of what became known as Air Raid Precautions (ARP).

In the 1930s a new generation of bombers cast a long shadow over Europe. Analyzing the experience of World War I and the Spanish Civil War, British air planners pessimistically concluded that any future armed conflict would open with devastating bombing raids on centers of population, causing millions of physical and psychological casualties and leading to the breakdown of entire societies. The side that delivered the so-called knockout blow first would emerge as the victor.

At the same time, twelve autonomous Civil Defense regions were established. London—the major target in any anticipated bombing campaign—counted as a single region. The chain of command ran down from the regional headquarters, through group headquarters, to individual boroughs in each county. The borough headquarters was usually located in a town hall, integrating the civil defenses with local government. In most towns,

council staff shared civil defense responsibilities with a small number of full-time civil defense personnel and many local volunteers.
Below the borough lay the district and, at the bottom of the pyramid, the air raid wardens' posts.

In theory each post, heavily sandbagged and clearly marked,
was supposed to cover an area containing approximately five hundred people. In London there were about ten posts per square
mile. In an air raid, the air raid warden was to act as the eyes and
ears of the local Civil Defense Control Center, patrolling the
streets to enforce the blackout regulations, imposed from sunset to
sunrise, and controlling "incidents," the bureaucrats' euphemism
for every sort of disaster likely to be visited upon Britain's civilian
population by an air raid. The warden's report of an "incident"
would set in motion the civil defense team, summoning stretcher
parties, fire engines, heavy-rescue units, and mobile canteens operated by the Women's Voluntary Service (WVS)—all the services
required to care for the injured, comfort the survivors, and dispose
of the dead.

In 1939 there were some 1.5 million civil defense personnel.
Over two-thirds of them were volunteers, and many of them were
women. Initially, full-time male workers were paid three pounds a
week and their female counterparts two pounds (raised by an extra
five shillings in the summer of 1940). When they were on
"standby," the full-time men worked a seventy-two-hour week
and the women forty-eight hours. By June 1940 there were more
than fifty thousand women in full-time civil defense work. They
were to play a vital role in the Blitz, the German bombing campaign against mainland Britain, which lasted from September 1940
to May 1941. Throughout the Blitz, women served as firewomen
in the Auxiliary Fire Service (AFS), which had been established in
1938 to augment Britain's regional brigades, and as fire guards,
ambulance drivers, dispatch riders, nurses staffing first-aid posts,
and air raid wardens. At the start of the Blitz there were more
than five thousand women serving in London's AFS as drivers,
mechanics, wireless operators, cooks, and control-room staff. At
the height of the Blitz, in the winter of 1940–41, one air raid warden in every six was a woman.

In December 1940, full-time ARP staff peaked at 131,700, of whom some 19,500 were women. In 1941 the ARP service changed its title to Civil Defense to reflect the wider range of roles it was undertaking. By 1944, its full-time staff numbered just under 70,000, of whom approximately 10,000 were women. Another 799,400 men and 180,00 women served as volunteers in their spare time.

Reference: Tom Harrisson, *Living Through the Blitz,* **1976.**

CONSCRIPTION
United Kingdom, World War II

In the spring of 1941, an Order of the British Government, the Registration for Employment, required all women between the ages of eighteen and fifty to register in one of two categories, "mobile" and "immobile." The women in the latter category were usually those with dependents or with husbands serving in the armed forces or merchant navy. The "mobile" category comprised single women and married women with no dependents.

The Registration for Employment Order was followed by the National Service Act of December 1941. The act empowered the government to conscript unmarried or widowed women between the ages of twenty and thirty, and in 1942 women of nineteen became liable for conscription. In 1943 the upward age limit was raised to fifty-one, principally to release younger women for work in aircraft production. Married women who were not living apart from their husbands were wholly exempt, as were women with children under the age of fourteen.

The conscripts were given a choice between serving in the auxiliary services—the **Auxiliary Territorial Service** (ATS, see p. 153), the WRNS (**Women's Royal Naval Service,** see p. 214), and the **Women's Auxiliary Air Force** (WAAF, see p. 209), **civil defense** (see p. 157), or industry. The women who chose the auxiliary services were not required to handle a lethal weapon unless they signaled their willingness to do so in writing. About 25 percent of Britain's "mobile women"—some 460,000—chose the auxiliary services. A social survey conducted in 1942 revealed that 97 percent of women "emphatically agreed" that they should undertake war work.

By mid-1943, the proportion of British women who were serving in the forces, munitions work, and essential industries was double that of 1918, and the number of married women engaged in war work had risen from the 1939 level of 1.25 million to 3 million. Nine out of ten single women between the ages of twenty and forty were in the services or industry. It was almost impossible for a woman under forty to avoid war work unless she had heavy family responsibilities or was looking after a war worker billeted on her. (See also **Rosie the Riveter,** p. 180.)

Reference: His Majesty's Stationery Office, *Manpower: The Story of Britain's Mobilisation for War,* HMSO, 1944.

DACOWITS, see Defense Department Advisory Committee on Women in the Services, see below.

DEFENSE ADVISORY COMMITTEE ON WOMEN IN THE SERVICES
DACOWITS, United States, 1951–Present

In 1951, with the United States engaged in the Korean War, the US secretary of defense, General George C. Marshall, enlisted the aid of a number of prominent women with the aim of bringing more women into the armed forces, encouraging them to stay in the services, and giving them a wider range of career opportunities.

At the outset, DACOWITS comprised some forty women, the majority of whom had professional or academic experience. It also included women who had held key posts in the women's corps during World War II, but with the passing of the years the number of women serving on DACOWITS has declined. Marshall conferred the protocol rank of three-star general on the original members (a tradition that continues today), and in its first year of existence, it made fifteen official recommendations to the secretary of defense. But for the next twenty years, until the final phase of the American involvement in Vietnam, DACOWITS languished, a reflection of the low priority given by successive administrations to the role of women in the US military.

The next development came in the 1990s, when under the Clinton administration efforts were made to review the changing nature of the US armed forces, which by 1994 comprised 16 percent female recruits, and their possible employment in direct ground combat. Once again DACOWITS gained a higher profile and played a part in the lifting of the existing restrictions on the number of women in the services and the ranks they could attain. There was much talk among conservative critics of the Clinton administration of DACOWITS being in thrall to the liberal agenda advanced by "Pentagon feminists" such as Sara Lister, assistant secretary of the army for manpower and reserve affairs, who resigned in October 1997 after making a speech in which she referred to the US Marine Corps as "extremists" totally disconnected from society. To everyone's surprise, however, DACOWITS came out against the commitment of women to front-line combat.

DACOWITS has survived these storms and retained its overall aims, which have changed little in more than fifty years: to improve the nation's defense by enabling military women to serve as full partners to military men; to give women opportunities that are commensurate with their abilities, which are not to be calibrated by popular notions of a "woman's role"; to provide the support systems that encourage this outcome; and to foster respect for women in uniform, which underlies unit cohesion, morale, and good order and discipline.

Reference: Francine D'Amico and Laurie Weinstein, *Gender Camouflage: Women and the US Military*, 1999.

FIRST AID NURSING YEOMANRY (WOMEN'S TRANSPORT SERVICE)
FANY, United Kingdom, World Wars I and II

The First Aid Nursing Yeomanry (FANY) was conceived in 1907 as a nursing corps recruited from well-to-do women operating on horseback to tend the wounded in the aftermath of battles. In 1914 the FANY, now motorized and equipped with its own ambulances, crossed the English Channel to France with the British Expeditionary Force (BEF), in the process supplying the British army with its first female drivers.

After 1918 the FANY continued to operate in national emergencies, providing the army with extra drivers in the general strike of 1926. A year later the War Office officially recognized the FANY, and when the ATS came into being, many FANYs joined that branch of the service as drivers and were called up in 1939 to serve in the ATS's transport arm. Nevertheless, the FANY remained an independent entity.

In World War II the FANY, redesignated the Women's Transport Service (WTS), performed a bewilderingly wide range of tasks. Its ranks were initially filled with fashionable young women from wealthy backgrounds who often occupied confidential positions as "personal assistants," perhaps the most celebrated being the former fashion model Kay Summersby, who became General Dwight D. Eisenhower's driver and mistress.

Members of the FANY were often mocked as "society girls playing at war," but they played an important back-room role in the field of intelligence, particularly with the **Special Operations Executive** (SOE, see p. 366). Some two thousand FANYs served with the agency in Britain, Europe, and the Middle and Far East, many as wireless operators and decoders, others as housekeepers in the SOE's many holding stations.

One FANY, a Mrs. Barclay, was responsible for delivering directly to Winston Churchill the raw decrypts of intercepted Enigma traffic assembled at Bletchley Park, home of the Ultra secret. Seventy-three members of the FANY went behind enemy lines in occupied Europe, where some were captured, brutally interrogated, and executed. Self-assured young FANYs were relied on to move comfortably in this secret world, which was for the most part run by men from a similar social background. They all "spoke the same language." The motto of the FANY was "I cope."

Reference: Eric Taylor, *Women Who Went to War 1938–1946,* 1988.

HELFERINNEN
Women Auxiliaries, Nazi Germany

Adolf Hitler was implacably opposed to women playing an active role in the waging of war, a paradox in such a highly militarized state as Nazi Germany. For the Führer, women were defined by "the three Ks"—*Kinder, Kirche,* and *Küche*—children, church, and kitchen, which encompassed the National Socialist ideal of womanhood. The war work of good German women was to breed, in large numbers, the child of the future, the Aryan dream.

True to these views, one of the earliest Nazi Party ordinances in January 1921 had excluded women in perpetuity from holding any office in the party. The kernel of Nazi thinking on the woman question was a doctrine of inequality between the sexes as immutable as that between the Aryan and non-Aryan races. This was in line with developments throughout Europe where the rise of fascism, with its unbridled stress on masculinity and exaggerated virility, undermined almost all the gains made by women in the previous century of struggle for civic freedom and the vote. But even before the outbreak of war, the role of female auxiliaries, the Helferinnen, had become a key component in the administration of Germany's armed forces.

In World War II, there were a number of German women's auxiliary formations servicing the signal corps, the air force and its antiaircraft batteries, the army, the navy, and the Waffen-SS. The Helferinnen wore uniforms, were placed under military discipline, and received free rations, quarters, and clothing. However, they were not treated as members of the armed forces, and their senior officers were not ranked in a hierarchy that paralleled the male officers in the Third Reich's armed forces. A directive of 1942 limited the role of the Helferinnen to the provision of clerical and switchboard assistance.

Heinrich Himmler, chief of the SS, had a marginally more flexible approach to the role of women within his empire of concentration and extermination camps. In World War II there were some thirty-five hundred female camp guards, although even at Ravensbrück, the camp designated for the training of female SS personnel, they constituted less than 10 percent of its SS establishment.

In devising the overall role of the female SS auxiliaries, Himmler had drawn on a Finnish model, the **Lotta Svärd** (see p. 169), an organization whose aim was to discharge militia and soldiers from all tasks not directly concerned with combat. He also insisted that they would have to meet the same racial criteria as SS men. Although the SS women did not have their blood type tattooed on their arm or chest like the men, they could rise to a position of command as senior overseers in which they were the equal of their male counterparts.

The Helferinnen in the Luftwaffe played an increasingly significant role from 1943 as the Allied bombing offensive against Germany gathered pace. Many were recruited into the RAD (Reich Labor Service) to deal with bomb damage. Others served in radar stations, the fighter control network, and antiaircraft batteries. By the end of 1944, Allied raids had become so severe that Hitler was persuaded to turn over the operating of searchlight batteries to women. By 1945 some women were firing antiaircraft guns. At its peak the Luftwaffe Helferrinen numbered some 130,000.

It was not until March 1945, when the Red Army had advanced to within sixty miles of Berlin, that Hitler withdrew his order banning women from carrying arms. The aim was to form an all-female battalion as a propaganda tool to bolster the last-ditch defense of the Third Reich (see **Bochkareva, Maria,** p. 88, for a similar idea in World War I Russia, the women's Battalion of Death). But the Führer flinched from this final step, rescinding the order within a week. Only the women serving on antiaircraft batteries or guarding communications hubs were armed.

But as the Fatherland crumbled, some German women acted on their own initiative. There is photographic evidence of women being trained to fire the *Panzerfaust,* a handheld, recoilless antitank weapon issued in large numbers at the end of the war to the Volkssturm, the German equivalent of the British Home Guard. There is also credible documentary evidence of some German tank crews containing at least one female member at this stage in the war. In her autobiography, *The Gift Horse,* the German actress

Hildegard Knef tells of joining her boyfriend in a Volkssturm column marching to defend Berlin against the Red Army. She fell into Russian hands and spent three weeks in a prisoner-of-war cage before being released.

Reference: Gordon Williamson, *World War II German Women's Auxiliary Services,* 2003.

ISRAELI DEFENSE FORCES
1941–Present

In the independence struggle in Palestine, which culminated in November 1947 with the founding of the State of Israel, a number of Jewish organizations played important military roles, although they did not always act in concert. The largest of these was the thirty-thousand-strong Haganah, conceived not as a guerrilla force but as a broadly based self-protection umbrella for Jews in Palestine, which followed a policy of self-restraint and nonviolence. It acted as the parent body for the Palmach (from *Plugot Mahatz* or "shock troops"), which had been formed in May 1941, with the knowledge of the British who administered the Palestine mandate.

The Palmach fielded approximately four thousand members, of whom 15 to 20 percent were women. The Haganah ensured that the women in the Palmach received weapons and combat training alongside the men. Female members of the Palmach played a relatively minor role in the organization's so-called actions against the British in Palestine—the sabotaging of communications and attacks on British army bases—and in 1946 the organization renounced terrorism and turned its attention to nonviolent activities, for example, encouraging and aiding the arrival in Palestine of illegal Jewish immigrants.

There were two more militant armed Jewish organizations: Etzel, with a membership of some seven thousand; and a smaller, splinter faction, Lehi, a self-proclaimed terror group dedicated to the violent ending of the British mandate in Palestine. Lehi fielded about eight hundred fighters and often clashed bitterly with the Haganah. Along with Etzel, it used women as medics and messengers and, in common with World War II Resistance networks, employed women to smuggle ammunition and explosives. A celebrated member of Lehi was Geula Cohen, an announcer on its underground radio station, the Voice of Fighting Zion, who was famous for her lugubrious tones as she issued chilling threats to the British forces occupying Palestine. Cohen was later to pursue a political career and in the early 1990s became a junior minister in the government headed by Yitzhak Shamir, who had been a driving force behind Lehi in the 1940s.

On the day the United Nations voted in favor of the establishment of a Jewish state, November 29, 1947, a mixed-gender Haganah patrol in the Negev was ambushed by Bedouins and wiped out. Their dead bodies were then mutilated, which prompted an order from Haganah headquarters withdrawing women from combat units. However, in the Israeli War of Independence, which broke out in early 1948 as the British relinquished their mandate in Palestine, women played an active part in the fighting that flared as the fledgling state was assailed by its Arab neighbors. Some women served as escorts to convoys making their way to a besieged Jerusalem. The women were also responsible for concealed arms and ammunition, confident that British troops would not search them. A number of women also took part in Operation Nachshon, Israel's brigade-sized operations in the hill country to the west of Jerusalem. Among them was twenty-year-old Netiva Ben-Yehuda, who had joined the Palmach in 1946 and served in an engineer unit. More than thirty years later, she recounted her experiences in the War of Independence in three autobiographical novels.

In June 1948 the United Nations brokered a truce between Israel and its Arab enemies. This enabled the newly formed Israeli Defense Forces (IDF) to rest and regroup while they were reorganized and underwent intensive training as war matériel arrived from Europe. The IDF then decided to remove women from the front line. Some 10,600 women continued to serve throughout the war, which ended in July 1949, but they were tasked with medical and administrative duties in a Women's Corps whose members served in female battalions attached to but independent of male formations. In 1949 the Women's Corps was restructured and women soldiers were dispersed among male units. Thereafter one of its roles was to act as a support system for the women in the IDF's ranks.

The Women's Corps was known as Chel Nashim, which was contracted into the acronym CHEN (grace). It was closely modeled on the British **Auxiliary Territorial Service,** or ATS, of World War II (see p. 153), an organization in which CHEN's first head, Stella Levy, had served. The emergence of CHEN coincided with the passing, in 1949, of Israel's Defense Service Law, the first piece of legislation to introduce conscription of women in peacetime. At first the bare terms on which Israeli women were conscripted were the same as those applying to men—they were drafted to serve for two years when they reached the age of eighteen. However, when the men's period of service was extended to three years, the women did not follow suit. (In August 2001 the Women's Corps lost its independence when it was incorporated into the Israeli General Staff and its commander, Brigadier General Suzy Yogev, was appointed to serve as adviser on women's issues.)

The Defense Service Law had required all citizens and permanent residents of Israel to perform military service. All women between the ages of eighteen and twenty-six who were physically fit, unmarried, and had not borne children, and had not objected on grounds of religion or conscience, were obliged to fulfill their military obligation. But in 2003, during the hearing that imprisoned five young men for refusing to serve on the "political" grounds of opposing the Israeli occupation of territory annexed after the Six Day War of 1967, the court reinterpreted the exemption law for women. Thereafter women were obliged to go through the same channels as men to gain exemption, which remains at the discretion of the minister of defense.

In 2005 this change of procedure led to the imprisonment of a young Israeli woman, Idan Halili, after an initial refusal by a conscience committee to hear her argument for an exemption on the grounds of her feminist rejection of militarism. When her case was heard, the conscience committee handled the hot potato thrust into their hands by Halili with some circumspection. She gained exemption on the grounds that her feminism made her "unfit to serve."

Until recent years, conscript women in the IDF were largely confined to administrative duties. If they possessed the right qualifications and had the endorsement of their commander, they could attend officer school. However, after graduation they could only command other women. Those who chose to remain in the IDF faced a limited range of promotion prospects and could not command men.

Israel is a small country that since its formation has often been obliged simultaneously to confront a range of more populous enemies on its borders. In time of war it relies on the rapid mobilization of its reserve to meet any major threat. In 1973, for example, just before the outbreak of the Yom Kippur War, the active IDF numbered some 75,000, of whom one-third were regulars in the army, navy, and air force, with the balance supplied by on-duty reservists and conscripts undergoing training. On mobilization in October, Israel's armed forces grew to 350,000. Women, however, rarely serve in the IDF reserve.

Nevertheless, since the 1990s women in the IDF have been making some, albeit limited, progress. This is a phenomenon that some military historians who are skeptical about the role of women in modern armies have linked to several interrelated factors. One of the most significant of these is the growing reluctance, since Israel's invasion of Lebanon in 1982, of a small but statistically significant number of Israeli men to undertake military service. Some of the gaps this has opened up have been filled by the introduction of women into a number of military occupational specialties (MOS) that had previously been the preserve of men.

Following a 1995 ruling of the Israeli Supreme Court, which upheld an appeal by Alice Miller, a Jewish immigrant from South Africa, women became eligible for training as aircrew in the Israeli air force. Miller did not make it through pilot training, but in 2001 Lieutenant Roni Zuckerman became the fourth Israeli woman to complete the air force's flight course and the first to reach the status of F-16 fighter pilot, ranking sixth in a class of seventy. Previously, several women had qualified as navigators. From 1997, women in the IDF have joined antiaircraft units, and in 1998 the navy removed its barriers to the recruitment of female shipboard personnel, although women do not serve in submarines. By 2005, women were able to serve in 83 percent of the MOS in the IDF. Combat, however, remains voluntary. Those women who volunteer for combat duty are among the small number of female personnel required to undertake active reserve duty, and this for only a period of two years after their active service. Currently some five hundred women serve in combat units of Israel's security forces, principally the border police. These volunteers may be required to serve for three years because they must undergo lengthy training.

However, women still have a long way to go in the IDF. In 2002 some 33 percent of the IDF's junior officers were female, a percentage that fell to 21 percent in the case of middle-ranking officers (majors and captains) and plummeted to only 3 percent in the senior ranks. Significantly, as women have become integrated more fully into the structures and operations of the IDF the number of exemptions from service for women—principally for religious reasons—has risen. It remains to be seen if the aftermath of Israel's invasion of southern Lebanon in July 2006 effects long-term changes in IDF morale and composition.

See also **Meir, Golda,** p. 48.

Reference: Chaim Herzog, *The Arab-Israeli Wars: War and Peace in the Middle East,* 1982.

LOTTA SVÄRD
Finnish Female Auxiliaries, World War II

Women had played an active voluntary but noncombat role in the Finnish independence movement and civil war (1918). In 1921 the Lotta Svärd emerged as an auxiliary to the Finnish Civil Guard, providing moral and medical support and assisting with provisioning and fund-raising. The organization was named after the heroine of a patriotic poem of the early nineteenth century, Lotta Vraede. The model was imitated in Sweden, Norway, Estonia,

and Denmark and encouraged the foundation of a number of asso-
ciations in the United States. It also influenced Heinrich Himmler
in his organization of female SS auxiliaries (see **Helferinnen,**
p. 163).

The Lotta Svärd had a center-right political bias and until the
Winter War between Finland and the Soviet Union (1939–40) it
was not open to those with socialist or Communist beliefs. Its
principal thrust was religious and moral, and its membership was
divided into two categories—an "acting" Lotta, which had received
training in specific tasks like nursing, provisioning, air surveillance,
signaling, or anti-chemical-warfare measures, and a reserve. By 1939
the Lotta deployed eight field hospitals, staffed by nurses dressed
soberly in gray and sporting white sheepskin hats in winter. Lotta
members wore a distinctive pin in the shape of a Finnish swastika.

In the Winter War, the Lotta Svärd became an auxiliary of the
Finnish armed services. Its members assisted with the evacuation of
civilians, worked in air-defense posts, staffed hospital trains and
field hospitals, and supplied the Finnish army with clothing. Many
Lottas worked in "centers for the fallen," washing and preparing
the bodies of dead soldiers before their dispatch to their home-
towns for burial. The Lottas were initially unpaid, receiving only
food and lodging, but later the Finnish Defense Ministry introduced a system of daily allowances for those members of the Lotta
who served outside their locality.

After the Winter War, the Finns had to yield territory to the
Soviets. In the 1941–44 War of Continuation, as the ongoing
struggle against the Soviet Union was known, Lottas were once
again mobilized. Typically, each Finnish division of twelve to fifteen thousand men had an auxiliary of one hundred to two hundred Lottas. They remained noncombatants and received no
weapons training, although some Lottas serving near the front line
were unofficially issued with weapons and given basic training in
their use. Adolf Hitler was sufficiently impressed by them to sum-
mon the Lotta leader, Fanni Luukkonen, to Berlin, where he
presented her with a medal for her "outstanding fight against Bol-
shevism." By 1944 the Lotta Svärd included 240,000 volunteers
from a Finnish population of four million.

This did not impress the Soviets, and at the conclusion of the War of Continuation, they demanded that the Finns disband a number of organizations they deemed to be "fascist," including the Lotta Svärd, which was wound up in November 1944. During World War II, 113 members of the Lotta Svärd died as the result of enemy action. Today the Lotta Svärds work has devolved to a successor organization, the Lotta Svärd Foundation.

Reference: A 2005 movie, *Lupaus* (Promise), describes the work of the Finnish Lottas in World War II.

NATO ARMED FORCES
1949–Present

The North Atlantic Treaty Organization (NATO) was formed in the spring of 1949, at the beginning of the Cold War, when military groupings coalesced around the United States on the one side and the Soviet Union on the other. It was the start of a standoff that lasted until the collapse of the Soviet Union in 1991.

In 1976, NATO's highest authority, the Military Committee, recognized the Committee on Women in the NATO Forces. Since then, the status of women in NATO forces has changed beyond recognition. Between 1976 and 2001 the number of females in NATO uniforms rose from 30,000 to nearly 300,000. The pace and scale of integration, however, differs from country to country within NATO.

In April 1949, acting in response to the Soviet land blockade of West Berlin, the United States and Canada had combined with Belgium, Denmark, France, Iceland, Italy, Luxembourg, the Netherlands, Norway, Portugal, and the United Kingdom to form NATO to provide for the collective defense of the major Western European states and the North American states against the perceived military threat from the Soviet Union.

Since 1949, NATO has undergone successive enlargements, and following the disintegration of the Soviet Empire has been joined by a number of Eastern European states that in the Cold War were members of the Warsaw Pact, the Soviet counterweight to NATO formed in 1955 and dissolved in 1991. In 2006, full members of NATO were Belgium, Canada, Denmark, Iceland, Italy, Luxembourg, the Netherlands, Norway, Portugal, the United Kingdom, the United States, Turkey, Germany, Spain, the Czech Republic, Hungary, Poland, Bulgaria, Estonia, Latvia, Lithuania, Romania, Slovakia, and Slovenia.

In some respects, Norway and Denmark have made the most striking progress toward the integration of women into the military. Norway was the first NATO country to allow women to serve on submarines, and since 1985 women have been allowed into all other combat functions. In 1988, Denmark opened all functions and formations in its armed services to women following a series of combat-arms trials conducted between 1985 and 1987. Women in Norway and Denmark have only been held back from entry into the para-rangers and marine commandos, both functions in which they have not met the entry requirements. Otherwise, female soldiers train, work, and are deployed on equal terms with men.

Nevertheless, representation of women in the armed forces of Norway and Denmark remains relatively low, at, respectively, 3.2 percent and 5 percent. Norway appointed its first female defense minister in 1999, but few female soldiers have progressed to senior ranks, and it was not until November 1999 that Norway appointed its first female colonel. One reason for this is that many female officers change from operational to administrative duties after maternity leave, reducing their chances of being selected to study at military academies.

The NATO nation with the highest representation of women in the armed forces is the United States, with 14 percent. The breakthrough for US servicewomen came with the creation of the all-volunteer force in 1973. At the time, disillusionment with the military in the aftermath of the Vietnam War meant that men were reluctant to serve, and as a result female recruits were welcome. By 2001, 8.6 percent of US troops deployed worldwide were women and nearly 11,500 had supported NATO peacekeeping operations. (For US Army, US Navy, and US Air Force, see **United States Armed Forces,** p. 185.)

In Canada, women have been able to serve in almost all

military functions and environments, including submarines, since 1989. However, most women in the Canadian armed forces—at 7,900, some 15 percent of regular personnel—are to be found in traditional fields and there has been only patchy progress toward integrating them into the combat arms—infantry, artillery, field engineering, and armor—where representation hovers around 2 percent. In May 2006, Canada suffered its first loss of an active-combat female soldier when Captain Nichola Goddard, one of 230 female Canadian forces personnel serving in Afghanistan, died in an engagement with Taliban forces.

France, which withdrew from NATO's military-command structure in 1966, granted female soldiers equal status in the early 1970s but retained quotas until 1998. Currently some 23,500 women make up just under 10 percent of the 260,400 active personnel in France's front-line armed forces. Of France's 6,800 naval aviators, 480 are women. Of the 64,000 air force personnel, some 7,000 are women. The French army comprises 137,700 personnel, of whom 12,500 are female.

In the United Kingdom, women in the armed forces were segregated into women's corps until the early 1990s, at which point the role of women underwent considerable changes. Women were able to serve at sea in surface ships and in all aircrew roles. In the Royal Air Force over 95 percent of posts are open to women, and approximately 70 percent in the army and navy.

British women in the military now serve alongside men in nearly all specialties, with an exception being units whose primary duty is "to close with and kill the enemy," where it is still felt that their presence would impair combat effectiveness. This restriction is consistent with a ruling of the European Court of Justice that allows women to be excluded from certain posts on grounds of combat effectiveness and leaves the final decision on the precise definition of the term to national authorities.

At present British servicewomen are not allowed to drive tanks, serve in the front-line infantry, or work as mine-clearance divers. They cannot be part of the Infantry, Royal Armored Corps, Royal Marines, or the RAF Regiment, and are also barred from submarine posts. In 2006 the British army's 7,432 women comprised 6.7 percent of the force; there were some 5,000 women (8.9 percent) in the Royal Air Force; and 2,890 (7.8 percent) in the Royal Navy, with 745 at sea aboard fifty ships.

The role of women in the modern navy was thrown into sharp relief by an international incident in March 2007. A fifteen-strong boarding party from the frigate *Cornwall,* which was patrolling an area south of the Shatt-al-Arab waterway in Iraqi waters in the Persian Gulf, was taken prisoner by two Iranian fast boats. One of *Cornwall's* boarding party was a woman, Acting Leading Seaman Faye Turney, the mother of a three-year-old child. The captured Britons were taken to Tehran and subjected to a sustained campaign of psychological harassment. Initially, Turney was separated from her colleagues, who were told that she had been sent home. She later appeared on Iranian television, wearing a hijab and making a confession that the boarding party had crossed into Iranian waters. After two weeks the boarding party was released and returned to the United Kingdom, having incurred considerable criticism for appearing to cooperate with their Iranian captors during their incarceration. Later Turney and another member of the boarding party, Arthur Batchelor, and their navy handlers, incurred even more criticism for selling their stories to British newspapers and television.

There were five fatalities among British women serving in Iraq between the invasion in March 2003 and April 2007. The overall figure for fatalities during the same period was 140. In a war with no front line in the traditional sense, British servicewomen increasingly found themselves in the fighting as medics, signalers, and in logistics crews. Private Michelle Norris, a teenage medic with the Princess of Wales Royal Regiment, was awarded the Military Cross for rescuing her wounded patrol leader during a fierce firefight in al-'Amarah, Iraq, in the summer of 2006.

In the spring of 2007 there were some 1,600 female troops on operations in Iraq and Afghanistan, and for much of the time they were exposed to the lethal hazards of roadside bombs and mortar fire. There are no restrictions on women deploying on operations unless they are pregnant. Although they cannot join a unit whose primary duty is "to close with and kill the enemy"—for example, the infantry and cavalry—women undertake a number of postings fraught with risk, and their deployment has its critics.

Colonel Bob Stewart, the first commander of British forces under UN command in Bosnia, opposes women being close to combat, arguing that their deaths or injuries have a debilitating effect on male comrades. One female soldier died in his arms in Northern Ireland, and the trauma rendered him inconsolable and effectively unable to operate. Stewart reflected, "If you put women in the front line because they are equal, then you have to expect that there will be operational casualties."

Belgium's armed forces, which were opened to women in 1975, now contain just over 7 percent female personnel, a number that continues to rise. All functions are open to women, but the majority occupy administrative and logistic posts. In Luxembourg, which has no air force or navy, women were allowed to enter the army in 1987, and today they make up 0.6 percent of personnel.

Most Mediterranean countries began opening their armed forces to women in the 1980s and 1990s. In 1979, Greece admitted women noncommissioned officers to support functions, but military academies remained closed to them until 1990, and full access to military education has still not been achieved. Women are excluded from combat roles but can go to sea, and, since 2001, have served as aircrew in the Greek air force. Spain began to recruit women in 1988, followed by Portugal in 1992, and in both countries female servicewomen make up some 6 percent of total strength. In Spain, combat positions are open to women, but over half serve in administrative posts. Portuguese women can in theory apply for all posts, but in practice posts in the marines and combat specialties remain closed to them.

In Turkey, women were accepted into military academies in the late 1950s, but this policy was reversed in the 1960s, and it was not until 1982 that they were readmitted to military education, a process that only got under way in the early 1990s. As a result, women in the Turkish armed forces make up a mere 0.1 percent of personnel. They can serve as officers but are restricted from serving in the armored and infantry fields and in submarines.

Italy was the last NATO member to admit women to the military. In September 1999, after a long and vociferous campaign mounted by La Associazione Nazionale Aspiranti Donne Soldato (Association of Aspiring Women Soldiers), the Italian Parliament passed legislation enabling women to serve in the armed forces. The first female recruits reported for duty in 2000, and in June 2001, to mark this success, the Committee on Women in the NATO Forces met in Rome. The Italian armed forces are taking a gradualist approach to the integration of women, bringing them into general support rather than operational positions and maintaining restrictions on their admission into military academies.

In the countries that have become members of NATO in recent years, simultaneous preparations for accession to the European Union stimulated the introduction of equal opportunities for women in the military. In the Czech Republic, servicewomen represent nearly 4 percent of service personnel. The figure in Hungary is higher, around 9 percent, but women are largely restricted to traditional roles. In Poland the figure is very low, at about 0.1 percent, and most servicewomen fill medical posts.

In Germany, until 2000 approximately 3,800 women made up 24 percent of the military's medical service. Another 37 women served in military bands. These were the only two branches in which women were allowed to serve, as they were prohibited by law from rendering service that involved the use of arms.

In February 2000 the European Court of Justice ruled, after a challenge by a German woman, Tanja Kreil, who wanted to enter the army as a maintenance technician, that it is contrary to European law that women are not allowed into nearly all branches of the military. The policy of recruiting women to the German armed forces was reconsidered, and from 2001 women were able to enter all branches and careers in the military. In 2005, there were some 7,200 women in the German army; 2,350 in the air force; 1,600 in the navy; and 5,600 in the medical corps.

Reference: Rebecca R. Moore, *NATO's New Mission: Projecting Stability in a Post–Cold War World,* 2007.

RED ARMY WOMEN SOLDIERS
Soviet Union, World War II

On September 1, 1939, Article 13 of the universal military law was ratified by the Fourth Session of the Supreme Soviet, enabling the Red Army to accept women trained in critical medical and technical areas. During the Great Patriotic War, some 40 percent of the front-line medical personnel would be women, fighting against Hitler's invasion.

In May 1941, on the eve of Operation Barbarossa, the German invasion of the Soviet Union, the Red Army's strength stood at some five million men. By the end of December, when Barbarossa had blown itself out, the Soviets had lost more than three million men taken prisoner in a series of massive "cauldron battles" (battles of encirclement). The exact figure for casualties has never been determined. Continuing losses in 1942 nearly bled the Red Army white and significantly changed the reluctance of the Soviet high command (Stavka) to recruit women into a fighting role.

In the summer of 1942, a recruiting drive aimed at women began; in part its aim was to shame the men of the Red Army into greater efforts, and also to accelerate the integration of Soviet women into war industry. During the war some 800,000 Soviet women served in combat formations, 8 percent of the Red Army's personnel.

Due to Stavka inefficiency and lack of foresight, women faced formidable problems of integration. They struggled with male uniforms and boots that were often several sizes too big. There was no female underwear and no segregated latrines. In a surreal move, considering the savagery that characterized the fighting on the Eastern Front, Stavka introduced forty-three mobile tearooms for female troops, which also fielded cosmetic counters and hairdressers. Women who did not smoke were given chocolate rations. However, they had to wait until the end of the war for uniforms specially designed for the female physique.

Some 70 percent of the women serving in the Red Army were posted to the front, but they were often kept away from the sharp end of the fighting and assigned to antiaircraft (AA) batteries or engineer battalions, where they performed their duties on an equal footing with men (see **Mixed Antiaircraft Batteries,** p. 233). Approximately 300,000 served in AA units and, in contrast to their British counterparts, performed every function, including the firing of the guns. Klavdia Konovaluva from the Georgian Republic, who served with 784th AA regiment, had been a blacksmith in civilian life and joined her unit as a gunlayer. This Red Army Amazon quickly became a gun loader, which involved shifting thirty-six-pound shells at high speed, often under heavy fire.

There were some all-woman AA units in which a female military subculture flourished, encouraging a warmer approach to the generally ferocious military discipline of the Red Army. However, throughout the war male officers were reluctant to commit women to action, partly out of male shame and also from an apprehension that women "were not up to the job." "Why are you bringing these girls here?" the response of one disgruntled Red Army officer, was a common reaction.

Many were clearly up to the job. Some women trained tank crews (a practice that continues today in the **Israeli Defense Forces,** p. 165) and others drove tanks in the field. Mariya Oktyabrskaya bought a tank from her personal savings and fought as its commander, with the rank of guards sergeant, until she was mortally wounded in action in January 1944. Marina Lagunova graduated from a tank-training brigade as a driver-mechanic and later fought in the Battle of Kursk (1943) and the advance to the Dnieper River. In September 1943 her tank "brewed up" (received a direct hit) and she was so badly burned that both her legs were amputated. Once released from the hospital, she learned to drive again and returned to duty as a tank instructor.

One tank family went to a shared wartime grave. On the death of Colonel Koponets, his daughter Yelizaveta volunteered for the armored corps, serving as gunner/wireless operator, only to be killed in 1945 in the Battle of Berlin. With one exception, all the women who fought in tanks rode in the medium T-34.

The exception was Alexandra Boiko, who, with her husband, pulled a great many strings to gain a place at the Tank Technical School at Chelyabinsk. They eventually rode into battle in the heavy IS-2, which weighed forty-five tons. Alexandra commanded the behemoth, and her husband served as the driver/mechanic. The couple fought together in the great battles of 1944–45, in the Baltic States, Poland, and Czechoslovakia, and in the drive to Berlin.

Other Red Army women excelled in specialized duties, notably in the air war (see **Litvak, Lily,** p. 227, and **Night Witches,** p. 235). They also proved to be adept snipers, a deadly skill highly prized on the Eastern Front. Sergeant Ludmila Pavlichenko, who began the war as a history student in Kiev, accounted for more than three hundred Germans, seventy-eight of whom were snipers like herself, while serving with Twenty-fifth "Chapayev" Rifle Division.

Such was Pavlichenko's fame that in 1943 she toured the United Kingdom and the United States, where she was dubbed "Sniper Number One." Woody Guthrie wrote a song about her. In the wartime British movie *The Tawny Pipit* (1944), the strapping actress Lucie Mannheim played a visiting Soviet sniper, possibly based on Pavlichenko, who in real life was slight and attractive. Another female sniper, Nina Alexeyevna Lobkovskaya, fought her way from the steppes to Berlin, bringing down some eighty-nine of the enemy. The women in her company killed more than three thousand Germans.

In the Red Army, medical-support tasks were wholly integrated with combat units, and doctors and nurses served in the front line under heavy fire. All the nurses and some 40 percent of the doctors in the Soviet military were women. There were many instances of the heroism of Red Army medical personnel under fire, although some of them were in all likelihood embellished for reasons of propaganda.

In one example, Vera Krylova enlisted as a student nurse in 1941 and in front-line service dragged hundreds of wounded comrades to safety. In August 1941 at the height of Operation Barbarossa, when German armies were racing across the Soviet Union, the wounded Krylova is said to have taken command of an ambushed company whose officers had been killed and, riding a horse in a two-week running battle, led the survivors back to Soviet lines. A year later, in another improbable tale, she was

reported to have single-handedly charged a German tank formation, hurling grenades as she went and enabling her comrades to
evacuate their position.

Whatever the precise truth of these exploits, they nevertheless
reflect the courage of Red Army women in the front line. Perhaps
a more typical memory of a woman's war is that of one veteran
who remembered her service more prosaically:

> We didn't shoot. I cooked porridge for the soldiers. . . . I was
> given a medal for that. . . . I dragged cauldrons and mess tins
> about. Heaven knows, they were heavy. I remember our com-
> mander saying, "I'll shoot holes through those mess tins. . . .
> How are you going to give birth after the war?"

More than 100,000 Red Army women were decorated during the
war, including 86 who received the Hero of the Soviet Union
medal, the USSR's highest award for valor. Three women—
sniper Petrova, machine-gunner Stanilizhene, and air gunner
Zhurkina—were awarded all three classes (bronze, silver, and
gold) of the Order of Glory, the most highly respected soldiers'
decoration (see also **Partisans,** p. 107).

Reference: Catherine Merridail, *Ivan's War: Life and Death in the
Red Army,* 2006. For a more skeptical view of the role played by
women of the Red Army in World War II see Martin van Creveld,
Men, Women and War, 2001.

ROSIE THE RIVETER
US War Industry Women Workers, 1942–45

The collective nickname for the women who worked in the
American ordnance and aircraft plants and shipyards of World War
II was Rosie the Riveter. She was also the muscular and deter-
mined heroine immortalized by the artist Norman Rockwell on a
Saturday Evening Post cover in May 1943.

In 1942, Eleanor Roosevelt visited Britain on a fact-finding
tour of war industry. She found many women at work on the pro-

duction lines, filling jobs that in the prewar years had been reserved for men, although she noted that they were not paid
the same as men. In the United States in 1941–42, although the
quickening pace of the draft had absorbed much of the male unem-
ployment that persisted from the Depression years, employers were
still reluctant to hire women in areas other than retailing or light industry. Over 80 percent of production work was closed to females.

The timing of Roosevelt's mission to Britain coincided with the
low point in the United States' fortunes in the war. The Japanese
had run amok in the Far East and the Pacific, seizing the islands of
Guam and Wake, bundling the Americans out of the Philippines,
and threatening the Aleutian chain and the approaches to Alaska.
However, President Roosevelt and the War Manpower Commission shrank from adopting measures similar to those that had been
introduced in Britain to conscript women into the labor force.

Rather, the administration encouraged state and city authorities to launch enrollment drives. The first of these, in Oregon,
produced a little more than 300,000 volunteers for war work. In
the city of Detroit, whose automotive industries were rapidly converting to the manufacture of tanks and artillery, 180,000 women
registered for war work. Initially, however, these women were
channeled into services that were still related to civilian occupa-
tions, in hotels, department stores, and office buildings. Significantly, when Gallup polled a cross-section of women on this
development, over 50 percent stated that they would be willing to
work in the war industry, while only one in five of the husbands
questioned approved of their wives' decisions to seek war work.

These developments took place against the background of a
War Manpower Commission projection that in 1943 at least two
million women would need to be introduced to the American
workforce, particularly in the armaments sector, to offset the
growing shortages of male workers and meet the administration's
ambitious production targets. A concerted recruiting drive was
launched, but in the final analysis, financial factors were to play as
important a role as patriotic sentiment. Nowhere was this more
evident than in the aviation industry: at the massive Boeing plant
in Seattle, where the assembly lines ran twenty-four hours a day,

women were to make up over 50 percent of the workforce. Tools and equipment were modified to accommodate the female physique, and working conditions were vastly improved.

By 1944, 475,000 women were employed in the US aviation industry. It is significant that it was only in the aircraft industries of southern California that African-American women were able to work alongside white women. In many other plants they were segregated. Another sector in which African-American women made limited progress was the munitions industry, which for reasons of safety tended to be located in remote or rural areas and drew from a different labor pool than the Lockheed or Consolidated Vultee plants in California. Even so, African-American women were often the beneficiaries of these conditions only when the supply of white labor had been exhausted.

Of enormous significance in the American war effort was the shipbuilding sector, which from 1941 experienced a growth spurt of over 200 percent. The average construction time of a cargo-carrying Liberty Ship was forty-two days, and the record construction time for these maids of all work was five days from the laying of the keel to launch. These feats of mass production could not have been achieved without the introduction of female labor and the breaking down of managerial and union resistance.

Hiring and training of women to work in the shipyards began in the autumn of 1942, and within a year the workforce in some West Coast yards was 30 percent female (in 1939 the total number of women working in US shipyards had been thirty-six). Women also made up some 65 percent of new workers in the shipyards. The women riveters and welders became the heroines of wartime propaganda and the "Ships for Victory" campaign. Nevertheless, they had to be psychologically tough in the face of male hostility and sexual harassment. In the shipyards women eventually filled a wide range of jobs, which included pipe fitters, riggers, painters, electricians, and metal burners.

In some war plants, women were banned from wearing makeup to minimize flare-ups between the sexes. Boeing sent fifty-three women home for supposedly wearing their sweaters provocatively tight in the manner of Lana Turner. The long "peekaboo" hairstyle popularized by the elfin Veronica Lake in the movie *This Gun for Hire* (1942), was considered a safety hazard and was replaced by the turban. When Lake herself set a patriotic example by cutting her hair short, her career went into a decline from which it never recovered. Ever-resourceful advertising campaigns sought to glamorize women's work clothes—welding leathers or loose-fitting dungarees—and to sell beauty products by showcasing models driving cranes or tractors, thereby encouraging women to preserve their femininity in a "man's world." They were, in effect, expected to remain feminine but not too attractive.

In reality, many women experienced immense difficulty when attempting to run a home, look after children, and work on a production line. The result was a worrying level of absenteeism, but efforts to introduce a universal system of child-care facilities were blocked by Congress in response to the popular prejudice that it was wrong for the mothers of small children to be at work. There were private initiatives to remedy the problem, including the establishment of a branch of Bloomingdale's at the Sperry plant on Long Island to cut down on the time women took off to go shopping.

More tangible benefits of women's experience in war industry were lessons some of them learned in the use of organized labor to achieve better working conditions. By the end of the war, over 22 percent of the female labor force—some three million women—had joined a union. By the end of the war, discriminatory pay differences for many—but not all—women had been eliminated and maternity leave and other benefits had been secured.

Reference: Miriam Frank, *The Life and Times of Rosie the Riveter: The Story of Three Million Working Women in World War II,* 1982.

SOVIET WOMEN IN WAR INDUSTRIES
World War II

In the opening phases of Operation Barbarossa—the German invasion of the Soviet Union—the Soviet collapse in the summer and autumn of 1941 resulted in the massive mobilization of Soviet women as "fighters in overalls." In the prewar Soviet Union, women had been inured to hardship and hard work. Rationing was a fact of everyday life, housing shortages were severe, and in the back of people's minds lurked the threat of the labor camps, the gulags. By early 1940, women already made up some 40 percent of the Soviet Union's industrial workforce and over 50 percent of its land workers. But the colossal military and territorial losses sustained in Barbarossa were to worsen the stark conditions in which women lived in the Soviet Union.

In another terrible blow, the German army in the East had occupied territory where 45 percent of the population lived and where much of its industry was concentrated. By the beginning of October 1942, when most of the available resources had been mobilized for war, women made up 52 percent of the industrial labor force in armaments production and over 80 percent in light industry. But the eastward evacuation of millions of workers, which placed vital industries out of the range of German bombers, had not been matched by the provision of adequate housing. In one giant tank factory, some 8,500 workers lived in holes in the ground. Other factory workers were lodged in primitive "settlements" whose inhabitants, often numbering some fifteen thousand, had little or no fuel and running water. Discipline was harsh. An edict of December 26, 1941, made absence without leave punishable by imprisonment for up to eight years. The workweek was a minimum of sixty-six hours, with one rest day.

Women were also deployed to keep the trains running, a vital contribution to the war effort in view of the Soviet Union's vast size. In 1942 alone, approximately 165,000 young Soviet women underwent training to operate the railways as engine drivers and mates, station staff, members of track gangs, electricians, and mechanics. The first woman engine driver in the Soviet Union, Maria Aleksandrovna Arestova, who had mounted the foot plate in 1931, was brought out of retirement to drive "flying column" trains to the front, often coming under attack by low-flying Luftwaffe aircraft.

In the agricultural sector, acute labor shortages were felt almost immediately. This problem was exacerbated by a severe shortage of tractors. By 1944 over 80 percent of them were driven by women, who in the intervening years had supplied much of the missing motive power with their own muscle power. In 1940 women had made up some 40 percent of the workforce on the land; by 1945 they contributed over twice that, at just under 92 percent.

Reference: Stephen White, ed., *World War II and the Soviet People*, 1992.

UNITED STATES ARMED FORCES
1943–present

US Air Force

The first women to fly military aircraft in the United States were members of the Women's Air Force Service Pilots (WASP, see **Jacqueline Cochran,** p. 219). One of the outstanding WASPs was Ann Baumgartner, who, on October 14, 1944, became the first American woman to fly a jet aircraft, the experimental Bell YP59A Airacomet.

The WASP trained the first women to fly US military aircraft, but there would be a long wait before the newfledged trainees gained full access to commercial and military planes. The WASPs were not recognized as military pilots until 1977, when the US Congress declared them veterans of World War II. A year earlier, in 1976, women began pilot training for the United States Air Force (USAF). Captain Connie Engle, who graduated from a class of ten women pilots at Williams Air Force Base, Arizona, in September 1977, became the USAF's first female pilot to fly solo in a T–41 Mescalero, a military version of the Cessna 172, and the T–37 Tweet twin-engine jet.

In 1948 the Women's Armed Services Integration Act (see **US Army,** p. 188) had stipulated that women in the USAF "may not be assigned to duty in aircraft while such aircraft are engaged on combat missions." It was not until 1991 that Congress lifted the ban on women flying in combat aircraft, although Department of Defense policy still prohibited women from flying combat missions.

In 1993, Secretary of Defense Les Aspin allowed women to fly combat missions and opened combat aviation to enlisted female aircrew. In 1994 the first female mission-qualified USAF fighter pilot, Lieutenant Jeannie M. Flynn, graduated from F-15E Strike Eagle combat-crew training. Flynn went on to log more than two thousand hours in her F-15 by the end of 2002, including two hundred hours of combat time in Operation Allied Force, the NATO bombing of Yugoslavia (March–June 1999). By 1994, the USAF had seven female fighter pilots and two female bomber pilots.

The first woman in the USAF to fly her combat aircraft, an A-10 Thunderbolt, into enemy territory—the no-fly zone over Iraq—was Lieutenant Colonel **Martha McSally** (see p. 232). McSally, who at five feet three inches was one inch under the regulation height and had to get a waiver to fly, later recalled: "In 1984 I was attending the US Air Force Academy and told my first flight instructor that I was going to be a fighter pilot. He just laughed, but after Congress repealed the prohibition law in 1991, and I was named as one of the first seven women who would be put through fighter training, he looked me up and said he was amazed I had accomplished my goal."

At first progress was slow. In 1998 there were twenty-five female fighter pilots and eight bomber pilots in the USAF, but now a new generation of women pilots who had never experienced the combat exclusion ban was progressing through undergraduate pilot training with high marks.

Typical of the new generation was Captain Kimberly Dawn Monroe, who graduated from KC-135 refueling aircraft to the B-1 bomber and logged eighteen combat missions over Afghanistan between January and May 2002 in Operation Enduring Freedom. The mission of Monroe and her crew was to provide precision strikes with Joint Direct Attack Munitions (JDAMs)—conventional free-fall bombs converted with a guidance tail kit into accurate, adverse-weather "smart" bombs.

By 2004, the USAF had women flying virtually every combat aircraft in its arsenal, including the B-2 stealth bomber, the B-52, the A-10 Thunderbolt close-support attack aircraft, and the service's front-line fighters, the F-15 Eagle and the F-16 Falcon. Female aviators on refueling jets found themselves even closer to combat. In the war against Iraq in 2003, Operation Iraqi Freedom air commanders ordered the fleet to get as close as possible to strike aircraft, in order to cut down on travel time to and from targets. Captain Tricia Paulsen-Howe, a navigator on a KC-135 Stratotanker, flew for hours over hostile territory, refueling aircraft and searching for the two crew members of a downed F-15 north of Baghdad: "We supported all the search aircraft. On that particular day, we were refueling F-15s and F-16s that were actively searching. We went well out of our refueling airspace to go north of Baghdad to be right there so that the fighters would not have to fly very far to get gas. It was extremely hostile territory."

In 2005, there were 568 (4.1 percent) female pilots and 210 (4.6 percent) female navigators. Inevitably, the advancement of women in the service has not been achieved without controversy. In 1995 an outstanding graduate pilot, Lieutenant Kelly Flinn, mission-qualified as the deputy commander of a B-52H Stratofortress and subsequently flew on a Global Power long-range air strike during an international exercise. As something of a poster girl for the success of women pilots, she also participated in air shows at Andrews Air Force Base and featured in USAF recruitment advertisements. Flinn was later grounded after facing military charges of adultery, and was allowed to resign from the USAF rather than face a court-martial, a decision that provoked a media storm.

In 2003, the US Air Force Academy was embroiled in a sexual-assault scandal in which 12 percent of the women who graduated that year reported that they had been victims of rape or attempted rape during their time at the institution. During the course of integrating women into the armed services, equipping them with the necessary technical skills has proved much easier than regulating male and female sexual behavior (see also **US Army,** below).

US Army

The onset of the Cold War in the late 1940s prompted the US Congress to reconsider the employment of women in the armed forces. There were congressional hearings in 1948 where the star witness, General Dwight D. Eisenhower, the Allied Supreme Commander in Europe from 1943 to 1945, spoke in favor of women in the military, singling out the work of British **Mixed Antiaircraft Batteries** (see p. 233) as an example of what women could achieve. Eisenhower stressed the complexity of modern warfare in which armies could not function without an immense and complex support system to sustain the (male) troops at the cutting edge. World War II had made Eisenhower, originally a skeptic about the role of women in the military, into a believer in their indispensability in a total war.

Shortly afterward, with the passing of the Women's Armed Services Integration Act, Congress authorized the US military to recruit women on a permanent basis. Given the contentiousness of the issue, however, severe limits were placed on the intake of women and the posts they could fill.

The services' subsequent interpretation of the law tightened the screw: women were barred from combat and going to sea, with the exception of transport and hospital ships; they could not serve as aircrew and were prohibited from commanding men; they could achieve no higher rank than colonel or, in the US Navy, captain; their numbers in the services were set at 2 percent of the total strength for enlisted women and 10 percent of that number for officers. In a heavy-handed attempt to regulate sexual behavior, women were to be encouraged to be "ladylike," and lesbians were, as far as possible, weeded out.

The army could not come up with a definition of "combat" that satisfied Congress, and as a result the army secretary was given statutory authority to establish policy appropriate to the needs of the service while supporting Congress's intention of keeping women out of combat.

In practice, the 1948 act signally failed to meet the congressional target of 112,000 women. By 1952, the second year of the

Korean War, only 46,000 had been recruited, and throughout the 1950s recruiting remained stagnant. In a booming economy, the services could do little to attract women. Uniformed women trained on their own bases and, in the main, acted as secretaries, cooks, telephone operators, and aides for uniformed men.

By the middle of the 1960s, 93 percent of the women in the services worked as secretaries or in military hospitals. Of the approximately seven thousand women who served in Vietnam, some 70 percent were nurses (see **US Military Nurses and Doctors,** p. 270). One army woman who served in Vietnam, Evelyn Foote, later a brigadier general, recalled the surreal conditions:

> When I was in Vietnam in 1967, I was not weapons-qualified. In fact we were not permitted to carry weapons. I was up along the Cambodian border once with a field artillery battalion. The only thing I could do was run around with a purse—I called it my M-16 purse. I was wearing a baseball cap, no helmet, no flak jacket, no weapons, nothing. I was a liability to that unit.

It was the war in Vietnam, however, that marked a turning point in the history of women in the US armed services. In November 1967, two months before the Vietcong launched the Tet offensive, the 2 percent cap on the number of women in the armed services was lifted, along with the restrictions on the rank they could attain. Two years later the US Army boasted its first two female brigadier generals, Anna Mae Hays and Elizabeth Hoisington. These measures, encouraging though they were, came too little and late to have any effect on the course of the war in Vietnam, where the American will to "finish the job" was dealt a fatal blow by the Tet offensive.

Five years later President Richard M. Nixon ended the military draft and reintroduced an all-volunteer professional force. This presented two problems: it necessarily resulted in a force smaller than the pre-1973 model, and it immediately created a shortage of male, college-educated volunteers.

Although the military remained reluctant to expand the role of women in the army, it was obliged to explore the possibility of taking in more women in a wider range of military specialties. Another major event that concentrated the minds of the service chiefs was the bitter battle for the Equal Rights Amendment in the early 1970s, which focused attention on sex discrimination and the status of all women in the United States.

The army found a silver lining in this scenario. Drawing from experience in World War II, it anticipated that female recruits would be better educated (see **Women's Army Auxiliary Corps,** p. 203) and would pose fewer problems of discipline. World War II continued to cast its long shadow over the army's deliberations. The incoming women were intended to free male soldiers for combat, just as they had in the war years. No thought was given to placing women in the line of fire or considering their career ambitions.

Meanwhile, the number of military occupational specialties (MOS) open to women rapidly rose, although many were "blue collar" jobs. Nevertheless, the ground had begun to shift. By 1976, one in every thirty recruits in the US armed services was a woman. In the same year the military academies were opened to women, and the US Military Academy at West Point accepted its first female cadets. In the American courts there was a landmark judgment, *Crawford* v. *Cushman* (1976), which enabled pregnant women to remain in the service and return to duty after giving birth.

During the presidency of Jimmy Carter (1977–81) the US high command came under considerable pressure to sell the integration of women and the increase in their numbers as an unalloyed success story. Dissent was frowned on. Repeal of the combat exclusions was the order of the day; to enable the absorption of greater numbers of women, "combat" was redefined. Distance from the enemy was ruled out of the equation; the determining factor was the primary duty or mission of the individual or unit concerned.

In the late 1970s, in the sour aftermath of the Vietnam War, the US Army found it hard to recruit men. It was also shrinking in size, and the place it had once occupied in American life had grown correspondingly smaller. The Reagan administration, which took office in 1981, sought to spend its way out of the crisis. The defense budget was boosted, as was pay for servicemen and -women, and a massive rearmament program was initiated. Some critics detected an "anti-feminine" thrust to this program; the immediate result was an increase in the number of male recruits.

At the same time, the army continued to chew over its definition of "combat." The body charged with analyzing the issues and coming up with answers was the Women in the Army (WITA) Policy Review Group. It concluded that the overall effect of army policy had been to limit job opportunities for women while still exposing them to danger. Women were forbidden to serve in any MOS whose principal task was the killing of the enemy but could serve in positions that exposed them to the risk of being killed. The army could either admit that women were already in combat roles or take the drastic step of removing them from positions in which they were now well established.

The result of WITA's deliberations was Direct Combat Probability Coding (DCPC), in which "direct combat" fell into the same category as "close combat": the engaging of the enemy with individual or crew-served weapons while being exposed to direct enemy fire; a high probability of direct physical contact with enemy personnel; and a substantial risk of capture. Factoring all the elements into a number of scenarios enabled the army to come up with a sliding scale of combat probability running from P1 (the highest probability of direct combat) to P7. Women were to be excluded from all P1 scenarios.

The first occasion in which women in the US Army were placed in harm's way came in 1989 when, in Operation Just Cause, 800 women soldiers joined the 18,400-strong expeditionary force that invaded Panama. One of the small number of women in combat support was Captain Linda Bray of the 519th Military Police Battalion, who led a platoon of military police against a Panamanian Defense Force (PDF) compound near Panama City.

Under fire, Bray's unit secured the compound, ostensibly a group of dog kennels but actually a weapons store, and forced its defenders to flee. Bray became a heroine overnight, until the Pentagon remembered that by commanding under fire Bray had breached its ban on women in direct combat. The Pentagon backpedaled, to the evident bewilderment of the gallant Bray, who had gone from twentieth-century Amazon to military footnote in the blink of an eye. She left the army because of stress fractures she had sustained, which she blamed on the extra weight she claimed to have carried on road marches to prove her stamina to her skeptical male colleagues.

An unforgiving fact of military life—and another problem addressed by WITA in the 1980s—is the physical difference between men and women when it comes to the rigors of combat support, a role in which women have served since the Persian Gulf War and which can involve much lifting and loading. On average a female soldier is about five inches shorter than her male colleagues, has half the upper-body strength, lower aerobic capacity, and nearly 40 percent less muscle mass. In addition, she cannot urinate standing up, a factor in route marches that absorbed the attention of an entire army research study devoted to enabling women to urinate in a standing position in locations where there is sparse cover.

Since 1994 the US Army has introduced gender-integrated training programs designed to take into account—or ignore, as some critics suggest—the physical differences between men and women. The aim has been to weed out the "white male" as the norm. Those who oppose this approach argue that the lowering of physical standards and the encouragement of cooperative skills like map reading and first aid—at which women often excel—can compromise the integrity of integrated training programs that have been modified to accommodate women.

In 1987, an Army Research Institute Survey concluded that women are more likely than men to report that insufficient upper-body strength interferes with their job performance. In the case of light-wheel-vehicle mechanics, for example, 26 percent of the female soldiers interviewed for the survey found their work "very difficult" as opposed to 9 percent of the men in that MOS. It is too much to expect women soldiers to be Amazons in the mold of the Russian former blacksmith Klavdia Konovaluva (see **Red Army**

Women Soldiers, p. 177), and as many critics of the US Army's policy in this area have contended, it is unwise to ignore the problem in the hope that it will go away.

Another fact of life in an integrated army is women's childbearing capacity. In 1995–96, during the crisis in Bosnia, every three days one US servicewoman had to be evacuated from the theater because of pregnancy. An army spokesman blithely commented that it was no "different than appendicitis" (see also **US Navy,** p. 199). In such circumstances, women who wish to remain in the army receive six weeks' maternity leave.

The problem of sex in an integrated army has furrowed some brows. In the initial deployment to Bosnia and Herzegovina, which involved some fifteen hundred female troops, men and women shared tents with room for up to ten. Ranks were mixed, and privates occupied beds next to superiors. The troops were not allowed to drink alcohol or eat in restaurants, but if they were single, they were allowed to have sex provided that it was not with a subordinate or superior in their chain of command. A spokesman explained that the army does not prohibit heterosexual relations between consenting single soldiers, but it does not provide facilities for sexual relations. The lack of official facilities proved no obstacle to human nature.

The problem of nonconsensual sex in an integrated army was highlighted in 1997, three years after women were integrated into basic-training groups, by the scandal at the Aberdeen Proving Ground in which a number of male drill instructors were found guilty, after a military trial, of raping female trainees. The verdicts were followed by similar charges from women elsewhere in the army and led to a major investigation into sexual misconduct. In the Persian Gulf War, the army recorded twenty-four incidents it categorized as sexual assaults.

It was in Operations Desert Shield and Desert Storm, the defense of Saudi Arabia and the subsequent liberation of Kuwait (August 1990–February 1991), that the integration of women into the US Army was put to the test. When Saddam Hussein invaded Kuwait on August 2, 1990, more than 11 percent of those on active duty in the US armed forces were women. For the first time they would be called on to demonstrate their effectiveness in positions that had in recent history been reserved for men.

In Desert Shield, an international coalition of more than forty nations assembled an expeditionary force of some 700,000 troops, 1,600 aircraft, and 200 warships. The largest single contributor was the United States, with more than 400,000 troops, the first of whom began to arrive on August 9, 1990.

The US forces in the Persian Gulf eventually included some 37,000 women: 26,000 army, 3,700 navy, 2,200 marines, 5,300 air force, and 13 coast guard. Some 7 percent came from the active forces and 17 percent from the reserve and National Guard. On September 5 the first combined force of American men and women ever to ship out in wartime conditions left San Diego for the Persian Gulf. There was a heated debate in the United States about sending women, many of whom were wives and mothers, into danger.

When the women arrived in the Persian Gulf, there was also a clash of cultures. To Western eyes, the role of women in Saudi culture is severely restricted. Initially, the Saudi authorities were most reluctant to play host to female American and European soldiers. However, the female US troops were now so vital to the military machine that it was not practical to leave them at home. To smooth ruffled Saudi feathers, compromises were made. Female soldiers had to be escorted by men when off base, but they declined to modify their work practices and, to the scandal of Saudis, shed some of their clothes in the intense heat, which often reached 100 degrees F.

In Desert Shield and Desert Storm, women were called upon, among other things, to crew Patriot missile batteries, to fly helicopters on reconnaissance and search-and-destroy missions, and to drive convoys over the desert close to enemy positions. To do that, fuel, water, and ammunition had to be brought up to armored vehicles, trucks, and troop formations as they advanced through the desert. These missions could be dangerous. On January 31, 1991, Iraqi soldiers captured their first female prisoner of war, Specialist Melissa Rathbun-Nealy of the 233rd Transportation Company, when her twenty-five-ton tank transporter got stuck in the sand on the Kuwaiti-Saudi border. Rathbun-Nealy and her codriver, Specialist David Lockett, were released on March 3. They reported that they had been held in solitary confinement in Basra and had been well treated.

In the aftermath of the Persian Gulf War, the debate about female soldiers serving in combat was reignited. In the House of Representatives, the drive to repeal this remaining taboo was led by Congresswoman Patricia Schroeder, who based her case on the recommendation by the Defense Advisory Committee on Women in the Services (**DACOWITS,** see p. 160) that female soldiers should be allowed to become combatants. After the Gulf War, the so-called revolution in military affairs (RMA) encouraged a widespread view that the arrival of new high technologies had transformed the battlefield. In the brave new world of "push-button" warfare, Schroeder argued, the button could just as easily be pushed by a woman as by a man.

However, in 1994 the restrictions on women in combat formulated by WITA had been restated by Secretary of Defense Les Aspin and applied to support units that were "collocated"; that is, operating 100 percent of the time with direct ground-combat units. In these situations, the concept of a "front line" no longer exists. A bomb or rocket can strike anywhere, and in an era of asymmetrical warfare, insurgents can appear from nowhere when a convoy takes a wrong turn. Nevertheless, the Aspin formula remained in force through the war in Afghanistan, launched in late 2001 and still being fought in the summer of 2007, and the invasion and occupation of Iraq, to which there is likewise no clear end in sight.

The problem lies in the army's application of the formula. It has now developed the concept of deploying self-contained formations—"units of action"—specifically organized to undertake combat missions. The first of these formations to deploy to Iraq was the Third Infantry Division in the spring of 2005. Forward support companies (FSCs) would necessarily be an organic part of the "unit of action," but according to the Department of Defense's officially stated policy, they cannot contain women, obliging the army to shift its ground. It claimed that there were insufficient male soldiers to fill the FSCs, which they moved into gender-integrated brigade-support battalions, from which in theory the women can be withdrawn in the event of its parent formation going into action. Critics have argued that this is a recipe for chaos and have also pointed out that the army has ignored a statutory obligation to provide Congress with advance notification of what amounts to a rewriting of the Aspin regulations.

Between 2002 and 2006, more than 155,000 women were deployed to Afghanistan and Iraq, 15 percent of the active-duty force. However, not everyone welcomes the influx of women into the army. The military historian Martin van Creveld has argued that the feminization of the military is part symptom and part cause of the decline of the advanced military. Others have suggested that far from being in decline, the military is undergoing a rapid process of change in which it has to be more responsive to public opinion and must readjust to meet new demands on its skills, particularly in the field of peacekeeping. However, this is a role in which the US Army has often appeared ill at ease.

Reference: See also Lynch, Jessica, p. 229: England, Lynndie, p. 315: Hester, Leigh Ann, p. 223; Duckworth, Tammy, p. 221; and McSally, Martha, p. 232. Kayla Williams, *I Love My Rifle More Than You,* 2006.

US Marine Corps
1950–Present

After World War II, the US Marine Corps retained a small nucleus of Women Marines (WMs) in a postwar reserve. In 1948, Congress passed the Women's Armed Forces Integration Act, which authorized women in the Regular Component of the Corps. At the time, the women's reserve made up only 2 percent of the corps, and a woman could not hold permanent rank higher than lieutenant colonel. An exception was made for Katherine A. Towle, who in November 1948 was appointed director of Women Marines, after they were reconstituted as a regular component, with the temporary rank of colonel. In 1949, the corps established a training facility for women recruits at Parris Island, South Carolina, and a women's officer-training class at Quantico, Virginia.

In August 1950, when the Women Marines were mobilized for the Korean War, the number of women on active duty reached peak strength of 2,787. Their role was to take jobs in the United States to free men for active duty. In an era when the notion of "feminine mystique" was at its height, the US military was reluctant in the extreme to encourage the women in its ranks to look and act like men. Marine Corps women were required to wear lipstick and nail polish while on duty, as hostesses in Disneyland and Disney World are today.

The first WM to report for duty in Vietnam was Master Sergeant Barbara J. Dulinsky, on March 18, 1967. In theory at least, all WMs who served in Vietnam were volunteers, since nearly all of them had expressed a willingness to go and none had objected. WMs in Vietnam normally numbered ten enlisted women and two officers at any one time. They were based in Saigon and performed clerical duties with the Military Assistance Command, Vietnam (MACV) providing administrative support to marines assigned as far north as the Demilitarized Zone (DMZ).

The marine corps' principal preoccupation with the deployment of WMs to Vietnam seemed to be their clothing. Mindful perhaps of the World War II ordeal of army nurses in the Pacific (see **US Military Doctors and Nurses,** p. 270), the corps cautioned its women to take with them a supply of nylon stockings, sturdy cotton lingerie, summer uniforms, and a dozen pairs of heel lifts: "Heels can easily be extracted with a pair of pliers and new ones inserted with little difficulty." Vietnamese women were fascinated by the WMs, and Colonel Vera M. Jones later recalled walking down the streets of Saigon and being startled by the touch of a Vietnamese woman feeling her stockings. When two WMs visited Da Nang on an assignment, they noted that the US troops stationed there gained pleasure from the "unfamiliar click of the female high-heeled shoes."

The Tet offensive of January–February 1968 provided less agreeable experiences. At the time, enlisted WMs were still quartered at the Plaza Hotel dormitory, which took incoming enemy mortar fire and confined the WMs to their quarters. One of them wrote on February 3, 1969: "It's hard to believe that a war is going on around me. I sit here calmly typing this letter and yet can get up, walk to a window and watch the helicopters making machine gun and rocket strikes in the area of the golf course which is about three blocks away. At night I lie in bed and listen to the mortar rounds going off."

In 1974 the commandant, the most senior marine corps officer, authorized WMs to serve in specialized rear-echelon elements of the Fleet Marine Force. However, these women were prohibited from deployment with combat units or units that might be engaged in combat. Women were banned from all infantry, artillery, and armored units and could not serve as aircrew.

In May 1978, Brigadier General Margaret Brewer became the first WM to reach general grade in the role of director of information. In 1992 Lieutenant General Carol A. Mutter assumed command of the Third Force Service Support Group, Okinawa, the first woman to lead a fleet marine force at the flag level. Four years later, Mutter became the first WM, and the second woman in the history of the US armed forces, to be awarded three stars. She later became a member of **DACOWITS** (see p. 160), the body charged with advising on the role of women in the US armed forces.

During the Persian Gulf War, approximately one thousand WMs were deployed to the Gulf for Operations Desert Shield (1990) and Desert Storm (1991). In 1993, the marine corps accepted women into naval aviation pilot training, and in July 1993 Second Lieutenant Sarah Deal became the first WM to begin training. She graduated with her Golden Wings in April 1995 and went on to pilot one of the corps' heavy-lift CH-53E helicopters. She later served as adjutant for the commanding officer of the Marine Aircraft Group 16 at Marine Corps Air Station Miramar at San Diego. In 2003, in Operation Iraqi Freedom, WMs flew close-support and attack AH-1W helicopter combat missions for the first time. The corps also saw another first in Iraqi Freedom, when one of its enlisted women gave birth in a war zone aboard a combat ship.

The marine corps remains the only US armed service that maintains separate boot camp training units for men and women recruits. Basic training remains separate and, in theory at least, equal. Women in the marine corps serve in 93 percent of military occupation specialties and make up some 6 percent of the corps's strength, the lowest percentage in the US armed forces and possibly the result of the corps's well-earned reputation for toughness. Two more reasons are that a significant number of the corps's rear-echelon services are provided by the US Navy, and the marines spend much of their time aboard ship in forward deployment.

US Navy

On August 7, 1972, Admiral Elmo Zumwalt issued one of his famous "Z-grams," No. 116, whose subject was "Equal Rights and Opportunities for Women" in the US Navy. Zumwalt opened with a bold statement of intent:

> There has been much discussion and debate with respect to equal opportunity for women in our country over the past few years. My position with respect to women in the Navy is that they have historically played a significant role in the accomplishment of our naval mission. However, I believe we can do far more than we have in the past in according women equal opportunities to contribute their extensive talents to achieve full professional status.

Zumwalt's response to the imminent arrival of an all-volunteer navy was to be ring-fenced with qualifications. In 1976 women were admitted to the US Navy's academy at Annapolis, but they were still barred from being assigned to duties on all seagoing vessels, both combat and noncombat. In 1978, in the case of *Owens* v. *Brown,* a number of navy women successfully brought a class-action lawsuit against the navy, arguing that the prohibition violated their due-process rights under the Fifth Amendment. However,

the judgment noted that in certain circumstances, such as on transport vessels or in combat postings, the navy's position might be
justified. In the aftermath of *Owens* v. *Brown,* Lawrence Korb, assistant secretary of defense during the first Reagan administration
(1980–84), claimed that the issue of women in the navy took up
more of his time than any other.

The navy's immediate response to the *Owens* decision was the
Women in Ships Program, in which 54 female officers and 367
enlisted women were deployed on a number of support ships. The
program was expanded in 1983 and was seen as a qualified success.
Further impetus toward the concerted integration of women in
ships at sea was given by the Tailhook scandal (see below), which
exposed systemic harassment of women in the US Navy.

By 1991 women made up 10 percent of navy personnel, and
the high command was now determined to champion their integration into the service. The result was the Defense Authorization Act of 1994, which included the establishment of "specific
gender-neutral physical requirements for any job specialty requiring strength, endurance, or cardiovascular capacity." Integration
was not uniformly easy, and in the early months of the new era
many women initially experienced physical and verbal harassment.
One female surface warfare officer (SWO) recalled that the commanding officer on her ship offered the commander of a cruiser
ten movies in exchange for the women serving under him.

Nevertheless, the barriers to career advancement that had existed twenty years earlier were coming down. The combat ban for
women was repealed in 1991, but it was not until 1993 that Kara
Spears Hultgreen enrolled in the F-14 Tomcat program at Naval
Air Station Miramar in San Diego. Hultgreen qualified in 1994 as
the first female carrier pilot and was assigned to the Black Lions of
VF-213, who were preparing for a tour of duty in the Persian
Gulf. On October 25, 1994, Hultgreen was killed when her F-14
crashed on approach to the carrier USS *Abraham Lincoln* after a
routine mission in the waters off San Diego.

Hultgreen's death sparked a heated debate about the role of
women in the navy. An exacerbating factor was the Tailhook
scandal and the controversy this had stirred. The term "tailhook"

derives from the arresting device used on the decks of US aircraft carriers to hook a landing aircraft. It also became notorious in 1991 after women attending a Tailhook convention in Las Vegas, a number of whom were serving officers in the US Navy, were subjected to assault and sexual harassment by gangs of drunken naval aviators. The navy launched a subsequent investigation that led to the resignation of the navy secretary H. Lawrence Garrett III and the early retirement of Rear Admiral Duval M. Williams, the commander of the navy's investigative service, which had dragged its feet over the affair. The reverberations of the Tailhook controversy rumbled through the debate that followed the death of Kara Spears Hultgreen. Her detractors cited the crash as evidence of Hultgreen's incompetence, while supporters argued that she was the victim of engine failure. The argument generated more heat than light.

Thereafter naval aviation moved relatively quickly to enable female pilots to fly combat missions. One who attracted much media attention in 2001 was a fighter pilot on the carrier *Carl Vinson,* who was American-born but the product of an English girls' public school and was flying daily bombing raids on targets in Afghanistan in Operation Enduring Freedom. In Afghanistan, navy women could fly combat missions under a policy approved by President Clinton but were not permitted to engage in direct ground combat, particularly the insertion and extraction of special forces, a prohibition that prompted a protest from **DACOWITS** (see p. 160). General Charles R. Holland, heading the Special Operations Command, did not agree, pointing out that these operations inevitably involved aircrew in close "collocation" (contact) with ground units, which often led to direct ground combat. The number of women flying combat missions from aircraft carriers remained small. In 2002, during the war in Afghanistan, there were only two on board the carrier *Theodore Roosevelt* out of a female crew component of 500 (total crew 3,600).

The US Navy's first gender-integrated warship was the *Eisenhower,* with 415 women among the crew of 4,967, which sailed in 1994. The arrival of the women necessitated expensive modifications to the carrier's living quarters: gynecologists were brought on board to treat specifically female conditions; the ship's barbers were retrained to cut women's hair; menus were modified; and *Eisenhower* stocked up on contraceptives. Elaborate care was taken to anticipate every eventuality except, it would seem, the most obvious one. Before *Eisenhower* set sail, twenty-four women were deemed "nondeployable" because they were pregnant, and another fifteen were evacuated once the carrier was at sea. The navy was adamant that this did not affect operational efficiency.

In May 2003, The US Marine Corps brought a female marine back home after she had given birth on a navy warship in the Persian Gulf. She told her superiors that she did not know she was pregnant.

One exception to the US Navy's policy of allowing women to serve on warships applies to submarines. The high cost of converting submarines, as opposed to that for surface ships, is usually advanced as the reason, although this calculation is based on the assumption of semi-segregation of the male and female crew and the considerable structural changes this would entail. At present the US Navy retains the tradition of "hot bunking," in which each sleeping berth is used by more than one man on a rotating basis.

Britain's Royal Navy has a similar policy, although it has placed much emphasis on the risk of a submarine having to surface, and abort its mission, if a female crew member gives birth. These fears have not deterred other navies. In 1995, the Royal Norwegian Navy became the world's first navy to appoint a female submarine captain. Three years later the Royal Australian Navy followed suit and allowed women to serve on combat submarines, followed by Canada and Spain.

Reference: Susan H. Godson, *Serving Proudly: A History of Women in the US Navy,* 2003.

VOLUNTARY AID DETACHMENT
VAD, United Kingdom, World War I

In 1914 there were several uniformed services in Britain that were open to women: Queen Alexandra's Imperial Military Nursing Service, the Territorial Force Nursing Service, the **First Aid Nursing Yeomanry** (FANY, see p. 161), and the Voluntary Aid Detachments, the last a voluntary and unpaid service formed in 1910 to provide medical assistance in wartime.

By the outbreak of World War I there were more than 2,500 Voluntary Aid Detachments in the United Kingdom staffed by 47,000 individual VADs, two-thirds of whom were women. Initially the British War Office was unwilling to accept VADs serving in theaters of war, but the scale of casualties on the Western Front meant that in 1915 the restriction was removed. Women volunteers over the age of twenty-three and with more than three months' experience were allowed to serve overseas, not only in France but also in the Middle East and on the Eastern Front.

By September 1916, some eight thousand VADs were serving in military hospitals. Most of them were working under the General Service Scheme, introduced in June 1916, under which the military authorities made direct payment to VADs who were employed not only on nursing duties but in cooking, storekeeping, dispensing, and clerical work. The inexperience of some of the well-born VADs inevitably resulted in friction with their professional nursing counterparts.

Between 1914 and 1918, more than 90,000 VADs worked as nurses, ambulance drivers, clerks, and cooks. In addition to their contribution overseas, VADs operated hospitals in Britain. For many of them the war proved a life-changing experience, their newfound personal freedom coinciding with the British Empire's almost unimaginable loss of nearly a million men. The VADs went on to perform sterling service in World War II.

Reference: Gail Braybon and Penny Summerfield, *Out of the Cage: Women's Experience in Two World Wars,* 1987.

WOMEN'S ARMY AUXILIARY CORPS
WAAC, Later Women's Army Corps, United States, World War II

The Women's Army Auxiliary Corps was the brainchild of US congresswoman Edith Nourse Rogers, who in 1941 introduced a bill to establish an army women's corps separate and distinct from the existing **Army Nurse Corps** (see p. 248).

In World War I, women had worked with the US Army as volunteer communications specialists and dieticians but had not enjoyed official status and had received no legal protection, medical care, disability benefits, or pension rights. Rogers wanted to ensure that in the event of another war, women would be able to serve in the army while enjoying the same legal protection and benefits as the men.

The army's high command, while welcoming Rogers's initiative, argued for the creation of a body that would pose no threat to army culture, and the bill that emerged represented a compromise. The Women's Army Auxiliary Corps was set up to work with the army "for the purpose of making available to the national defense the knowledge, skill and special training of the women of the nation." The army would provide up to 150,000 female auxiliaries with food, uniforms, living quarters, pay, and medical care. However, women would not be allowed to command men, a far cry from the days when an estimated 70,000 men flocked to fight under **Boudicca**'s command (see p. 12), and the ranking system and pay reflected their lower status.

Other discriminations abounded to remind the women of their inferiority. Members of the WAAC might serve overseas, but they would not receive overseas pay. They were not covered by government life insurance, veterans' medical coverage, and death benefits granted to regular army soldiers. If they were captured, they would not be protected under international conventions.

In spite of opposition from conservative southern senators, Rogers's bill passed Congress by 249 votes to 86. The Senate approved the bill by 38 votes to 27 on May 14, 1942, and the president signed off on it the next day. Secretary of War Henry L. Stimson appointed as the WAAC's first director Oveta Culp Hobby, an experienced newspaperwoman who worked with the War Department's Public Relations Bureau and had a firm grasp of national and local politics. From the outset, it was Hobby's stated intention that the auxiliaries of the WAAC would free men for combat. Applicants had to be US citizens between the ages of twenty-one and forty-five with no dependents. They had to be at least five feet tall and weigh no less than one hundred pounds.

The first auxiliary units to reach the field were assigned to the Aircraft Warning Service (AWS). By October 1942, twenty-seven WAAC companies had been activated at AWS stations on the eastern seaboard, tracking the movement of every aircraft in their station area. Initially, the majority of auxiliaries were assigned roles as typists, stenographers, and drivers, but over time a wider number of opportunities opened up for the Wacs, as they were known. Some 40 percent served in the United States Army Air Force (USAAF), working as weather observers and forecasters, cryptographers, radio operators, sheet-metal workers, parachute riggers, link trainer instructors, bombsight-maintenance specialists, aerial reconnaissance photograph analysts, and control-tower operators. They also operated statistical-control tabulating machines—early computers—which held service records.

A few Wacs in the USAAF were given flying duties as radio operators on training flights, and as mechanics and photographers. One Wac in the China-Burma-India theater was awarded an Air Medal for her work in mapping "the Hump," the Allied air-supply route over the eastern Himalayas from Assam to China, which was opened in April 1942 when the Japanese cut the Burma Road.

Wacs also served in the Army Ground Forces (AGF) or Services of Supply (redesignated Army Service Forces [ASF] in 1943) field installations. The latter included a bewildering range of duties. Some Wacs in the ASF were assigned to the Chemical Warfare Service to work in laboratories and in the field. They trained as equipment testers, trialing walkie-talkies or meteorology instruments, or as glassblowers, making test tubes for the army's chemical laboratories. More than twelve hundred Wacs served in the signal corps as telephone switchboard, radio, and telegraph operators, cryptanalysts, photographic technicians, or analysts of photo-reconnaissance mosaics. The army's medical services benefited from WAAC laboratory and dental technicians, medical secretaries, and ward clerks.

Wacs assigned to the Corps of Engineers played a part in the Manhattan Project, the joint research effort undertaken by the Allies to develop the atomic bomb. A key element in the program was the cyclotron in the Chemistry Division at Los Alamos, in New Mexico, run by Master Sergeant Elizabeth Wilson. Another important Wac member of the Los Alamos setup was Jane Heydorn, an electronics technician who was closely involved in the construction of equipment for the testing of the A-bomb. Wacs also played their part at the Manhattan Project's seventy-eight-square-mile plant at Oak Ridge, Tennessee, maintaining top-secret files on the A-bomb program. Another team, based in London, helped to coordinate the flow of information passing between British and American scientists engaged on the project.

The Army Ground Forces (AGF) received some 20 percent of WAAC assignments. They encountered resistance from the army high command, some of whom felt that women could be used more effectively on war-industry production lines (see **Rosie the Riveter,** p. 180) rather than being trained for a variety of tasks within the military. As a result, many of the Wacs assigned to the AGF felt that they were not made welcome and subjected to overbearing discipline. Three-quarters of the Wacs in AGF were involved in routine office work. Many of the remainder worked in motor pools, where the chances for transfer and promotion were very limited.

The first women in the WAAC to serve overseas were five officers, two of them French-speakers, who were posted to General Eisenhower's headquarters in North Africa in November 1942. Their ship was torpedoed during the Atlantic crossing, leaving them to be picked up from their lifeboats by Royal Navy destroyers and delivered with no uniforms and supplies to Algiers, where anxious officers greeted them with fruit and toiletries. They later served on Eisenhower's staff in the North African, Mediterranean, and European campaigns.

The campaigns in North Africa and Italy saw a cautious movement toward employing a WAC unit, 669th Headquarters Platoon, as close as six miles from the front line, handling a complex communications network plotting the movement of troops and the supply chain that sustained them.

Early in 1943, the progress made by the WAAC was temporarily slowed by a mounting public relations crisis that threatened moves by the War Department to post more women overseas. True to the age-old tradition of stigmatizing as harlots or whores any women who ventured out of their housewife roles, the WAAC had gained an entirely undeserved reputation among many enlisted men for low morals, and the War Department sought to address this problem by integrating the WAAC into the regular army.

In July 1943 the organization became the Women's Army Corps (WAC) and all its members were given the option of either joining the army as Wacs or returning to civilian life. Some 25 percent, many of them from the AGF, decided to leave. For those who stayed, life in the WAC was accompanied by a realignment of the ranking system, which in the case of enlisted women now mirrored that enjoyed by their male counterparts. Subsequently, enlistment never matched the high levels achieved in the opening months of the war but nevertheless enabled the War Department to meet its overseas posting requirements.

In the middle of 1943, American women came close to handling weapons when the US Army conducted an experiment to determine whether they could effectively operate antiaircraft guns. Not only did the women who participated succeed, they also performed better than their male counterparts.

But the US Army's chief of staff, General Marshall, with the support of Colonel Hobby, concluded that the US public was not ready for women to assume so "masculine" a role. The results of the experiment were subsequently classified as "secret" (see **Mixed Antiaircraft Batteries,** p. 233).

The first Wacs to arrive in the European theater of operations in the summer of 1943 were 557 enlisted women and 19 officers serving with Eighth Air Force. A detachment of 300 Wacs served with the Supreme Headquarters Allied Expeditionary Force (SHAEF), located outside London in Bushey Park, and followed it to France in July 1944.

Working as stenographers, typists, translators, legal secretaries, cryptographers, telegraph and teletype operators, radiographers, and clerks, they played their part in the planning of Operations Neptune and Overlord, the Allied invasion of northwest Europe. By May 1945 there were some 7,500 Wacs in the European theater, stationed in England, France, and Germany.

From the outset the WAAC and WAC had been a racially segregated organization, and it was not until February 1945 that a battalion of black Wacs received a foreign assignment when the 688th
Central Posting Battalion, commanded by Major (later Colonel)
Charity Adams, arrived in the United Kingdom before moving to
France. The battalion was responsible for the redirection of mail
to all US service personnel in the European theater. To clear
the backlog of Christmas mail, the Wacs worked three eight-
hour shifts seven days a week. At peak numbers, 4,040 African-
American women served in the WAC, 4.5 percent of the total
strength.

Wacs who were posted to the Southwest Pacific Area Command operated far behind the lines and, at first, in trying conditions. Many arrived in the tropical theater kitted out with winter
clothing, including ski pants, earmuffs, and heavy twill overalls. A
shortage of khaki trousers exposed the women to malaria-carrying
mosquitoes. Appropriate clothing remained a problem until the
end of war and was often the cause of dermatitis, a skin disease ag-
gravated by heat and humidity. Evacuations for health reasons
eventually ran at 267 per thousand. Nevertheless, in all theaters it
was recognized that health problems were no greater for women
than for men.

The morale of women of the WAC in the southwest Pacific
also suffered because they were confined to compounds surrounded by barbed wire and escorted to work by armed soldiers,
an imposition many regarded as irksome. Male soldiers joked
sourly that the Wacs in the theater were not releasing men for
combat because so many troops were required to guard them.

Experience in the wartime services demonstrated the differences between women and men in their ability to function within
a military hierarchy. The WAC director noted that "women need
to remain individuals." The stress on individuality, coupled with
women's lack of experience with the military hierarchy, was reflected in their greater readiness to treat one another as individuals
and not as part of a troop.

Moreover, many Wacs resented the "caste system" that separated officers from enlisted personnel, because it restricted enlisted

women's contact with close friends or family members who were male officers. However, the qualities most valued by the WAC leaders were fairness, unselfishness, and sincere concern for the troops. Selfish ambition, while it might be tolerated by males in the male officer corps, was considered an "absolutely disqualifying" drawback in WAC officers.

After VE Day in Europe, on May 8, 1945, the demobilization of the WAC began, and by the end of December 1946 the corps's strength had shrunk to less than 10,000, the majority of whom were stationed in the United States. During World War II, 657 Wacs received medals and citations. Sixty-two were awarded the Legion of Merit, marking exceptionally meritorious conduct in the line of duty. Sixteen received the Purple Heart, awarded to soldiers wounded by enemy action. The majority of the Purple Heart Wacs had sustained their wounds in V-1 attacks in 1944 when they were stationed in London. Another 565 were awarded the Bronze Star for meritorious service overseas. By the end of the war, the WAC was releasing the equivalent of seven US Army divisions for active duty.

In 1946 the army asked Congress for the authority to establish the WAC as a permanent corps, and in June 1948 it achieved the status of a separate corps in the regular army. It remained part of the US Army until 1978, when it was assimilated into all but the combat branches of the US Army.

Reference: Mattie E. Treadwell, *The Women's Army Corps,* 1954.

WOMEN'S AUXILIARY AIR FORCE
WAAF, United Kingdom and Commonwealth, World War II

The WAAF was formed just before World War II broke out in June 1939, although WAAF personnel had been on duty for nearly a year before in the Royal Air Force (RAF) companies of the **Auxiliary Territorial Service** (see ATS, p. 153).

The principal objective of the WAAF was to release men for combat posts. Initially, recruits were accepted between the ages of seventeen and forty-four, joining for the "duration," and had to be prepared to serve anywhere, at home or abroad. By the outbreak

of war, the WAAF numbered nearly eight thousand officers and airwomen.

From July to October 1940, the women of the WAAF were in the front line of the Battle of Britain. Their most important roles were as radar operators in the Chain Home network of radar stations strung around Britain's coastline, and as plotters tracking the course of incoming German air attacks in RAF Fighter Command's sector stations, group headquarters, and general headquarters at Bentley Priory outside London.

In August 1940, Fighter Command's radar and sector stations came under heavy attack by the Luftwaffe. On August 18 the radar station in Poling, Sussex, was hit by bombers, which dropped eighty 500-pound bombs and almost put it out of action. The station's radar operators worked in little more than garden huts protected by piles of sandbags, but Corporal Avis Hearn, at four feet ten inches the smallest woman in the WAAF, remained at her post throughout the raid.

For her devotion to duty, Hearn was decorated with the Military Medal, an award usually reserved for men, by King George VI at Buckingham Palace. The key sector station at Biggin Hill, situated on the southern approaches to London, was also badly hit on August 18, and three more WAAFs—Corporal Elspeth Henderson and Sergeants Helen Turner and Elizabeth Mortimer—all won Military Medals for their bravery on that and subsequent days. In World War II there were only six awards of the Military Medal to members of the WAAF.

WAAF women eventually served in some eighty trades, including the highest trade group in RAF—that of fitter. They also served as flight and instrument mechanics, electricians, and armorers. On RAF Bomber Command stations they maintained and drove the tractors that towed "trains" of bombs to aircraft waiting on the hardstandings for their load.

For Bomber Command they also played a vital intelligence role in the interpretation of photographs of enemy targets and in debriefing the aircrew who attacked them. It was a WAAF section officer, Constance Babington Smith, who was the first to spot evidence of Hitler's V-weapon program when studying

reconnaissance photographs of the German research establishment at Peenemünde on the Baltic island of Usedom.

One of the most physically demanding wartime tasks under-taken by women was the operation of balloon sites, an important element in Britain's air defenses, which deterred low-flying bombers from attacking important targets and kept them at a height where they were more vulnerable to antiaircraft fire. In the spring of 1941, WAAFs began training to take over the flying of balloons. Crews of ten airmen were replaced by sixteen airwomen, and by the end of the year three balloon sites a day were being handed over to the WAAF, which eventually operated 1,029 sites and provided 47 percent of the personnel.

These women often lived in primitive conditions and at regu-lar intervals were exposed to danger from the unforgiving system of ropes, cables, and wires that raised and held the balloon aloft. Because they were not working with aircraft, these WAAFs were regarded as a "Cinderella service."

By 1944, nearly all the service meteorological officers of the Flying Training Command were women. By March 1945, there were some 180,000 women serving in the WAAF, constituting 22 percent of RAF strength in Great Britain. During the course of the war, 187 lost their lives, 420 were wounded, and 4 went miss-ing. Among the decorations awarded to WAAF members were three George Crosses (the gallantry award second only to the Vic-toria Cross), six Military Medals, 1,489 Mentions in Dispatches, and two Commendations for Brave Conduct (see also **Air Trans-port Auxiliary,** p. 151).

Reference: Squadron Leader Beryl Estcott, *Women in Air Force Blue,* 1989.

WOMEN'S AUXILIARY ARMY CORPS
WAAC, Later Queen Mary's Army Auxiliary Corps,
United Kingdom, World War I

On December 8, 1916, the War Office instructed Lieutenant General H. M. Lawson to prepare a report on the numbers and condition of the British troops employed in France. A month later, Lawson's report contained a recommendation that women be employed on the Western Front.

This arrived in the middle of an ongoing debate about the use of women in the British army. In March 1917, the British commander-in-chief in the field, General Sir Douglas Haig, told the War Office that he accepted the proposal in principle, although he had a long list of "objections and difficulties."

By then, however, the wheels were already in motion and a recruiting program had been launched through the office of the director-general of National Service. On July 7, 1917, the Army Council's Instruction 1069 became the formal basis of the WAAC, which was led by a chief controller, Mrs. Chalmers Watson, a distinguished medical woman from Edinburgh and the sister of the director-general of National Service, Sir Auckland Geddes.

Because a commission from the Crown could be held only by male subjects, the WAAC had no military ranks: "controllers" and "administrators" took the place of officers, NCO equivalents were called "forewomen," and privates were "workers." As with the **Voluntary Aid Detachment** (**VAD,** see p. 202), the intention was to restrict the WAAC, as far as possible, to middle- and upper-class women, but the majority of the rank and file consisted of women from the working class. They messed separately from the controllers and administrators.

Members of the WAAC who remained in Britain could live at home, provided that this did not interfere with the efficient performance of their duties. Many of the working-class recruits joined the WAAC with no warm underclothing and a surfeit of head lice. As a result, Mrs. Chalmers Watson issued a remarkably optimistic list of recommended items for each recruit before she joined an active unit:

1 pair strong shoes or boots (this of course being in addition to the free issue)

1pr low-heeled shoes for house wear

2prs khaki stockings (this of course being in addition to the free issue)

2prs at least warm combinations

2prs dark coloured Knickers with washable linings

2 warm Vests of loosely woven Shetland wool

1 doz khaki Handkerchiefs

2prs Pyjamas or 2 strong Nightdresses

Burning Sanitary Towels

It is advisable if possible to bring as well, a Jersey or Golf Jacket which should be worn under the frock coat in cold weather

The WAAC claimed that the women in its ranks "do all kinds of work which a woman can do as well as a man, and some of which she can do better." The aim, however, was for each member to release a man for combat duty, just as it would be for the ATS and other auxiliary services in World War II. Most of the duties undertaken by the WAAC lay in the traditional female domain—cooking and catering, telephony and clerical work—but its members also worked on lines of communication, as printers and as motor mechanics.

In April 1918, the WAAC was renamed Queen Mary's Army Auxiliary Corps, but the new title was not generally adopted and its members remained Wacs. By the following month there were just under seven thousand WAAC officers and other ranks serving in France, some of them with the American Expeditionary Force. They were restricted to the communications zone, which meant that with the exception of air attacks, they were always out of the firing line. To minimize external sex differences, the salute and other forms of military comportment were introduced, along with strict rules of movement, dress, and behavior. The women's uniforms were subtly defeminized by removing the breast pocket, a measure that was thought to deemphasize the bust.

In spite of the application of strict rules of fraternization, the presence of several thousand Wacs in France encouraged rumors of promiscuity. This led in February 1918 to the appointment of an all-woman commission of inquiry, which produced this magisterial conclusion:

We can find no justification of any kind for the vague accusations of immoral conduct on a large-scale which have been circulated about the WAAC. The chief difficulty of our task has
lain in the very vague nature of the damaging charges we were
requested to negotiate. It is common knowledge that fantastic
tales have passed from mouth-to-mouth of the numbers of
WAAC women returned to England for misconduct of the
gravest character.

In other words, not guilty as charged. This was neither the first
time nor the last that accusations of immorality would be made
against women acting independently and out of the direct control
of men (see **US Women's Army Auxiliary Corps,** p. 203).

Reference: Arthur Marwick, *Women of War, 1914–18*, 1977.

WOMEN'S ROYAL NAVAL SERVICE
WRNS, United Kingdom, World War II

The WRNS, universally known as the Wrens, had been formed in
World War I and was demobilized in 1919. When it was re-
formed in April 1939, many of its original members enrolled again.
Others often came from the families of naval personnel living in
the ports in which Wren units were being formed. Many of these
Wrens continued to live at home and were classed as "immobile."
As the war progressed, many volunteered for "mobile" service not
only in the naval shore establishment in the United Kingdom but
also in the Middle and Far East.

In line with the other British auxiliary services, the WRNS
had as its principal aim the replacement of naval personnel in shore
establishments, releasing men for front-line service. Although the
bulk of Wrens served in shore establishments, they adopted the
language of the Royal Navy, always cooking in a "galley" rather
than a kitchen and sleeping "below decks" in "cabins"; Portsmouth,
a great naval city, was "Pompey," a midmorning snack was a "stand
easy bun," and "Jimmy the One" was a first lieutenant.

For the British, the Battle of the Atlantic was the longest and most crucial campaign of World War II, fought from the very first day to the last. The daily progress of the battle was plotted by Wrens in the operations room of the Western Approaches Command. Many were also employed in top-secret naval communications, decoding encrypted messages of the Kriegsmarine and later the Imperial Japanese Navy.

In general, Wrens were not allowed to go to sea, but a few exceptions were made. Wrens served on troopships in the Atlantic and were tasked with signaling and code-breaking duties. When Prime Minister Winston Churchill sailed to Casablanca for the big Allied conference of January 1943, twelve Wrens accompanied the British contingent.

Away from the spotlight, Wrens manned harbor craft in all weathers; served as signalers, coastal mine spotters, and air and radio mechanics; trained as welders, carpenters, and electricians; handled torpedoes and depth charges; and maintained and repaired ships in naval bases. By March 1945 there were some 73,200 women serving in the WRNS. Following the German surrender, a Wren contingent assisted in the Allies' disbanding of the German women's naval auxiliary, the **Helferinnen** (see p. 103). In World War II, 102 Wrens were killed and 22 were wounded.

Reference: Ursula Stuart Mason, *The Wrens, 1917–1977, A History of the Women's Royal Naval Service,* 1977.

7

AT THE SHARP END

―∞∞∞―

Modern Women Soldiers, Sailors, and Airwomen

We are the pointing end of the spear. I understand the marching orders, and we will be prepared to deploy . . . with an aggressive attitude that we will win. I hope I am a role model to both men and women, because we are a fighting force and should not be concerned with the differences between us.

—Lieutenant Colonel Martha McSally, taking command of the US Air Force 354th Fighter Squadron, based at Davis-Monthan Air Force Base, Arizona, 2004

In World War II, the physical demands made on those delivering combat aircraft, or flying them in action, were considerable. The stamina, strength, and determination required of a Red Air Force fighter pilot such as **Lily Litvak** (see p. 227) demand respect. But in the postwar world, as women's emancipation gathered speed in the West, twentieth-century technology kept pace with twentieth-century freedoms to offset the difference between the sexes.

As a result, the introduction of women to combat in the armed forces of the late twentieth century has been accomplished with the least difficulty in navies and air forces, where technology has removed a number of the demands previously made on muscle power and upper-body strength (see also **US Army**, p. 188). Litvak was a slight figure, like the German aviator **Hanna Reitsch** (see

p. 231) and the modern US combat pilot **Martha McSally** (see p. 232), for whom the USAF had to modify its height requirements to enable her to serve. Nevertheless, aloft in her A-10, McSally could pull g-forces with the best of them.

In the 1930s, governments of all political persuasions had encouraged their populations to become more "air-minded," and female flyers came to the fore as pioneering figures of long-distance aviation. Some, like the Soviet **Marina Raskova** (see p. 236), the American **Jacqueline Cochran** (see p. 219), and Reitsch herself became national heroines, carving out careers in a previously male-dominated environment. Photographs of the diminutive Reitsch, surrounded by burly Luftwaffe officers in creaking leathers, are both touching and, in view of Reitsch's subsequent career in World War II, slightly sinister.

The trajectory of Raskova's, Reitsch's, and Cochran's careers in the war years provides an insight into the contrasting Soviet, German, and American approaches to the employment of women in the front line of the national struggle. The Soviets proved the least squeamish when it came to training and deploying women at the sharp end (see **Night Witches,** p. 235). The Americans and their British allies shrank from following suit but nonetheless channeled the enthusiasm and courage of many women aviators into two organizations, the **WASP** (see p. 220) and the **ATA** (see p. 151), which played a vital role in the ferrying of warplanes to the airfields where they were needed.

Reitsch, however, plowed a lonely furrow in Nazi Germany, where ideological reluctance to commit women fully to the war effort was addressed only when the tide of war was flowing inexorably against Germany. It was typical, perhaps, of Reitsch's misplaced fervor for the Nazi regime that she was, quite literally, in at the death of the Third Reich, piloting a light aircraft into a blazing Berlin in April 1945, to deliver a high-ranking comrade to a futile conference in Hitler's bunker.

Unlike Reitsch, most of these modern women warriors had no military background or previous training. But under pressure of events, they rapidly became proficient and like many women in other areas of war often discovered talents they did not know they had. New forms of transport offered a new dimension of war, with opportunities few women had dreamed of. For Cochran, McSally, and others, the challenge of flight and the chance to gain equal footing with men was a major part of the appeal. One of the pioneers of women's aviation, Amelia Earhart, observed: "I want to do it because I want to do it. Women must try to do things that men have tried. If they fail, their failure must be but a challenge to others."

These new fields of endeavor offered unprecedented opportunities to exceptional women such as the US Navy's **"Amazing" Grace Hopper** (see p. 225), a prime mover in the invention of the computer language COBOL, who helped to shape one aspect of the technology that had itself shaped the entry of women into the "senior service" of the sea. As navies became more technologized, numbers of women began to sign up along with men, striking out for new freedoms and, in doing so, reclaiming the old. In 1998, US Navy captain **Kathleen McGrath,** the first woman to command a US warship (see p. 231), was hailed as breaking fresh ground. In reality, she was following in the footsteps of other female sea captains like the redoubtable Artemisia of ancient Greece, renewing a tradition dating back thousands of years.

There is nonetheless a groundswell of continuing dissent arising from those who are profoundly dismayed by what they see as the feminization of the modern military. In the spring of 2000, US Navy lieutenant John Gadzinski observed of the aircraft carrier USS *Eisenhower,* "This is a boat where our job is to put bombs on target, missiles on target." He then went on to complain that *Eisenhower's* maiden cruise with a crew that was 10 percent female was a PR exercise aimed at spinning the success of a gender-integrated navy. Gadzinski claimed that female sailors who worked in data processing were placed on the flight deck and the control tower "to make a pretty picture for the VIPs on their walk through."

Despite such skepticism, nations with entrenched traditions of female subjection have also taken small but significant steps toward the training of female combat aircrew. Few countries could be less friendly to the integration of women into the armed forces than those of the Indian subcontinent, but the Pakistan Air Force (PAF) inducted four women as fighter pilots in March 2006.

At the passing-out parade at the PAF academy at Risalpur, one of the women, Nadia Gul, received the trophy for the best academic achievement along with two of her male colleagues. Despite Gul's success, the PAF remains male-dominated, and only time will determine the impact of the presence of a small number of women on the academy's male commanders and cadets.

As all modern air forces were modeled on established military organizations, women worldwide are still a minority of pilots and aircrew and have by no means conquered all the resistance of tradition and good old-fashioned misogyny. Nevertheless, women of every country start off in their air force in conditions of greater parity with men than they can ever hope to achieve as latecomers to the far older services of the army and the navy, whose history reaches back hundreds if not thousands of years. For this reason and with America once again leading the way, the United States Air Force achieved a significant international first when **Jeanne Holm** (see p. 224) was promoted to two-star general, making her the highest-ranking airwoman in the world.

COCHRAN, JACQUELINE
US Aviator and Head of World War II Women's Airforce Service Pilots, WASPs, 1910–80

Born an orphan in Florida, Jacqueline Cochran was raised in poverty by foster parents. Nothing in her background indicated the talent that would make her a pioneering aviator and leader in World War II. She was eight years old before she was given her first pair of shoes and two years later was working in a cotton mill. She had virtually no formal education and in later years would take an oral examination for her pilot's license.

She worked in a beauty parlor in Montgomery, Alabama, before moving to New York in 1929 and becoming a hairdresser at Saks Fifth Avenue. In 1932, while in Miami, she met the wealthy entrepreneur and aviator Floyd Odlum, whom she later married.

Odlum encouraged Cochran to fly, and in the summer of 1932 she obtained a pilot's license in just three weeks.

In 1934 Cochran set the first of many records when she flew and tested the first supercharger installed on an aircraft engine. In the same year she achieved another first, piloting an unpressurized biplane to 34,000 feet while wearing an oxygen mask. Cochran then became the first woman to fly in the 1935 Bendix transcontinental race, winning the overall title in 1938 in an untried Seversky fighter. In 1938 she received the General William E. Mitchell memorial award for making that year's greatest contribution to aviation.

In June 1941 Cochran became the first woman to pilot a US Army Air Force Lend-Lease bomber across the Atlantic. On her arrival in Britain, she liaised closely with Pauline Gower, the head of the women's division of the ATA (**Air Transport Auxiliary, p. 151**). In 1943 Cochran was the driving force behind the formation of the Women Airforce Service Pilots (WASP), the US equivalent of Britain's Air Transport Auxiliary, and was appointed its director. More than 25,000 women applied for training with the WASP, and eventually 1,074 graduated from its rigorous training program. They were to fly some sixty million miles for USAAF, suffering thirty-eight fatalities, approximately one for every sixteen thousand hours flown. For her services to her country in World War II, Cochran received the Distinguished Service Medal. More than thirty years later, in 1977, she was among those who successfully lobbied the US Congress for veteran benefits for the WASP. From 1948 to 1970 she served in the Air Force Reserve with the rank of colonel.

With the war over, she returned to record breaking, forming a close alliance with Colonel Fred. J. Ascani and Captain Chuck Yeager of the air force. In May 1953, flying a North America F-86 Sabre jet and with Yaeger flying on her wing, Cochran set a new world speed record of 652.3 miles per hour, and broke the sound barrier, at Edwards Air Force Base, California. Early in 1954 she was awarded the Harmon trophy as the outstanding female pilot of the year.

In 1961 she set a succession of speed records flying a Northrop

T-38 Talon trainer and, flying the notoriously unforgiving Lockheed F-104G Starfighter, recorded a speed of 1,429.3 miles per hour, the fastest by a woman. She also claimed a five-hundred-kilometer record with the F-104, recording a speed of 1,127.4 miles per hour. A pilot to rate alongside the finest of the heroic age of jet-powered aviation, Cochran subsequently became active in politics and journalism and headed her own cosmetics company.

Reference: Jacqueline Cochran, *Jackie Cochran: An Autobiography*, 1987.

DUCKWORTH, TAMMY
US Army Major, Iraq War Veteran, and Politician, b. 1968

Like the British World War II Hurricane pilot Douglas Bader, Ladda "Tammy" Duckworth lost both her legs when her helicopter was shot down in Iraq. In recovering to launch a political career as a fierce critic of the war, she displayed a courage comparable to that of Bader himself, the legendary "legless ace" of RAF Fighter Command.

Duckworth was born in Thailand, the daughter of an American father and a Thai mother. Her family later moved to Hawaii, where she graduated from the University of Hawaii in 1989 with a degree in political science, to which she added a master's degree in international affairs from George Washington University. While she was working toward her PhD at George Washington, Duckworth joined the Reserve Officers' Training Corps (ROTC) in 1990 and two years later became a commissioned officer in the Army Reserve, attending flight school, where she chose to fly helicopters because it was one of the few combat jobs open to women.

As a member of the Illinois Army National Guard, Duckworth was subsequently deployed to Iraq. On November 12, 2004, the UH-60 Black Hawk helicopter she was copiloting was hit by a rocket-propelled grenade (RPG) fired by Iraqi insurgents. In the explosion and crash, she suffered massive injuries to her legs and severe damage to her right arm. It took eight days for Duckworth to regain consciousness, and when she came around she asked why her feet hurt, unaware that she had lost both her legs.

On December 3, 2004, Duckworth was awarded the Purple Heart, and three weeks later was promoted to the rank of major at the Walter Reed Army Medical Center, also receiving the Air Medal and the Army Commendation Medal. She was fitted with artificial legs, which enabled her to regain mobility and play a part in establishing the Intrepid Foundation, dedicated to the care and rehabilitation of injured veterans.

Duckworth quickly became a vocal critic of the Bush administration's policy on the provision of veteran care and the US Army's slowness in addressing the problem. She stated that although she had disagreed with Bush's decision to go to war, she had nevertheless done her duty, adding that the United States would have been better advised to pursue those behind the attacks on Washington and New York on September 11, 2001, particularly Osama bin Laden, rather than invade Iraq.

In March 2006 Duckworth became the Democratic nominee for the US House of Representatives in the Sixth District of Illinois, a Republican stronghold. The following September she was chosen by the Democratic Party to respond to President George W. Bush's weekly radio address. Duckworth went straight on the attack:

> Instead of a plan or a strategy, we get shallow slogans like Mission Accomplished and Stay the Course. . . . Those slogans are calculated to win an election. But they won't help us win our mission in Iraq. . . . I didn't cut and run, Mr. President. Like so many others, I proudly fought and sacrificed, my helicopter was shot down long after you proclaimed "mission accomplished."

In her campaign, Duckworth was also fiercely critical of the wasteful management of the war in Iraq, pointing out that the lavish meals with which she and her colleagues were provided were no substitute for properly equipped and maintained hardware. She singled out the waste of huge sums of money on civilian contractors to perform tasks that could have been undertaken at a fraction of the cost by the US military. Her Republican opponents launched an expensive mailing campaign against Duckworth, attacking her as "unhinged," and she failed to be elected.

Reference: www.TammyDuckworth.com.

HESTER, LEIGH ANN
US National Guardswoman, b. 1982

Hester was the first woman to receive the Silver Star, the third-highest US military service award, since World War II. Her undoubted courage nevertheless highlighted the dilemma facing the US military over the role played by its female personnel on active service (see p. 194–196).

Born in Bowling Green, Kentucky, Hester joined the National Guard in April 2001 and was posted to Iraq as a sergeant in the 617th Military Police Company. On March 20, 2005, Hester's squad was shadowing an unarmed supply convoy when it was caught in an insurgent ambush south of Baghdad. Under fire from rocket-propelled grenades, Hester maneuvered her ten-man squad into a flanking position to cut off the insurgents' line of retreat, before launching an attack on the trenches from which they were firing.

Working with her squad leader, Sergeant Timothy Nein, Hester attacked the trench line with M203 grenade-launcher rounds and M4 rifle fire, killing three of the insurgents. At the end of a fierce skirmish, twenty-seven insurgents were dead, six were wounded, and one had been taken prisoner. Nein was also awarded a Silver Star for his part in the action.

Reference: Thomas E. Ricks, *Fiasco: The American Military Adventure in Iraq,* 2006.

HOLM, JEANNE
First American Woman to Rise to the Rank of Two-Star General,
USAF, b. 1921

Holm joined the US military in 1942 and retired three decades later after becoming the first woman in any branch of the service to rise to the rank of two-star general.

Born in Portland, Oregon, she trained as a silversmith and enlisted in 1942 after Congress established the Women's Army Auxiliary Corps (WAAC). In 1943 she was commissioned as a third officer, the WAAC equivalent of a second lieutenant. By 1945 she was a captain in charge of a woman's training regiment. At war's end she returned to civilian life to earn a university degree.

In 1948, during the Berlin blockade, Holm was recalled to active duty and in 1949 transferred to the United States Air Force (USAF), advancing through the grades to become a major general in 1973, the highest rank achieved by any woman in the US armed forces.

One of her early assignments was to the post of war plans officer for the Eighty-fifth Air Deport Wing in Germany during the Berlin Airlift and the early stages of the Korean War. She was the first woman to attend the Air Command and Staff School and from 1957 to 1961 was based in Naples, responsible for supervising manpower needs at the headquarters of the Allied Air Forces for Southern Europe. From 1961 to 1965 she served in Washington as a congressional staff officer, after which she was appointed director of female personnel in the USAF. In this position Holm was a powerful force for the opening up of career opportunities for women in the USAF and the abolition of discriminatory regulations.

She spent her last two years before retirement as director of the Secretariat of Air Force Personnel. After her retirement Holm remained immensely active, working on the Defense Manpower Commission and serving as a member of the Defense Advisory Committee on Women in the Services. A strong supporter of the women's rights movement, Holm is a member of the

National Women's Political Caucus and founder and first chairperson of Women in Government.

Reference: Jeanne Holm, *Women in the Military: An Unfinished Revolution,* 1986.

HOPPER, "AMAZING" GRACE
Wartime Naval Officer and US Navy Computer Expert, b. 1906, d. 1992

Dubbed "Amazing Grace" and "the First Lady of Software," Hopper chaired the committee that developed COBOL, the automatic programming language that in the 1940s launched computers as a universal instrument. She was also credited with coining the term "bug" to describe the problems that beset computers and their programs. Her lifelong love affair with electronics began when World War II drew her out of teaching math and into the US Navy Reserve.

She was born in New York. Her grandfather was a civil engineer commissioned to lay out a section of the Bronx, and as a small girl she spent many happy hours trailing around after him, carrying his measuring stick. The experience fostered a love of geometry and maps, and Hopper later confessed that she would have become an engineer herself on graduating from Vassar with a degree in mathematics, had that career path been open to women in the 1920s. She contented herself with a doctorate in mathematics from Yale and in 1931 returned to Vassar to take up a teaching post.

In December 1943 Hopper joined the navy reserve and was posted to the computer laboratory at Harvard, where she had a life-defining encounter with the first large-scale digital computer in the United States, the Mark I. In 1945, when Hopper was a lieutenant assigned to the Bureau of Ordnance computation project, a breakdown in one of the Mark I's circuits was found to have been caused by a trapped moth, which was removed with tweezers and prompted Hopper to coin the word "bug."

Hopper had had a much better war than most and developed a liking for the service. When she was demobilized, she was informed that she was too old (at forty) to join the navy proper, but she retained her place in the reserve and joined a company that was building Univac 1, the first commercial computer. The company subsequently merged with the Sperry Corporation, and it was with Sperry that Hopper worked on the programming idea that led to COBOL. In 1966, Hopper retired from the reserve, only to find that she was still needed. She was recalled a year later to active duty with the Naval Data Automation Command (NDAC), where she was tasked with imposing a standard on the US Navy's plethora of computer languages.

In 1975, Congress passed legislation enabling the navy to promote Hopper to the rank of captain, as she was still theoretically on the retired list. In 1983 she received a special presidential appointment to the rank of rear admiral. She became head of the NDAC and for two decades worked at the Pentagon. A slight woman of intense vigor, Hopper was a firm believer in giving her juniors (or "kids," as she called them) complete creative freedom. She found Pentagon bureaucracy irksome and was happy to encourage her "kids" to cut through red tape, observing, "You can always apologize later."

Hopper had even less time for feminism and in 1969 was delighted to be named the First Computer Sciences Man of the Year. She once remarked, "I'm thoroughly in the dog house with the women's liberation people. They once asked me if I had ever met prejudice, and I said I've always been too busy to look for it." Hopper chose to go her own way, a self-professed "old-fashioned patriot" who wore a full medal-beribboned uniform at every opportunity and smoked like a chimney. Sadly, she was not granted her wish to live until the age of ninety-four and witness the ending of the year 1999, when she would have been able to whoop it up at the parties given to usher in the millennium. After that, she declared, she would like to "retire to a mountaintop with a computer and send messages to everyone telling them where they are going wrong."

Reference: Patricia J. Murphy, *Grace Hopper: Computer Whiz,* **2004.**

LITVAK, LILY
"The White Rose of Stalingrad," Red Air Force Fighter Pilot,
b. 1921, d. 1943

Litvak was not only a seasoned World War II fighter ace but also a gift to Soviet propaganda during a key passage of the war on the Eastern Front. Such was the respect in which she was held by her opposite numbers in the Luftwaffe that, according to legend, it required no fewer than eight of them to put an end to her life.

From her teenage years, Litvak was "air-minded," and at the age of fourteen she joined her local Aeroklub, making her solo debut a year later and subsequently joining the Soviet paramilitary air formation, the Osoaviakhim, as a flight instructor.

In the opening phase of the German invasion of the Soviet Union, Operation Barbarossa, the Red Army Air Force (VVS) suffered grievous losses at the hands of the Luftwaffe. On the first day of Barbarossa, Luftflotte 2 (Second Air Fleet), supporting Army Group Center, destroyed 528 Soviet aircraft on the ground and 210 in the air. Between June and October 1941 the VVS lost 5,316 aircraft, many of them on the ground. However, in the depths of disaster lay the seeds of recovery. The large numbers of obsolete aircraft destroyed on the ground did not entail the loss of aircrew, who were retrained on the potent new types that the VVS was bringing into service.

The disastrous performance of the VVS in the first two months of Barbarossa encouraged the formation of female aviation groups. The driving force behind this innovation was **Marina Raskova** (see p. 236), a celebrated record-breaking aviatrix of the 1930s, who secured the formation of three complete women's air regiments, the 586th Fighter, the 587th Bomber, and the 588th Night Bomber Regiments.

Litvak joined the 586th Fighter Regiment, which had been intended as a reserve formation flying support missions. However, in the spring of 1942 the attrition of the air war on the Eastern Front thrust the 586th into the front line.

Litvak and a number of other women, including Katya Budanova, earned transfers in September 1942 to the all-male 437th

Fighter Regiment flying over Stalingrad. On September 13, piloting a Lavochkin La-5 fighter, Litvak scored her first victory, shooting down a Junkers Ju88 fighter-bomber. She scored two more victories with the La-5 before switching to the durable Yakovlev Yak-1, with which she scored all her subsequent kills. In late 1942, Litvak was transferred to the Ninth Guards Fighter Regiment and then, in January 1943, to the crack 296th Fighter Regiment (subsequently redesignated Seventy-third Guards Fighter Regiment), flying "free hunt" missions against targets of opportunity. Shortly afterward she received the Order of the Red Star to add to the Order of the Red Banner and the Order of the Patriotic War. Twice she had to make forced landings due to battle damage, and twice she was wounded.

In February 1943 Litvak married Aleksei Solomatin, a fellow pilot from the Seventy-third Guards Fighter Regiment, who was killed in May of that year. A month later, she lost her comrade Budanova, who also died in air combat. Litvak was by now a national heroine, albeit a most reluctant one who was physically and emotionally exhausted by the strain of combat flying. Photographs of the time show a slim, fair-haired woman with a steady but anxious gaze. She became expert at giving Red Army photographers the slip.

On August 1, 1943, while escorting ground-attack aircraft on her third sortie of the day, Litvak's fighter was intercepted and shot down by a gaggle of German fighters. Her aircraft was not found, prompting the Soviet high command to surmise that she might have been captured, and thus to deny her the award of Hero of the Soviet Union.

It was not until 1979 that the crash site was found. Litvak's remains lay beneath her aircraft's wing and indicated that she had succumbed to a head wound. She had flown 168 combat missions, gaining twelve individual kills and three shared victories. Ten years later Litvak was given an official burial, and in May 1990 President Mikhail Gorbachev posthumously made her a Hero of the Soviet Union.

Reference: Reina Pennington, *Wings, Women, and War: Soviet Airwomen in World War II Combat*, 2002.

LYNCH, JESSICA
US Prisoner of War in Iraq, b. 1983

When PFC Jessica Lynch was freed from a hospital in An Nasiriya, Iraq, on April 1, 2003, it was the first rescue of an American POW by US forces since World War II, and the first ever of a woman. However, soon after the operation had been completed, it became clear that the US Army's account of her capture and rescue was not wholly accurate. As it turned out, the pretty, petite, blond and blue-eyed Lynch was rescued only to be exploited as a propaganda tool.

Lynch was born in Palestine, West Virginia and, while serving in Iraq as a supply clerk with the 507th Maintenance Company, was captured by Iraqi forces after the convoy with which she was traveling on March 23 made a wrong turn and was ambushed near An Nasiriya, a major crossing point over the Euphrates River northwest of Basra. Eleven soldiers were killed in the ambush, including Lynch's friend PFC Lori Piestewa. Lynch was initially listed as missing in action.

After a period in the custody of the Iraqi unit that had taken her prisoner, Lynch was taken to the Saddam hospital in An Nasiriya. After her rescue, staff at the hospital, including two doctors, Harith al-Houssona and Anmar Uday, stated that they had done their best to protect Lynch from the Iraqi fedayeen and government agents who were using the hospital as a base for their operations. When she was rescued, Lynch was suffering from a head laceration, an injury to her spine, and fractures to her right arm, both legs, and her right foot and ankle. Most of these are consistent with the injuries noted on her arrival at the hospital by Dr. al-Houssona. However, al-Houssona was later adamant that Lynch had not sustained gunshot and stab wounds, nor had she been raped and sodomized, as claimed in an authorized biography of Lynch written by Rick Bragg, *I Am a Soldier, Too*. When first seen by al-Houssona, Lynch was fully clothed and exhibited no signs of having being raped or mistreated.

Much of the credit for Lynch's rescue was later given to Muhammad Odeh al-Rahaief, a local lawyer, who insisted that his wife was a nurse at the hospital, a claim the hospital later denied. Muhammad was also to assert that while he was in the hospital he had seen an Iraqi colonel physically assaulting Lynch and was so shocked that he felt impelled to reveal her whereabouts to the Americans. Lynch has no memory of this incident.

Muhammad seems to have been one of a number of Iraqis who told American troops that Lynch was in the hospital. It is possible that he was also the so-called agent who was briefed by US intelligence and sent back into the hospital to film its layout with a concealed camera, revealing the route to Lynch's room, where she occupied the only specialist bed in the facility.

On the night of April 1, 2003, while US Marines staged a diversionary attack, a team of elite special forces, including members of the US Navy's counterterrorism formation (DEVGRU), the Air Force pararescue men, and a security unit of US Army Rangers, launched a successful raid to extract Lynch; the raid was filmed from start to finish. Staff at the hospital later accused the special forces of behaving with excessive zeal, particularly as they were quick to inform the American troops that the site had been abandoned by the Iraqi military twenty-four hours before their arrival, and Lynch was not under guard. It is safe to say, however, that while conducting an operation like this, the special forces do not necessarily take bystanders, whether innocent or not, unquestioningly at their word.

What is more questionable is the subsequent handling of the story by the US military, which, at a difficult moment in the prosecution of the war, felt it needed a broad-brush, "feel-good" item to cheer American audiences at home. Rushing a swiftly edited version of the rescue onto American television screens mattered more than scrupulous adherence to the facts. Thus Lynch was credited with having fought on after the ambush until she was wounded, a claim that she denied months later during a television interview in which she stated: "They [the Pentagon] used me to symbolize all this stuff. It's wrong. I don't know why they filmed [my rescue] or why they say these things." She also said, "I did not shoot, not a round, nothing. I went down praying to my knees. And that's the last I remember."

The Pentagon has also been criticized for the contrasting treatment of African-American specialist Shoshana Johnson, another member of 507th Maintenance Company, who was one of four soldiers who had also been taken prisoner near An Nasiriya on March 23. Johnson was the first American female POW since the lifting in 1994 of the so-called risk rule, allowing women to undertake duties in combat that exposed them to hostile fire or capture.

Johnson was shot in both legs and held prisoner for twenty-two days, during which she appeared, tearful and distressed, on Iraqi television. She was released the day after Lynch's dramatic rescue. Lynch was released from the Walter Reed Army Medical Center in Washington, D.C., on July 22, was awarded the Bronze Star, and on August 27 was given an honorable medical discharge with an 80 percent disability benefit. In August 2005, Lynch announced that she would be attending West Virginia University on a full scholarship stemming from her military service.

By contrast, there were no television movies, ghosted books, and military scholarships for Johnson, who received a benefit of only 30 percent. This prompted the Reverend Jesse Jackson to accuse the US Army of double standards, since Lynch was personable and white, while Johnson was less articulate, less newsworthy, and black.

Reference: Rick Bragg, *I Am a Soldier, Too: The Jessica Lynch Story,* 2004, an unreliable source.

McGRATH, KATHLEEN
US Navy Captain, b. 1952, d. 2002

The first woman to command a warship of the US Navy, Kathleen McGrath attracted much media attention when she took command of the frigate *Jarrett* in 2000 to conduct maritime interception operations in the Persian Gulf.

The daughter of a USAF pilot, McGrath was born in Columbus, Ohio, and raised in military bases around the world. She studied forestry at California State University, Sacramento, and after a stint with the US Forest Service joined the navy.

She earned a master's degree in education at Stanford and underwent training at the Surface Warfare Officers (SWO) School. In 1987 she became operations officer on the USS *Cape Cod* and subsequently on the USS *Concord*. These assignments took her to the Indian Ocean, the Mediterranean, and the Red Sea, including stints on Operations Sharp Edge and Desert Shield.

In 1993, McGrath took command of the rescue-and-salvage ship USS *Recovery*. In 1998, four years after the opening of warships to women, she became chief staff officer of a destroyer squadron serving in the western Pacific and Persian Gulf. That year she became the first woman to command a US warship when she was appointed to the USS *Jarrett,* a frigate with crew of 262. She completed one deployment with the *Jarrett* as it patrolled the Persian Gulf to intercept oil smugglers.

McGrath then transferred to the Institute for Defense Analyses in Alexandria, Virginia, for what turned out to be her final tour of duty. She died of cancer at the National Naval Medical Center in Bethesda, Maryland.

Reference: Susan H. Godson, *Serving Proudly: A History of Women in the US Navy,* 2003.

McSALLY, MARTHA
US Air Force Combat Pilot, b. 1966

In her career with the USAF, McSally has scored two notable firsts. She was the first woman to fly combat operations and subsequently became the first woman in the service to command an air-combat unit. She later recalled: "In 1984 I was attending the US Air Force Academy and told my first flight instructor that I was going to be a fighter pilot. He just laughed, but after Congress repealed the prohibition law in 1991, and I was named as one of the first seven women who would be put through fighter training, he looked me up and said he was amazed I had accomplished my goal."

McSally graduated from the US Air Force Academy in 1988 and studied for a master's degree at Harvard University's School of Public Policy. In 1993 she was one of the first seven women to be trained as fighter pilots by the US Air Force. In 1995–96, during a tour of duty in Kuwait, she became the first woman in the service to fly a combat mission, piloting a Fairchild Republic A-10 Thunderbolt close-support attack aircraft over southern Iraq to enforce the no-fly zone. In 2001, while based in Saudi Arabia, McSally was embroiled in a dispute with the US military over a directive requiring female service personnel to wear an *abaya*—an Islamic head-to-toe robe—when not on duty. McSally, a devout Christian, deemed the dress code "ridiculous and unnecessary" and argued that women serving in the military in Saudi Arabia should be able to wear their uniforms on official business and dress in long pants and long-sleeve shirts when off duty. She would not back down and successfully argued her case in the US Supreme Court before accusing the USAF of discriminating against her for rocking the boat in an admittedly sensitive policy area.

In 2004 Lieutenant Colonel McSally was vindicated when she took command of 354th Fighter Squadron, based at Davis-Monthan Air Force Base, Arizona. Characteristically, McSally said of her new command, "We are the pointing end of the spear. I understand the marching orders, and we will be prepared to deploy . . . with an aggressive attitude that we will win."

McSally subsequently served in Afghanistan, where her squadron flew some 2,000 missions, accumulated more than 7,000 combat flight hours, and expended more than 23,000 rounds of thirty-millimeter ammunition. She became a full colonel in December 2006. She reflected, "I hope I am a role model to both men and women because we are a fighting force and should not be concerned with the differences between us."

Reference: www.defenselink.mil/

MIXED ANTIAIRCRAFT BATTERIES
United Kingdom, World War II

During World War II, women of the **Auxiliary Territorial Service** (ATS, see p. 153) played a vital role in the nation's Anti-Aircraft (AA) Command. The idea had first been taken up in 1938 by General Sir Frederick Pile, the wartime commander of AA Command, who had taken advice from Caroline Haslett, a distinguished engineer, on the suitability of women for this role in home defense. Training for mixed-AA batteries began in the spring of 1940, to meet an estimated shortfall in AA Command of some eleven hundred officers and eighteen thousand men, and the first mixed battery was deployed on August 21, 1941, in Richmond Park, on the outskirts of London. The first German aircraft to be shot down by a mixed battery crashed near Newcastle on December 8, 1941.

At full strength a mixed battery contained 189 men and 229 women, including officers. At the outset, each battery had eleven male and three female officers, the latter performing administrative and welfare duties. However, in 1943 the first female technical control officers began to assume operational responsibilities on gun sites in Home Command.

On the site, women operated all the equipment except the guns, handling the radar, predictors, and radio communications. Pile, an unlikely feminist, saw no logical reason why women should not fire the guns, but he was overruled. The wartime history of AA Command patronizingly observed of the women in mixed batteries, "They have the right delicacy of touch, the keenness and the application which is necessary to the somewhat tiresome job of knob twiddling, which are the lot of the instrument numbers. In principle, also, women will take on all the duties of mixed searchlight detachments." The searchlight batteries had been the first operational ATS units within AA Command, a pioneer "experimental" battery having been established in April 1941 and manned by an all-ATS crew wearing male battle dress. An ATS version of battle dress was subsequently introduced in specifically female sizes and in a finer "Saxony serge." But however finely dressed, the women on searchlight duty were still not allowed to return fire if machine-gunned by enemy aircraft.

Work on the searchlight batteries was demanding and included the shifting of tons of earth, filling and laying sandbags, renovating derelict sites, logging all aircraft, and transmitting messages between command posts and gun operations rooms. Mary Churchill, daugher of British wartime leader and prime minister Winston Churchill, was one of the first women to volunteer for duties with a mixed battery.

The idea of men and young women working together, sometimes in remote and physically arduous conditions, was approached with caution by the army. Initially, it was decided to combine ATS volunteers with men who had just joined up, on the basis that the latter's lack of military experience would not prejudice them against working alongside women. Great care was also taken in the appointment of male officers, often relatively older, fatherly or schoolmaster types, in an attempt to minimize friction.

The mixed batteries played a particularly important role between June 1944 and March 1945, when a significant proportion of the AA Command's resources was deployed to southern England to deal with the threat posed by German V-1 flying bombs.

Reference: General Sir Frederick Pile, *Ack-Ack: Britain's Defence Against Air Attack During the Second World War,* 1949.

NIGHT WITCHES
Soviet Women Combat Pilots in World War II

Of the three all-women air regiments for which **Marina Raskova** (see p. 236) was responsible, the most celebrated was the 588th Night Bomber Regiment, known as "the Night Witches."

The regiment's aircrew flew obsolete wood-and-fabric Polikarpov Po-2 biplanes on night operations against targets in the enemy's rear areas. The strategic importance of these missions was not high, but the psychological effect was often considerable on exhausted German formations recovering from heavy fighting. With its 110-horsepower engine, the highly maneuverable Po-2 had a maximum speed of only 94 miles per hour, lower than the stall speeds of the high-performance German Messerschmitt-109 or Focke Wulf-190 fighters, which made it very hard to shoot down as it flew along the deck to launch its bombing run. Near the target, the Po-2's pilots would cut their engines and glide into the attack, the whistling of the wind against the aircraft's bracing wires prompting the Germans to coin the phrase "Night Witches." In a practice that recalled the early bombing operations of World War I, the bomb load was sometimes stored inside the Po-2 and tossed overboard by the aircrew. Most of the women declined to wear parachutes, preferring death to becoming prisoners of war.

The 588th Night Bomber Regiment, commanded by Yevdokia Bershanskaya, was in action from 1942, when it was deployed to the Kuban region in the southern Soviet Union, up to the fall of Berlin in 1945. In February 1943, in recognition of its outstanding service, it was redesignated the Forty-sixth Guards Night Bomber Regiment, and by the end of the war it had flown 24,000 combat missions, dropping 23,000 tons of bombs. No fewer than 23 of its aircrew became Heroes of the Soviet Union (the title Mother Heroine of the Soviet Union was reserved for women who patriotically produced large numbers of children).

Reference: Reina Pennington, *Wings, Women, and War: Soviet Airwomen in World War II Combat,* 2002.

RASKOVA, MARINA
Pioneering Soviet Aviatrix, b. 1912, d.1943

Raskova was a record-breaking pilot in the interwar years, and in World War II the driving force behind the formation of three female combat formations that flew more than thirty thousand sorties for the Red Air Force (VVS) on the Eastern Front.

Raskova was a polymath, an excellent musician, a fluent French- and Spanish-speaker, a scientist, and an airwoman. Trained as a navigator, she acquired a pilot's license in 1935 and two years later, while teaching at the Zhukovsky Air Academy, embarked on a series of record-breaking endurance flights. At the age of twenty-six she was awarded the Gold Star of Hero of the Soviet Union and was often referred to as "the Soviet Amelia Earhart."

After the German invasion of the Soviet Union in June 1941, Raskova used her personal influence with Joseph Stalin, and her position on the People's Defense Committee, to secure the establishment of Aviation Group 122, a training formation in which both the air and ground crews would be female.

Raskova oversaw the recruitment and training of the intake and their eventual assignment to three air regiments—the 586th IAP (Fighter), the 587th BAP (Bomber), and the 588th NBAP (Night Bomber). She assumed command of the 587th BAP, which was equipped with the rugged Petlyakov Pe-2 attack bomber, an outstanding combat aircraft that had entered service in 1940 and was frequently upgraded throughout the war. On January 4, 1943, while leading a flight of Pe-2s to reinforce the Stalingrad front, Raskova crashed in a heavy snowstorm and was killed. She received the first state funeral of the war and was buried in Red Square. In September 1943 the formation she had commanded was redesignated the 125th M. M. Raskova Guards Bomber Aviation Regiment.

Reference: Reina Pennington, *Wings, Women, and War: Soviet Airwomen in World War II Combat,* 2002.

REITSCH, HANNA
Hitler's Test Pilot, 1912–1979

Diminutive, dynamic, and burning with an almost mystical belief in the magic of flight, Reitsch became an ambassadress for Nazi aviation in the 1930s, gaining a reputation from which she struggled to distance herself in the postwar years. When she died, one of the kinder obituaries referred to her as a "politically naïve patriot who had believed that she had only served her Fatherland."

Reitsch was raised in an intensely patriotic family in the eastern German province of Silesia. Bitten by the flying bug, she abandoned her medical studies for gliding, which had been developed in Germany in the 1920s as a means to circumvent the ban on powered flight imposed on Germany in 1919 by the Treaty of Versailles.

International success as a gliding champion took Reitsch around the globe as a woman in an almost exclusively male world. In the 1936 Berlin Olympics she was a member of an elite German team tasked with giving aerobatic displays. On the insistence of Ernst Udet, the World War I flying ace who in 1936 became the technical director at the German Air Ministry, Reitsch was appointed *Flugkapitan,* a rank normally reserved for the most senior pilots of Lufthansa, the German national airline.

In September 1937, Udet invited Reitsch to join a team of test pilots at Rechlin, an air base at which new aircraft designs were flown and evaluated. Here she tested the dive breaks on the Junkers Ju 87 bomber and flew an early helicopter, the Fa61, in the presence of Charles Lindbergh. Photographs of the period show a small, intensely feminine figure dwarfed by Luftwaffe officers in bulky leather overcoats.

In the early war years, Reitsch remained at Rechlin as a test pilot, helping to develop and fly the Messerschmitt Me321 Gigant, a massive transport glider capable of carrying one hundred fully equipped troops plus a crew of seven or 21,500 pounds of cargo. A powered version was later used extensively as a heavy transport machine.

Reitsch also tested the Me163 Komet, a unique ultra-short-range defensive jet fighter, which had an alarming tendency to explode like a bomb as it landed on its ski undercarriage. Reitsch later likened flying the Komet to "thundering through the skies on a cannonball." On October 30, 1942, while flying an unpowered Me163, she crashed and sustained severe injuries.

This setback did not deter Reitsch, and after the award of an Iron Cross she embarked on another hazardous assignment, test flying a manned version of the V-1 missile, which was launched from the underside of a modified He111 bomber. Reitsch advocated the employment of this weapon on suicide missions against Allied shipping, but it never went into service.

On April 26, 1945, as the Third Reich entered its death throes, Hitler summoned the Luftwaffe general Robert Ritter von Greim, then commander of Luftflotte 6 and an old friend of Reitsch, to the *Führerbunker* in Berlin. They flew into the besieged city in a Fieseler Fi 156 Storch light aircraft, piloted by Reitsch after Greim had been badly wounded in the foot by ground fire. Trapped in Hitler's bunker in the grounds of the Reich Chancellery, Greim

was promoted to the rank of field marshal and appointed commander of what remained of the Luftwaffe. On April 29, he was
ordered to fly out of Berlin with Reitsch to arrest Heinrich
Himmler. The historian Hugh Trevor Roper dryly commented
that Reitsch's fervent character was "well suited to the atmosphere
in that last subterranean madhouse in Berlin." She and Greim took
off from Berlin's east-west axis in a small Arado aircraft, shells
bursting around them, a sea of flame below, and flew on to Grand
Admiral Dönitz's headquarters at Plon, on the Baltic. Greim committed suicide on May 24, 1945 and Reitsch was taken into US
custody.

Reitsch's postwar career was marked by more international
gliding triumphs, a rapprochement with aviation enthusiasts in the
United States—she was invited to the White House in 1961—and
a protracted battle to clear her name of the taint of Nazism. In the
1930s she had regarded Nazism as "the most natural way of life"
and had, perhaps naïvely, allowed the German propaganda machine to exploit her femininity. The attention she had received in
the 1930s and early 1940s was unsought but not unwelcome, and
in the 1960s and 1970s she paid the price in the form of a number
of libel actions. She continued to set gliding records up to her
death, on August 24, 1979, from a heart attack.

Reference: *Fliegen mein Leben, Hanna Reitsch,* 1968; and Judy
Lomax, *Flying for the Fatherland,* 1988.

ROSSI, MARIE T.
US Helicopter Pilot, b. 1959, d. 1991

Major Rossi was the first US woman soldier to fly operationally
into Iraqi-held territory in the Persian Gulf War. She was killed
in an air accident the day after the cease-fire had been declared in
Operation Desert Storm.

A graduate of River Dell Regional High School, New Jersey,
she studied psychology at Dickinson University, where she was an
outstanding cadet in the ROTC (Reserve Officers' Training
Corps). In the Gulf War, Rossi commanded Company "B" of the

159th Aviation Battalion, 24th Infantry Division, which played an important role in Desert Storm, ferrying fuel and ammunition to the 101st and 82nd Airborne Divisions. Three days before she lost her life, Major Rossi made these comments to a CNN interviewer:

> Sometimes you have to disassociate how you feel personally about going into war and, you know, possibly see the death that's going to be there. But personally, as an aviator and a soldier, this is the moment that everyone trains for—that I've trained for—so I feel ready to meet the challenge. I don't necessarily personally like it; if I had the opportunity and they called a ceasefire tomorrow that would be great.

Major Rossi died on March 1, 1991, when the CH-47 Chinook transport helicopter she was piloting flew into an unlighted microwave tower at night and in bad weather near her base in Saudi Arabia. Three other crew members died in the crash. Major Rossi is buried in Arlington National Cemetery; her epitaph reads, "First Female Combat Commander to Fly into Battle Operation Desert Storm."

Reference: Marie T. Rossi-Cayton, www.ctie.monash.edu/.

WARSAW GHETTO UPRISING
World War II

One of the rare engagements of World War II in which women fought side by side with men, the Warsaw Ghetto uprising proved beyond doubt what women were capable of when given weapons and allowed to take part in combat. The heroism of the Jewish women involved in the Warsaw Ghetto uprising was such that it commanded the attention of the German commander of the forces against whom they made their courageous but doomed last stand.

At the outbreak of World War II, there were some 3 million Jews in Poland, of whom about 300,000 lived in the capital, Warsaw, where they formed about one-third of the city's population. The Warsaw Ghetto was established by Poland's German occupiers in the autumn of 1940. In a matter of days, an eleven-mile wall, ten to twenty feet high and topped with broken glass and barbed wire, was built to isolate an area of 2.5 square miles east of the Vistula River.

The original population of the area had been moved out and replaced by some 138,000 Jews. No Jews were allowed to leave the area, with the exception of a few employed in war-related industries. Thousands more Jews were transported to Warsaw from cities and towns across Poland, and eventually some 433,000 Jews were incarcerated in the ghetto. Thousands of its inhabitants died every month from starvation and disease. Communication with the outside world was both illegal and fraught with danger (see **Sendlerowa, Irena,** p. 363).

July 1942 saw the first shipments from the Warsaw Ghetto to the gas chambers of Treblinka, a death camp only fifty miles away. The Jewish Council, a body established by the Germans, was ordered to supply six thousand people a day for "resettlement." Few believed that this was a death sentence. A German poster offered three kilos of bread and a kilo of jam to those who reported for resettlement between July 29 and 31.

However, the truth about Treblinka was discovered by a member of the Bund, the underground Jewish socialist party in Poland. The news was published in the Bund newspaper but had made little or no impact on the situation. By September 1942, the population of the ghetto had fallen to sixty thousand. The decision to resist the liquidation of the ghetto was led by the Jewish Fighting Organization (ZOB), a group of some five hundred young male and female Zionists opposed to the Bund, who up to that point had remained isolated and powerless. From December 1942, the ZOB began to acquire arms with the help of the Polish Home Army (the clandestine force formed after the fall of Poland in 1939), although on a pathetically small scale.

On January 18, 1943, the Germans launched a renewed roundup in the ghetto. This time they met armed resistance, and the roundup was abandoned after four days of fighting. The mood of fatalism that had previously pervaded the ghetto was lifted. Taxes were imposed on wealthy inhabitants of the ghetto to obtain fuel and arms from outside its walls, and the ZOB received additional weapons from the Polish Home Army. Training and weapons drills were stepped up. Bunkers were prepared with supplies of food and water.

On April 19, three thousand SS troops, supported by tanks and flamethrowers and commanded by SS general Jürgen Stroop, were sent into the ghetto with orders to clear it out and destroy the buildings. They were met with small-arms fire and grenade attacks. Small detachments of armed Jews totaling some 750 male and female fighters armed with grenades, Molotov cocktails, seventeen rifles, and a handful of pistols engaged the SS in a running battle.

The Jews were meant to go like lambs to the slaughter, but they fought like tigers, using hidden bunkers and secret escape routes. Stroop himself reported on the battle in the ghetto: "Jews and Jewesses shot from two pistols at the same time. . . . Jewesses carried loaded [weapons] in their clothing. . . . At the last moment they would pull out hand grenades . . . and throw them at the soldiers."

The battle lasted twenty-seven days. On May 8 the headquarters bunker of the ZOB was overrun and its leader, Mordecai Anielewicz, killed. Eight days later Stroop announced that the fighting was over. He had proceeded methodically, using fire rather than the sword. Water, gas, and electricity were cut off and buildings set aflame block by block. Cellars were cleared with "smoke candles." When their occupants emerged, they were mown down.

At the final count, more than twenty thousand inhabitants of the ghetto were killed and some sixteen thousand remained for transport to Treblinka. Around three hundred Germans had died in the fighting. The Polish Jews had provided their fellow Poles with a heroic example. Their cause had been hopeless, but their courage was superb. In the process they had demonstrated the effectiveness of urban guerrilla warfare waged with unflinching determination against a better-armed and more numerous enemy.

Reference: Norman Davies, *Rising '44: The Battle for Warsaw,* 2004.

8

HEALING HANDS

⸻

Doctors, Nurses, Medics, and Health Workers

*The picture came back to me of myself standing alone in a newly created
circle of hell during the "emergency" of March 22nd 1918, gazing
half-hypnotised at the dishevelled beds, the stretchers on the floor, the
scattered boots and piles of muddy clothing, the brown blankets turned
back from smashed limbs bound to splints by filthy bloodstained bandages.
Beneath each stinking wad of sodden wool and gauze an obscene horror
waited for me, and all the equipment that I had for attacking it in this
ex-medical ward was one pair of forceps standing in a potted-meat
glass half full of methylated spirit.*

—Vera Brittain, working as a VAD sister in a field hospital
in Étaples, France, recalled in *Testament of Youth* (1936)

MY GOOD LADY, go home and sit still!" The British War Office
bully who gave this insulting advice to **Dr. Elsie Inglis** in World
War I (see p. 262) was clearly ignorant that women of all kinds had
been vital attendants at battlefields for thousands of years. All wars
everywhere have needed doctors and nurses, a reality recognized
by **Isabella I,** the fifteenth-century warrior queen of Spain, when
she set up one of the earliest known military field hospitals in the
Western world (see p. 44).

Despite some notable exceptions, for thousands of years doctors

243

were male, and women were restricted to nursing roles until the turn of the twentieth century, when medical schools finally opened their doors to female students. As with the entire story of women at war, women's struggle to gain entry to medical training and also to be admitted to front-line service mirrors their fight for freedom and equality in the wider world.

Inglis herself had benefited from these greater freedoms to qualify as a doctor in Scotland, and eager to put her healing skills to good use, she had offered to provide the British army with fully staffed female medical units for the battlefronts of World War I. Whether she knew it or not, Inglis was working within an ancient tradition. Early myths and legends place goddesses and women on every battlefield, both as combatants and hostile scavengers and as their polar opposite, healers in time of need. The Roman historian Tacitus records that Celtic warriors fighting the Roman armies from the first invasion of Britain in 43 CE always brought their women to the battlefield because "it is to their mothers that they go to have their wounds treated, and the women are not afraid to count and compare the gashes."

In Arabia before Islam, women similarly went to war with their men to help the wounded, when they were not fighting themselves (see **Al-Kind'yya, Khawlah bint al-Azwar,** p. 9). Records show that during the early period of Islam in the seventh century, there are many women who appeared on the battlefield, including some of Muhammad's wives. Women known as "the companions of the Prophet" accompanied the men to battle to nurse the wounded and to supply food and drink: Umm Ayman, Muhammad's nurse and freedwoman, was present at the Battle of Uhud in 625 CE, at Khayber in 628 CE, and at Hunayn in 630 CE. Several other women companions, such as Umm Sinan al-Aslamiyya and Ku'ayba bint Sa'd al-Aslamiyya, were active in a number of battles, tending the sick and the wounded. Al-Aslamiyya is said to have set up a tent in the mosque at Medina to serve as a makeshift hospital for the wounded, which would make it one of the very first field hospitals in the world.

The history of military medicine can be traced to the origins of organized warfare in the Sumerian city-states of southern

Mesopotamia around 3000 BCE, when the so-called Vulture Stele of the city-state of Lagash around 2500 BCE shows the gory fate of the defeated enemy, whose abandoned corpses are being picked over by vultures: men whom their battlefield nurses had been unable to save.

The Romans, masters of order and organization, understood the link between their troops' health and fighting strength, but patriarchs to a man, they had no room for women in their first medical corps, formed in the reign of its first emperor Augustus between 27 BCE and 4 CE. Centuries ahead of their time, the Roman army's *medici* (physicians) cleaned wounds with *acetum* (vinegar, a simple fatty acid more efficient than the carbolic acid used by Joseph Lister, the founder of nineteenth-century antiseptic surgery), and boiled their surgical instruments before every use. With an equally advanced organization of military hospitals and wards staffed with medical orderlies and designated bandagers *(capsarii),* they provided the troops with a standard of medical care in times of war and peace that was not to be equaled until the work of **Florence Nightingale** and others in the late nineteenth century (see p. 264).

Medical care of this standard was one of the rewards a grateful empire bestowed on the soldiers who sustained it, and the exclusion of women from the knowledge and experience of the army doctors meant that vital information never spread into the civilian world beyond the military. Incalculable death and loss would have been avoided if midwives attending women had known about sterilization and antisepsis, for example. Nevertheless, a parallel tradition persisted of local wise women who were expert in treating war wounds, like the crone reputed to have saved a feverish Alexander the Great from a particularly vicious sword gash. She packed the gaping hole with spiderwebs, a remedy dismissed by later physicians as filthy old wives' nonsense until modern science showed them to be full of penicillin.

Nevertheless, in succeeding centuries, women continued to be banned from both the armed services and from enrolling as doctors. Throughout Europe from the Dark Ages to the twentieth century, nurses were treated as no better than domestic servants and given only rudimentary training at best. Surgery was performed without any anesthetic except the occasional use of alcohol and never with sterilized instruments, antiseptics were not in general use, and hygiene was primitive or nonexistent. With no clear idea of good practice until **Florence Nightingale** (see p. 264) began her program of reform, the administration and design of wards were matters of chance, and treatment was haphazard at best. The women who tended the sick were also notorious for their addiction to the bottle, and were often drunk (see **Seacole, Mary,** p. 268).

British journalists investigating the campaign in the Crimea between 1853 and 1856 exposed these and other chronic levels of mismanagement by the military authorities in Britain that ensured that malnutrition and disease took a deadly toll. The resulting national scandal brought down the British government and stimulated reforms aimed at improving the welfare of British troops.

One determined woman grappled with this tangle of problems. At the request of Britain's secretary for war, Florence Nightingale led a team of nurses to reorganize the care of the wounded at the British army's base hospital at Scutari. A small band of equally determined women in the American Civil War (1861–65) followed the standards set by Florence Nightingale, **Dorothea Dix** (see p. 258) among them. Like Nightingale, Dix battled against entrenched male hostility to establish the Union's Army Nursing Corps, as did **Clara Barton,** the founder of the American Red Cross (see p. 253). The Civil War boasted another remarkable medical and military cross-dresser like **James Barry** (see p. 69), **Mary Edwards Walker,** who became the first female doctor in the Union army's medical corps (see p. 278).

In spite of these significant advances, the American and British armies of the late nineteenth and early twentieth centuries remained strongly male institutions, with little tolerance for women except as nurses. A small number of British nurses saw service in the Zulu War of 1879 and between 1882 and 1885 in Egypt and the Sudan. The British Army Nursing Reserve was established in 1897, and in the United States the American Nurse Corps followed in 1901.

In the twentieth century, the scale of both world wars drew

tens of thousands of American and British women into work as nurses, and increasingly near the front line (see **Army Nurse Corps,** p. 248). In World War I, there was still room for remarkable and often crazily heroic freelances who provided medical care (see **Chisholm, Mairi,** and **Knocker, Elsie,** both p. 257). But the industrial scale on which that conflict was waged—more than 90,000 women served in **Voluntary Aid Detachments** (see p. 202) alone—left little room for quirky individualism.

America's entry into World War II brought some 59,000 women into the Army Nurse Corps over time, and the sophisticated "chain of evacuation" they developed in North Africa, Italy, and northwestern Europe became standard practice until the end of the war. Twenty years later, the experience the corps gained in air evacuation proved invaluable in the Vietnam War, when nurses formed the majority of female service personnel in the war zone. Later, the work of the corps laid the foundation for medical care during the Persian Gulf War and the subsequent invasion of Iraq.

Modern warfare is frequently described as more "technologized" and more "professional" than the wars of the past. But war wounds remain as horrific as ever, if not worse, and nurses continue to serve armies worldwide, often at the risk of their own lives.

ANG, SWEE CHAI
"Small Miss," Singaporean Orthopedic Surgeon and Refugee Camp Doctor, Beirut 1982, b. ca. 1952

An orthopedic surgeon by training, the less-than-four-foot-nine-inch Swee Chai Ang volunteered to join a humanitarian mission to Lebanon after hearing an international SOS for a surgeon to treat war victims in Beirut. She found the hospitals bombed and without electricity or water. She was working in the Palestinian refugee camps of Sabrah and Shatila when, only weeks after her arrival, Israel invaded West Beirut and the people of the camps fell victim to the notorious massacre of 1982. The killing of an estimated 800 to 3,500 Palestinians was carried out by Lebanese

Christian militiamen, and controversy continues to surround Israel's role in the outrage.

"Frightened people were pouring into the hospital," Ang recalled. "The first woman . . . had her entire elbow joint missing . . . she had been shot as soon as she stepped out of her front door. After her came a stream of women, shot in the jaw, the head, the chest, the abdomen . . . shot in the streets while going out for food or water for their families." These were the lucky ones. Many more were raped, tortured, and horribly killed.

Ang and her colleagues worked throughout the crisis, treating all comers. Later that year she gave evidence to the Israeli Commission of Inquiry into the massacre, then returned to Beirut, where she worked for six more years. Subsequently she devoted much of her time to work with the charity Medical Aid for Palestinians (MAP).

Reference: Dr. Swee Chai Ang, *From Beirut to Jerusalem: A Woman Surgeon with the Palestinians,* 1989.

ARMY NURSE CORPS
United States, World War II

American nurses served in the Spanish-American War of 1898 and were officially established as the Nurse Corps in 1901. Although the American military continued to see itself as an all-male preserve, extending only a grudging tolerance to nurses, the value of the nursing service was effectively demonstrated in World War I.

In World War II, more than 59,000 nurses served in the US Army Nurse Corps. They came under fire in field hospitals and hospital ships and as flight nurses on medical transport aircraft. Their dedication, combined with advances in medical science, contributed to the low mortality rate among US troops who received medical care in the field or underwent casualty evacuation.

On December 7, 1941, the day that the carrier-borne aircraft of the Japanese Imperial Navy attacked the US Pacific Fleet anchored at Pearl Harbor in Hawaii, there were fewer than a thousand nurses in the US Army, of whom eighty-two were stationed on the island of Oahu. First Lieutenant Annie G. Fox, the chief nurse at Hickam

Field, on Oahu, was the first nurse of World War II to be awarded the Purple Heart for her "calmness, courage and leadership" during the Japanese attack.

The attack on Pearl Harbor was only one element in Japan's preemptive strike in the Pacific. On December 8, Japanese forces landed in the Philippines, where more than one hundred members of the Nurse Corps were stationed, most of them in Manila. With the fall of Manila on January 2, 1942, the nurses were evacuated to the island fortress of Corregidor and then, after leaving some of their number behind, transferred to the Bataan peninsula, where they were ordered to prepare two emergency hospitals for the US and Filipino forces fighting there.

By the end of March, the hospitals were massively over-crowded, short of medicine, food, and clothing, and under Japanese air attack. A month later the twenty nurses left on the peninsula were evacuated on two US Navy aircraft. One aircraft made a forced landing, and all those aboard were taken prisoner by the Japanese. On May 7, the defenders of Corregidor surrendered, along with the fifty-five nurses who had remained there. The nurses who had fallen into Japanese hands in the opening campaign of the Pacific war were interned in Manila and remained prisoners of war until their liberation by US forces in February 1945.

By May 1942, there were 12,000 nurses in the corps, although it was not until over a year later that a formal month's training course was introduced for new recruits. In the next two years, some 27,500 newly inducted nurses graduated from fifteen army training centers. A three-month program was introduced to train nurses in the treatment of shock and battle stress, a condition that by the end of the war led to the discharge of many thousands of soldiers.

In World War II, the US Army was racially segregated, and by 1945 it had accepted fewer than five hundred black nurses in a corps of approximately fifty thousand. Nevertheless, adverse public reaction to the reluctant recruiting of black nurses led in 1944 to the enrollment of two thousand black students in the Cadet Nursing Program. The first black medical unit to serve overseas was the Twenty-fifth Station Hospital Unit, which deployed to Liberia in 1943.

In November 1942, sixty nurses of the Forty-eighth Surgical

Hospital came ashore under fire in North Africa in Operation Torch, the landings in Morocco and Algeria. The North African theater was the test bed for the US Army's evolving "chain of evacuation," which was to become standard practice in every theater for the rest of the war. The first links in the chain were field and evacuation hospitals, which remained in close contact with combat formations. Each field hospital was staffed by 18 nurses, who were responsible for up to 150 patients. A field hospital could perform about 80 operations a day, and over 85 percent of the troops who underwent operations in field hospitals survived.

Patients at the field hospital who were strong enough to travel went by ambulance to an evacuation hospital, which was usually staffed by 53 nurses and could handle up to 750 patients. Hospital trains, ships, and aircraft then carried patients to station and general hospitals housed in semipermanent locations with running water and electricity. These facilities, although not exposed to direct enemy fire, were frequently subjected to air attacks. The white hospital ship with red crosses prominently displayed operated under the terms of the Hague Convention but on occasion was attacked by enemy aircraft. In the Pacific theater in April 1945 the US hospital ship *Comfort* came under repeated bomber attacks off the island of Leyte; six nurses died.

The evacuation of wounded troops by aircraft, which began early in 1943, was another innovation of the North African campaign and was subsequently to feature in every theater in World War II. Flight nurses received special training, including crash procedures and survival in hostile environments, before assignment to the Air Force Surgeon General's Office. They were at greater risk than their counterparts on the ground, as the aircraft in which they flew doubled as military transports and could not display red crosses. Of some five hundred Army nurses who served as members of thirty-one medical air-evacuation transport squadrons operating across the world, seventeen lost their lives. As a testament to their skill and dedication, of the 1.2 million patients who underwent air evacuation, only forty-six died en route.

In the campaigns in Sicily and southern Italy, army nurses worked through enemy artillery bombardment and dive-bomber attacks and battled first with extreme heat and malaria and then with drenching winter rain. On November 8, 1943, a Douglas C-54 Skymaster ferrying thirteen flight nurses and thirteen medical technicians (corpsmen) of the 807th Medical Air Evacuation Transport Squadron from Sicily to Bari, on Italy's east coast, flew into a heavy storm, which blew it off course. Icing forced the Skymaster down in the mountains of Albania, miles behind German lines.

From there, the Americans were rescued by Albanian partisans, who, in an epic journey of eight hundred miles in severe weather, escorted all but three of the party to safety. The three nurses left behind were suffering from frostbite and dysentery, and had been hidden from the Germans in the homes of partisans in the town of Berat. In March 1944 they left Berat disguised as Albanians and traveled by donkey across the mountains to make a rendezvous on the coast with an Allied torpedo boat. They arrived in Otranto, on the heel of Italy, on March 21.

The return of the "Balkan Nurses" coincided with fierce fighting in the congested Anzio beachhead, where Allied forces had been bottled up after the failure to exploit an amphibious landing behind the German Gustav defensive line. The Thirty-third, the Ninety-fifth, and the Ninety-sixth field hospitals, with approximately two hundred nurses, had arrived at the beachhead on January 22, 1944, and came under heavy artillery and aerial bombardment. On February 10, the battered Ninety-fifth was replaced by the Fifteenth Evacuation Hospital; on that day, the Thirty-third was hit by long-range artillery fire, which killed a number of medical staff, including two nurses. For their bravery under fire, four nurses received the Silver Star, the first such award to women in the US Army.

The first nurses to arrive in Normandy after the launching of Operation Overlord in June 1944 were members of the Twelfth Evacuation Hospital, which deployed to France at the beginning of August. During the drive into Germany, the US Army sustained heavy casualties. In one fifty-six-hour period in mid-April 1945, the Forty-fourth Evacuation Hospital admitted 1,348 patients from the Third Armored Division. Simultaneously, the Seventy-seventh Evacuation Hospital was receiving released American and British prisoners of war, many of whom were weak and malnourished. In a far more terrible condition were the concentration camp survivors cared for by nurses of 116th and 127th Evacuation Hospitals. By June 1945, the number of army nurses in the European theater had peaked at 17,400.

In the Pacific theater, where the climate and terrain were less forgiving than in Europe and behind-the-lines Japanese operations posed a constant threat, the US high command limited the nurses' combat-support role to the rear areas. The sheer size of the theater was also a significant factor in keeping nurses in the rear echelon, and until the closing months of the war in the Pacific, they worked far from the combat zone, in which medical corpsmen performed the role of nurses. New Caledonia, in the South Pacific, with its benign, malaria-free climate, became home to seven station and two general hospitals.

The nature of the "island-hopping strategy" employed in the Pacific, and the small size of many of the islands seized as stepping-stones to the Japanese home islands, ensured that nurses arrived only when an island had been cleared and secured. Guadalcanal, in the Solomons chain, had been secured by US forces in February 1943, but nurses of the Twentieth Station Hospital did not arrive there until June 1944, sixteen months after the deployment of male medical members of the unit.

One reason for the long delay was the unhealthy Guadalcanal climate, hot, humid, and rainy, which encouraged malaria, dysentery, and dengue fever. Victims of these diseases outnumbered battle casualties by four to one. Conditions were similar in New Guinea, where in 1943 malaria disabled nearly 8,600 of the occupying 14,700 troops. Blanket spraying with DDT brought the problem under control, eventually reducing the incidence of malaria from 172 per thousand to less than 5 per thousand. Dengue fever, however, remained a constant problem, and in the late summer of 1944 an outbreak on Saipan invalided half of the nurses posted there.

In 1944, as the American advance closed on Japan, the military hospitals set up at the start of the Pacific campaign in New Zealand, the Fiji Islands, and the New Hebrides were closed down and nurses followed US forces to the Solomons, the Marshalls, and the Marianas. Nurses stationed in secured islands lived in fenced quarters guarded around the clock by armed sentries who also escorted them to the hospitals and always accompanied them when they were off post, an oppressive regime that led to a dip in morale.

The invasion of the Philippines, launched on October 20, 1944, gave army nurses in the Pacific their first opportunity to tend battle casualties in the field, a radical change in their responsibilities that led to a rapid raising of morale. However, this was tempered by a soaring casualty ratio in the land fighting of one killed to every three wounded. Naval losses to kamikaze attacks were also heavy, and approximately three thousand naval wounded were evacuated to New Guinea between October and December.

In World War II, army nurses won 1,619 medals, citations, and commendations. Sixteen medals were awarded to nurses who died in battle. Between 1941 and 1945, 20 nurses died while serving in the US Army.

Reference: Edith A. Aynes, *From Nightingale to Eagle: An Army Nurse's History,* 1973.

BARTON, CLARA
US Nurse and Founder of the American Red Cross, b. 1821, d. 1912

In a long career of public service, Barton was a teacher, a trailblazer for female civil servants, a battlefield nurse and organizer, and president of the American Red Cross.

She was born on December 25, 1821, in North Oxford, Massachusetts, the last of five children, and as a child she loved to play nurse while tending sick pets. At the age of eleven she nursed one of her brothers after he had fallen from a roof. After teaching in local schools she attended the Liberal Institute at Clinton, New York, before founding one of New Jersey's first "free" or public schools. She resigned when a man was appointed over her head. She then took a clerkship in the Patent Office, becoming possibly the first regularly appointed woman civil servant, and from 1854 she was based in Washington, D.C.

When the Civil War began in 1861, Barton advertised for provisions and medical supplies for the wounded and traveled to the front line by mule team to distribute them, earning the title "the Angel of the Battlefield." She remained independent of the US Sanitary Commission and **Dorothea Dix's** Army Nursing Corps (see p. 258), often paying her own way. In the latter part of the war, Barton was appointed head nurse of the Army of the James and a network of hospitals in Virginia. She spent the greater part of 1865 amassing information on missing soldiers and marking graves. After the war she became a persuasive public speaker and was acknowledged as a war heroine.

In 1868 she suffered a nervous collapse and traveled to Europe to recuperate. In Switzerland she was introduced to the work of the Red Cross, which had been formed in 1863 to provide relief for the wounded on the battlefield. In France in 1870, she worked with the organization to establish military hospitals in the Franco-Prussian War. When she returned to the United States, she agitated for American alignment with the movement to bring a measure of humanity to the battlefield, and in 1881 she presided over the formation of the American Association Red Cross, remaining its autocratic president until 1904. In 1881 the United States signed the Geneva Treaty, including the provisions Barton had made for the association's role in dealing with peacetime disasters. In the Spanish-American War of 1898, Barton, at the ripe old age of seventy-seven, worked again as a nurse in a mule train.

Reference: Stephen B. Oates, *A Woman of Valor: Clara Barton and the Civil War,* n.d.

BICKERDYKE, MARY ANN
US Civil War Hospital Administrator, 1817–1901

The formidable "Mother" Bickerdyke, chief of nursing for the Union army, was so beloved by its men that soldiers would cheer her when she appeared, just as they would a general. The Union generals treated her with wary deference. When the commander-in-chief, General Ulysses S. Grant, was asked what he was going to do about the outspoken and often insubordinate Bickerdyke, he replied, "She outranks me. I can't do a thing in the world."

Born in Ohio, she later moved to Illinois. She was widowed in 1859 and supported herself and her two young sons by practicing as a "botanic physician" in Galesburg, Illinois. After the outbreak of the Civil War in 1861, a young volunteer doctor from Galesburg wrote home about the squalid conditions in the military hospital in Cairo, Illinois, prompting the citizens of his hometown to raise five hundred dollars' worth of supplies, which they entrusted to Bickerdyke to deliver.

Bickerdyke remained in Cairo as an unofficial nurse and set about establishing order out of chaos. She received backing from Grant, who placed her in charge of the establishment of new medical facilities as the Union army moved south. It was said that Grant was so impressed by her that she was the only woman he allowed in his camp. If challenged, she could be imperious and was known to outplay the military men at their own hierarchical game. When a surgeon questioned her authority, Bickerdyke replied that she was acting "on the authority of God Almighty, have you anything that outranks that?"

By the end of the Civil War, and with the cooperation of the US Sanitary Commission, Bickerdyke had built three hundred hospitals and had organized medical care for the wounded on nineteen battlefields. When the war ended, at the request of General William T. Sherman, she rode at the head of the XV Corps in the Grand Review held in Washington. Bickerdyke went on to work for the Salvation Army in San Francisco and became a lawyer, assisting Union veterans with their legal problems. In 1886 she was awarded a special pension by Congress.

Reference: Adele de Leeun, *Civil War Nurse Mary Ann Bickerdyke*, 1973.

BULLWINKEL, VIVIAN
Australian World War II Nurse, b. 1915, d. 2000

On February 12, 1942, three days before the British capitulation to the Japanese, the SS *Vyner Brook,* a small tramp steamer, set sail from Singapore. On board were some three hundred civilian evacuees and sixty-four nurses of the Australian Army Nursing Service, one of whom was the twenty-six-year-old Bullwinkel.

The *Vyner Brook*'s destination was Batavia, in Java, but the voyage ended in the Banka Straits, four hundred miles southeast of Singapore, when the freighter was attacked and sunk by six Japanese warplanes. Bullwinkel, with twenty-one of the nurses on the ship and a large number of men, women, and children, came ashore at Radji Beach on Banka Island. The following day they were joined by twenty British soldiers who had survived the sinking of another vessel.

The decision was made to surrender to the Japanese, and the nurses remained with the soldiers and stretcher cases on the beach while other members of their party went in search of food and the enemy, who arrived in a patrol consisting of an officer and ten men, on February 16.

The Japanese officer ordered all the men who could walk to proceed around a nearby headland, where they were shot and bayoneted. One of them, Private Kinsley, survived and managed to crawl away. The Japanese then turned to the nurses, who were ordered to walk into the sea. The senior nurse, Matron Drummond, who had been wounded in the attack on the *Vyner Brook* and had to be supported by two of her colleagues, told them, "Chin up, girls, I'm proud of you and I love you all."

When the water reached waist height, the women were raked by machine-gun fire and all were killed, with the exception of Vivian Bullwinkel, who floated away, wounded in the hip. When the Japanese left the beach, she struggled ashore. Three days later she stumbled across Private Kinsley, dressed his wounds, and helped him into the jungle, from which they eventually emerged to give themselves up to the Japanese. They concealed their wounds, saying that they had survived a shipwreck and had swum ashore. Kinsley succumbed to his wounds shortly afterward, but Bullwinkel survived the war to give evidence about the massacre at the Tokyo War Crimes Tribunal, although the officer thought to have ordered it had committed suicide in 1945.

After the war, Bullwinkel rose to the top of her profession, retiring as matron of the Queen's Memorial Infectious Diseases Hospital,

Melbourne. In 1947 she received the Red Cross's Florence Nightingale Medal. She was appointed MBE (Member of the Order of the
British Empire) in 1973 and made an officer of the Order of Australia
in 1993, the year in which she attended the unveiling ceremony of a
memorial to the nurses who had died on Banka Island.

Reference: Peter Thompson, *The Battle of Singapore,* 2005.

CHISHOLM, MAIRI, AND ELSIE KNOCKER
British World War I Nurses

In August 1914, Dr. Hector Munro, a Scotsman, organized a flying ambulance unit to work with the Belgian army. Munro was a
feminist and included four women in the unit: an American, Helen
Gleason; two Englishwomen, Lady Dorothea Fielding and Elsie
Knocker; and the eighteen-year-old Mairi Chisholm, a fellow Scot.

Elsie Knocker was a widow who had some nursing experience
and who shared with Chisholm a passion for motorcycling. After
two months of operating with the ambulance corps in Belgium,
Knocker decided to establish a first-aid post immediately behind
the front line. In November 1914, Knocker and Chisholm set
themselves up in a cellar in the Belgian town of Pervyse, which
had been leveled by German shelling and lay just behind the front-
line trenches. Such proximity to the front line was in contravention
of British regulations, and until 1918 the two women worked with
Belgian drivers and orderlies. By early 1915, British newspapers had
dubbed them "the Heroines of Pervyse," and King Albert of Belgium had personally pinned on their tunics the Order of Leopold.

As Mairi Chisholm confided to her diary, the motor-ambulance
drive to the rear was fraught with difficulty and danger:

> Taking wounded to hospital 15 miles back at night was a very
> real strain—no lights, shell-pocked, mud-covered roads, often
> under fire, men and guns coming up to relieve the trenches, total
> darkness, yells to mind one's self and get out of the way, mean-
> ing a sickening slide off the pavie [road] into deep mud—
> screams from the stretchers behind one and thumps in the back

through the canvas—then an appeal to passing soldiers to shoulder the ambulance back on the pavie. Two or three of these journeys by night and one's eyes were on stalks, bloodshot and strained. No windscreen, no protection, no self-starters or electric lights to switch on when out of reach of the lines—climb out to light with a match, if possible, the carbide lamps.

After heavy shelling destroyed their first post, the two women moved into the ruins of a house and, after a fund-raising tour in Britain, found a new home in a concrete structure swathed in sandbags and hidden inside the ruins of another house. In this desolate landscape of flooded shell craters and rotting corpses, Elsie Knocker was married to an aristocratic Belgian airman, who had been brought down in no-man's-land near the post, and became the Baroness de T'Serclaes. Amid the carnage, Mairi Chisholm still had time to see beauty. One of her diary entries comments: "The ruins by moonlight were strangely beautiful and when it reigned over the trenches it was hard to believe that life was at a premium."

In 1917 the two women of Pervyse were awarded the Military Medal, which had been created in 1916 and was open to women (the first woman to receive the award had been their colleague from the flying ambulance days, Lady Dorothea Fielding). Early in 1918 both women were badly injured in a German gas attack. The baroness never returned to the trenches, and after suffering more wounds in a second gas bombardment, Knocker was forced to call it a day, and the Belgians closed down the post.

Reference: Elsie Shapter Knocker T'Serclaes, *Flanders and Other Fields: Memoirs of the Baroness de T'Serclaes,* 1964.

DIX, DOROTHEA
US Nurse and Social Reformer, b. 1802, d.1887

Born in Hampden, Maine, to farming stock, Dix had an unhappy childhood and lived with her grandmother in Boston from the age of twelve. At nineteen, she opened a school in her grandparents' house and also wrote elementary science textbooks and religious works.

On a visit to England in 1830s, Dix was influenced by a number of social reformers. When she returned to America in 1841, she taught at a Sunday school in Cambridge's House of Correction, in which she discovered to her horror that insane women were confined in barbaric conditions. Dix's response was to make a detailed investigation of local prisons, almshouses, and insane asylums and presented a report to the Massachusetts legislature. The report, combined with tireless speech-making and pamphlet-writing, led to a substantial investment in new facilities dedicated to the humane treatment of the mentally ill. As a direct result of Dix's efforts the number of asylums in the United States increased from 13 in 1843 to 123 in 1880, and she later undertook reforming missions to Scotland, the Channel Islands, France, Turkey, and Russia.

At the start of the American Civil War, Dix offered her services to the Union, and in June 1861 was placed in charge of all women nurses working in army hospitals. Like **Florence Nightingale** (see p. 264) she met with official hostility and skepticism that nurses could satisfactorily perform their duties in a military environment. Nevertheless, the determined Dix put her stamp on the Army Nursing Corps, recruiting more than 3,000 women and turning public buildings into hospitals. Her methods, however, were autocratic: she declined to accept applicants from religious sisterhoods and those under the age of thirty. She authorized a uniform of plain black or brown and forbade the wearing of jewelry. Unsurprisingly, she became known as "Dragon Dix," a nickname she confirmed by regularly clashing with military bureaucrats and pointedly ignoring administrative details.

Under Dix's leadership the standards of military nursing markedly improved. She was concerned with the welfare of her corps and the men they cared for, often obtaining medical supplies from private sources when the government proved unforthcoming. At the end of the Civil War, Dix returned to her work for the mentally ill. She spent her last days in the hospital that she had founded in Trenton, which she called her "firstborn child."

Reference: Barbara Witteman, *Dorothea Dix, Social Reformer* (Let Freedom Ring), 2003.

ETHERIDGE, ANNA
US Civil War Nurse, b. 1839, d. 1913

In *Women of the War,* published in 1866, "Gentle Anna's" service in the Civil War was commended in the following words: "Few soldiers were in the war longer, or served with so slight intermission, or had so little need of rest."

Born Anna Lorinda Blair to prosperous parents in Wayne County, Michigan, she married unsuccessfully at sixteen. In the summer of 1861, while in Detroit, Etheridge enlisted in the Second Michigan Volunteers. She was one of twenty young women who offered their services as **vivandières** (see p. 146) to the regiment. Within a few months only Etheridge remained.

She first saw action at Blackburn's Ford, Virginia, nursing the wounded on the battlefield and bringing water to the dying (see also **Molly Pitcher,** p. 106). After the second Battle of Bull Run (1862), and at the urging of General Philip Kearny, the regiment provided her with a horse, which she rode side-saddle into the front line, frequently dismounting to come to the aid of wounded men while fighting continued around her. Having bound up their wounds and given them water or some other "stimulating drink," Etheridge would then gallop off on her mission of mercy undeterred by the musket balls that often passed through her clothes. She was armed at all times with two pistols. Her brigade commander, General Berry, declared that Etheridge remained cool and self-possessed under fire as fierce as any he had experienced himself. The gallant General Kearny suggested that Etheridge be made a regimental sergeant, but he was killed shortly afterward and Etheridge never received a sergeant's rank or pay. She was, however, awarded a medal, the Kearny Cross.

When not in the field or working in military hospitals, Etheridge oversaw the cooking at brigade headquarters. On the march, she accompanied the ambulances and the surgeons. At the nightly bivouacs, she wrapped herself in a blanket and slept on the ground "with the hardihood of a true soldier."

Etheridge was present at the First Battle of Bull Run (1861) and at Antietam (1862), after which Second Michigan was sent to Tennessee. She decided to remain with the Army of the Potomac and enlisted with the Third and then the Fifth Regiments, serving at Fredericksburg (1862) and Chancellorsville (1863), where she was wounded when a Union officer hid behind her in a vain attempt to save his life. On several occasions she rallied demoralized troops and, seizing the colors, led them in a charge. She faltered only once, at the Battle of the Wilderness (1864), when a teenage orderly to whom she was talking fell into her arms, killed instantly by a bullet to the heart. Etheridge was so disoriented that she ran into the advancing Confederate line, through which she passed unharmed. The Union troops dubbed her "the brave little soldier in petticoats."

In September 1864, General Ulysses S. Grant ordered that all women be removed from military camp in his theater of operations, and thereafter Etheridge worked in the hospital at City Point, Virginia, although it seems she was with Fifth Michigan when it mustered out in July 1865.

After the Civil War, Etheridge found temporary employment at the Treasury Department and in 1886 formally requested a pension of fifty dollars a month. A year later Congress granted her a monthly pension of twenty-five dollars. She was buried in Arlington National Cemetery. A poem of 1866 celebrates Etheridge's Civil War exploits:

Hail, dauntless maid! whose shadowy form,
Borne like a sunbeam on the air,
Swept by amid the battle-storm,
Cheering the helpless sufferers there,
Amid the cannon's smoke and flame,
The earthquake roar of shot and shell,
Winning, by deeds of love, a name
Immortal as the brave who fell.

Reference: P. Brockett, *Women's Work in the Civil War: A Record of Heroism, Patriotism and Patience,* 1867.

KNOCKER, ELSIE, see CHISHOLM, MAIRI, and ELSIE KNOCKER.

INGLIS, ELSIE
British World War I Doctor, b. 1864, d. 1917

The daughter of an official in the Indian Civil Service, Inglis was born on a Himalayan hill station. Her parents ensured that she had a good education, and she attended the Edinburgh School of Medicine for Women, studying under Dr. Sophia Jex-Blake, the first woman physician in Scotland, before moving to the University of Glasgow to promote a rival women's faculty and winning the right to read medicine alongside men.

In 1892 Inglis had qualified as a licentiate of all the Scottish medical schools. She then moved to London, where she was horrified by the shoddy standards of care endured by many female patients. In 1894 she returned to Edinburgh and with another female doctor, Jessie MacGregor, established Scotland's only maternity center run by women. She traveled widely, visiting clinics in Europe and the United States, including the Mayo Clinic in Minnesota. She also became politically active and was one of the founders of the Scottish Women's Suffragette Federation. A philanthropist, Inglis frequently waived her fees and personally funded the convalescence of poor patients.

On the outbreak of World War I in 1914, Inglis offered to provide the British army with fully staffed Scottish Women's Hospital (SWH) medical units, only to be told by a War Office official, "My good lady, go home and sit still." However, the French took Inglis seriously, dispatching two of her units to France and a third, headed by Inglis herself, to Serbia. She dealt with a typhus epidemic before she and the members of her unit became prisoners of the Austrians, who overran Serbia in the autumn and winter offensives of 1915. Thereafter Inglis and her team tended both Serb and Austrian wounded in military hospitals in Krusevac.

Repatriated in February 1916, Inglis immediately organized and accompanied an SWH medical team, which was dispatched by sea to Russia. She also ensured the establishment of an SWH hospital at Salonika, in northeast Greece, where an Anglo-French expeditionary force and the rebuilt Serbian army had been bottled up since the spring of 1916.

By 1917, Inglis had organized fourteen medical units for the Belgian, French, Russian, and Serbian armies. When she sailed back to England from Russia in November 1917, she was exhausted and stricken with cancer. With a huge effort, she said farewell to her Serbian staff and, after the ship docked, managed to walk ashore. She died the next day.

Inglis's life was devoted to her twin passions, suffrage and surgery. Her name lives on in the Elsie Inglis Unit of the Scottish Women's Hospitals, a children's home in Yugoslavia, and a wing of the Royal Infirmary in Edinburgh.

Reference: Margo Lawrence, *Shadow of Swords: A Biography of Elsie Inglis,* **1971.**

KEIL, LILLIAN KINKELA

US Military Flight Nurse, World War II and Korea, One of the Most Highly Decorated Women in US Military History, b. 1916, d. 2005

During her service, Lillian Keil was awarded the impressive total of nineteen medals and ribbons, including four Air Medals, two Presidential Unit Citations, a World War II Victory Medal, four World War II battle stars, and a Korean Service Medal with seven battle stars.

She was born in Arcata, California and, after her father left the family home, was brought up by her mother in a convent where she worked as a cleaner. Following high school, she enrolled in a nursing program at St. Mary's Hospital in San Francisco. She later became a flight attendant with United Airlines, which then required its stewardesses to be registered nurses.

In World War II she enlisted as a flight nurse with the US Army Air Corps, attending wounded soldiers on casualty evacuation flights from combat zones to hospitals in the rear areas. In that war, and later in Korea, Keil took part in eleven major campaigns, including Normandy and the Battle of the Bulge (both 1944) and the Inch'on landings in Korea (1950). It is estimated that in these conflicts Keil tended some ten thousand US troops. In the air she was careful to remain well groomed and made up, to raise the morale of her wounded charges, and to remind them of girlfriends back at home.

A 1954 Hollywood movie, *Flight Nurse,* starring Forrest Tucker and Joan Leslie, was in part based on Keil's wartime experiences. Seven years later Keil appeared on the television show *This Is Your Life,* generating a flood of correspondence from veterans for whom she had cared in northwest Europe and Korea.

Reference: **Barbara Tomblin, G. I. Nightingales: The Army Nurse Corps in World War II, 1996.**

NIGHTINGALE, FLORENCE
British Nurse and Administrator, b. 1820, d. 1910

A pioneer of modern nursing and hospital-sanitation reform, Florence Nightingale was also a trailblazer in the use of statistics to demonstrate that social phenomena can be objectively measured and subjected to mathematical analysis. Known to British troops in the Crimea as "the Lady with the Hammer" for her prowess in breaking into a locked cupboard full of medical supplies, she was equally fearless whether fighting wartime dysentery and disease or mounting pitched battles with the boneheaded, reactionary, and misogynistic military commanders who stood in her way.

Nightingale was the second daughter of wealthy and well-connected parents who were traveling in Italy when she was born and named her after the city of her birth (her sister Parthenope was named after the ancient city that is now Naples). Florence was very close to her father, William, who taught her classics and mathematics and encouraged her to study modern languages.

At the age of seventeen Nightingale underwent the first of a number of religious experiences calling her to nursing, a prospect that dismayed her mother, who was determined that Florence make a good marriage. Active involvement in Poor Law reform hardened Nightingale's resolve. In 1850, while traveling in Europe, she visited an innovative hospital at Kaiserswerth, Germany, which was staffed by an order of Lutheran deaconesses. She also received encouragement from Elizabeth Blackwell, who had been the first woman to earn a medical degree in the United States and who worked for a time in London at St. Bartholomew's Hospital.

Nightingale's nursing career began in earnest in 1851, the year when, to the distress of her mother, she rejected a proposal of marriage from the poet and politician Richard Monckton Milnes, the first Baron Houghton. Overcoming the strenuous objections of her family, she proceeded to Kaiserswerth, where she received four months' training as a deaconess. This deliberate choice of the single life in an era when a "spinster" was widely derided and despised was highly controversial, but guaranteed Nightingale her lifelong independence.

In August 1853, thanks to a five-hundred-pound annual allowance from her father, Nightingale was able to assume the post of unpaid superintendent at the Institute for the Care of Sick Gentlewomen in London, where she gained her first experience of day-to-day administration. In 1854 she was recruited by an old friend, Sidney Herbert, secretary of war, to train and lead a contingent of thirty-eight volunteer nurses to the Crimea, where Britain, France, and Turkey were at war with imperial Russia. Reports in the *Times* of London filed by its correspondent in the field, William Howard Russell, had been highly critical of the British army's treatment of its wounded.

The British expeditionary force had arrived on the Crimean Peninsula singularly ill equipped to deal with the scourge of cholera then raging in southern Europe. At the vast military hospital in Scutari, on the Asian shore of the Bosporus, men were kept in filthy conditions without blankets or decent food, and slept in uniforms "stiff with dirt and gore." Wounds accounted for only one death in six, and the overall death rate from disease was running at 60 percent.

Nightingale arrived at Scutari (modern-day Usküdar, a suburb of Istanbul) on November 4, 1854, on the eve of the Battle of

Inkerman. Herbert had promised her "unlimited power of drawing on the government for whatever you think requisite for the
success of your mission." However, she had first to overcome
the hostility of the army's male medical staff, who regarded her arrival as a slur on their own professionalism. Nevertheless, by the
end of 1854, Nightingale had brought a degree of order to
the chaos at Scutari. Another forty-six nurses had arrived from
England, kitchens and laundries had been established, and the
wives and children of the soldiers at Scutari were cared for.

Nightingale regularly worked a twenty-hour day and was the
only woman permitted to enter the wards after eight at night,
when the nurses were replaced by orderlies. The Grecian lamp she
carried on her nightly rounds at Scutari earned her enduring fame
as a Victorian icon, when the *Times* war correspondent adapted
the troops' admiring nickname of "the Lady with the Hammer"
into something more feminine and acceptable to readers back
home, "the Lady with the Lamp." More practically, it also provided illumination for her meticulous updating of medical records.
This painstaking work led to her invention of the "coxcomb," a
graphic depiction of changing patient outcomes similar to a modern pie chart, which was to become a vital tool in her subsequent
campaign for hospital reform.

Early in 1855 the hospital at Scutari suffered a setback when its
defective sewage system, which Nightingale had not tackled, led
to a renewed outbreak of cholera and typhus fever. To these were
added frostbite and dysentery contracted in the trenches before
Sebastopol. In February 1855 the death rate was still an alarming
42 percent. The War Office intervened to order the immediate
implementation of sanitary reforms, and within four months the
death rate fell to 2 percent.

In May 1855, Nightingale fell ill with "Crimean fever" while
visiting hospitals on the front line. She returned to the Crimean
Peninsula in March 1856 and remained there until August, when
she sailed to England to be received as a national heroine. She
compiled an exhaustive and confidential report based on her
experience in the Crimea, and in 1858 published *Notes on Matters Affecting the Health, Efficiency and Hospital Administration in the*

British Army. That year she gave evidence to the Royal Commission on the Army, which led to the formation in 1859 of the Army Medical College at Chatham and in 1861 to an army hospital in Woolwich. As a woman, Nightingale could not sit on the commission, but she wrote its one-thousand-page report, compiled its exhaustive tables of statistics, and was closely involved in the implementation of its findings. She subsequently developed a Model Hospital Statistics Form, enabling hospitals to collect and generate consistent data. She had been elected a fellow of the Royal Statistics Society in 1858 and in 1874 became an honorary member of the American Statistical Association.

In 1860 she used the forty-five thousand pounds raised by public subscription for the Nightingale Fund to establish a training school for nurses at St. Thomas's Hospital (now part of King's College, London). The same year saw the publication of *Notes on Nursing,* which remains a classic introduction to the field. But although Nightingale urged the removal of restrictions that prevented women from pursuing professional careers, she remained convinced that it was more important to have better-trained nurses than women doctors and withheld her support from feminist campaigners such as Elizabeth Garrett Anderson, the first woman in England to qualify as a doctor.

Following the Indian Mutiny of 1857, Nightingale became a political expert on imperial India, writing influential papers on the improvement of health and sanitation on the subcontinent. In all these endeavors she preferred to work behind the scenes, living the reclusive life of an invalid. This was possibly caused by her exertions in the Crimea or the result of a psychosomatic condition that may also have triggered her early religious experiences. From 1896 she was bedridden.

In her old age Nightingale received many honors, and in 1907 she became the first woman to be awarded the Order of Merit. She died in 1910 at the age of ninety and was buried, according to her wishes, at St. Margaret's, East Wellow, near her parents' home in Hampshire. After the queen herself, she was probably the best-known woman of the Victorian era.

Reference: Florence Nightingale, *Notes on Nursing,* **2007.**

SEACOLE, MARY "MOTHER"
Jamaican Nurse and Writer, b. 1805, d. 1881

A heroine of today's multicultural historians, Mary Seacole was one of the most remarkable women of the nineteenth century, an intrepid traveler, a pioneer of military nursing, and a beacon of cheerful self-reliance. She once observed, "Whenever the need arises—on whatever distant shore—I ask no higher or greater privilege than to minister to it."

She was born in Kingston, Jamaica, the daughter of a Scottish officer and a free black woman who ran a boardinghouse for British officers. Being of mixed race, Seacole was technically free but enjoyed few civil rights: she could not vote, hold public office, or enter a profession.

In her early years Seacole's love of travel resulted in two trips to England, where she was the butt of racial taunts that prompted her to protest, "I am only a little brown—a few shades duskier than the brunettes whom you all admire so much." She was briefly married to Edwin Horatio Seacole (one of Admiral Nelson's god-children) but after his death resolved to live an independent life as a hotel keeper and nurse, acquiring much practical experience during the cholera and yellow fever epidemics that were a regular feature of life in Jamaica. During a yellow fever outbreak, Seacole supervised the nursing at Up Park Military Camp. She also made a postmortem dissection of an infant cholera victim in an attempt to discover more about the disease.

After the loss of her mother, Seacole joined her brother in New Granada (now Colombia and Panama), which was a magnet for adventurers and gold prospectors. Here the resourceful Seacole combined work as a hotelier with prospecting and nursing.

After the outbreak of the Crimean War in 1854, Seacole traveled to England and badgered the War Office to send her to the theater of war as a nurse. She was cold-shouldered by the military and by Elizabeth Herbert, the wife of the secretary of war, who was recruiting nurses. Undaunted, Seacole made the three-thousand-mile journey to the Crimea as a sutler, supplying provisions to the troops, and established the British Hotel at Spring Hill, two miles from Balaklava, to provide a "mess table and comfortable quarters for sick and convalescent officers."

Both officers and other ranks found hospitality and a warm welcome at Spring Hill. The French chef Alexis Soyer, who was to revolutionize army catering in the Crimea, praised Seacole's "soups and dainties." She also provided sound medical treatment based on traditional Caribbean remedies to combat diarrhea, dysentery, and cholera. Armed with her medicines, lint, bandages, and needle and thread, "Mother" Seacole treated the wounded on the battlefield, and on September 8, 1855, was the first woman to enter Sebastopol.

Seacole's work in the Crimea drew only faint praise from her contemporary **Florence Nightingale** (see p. 264). While conceding that Seacole had done "some good," Nightingale discouraged her nurses from visiting Spring Hill, which she wrongly considered to be a nest of "drunkenness and improper conduct." Nightingale's uncharitable attitude was colored by the fact that Seacole had secured the support of one of her old enemies, Dr. John Hall, inspector general of hospitals in the Crimea.

In 1856, after the conclusion of the Crimean War, Seacole returned to England in debt and in poor health. When she was forced to declare herself bankrupt, a veteran of the Crimean War wrote to the *The Times* to ask whether "while the benevolent deeds of Florence Nightingale are being handed down to posterity with blessings and imperishable renown, are the humbler actions of Mrs. Seacole to be entirely forgotten, and will none now substantially testify to the worth of those services of the late mistress of Spring Hill?"

The answer came when the press highlighted Seacole's plight and in July 1857 money was raised by a four-night benefit in her honor at the Royal Surrey Gardens. Seated in the place of honor, surrounded by members of the military establishment, Seacole received the acclaim of the public. Sadly, much of the money raised by the benefit was mismanaged, but she recouped her losses with the publication of a successful autobiography, *The Wonderful Adventures of Mrs. Seacole in Many Lands,* which is suffused with her sense of humor, indomitable self-confidence, and practical good sense. The book conveys "how hard the right woman had to struggle to convey herself to the right place."

Reference: Jane Robinson, *Mary Seacole: The Charismatic Black Nurse Who Became a Heroine of the Crimea,* 2005; and Mary Seacole, *The Wonderful Adventures of Mrs. Seacole in Many Lands,* 1857.

US MILITARY NURSES AND DOCTORS
1950–Present

Korea

Occupied by Japan in World War II, Korea had been divided along the 38th Parallel at the end of the war, with Soviet troops occupying the North, and US forces the South. The president of North Korea, Kim Il-Sung, claimed the whole of the country, but elections in the South produced a government that was friendly toward the United States, and by 1949 both Soviet and US troops had been withdrawn. In June 1950 the North Korean People's Army (KPA) invaded the South.

At that time only one US Army nurse, Captain Viola B. McConnell, was stationed in Korea. For her work in helping to evacuate seven hundred Americans to Japan, she received the Bronze Star. Within weeks the KPA had occupied all of South Korea with the exception of a small area around Pusan in the southeast, where a multinational force dominated by the Americans had been assembled under the banner of the United Nations.

US combat troops had begun to arrive in South Korea at the beginning of July, and with them came some sixty members of the **Army Nurse Corps** (ANC, see p. 248). Within a few days, twelve nurses moved forward with a mobile army surgical hospital (MASH) to treat critically wounded casualties before they were evacuated to army hospitals or US Navy hospital ships.

By 1951, there were 540 army nurses in Korea, the majority of them veterans of World War II who on demobilization had joined the reserves (see **Keil, Lillian Kinkela,** p. 263). Members of the

ANC served throughout the Korean Peninsula: army nurses supported combat troops defending the Pusan perimeter; they were present during the amphibious landings at Inch'on in September 1950; and they accompanied advance troops across the 38th Parallel to the Yalu River on the Manchurian border. They also supported the UN forces in their withdrawal south to the 38th Parallel after the Chinese launched a counteroffensive in November 1950.

Conditions sometimes recalled those that had confronted army nurses in World War II during the Allied landings in Italy. The thirteen nurses of the MASH that arrived shortly after the landings at Inch'on took over a civilian hospital where they endured conditions as primitive as those in which the GIs for whom they cared had fought and died. The nurses wore fatigues, combat boots, and steel helmets, which they used as washbasins, and lived in tents or shattered buildings. No army nurse was killed by enemy action in Korea, but Major Genevieve Smith, on her way to take up the post of chief nurse, died in an air crash.

In 1950, the number of navy nurses had been drastically reduced from World War II levels and there were only just under 2,000 regular and 440 reserve navy nurses serving on active duty. In August 1950, the hospital ship USS *Consolation* arrived in Korea and the USS *Repose* and *Benevolence* were taken out of the reserve fleet. During a trial run in the San Francisco harbor, *Benevolence* sank. There were fifteen navy nurses on board, one of whom died in the incident. In September 1950, eleven navy nurses died when the aircraft in which they were traveling crashed in the Pacific en route to the Korean theater on September 19, 1950. By 1951 the hospital ship USS *Haven,* with thirty nurses on board, was on station rotating with other ships between Korea and Japan.

The ships were a new type of mobile hospital, capable of performing different functions in different locations. They supported the Inch'on landings and aided the evacuation from Hamhung in December 1950. Two senior navy nurses, Commander Estelle Kalnoske Lange and Lieutenant Ruth Cohen, were awarded the Bronze Star for their work on the hospital ships.

Convalescent patients were sent to Yokosuka, in Japan, where

200 nurses worked in a hospital that had replaced a small prewar dispensary. By July 1951 the number of navy nurses in the theater had reached 3,200, all of them women, as men were not then permitted to join the Navy Nurse Corps.

The **United States Air Force** (USAF, see p. 185) came into being on September 18, 1947, and its nursing service underwent a baptism of fire in the Korean War. It went into action almost immediately, in the air evacuation of casualties. On December 5, 1950, the USAF's Nurse Corps assisted in the evacuation of about 4,000 patients after the Chinese intervention in the war. Flight nurses had to load between 30 and 40 patients onto each aircraft, calmly and efficiently arranging them to care for their wounds or illnesses. Extra litters often dotted the floor, making movement extremely difficult. Nurses had to cope with the rigors of flying at altitude, where the noise of the engines muffled cries for help and wounds and bodily functions displayed markedly different characteristics from those presented on the ground. Nevertheless, thanks to the interventions of the army's MASH teams and the efficiency of air evacuation, fewer than 2,000 of the 78,000 men who were wounded in Korea lost their lives. By the end of the war, the 2,990 air force nurses in Korea had evacuated some 350,000 patients.

Vietnam

The flood tide of Japanese conquest in 1941–42 sounded the death knell of the European empires in Southeast Asia. The French, more stubborn than most, hung on in Laos, Cambodia, and Vietnam until May 1954, when their departure left a Vietnam divided between the Communist North and a notionally democratic South.

The North's growing infiltration of the South, combined with a Communist insurgency in Laos and Cambodia, prompted the United States to step up its support for South Vietnam's president, Ngo Dinh Diem. In the late 1950s it progressed from training the new republic's army to deploying military advisers in the country, and by 1962 the arrangement had been formalized with the establishment of the Military Assistance Command (MAC). Within three years the number of US advisers had grown to twenty-seven thousand, and in March 1965 President Johnson's decision to commit combat troops to the war was symbolized by the landing of US Marines at Da Nang.

The first US Army nurses had arrived in 1956 to train the South Vietnamese and provide care for American military advisers. By the end of 1963 there were 215 nurses in the theater, working in mobile army surgical hospitals and evacuation hospitals in Vietnam and Thailand. Thereafter numbers began to rise.

Between 1963 and 1973, of the approximately 2.6 million US military personnel who served in Vietnam, some 5,600 were nurses in the army, navy, marine corps, and air force. Judith Baker Williams, an army nurse who served in the Sixty-seventh Evacuation Hospital in Qui Nhon, recalled:

> Our battlegrounds were the Emergency Room, Operating Room, Post-Op, Intensive Care Unit, and Surgical Wards. We served our country with pride. We were the youngest and most inexperienced nurses ever to have been sent into a war zone, but nothing could have prepared us for what we saw and what we had to deal with. But we met the challenge; the survival rate for the seriously wounded was 83 percent, the highest survival rate of any war.

Military nurses in Vietnam had routinely to deal with men seriously wounded from vicious *punji* sticks, booby traps, claymore mines, and high-velocity bullets. The speed with which helicopters were able to convey wounded soldiers from the battlefield to a hospital placed an immense strain on medical personnel, who had to make instant triage assessments of each patient's chances of survival, often while under rocket and mortar attack.

In 1963, four of the navy nurses stationed at the US Naval Station Hospital in Saigon were the first military women to be awarded the Purple Heart after they cared for the victims of a car-bomb attack in spite of sustaining injuries themselves in the blast.

The navy hospital that opened in Da Nang in 1966 was a regular target of rocket attacks and was shelled during the 1968 Tet offensive. In 1969 its operating rooms were in use around the clock.

USAF flight nurses were stationed in Saigon, and clinical nurses were placed in other locations in Vietnam and Thailand. The USAF hospital at Cam Ranh Bay was far from the fighting, and the greater part of its work was not focused on combat wounds, allowing many nurses to work regular shifts and to do voluntary work among the local Vietnamese. Air-evacuation duties were assigned to two teams: the Military Airlift Command, with sixty-seven nurses who escorted patients aboard Lockheed C-141 Starlifter aeromedical transport aircraft bound for the United States; and the Pacific Air Force (PACAF), which deployed fifty-four flight nurses on Lockheed C-130 Hercules multirole transports flying to the Philippines, Okinawa, and Japan. When operating in areas that had not been secured, the nurses were armed and trained to fire an M-16 machine gun. For loading patients under enemy fire at Da Nang, First Lieutenant Jane A. Lombardi was awarded the Bronze Star.

Between 1965 and 1970, of 133,000 patients treated by US military nurses, only 2.6 percent died. Seven female army nurses died in the conflict. First Lieutenant Sharon Ann Lane, who was killed at work by an enemy rocket attack, was awarded a posthumous Bronze Star.

A number of advances in military nursing were made during the Vietnam years. In 1964, Margaret E. Bailey became the first African-American nurse to be promoted to the rank of lieutenant colonel and in 1970 was made full colonel. In 1964, married women were allowed to receive direct appointments into the regular army, and two years later male nurses were authorized commissions. In 1970, a married, pregnant officer was able to stay on active duty. In 1972 Alene B. Duerk, a veteran of World War II, Korea, and Vietnam, became the first navy nurse to be promoted to the rank of admiral.

In 1973, when the US military became an all-volunteer force, women made up only 2 percent of its personnel. Nevertheless, the way was now open for significant changes. For example, in 1979,

Hazel W. Johnson, director of the Army Nurse Corps, became the first African-American officer in the entire military to reach the rank of general. In 1980, Captain Frances T. Shea became the first female navy nurse to command a naval hospital.

Global Operations, Kuwait and Iraq

In 1982 one female and two male army nurses were assigned to the United Nations peacekeeping force in Sinai. In October 1983, in Operation Urgent Fury, the invasion of the island of Grenada, the United States launched the first major military operation since the Vietnam War. Sixteen army nurses of the Fifth MASH and 307th Medical Battalion at Fort Bragg took part in Urgent Fury, and six received decorations. In 1984 a policy change permitted the deployment of up to two hundred nurses to support military units in the field. In December 1989, in Operation Just Cause, the US invasion of Panama and the toppling of its dictator, Manuel Noriega, army nurses of the 44th Medical Brigade, from Fort Bragg, were assigned to medical facilities in the theater.

In the 1980s, when the Cold War was at its height, US defense planners estimated that another thirty thousand military nurses, with experience across the medical spectrum, would be needed. The time when they might be needed seemed to have arrived in the wake of the Iraqi invasion of Kuwait in August 1990 and the subsequent Persian Gulf War.

The planning and execution of the removal of Iraqi forces from Kuwait, in Operations Desert Shield and Desert Storm, presented the US military with a series of new challenges for women. The successful mounting of both operations depended on the mobilization of reservists and the medical corps. Thousands of reservists, including female nurses, doctors, and surgeons, were deployed to the Persian Gulf. By February 1991, 2,265 army, 1,350 navy, and 336 air force nurses had landed in Saudi Arabia. They were to serve in forty-four hospitals, one of which, deployed on the Iraqi border, was farther forward than coalition troops when Desert Storm was launched on February 24.

In Desert Storm, medical personnel served in several different kinds of medical facilities: huge tents surrounded by sandbags; temporary, air-conditioned buildings quickly assembled from pre-fabricated materials; battalion aid stations nearer the front line, where injured soldiers were brought for assistance and evaluation of their wounds; and mobile army surgical hospitals (MASH units) located some fifty miles behind the front line and following the troops. Combat-support hospitals were located some hundred miles behind the front line and treated the local population as well as coalition military. Evacuation hospitals, established near air-fields, provided care for soldiers awaiting aircraft to fly them for specialized treatment in Europe.

Medical care was also provided by the US Navy in the form of fleet hospitals and the hospital ship USNS *Comfort,* a former oil tanker and the third navy ship to bear that name. With 956 naval hospital staff, including 157 nurses, and 12 operating rooms, *Comfort* was capable of handling 1,000 patients.

In the buildup to Desert Storm, many chilling predictions were made about the use of chemical and biological weapons by the Iraqi dictator Saddam Hussein and the inevitability of heavy coali-tion combat casualties. But in the face of overwhelming force, the Iraqi will to fight rapidly crumbled, and in the first hundred hours of fighting, some eighty thousand of Saddam's troops surrendered. Rather than dealing with mounting US casualties, medical person-nel found they were coping with wounded Iraqi prisoners, acci-dental injuries, and medical problems caused by desert conditions, the most common of which was dehydration. One hospital treated eight thousand outpatients. In Desert Storm, the final death toll in all three US services was 148.

In previous conflicts, nurses usually remained well behind the battle lines. However, in Desert Storm at least one woman, Major Rhonda Cornum, an Army flight surgeon, went into enemy terri-tory on a rescue mission. On February 27, 1991, Cornum and a seven-man flight crew flew by helicopter to extract an injured pilot who had come down some sixty miles behind the Iraqi bor-der and had radioed for help. The helicopter was hit by ground fire and crashed in the desert, killing five of Cornum's comrades.

The seriously injured Cornum became one of two US service-women taken prisoner during the Gulf War. Both her arms had been broken in the crash, and she was unable to fight off a sexual assault by one of her captors (for another American servicewoman in Iraqi hands, see **Lynch, Jessica,** p. 229). She and the other two survivors of the crash were released on March 6. She was awarded the Distinguished Flying Cross and the Purple Heart.

Shortly after the conclusion of the Persian Gulf War, many soldiers who had served in the theater began to exhibit a variety of symptoms, including memory, hair, and weight loss; insomnia; severe fatigue; and diminished powers of concentration. Initially identified by the Department of Defense as post-traumatic stress disorder, these symptoms were eventually attributed to Gulf War syndrome. In veterans of the Gulf War, the condition seems to have been triggered by exposure to a combination of factors, any one of which might have a malign effect: vaccination against chemical or biological attacks; exposure to equipment or munitions containing depleted uranium or struck by shells that incorporate this dangerous material; smoke and chemical pollutants produced by burning oil wells; and bites from sand flies indigenous to the Persian Gulf.

Between 1991 and 1993, an army doctor, Paula K. Underwood, treated more than seventy cases of Gulf War syndrome. In 2003, in the buildup to the Second Gulf War, Underwood and other army doctors worked together on a project to protect the health of the 250,000 soldiers sent to the theater and to establish an automatic screening program for them on their return.

When the Iraq War began in March 2003, the USNS *Comfort* was once again in the Persian Gulf. Seven of its 157 nurses had served in Desert Storm. Military nurses and doctors were also busy on land, in Iraq and Kuwait. The Forty-seventh Combat Support Hospital, in the Kuwaiti desert, was a three-hundred-bed medical complex, covering twelve acres and boasting state-of-the art facilities in air-conditioned tents that were pressurized to keep out the dust. Conditions in some of the makeshift hospitals in Iraq were more testing. The Eighty-sixth Combat Support Hospital near An Nasiriya was often filled with choking dust, stirred up by the desert wind, which forced its staff and patients to don surgical masks.

Reference: Karen Zeinert and Mary Miller, *The Brave Women of the Gulf Wars: Operation Desert Storm and Operation Iraqi Freedom,* 2006.

WALKER, MARY EDWARDS
US Feminist and Civil War Doctor, b. 1823, d. 1919

A forceful proponent of women's rights and dress reform and one of the first female journalists in America, Walker was awarded a Congressional Medal of Honor for her service as a physician in the Civil War and refused to return it when the award was revoked in 1917.

Born in Oswego County, New York, she was a pioneering advocate of women's rights and adopted the wearing of "bloomers" long before the craze for bicycling made them fashionable. In 1855 she became one of the United States' first female physicians when she graduated from Syracuse Medical College. She married a fellow student, Albert Miller, wearing trousers and a dress coat at the ceremony, in which she did not promise to obey her husband. Nor did she take his name when they set up a medical practice together. Unfortunately, their patients did not take to a female physician, and neither the marriage nor the practice lasted long.

In 1861, at the start of the Civil War, Walker offered her services to the Union army but was not accepted. Undaunted, she worked as a nurse in the Patent Office Hospital in Washington and treated wounded soldiers at the First Battle of Bull Run (1861). In 1862, however, she was engaged by the army as an assistant surgeon with the Fifty-second Ohio Infantry, the first woman doctor to serve with its medical corps. Walker took risks in crossing Confederate lines to attend civilians and also undertook spying missions. In 1864 she was captured by Confederate troops and imprisoned for four months before being returned to the Union lines in an exchange of prisoners. She worked the closing months of the Civil War in a women's prison in Louisville, Kentucky, and at an orphans' asylum in Tennessee. During the war she habitually wore a man's uniform jacket and a pair of trousers under her skirt, and she carried two pistols.

When Walker received the Congressional Medal of Honor in January 1866, the citation noted that she had "devoted herself with much patriotic zeal to the sick and wounded soldiers, both in the field and in hospitals, to the detriment of her own health." After resigning from the army, Walker worked as a journalist in New York, lectured on women's rights, and wrote two books— *Hit: Essays on Women's Rights* (1871), a fictionalized autobiography, and *Unmasked, or the Science of Immorality* (1878)—and many broadsides against tobacco and alcohol. On formal occasions she invariably appeared in men's full evening dress and silk top hat, although she wore her hair in curls to show that she was a woman. This did not prevent her being arrested on several occasions for "masquerading in men's clothes." One of her best-known sayings was "Let the generations know that women in uniform also guaranteed their freedom."

In 1897 she founded a colony for women called Adamless Eve. When in 1917 the US government reacted to widespread abuse by revoking the award of some nine hundred Congressional Medals, Walker refused to return hers and wore it until her death two years later. In 1977 President Carter restored the medal, making her the only female recipient, and it can be seen today in the Women's Corridor at the Pentagon.

Reference: Mercedes Graef, *A Woman of Honor: Dr. Walker and the Civil War,* 2001.

9

RECORDING ANGELS

—◦◦◦—

Singers, Entertainers, Artists,
Propagandists, and Chroniclers of War,
the Good and the Bad

*I'm going to Spain with the boys. I don't know who the boys are,
but I'm going with them.*
—US war reporter Martha Gellhorn on the Spanish Civil War, 1936

EVERY WAR NEEDS its interpreters and chroniclers, those who
write, sing, or speak on behalf of all the others out either on active
service or left behind at home. Women have undertaken a far
greater and more varied share of this work than is generally realized. Like CNN's **Christiane Amanpour** (see p. 284), they have
made their mark in many areas and penetrated almost every arena
of war, leaving intensely personal records of their experience that
have survived the test of time, like the haunting songs of "the
Forces' Sweetheart," British World War II vocalist **Vera Lynn** (see
p. 302), or the gritty prose of war reporter **Martha Gellhorn**
(see p. 293).

Many of these reporters, artists, and activists were reaching out
for a life otherwise barred to them by virtue of their sex. Most of
them were active in the modern era, when the constraints against
women's education, choice of profession, and freedom of movement were beginning to break down. The honor of being America's first female war correspondent went to the pioneering **Peggy**

Hull Deuell in World War I (see p. 289). However, it was not until the eve of World War II, when many barriers to women's advancement were beginning to crumble, that women in any numbers were able to work as war correspondents or "warcos." Inevitably they still had to overcome much lingering prejudice in World War II, from the belief that war was a wholly male activity that they were unable to grasp, to the pseudo-chivalric argument that they were too frail and weak to stand up to the hardships that the task entailed.

A third school of thought focused on the practical difficulties presented by the presence of women in theaters of war. Most of this seemed to focus rather pruriently on the vexed matter of having to provide them with latrine facilities. When in 1944 this was advanced as a reason for preventing the formidable **Helen Kirkpatrick** (see p. 298) from reporting from the beachhead in Normandy, one of her supporters pointed out that she could "dig a latrine faster than anyone in this room."

The growing number of female war correspondents in part reflected the vital contribution women were making to the war effort in the United States, Britain, and the Soviet Union. Nevertheless, it was only with the greatest reluctance that the Allied high command contemplated admitting female war correspondents to the front line. On January 22, 1943, the remarkable **Margaret Bourke-White** (see p. 286) crashed this barrier with her aerial camera firmly in her grasp when she became the first woman to fly on a combat mission with the United States Army Air Force.

The ability of women such as Bourke-White, Kirkpatrick, and Gellhorn to focus single-mindedly on their work and also to be in the right place at the right time often enabled them to scoop their distinguished male counterparts. In Gellhorn's case it also played a part in the collapse of her marriage to Ernest Hemingway, whose grandstanding antics as a war correspondent were overshadowed by the more steely journalistic skills of his wife.

Also playing their part in recording conflicts near and far are women with more complex and sometimes compromised histories: **Tokyo Rose,** the voice of Japanese wartime radio propaganda

(see p. 306); **Mildred Elizabeth Gillars,** the American propagandist
for the Third Reich (see p. 296); **K'tut Tantri,** a woman of many
aliases and the eccentric voice of postwar Indonesian nationalism
(see p. 300); and a figure of the more recent past, the Russian journalist **Anna Politkovskaya,** investigative reporter of the war in
Chechnya and victim in 2006 of an assassin's bullet (see p. 303).

In the final analysis, the experience of battle is like having
sex—something almost impossible to communicate to an outsider.
After she had seen firsthand the siege of Sarajevo by Bosnian Serbs
in the early 1990s, Susan Sontag summed it up:

> We don't get it. We truly can't imagine what it was like. We
> can't imagine how dreadful, how terrifying war is, and how
> normal it becomes. Can't understand, can't imagine. That's
> what every soldier, and every journalist and aid worker and in-
> dependent observer who has put in time under fire, and had
> the luck to elude the death that struck down others nearby,
> stubbornly feels.

AL HAIDERI, SAHAR HUSSEIN
Iraqi Journalist, 1962–2007

A brave example of a new generation of Iraqi journalists, Haideri
took advantage of the accelerating violence in her country during
the American occupation to write about issues that were increasingly difficult if not impossible for the international media to
cover. For this boldness she paid with her life.

A print and radio journalist, she wrote for the Aswat al Iraq
(Voice of Iraq) news agency and local press as well as contributing
articles to the Institute for War and Peace Reporting (IWPR).
Born in Baghdad into a professional family and educated at Baghdad University, her career as a journalist began only after the
toppling of Saddam Hussein in 2003 when she joined a training
program run by Reuters and IWPR.

Based in Mosul in northern Iraq, she filed her first story in

2005. It dealt with attempts by local insurgents to impose Taliban-style restrictions on women in Mosul and described how female lecturers and civil servants were being targeted. However, staying at home was not an option she considered for herself. She chronicled the violent struggle for control over Mosul—she was herself a Shia whose husband was a Sunni—and in particular how this affected the women of the city.

Some of her reports had, to Western eyes, an almost surreal quality. She wrote about the covering of the heads of female mannequins in shop windows and the serving of tomatoes and cucumbers on different plates because they were supposedly of different genders. One particularly poignant feature was about the chief of a Mosul morgue, considered to be inured to death until the arrival of a charred corpse on his investigation table, unrecognizable but for the class ring on one finger. It was the ring he had bought for his son at graduation.

Haideri was as scathing about police corruption as she was alarmed by sectarian extremism. She was obliged to publish a number of stories under pseudonyms and took every opportunity to leave Mosul to visit Syria or attend training courses in Jordan. She was saved from a kidnap attempt by a US patrol and wounded in the stomach in a firefight. In 2006 she moved her husband and four daughters to Syria for their own safety. In 2007, she told the *UK Press Gazette,* "Our psychological state is unbalanced because we live and think in fear and worry. But I never thought about quitting journalism, as journalism is my life." It is a very dangerous life. When Iraqi journalists attempt to cover car bombings or other atrocities, they come under threat from US troops at checkpoints who tend to assume that any person of Arab appearance who approaches a bomb scene instead of running away from it, must be a suicide attacker. The Iraqi government in turn banned journalists from the scene of bomb incidents, ostensibly to protect them from secondary explosions, but effectively to keep all information in their own hands.

Haideri, however, was not killed by Americans but by Iraqis. On June 30, 2007, as she was leaving her house in Mosul, she was confronted by gunmen from an extremist group, the Ansar al-Sunna, who executed her. Later a statement was issued, claiming that she was killed because she had published "falsehoods" and supported the authorities. In fact she published the truth and supported the people of Iraq. She was one of the 108 journalists killed in Iraq—86 of them Iraqis—between 2003 and June 2007.

Reference: Ali A. Allawi, *The Occupation of Iraq: Winning the War, Losing the Peace,* 2007.

AMANPOUR, CHRISTIANE
British-Iranian International War Correspondent, b. 1958

As CNN's chief international correspondent, Christiane Amanpour has filed reports from most of the world's trouble spots, including Iraq, Israel, Iran, Afghanistan, Pakistan, Somalia, Rwanda, and Bosnia, and has interviewed innumerable world leaders. Former US President Bill Clinton dubbed her "the voice of humanity," but the administration of his successor, George Bush, was less fulsome, accusing her of being overly emotional and biased. *Time* magazine called her the most influential foreign correspondent since Edward R. Murrow.

Shortly after her birth in London, her British mother and Iranian airline-executive father moved their family to Tehran, where they led a privileged life until they were forced to flee the Islamic revolution of 1979. At the age of eleven, Amanpour had returned to the United Kingdom to receive a Catholic education and later studied journalism at the University of Rhode Island, from which she graduated in 1983. Thereafter she worked as a journalist for an NBC affiliate, WJAR-TV, in Rhode Island before joining CNN.

In journalism, timing is all, and in 1989 Amanpour was posted to Frankfurt in West Germany, where she reported on the democratic revolution that was sweeping across the Communist countries of Eastern Europe. However, it was her coverage of the Persian Gulf War in 1991 that brought her into the public eye. She began to file live reports shortly after the arrival of US troops in Saudi Arabia in Operation Desert Shield, as one of one hundred women journalists in the television pool. Although women had filed filmed reports during the Vietnam War, few provided the amount and depth of coverage that Amanpour, equipped with gas mask and helmet, gave CNN viewers worldwide.

In 1991 she covered the disintegration of the Soviet Union and the subsequent fighting in Tbilisi, the capital of Georgia. In 1992 she reported on the conflict in the Balkans that followed the breakup of Yugoslavia and covered the US-led peacekeeping mission in Somalia, Operation Restore Hope. In the 1990s, Amanpour returned repeatedly to the Balkans and at the start of the new millennium was present at the trial of Slobodan Milosevic for war crimes at the international court in The Hague. In 2005 she was in the region again to mark the tenth anniversary of the massacre in Srebenica.

In the summer of 2004, she was in Baghdad for the opening of the war-crimes trial of Saddam Hussein. Amanpour was later sharply critical of the media's self-censorship during the Iraq War, believing the coverage had been skewed by Pentagon bullying and the disinformation campaign mounted by the Bush administration, aided and abetted by a compliant Fox News. The war had been a disaster, she claimed, a frank admission to make in a country that had made her famous and for whose "American Way" she professed to having always harbored an outsider's respect.

In a speech in 2000, after accepting the Edward R. Murrow Award for distinguished achievement in broadcast journalism, Amanpour concluded by quoting **Martha Gellhorn** (see p. 293): "In all my reporting life I have thrown small pebbles into a very large pond, and I have no way of knowing whether any pebble caused the slightest ripple. I don't need to worry about that." In a world of instant communication, however, the ripples can come thick and fast, and Amanpour has received a stream of rewards (she is said to be one of the highest-paid women in broadcasting) and awards, including nine Emmys, the 1997 Woman of the Year in Iran, and the Golden Nymph Award at the Monte Carlo Television Festival in 1997.

Since 1998, Amanpour has been married to James Rubin, a former State Department spokesman in the Clinton administration who now works in the media.

Reference: Christiane Amanpour's RTNDA 2000 speech is available at www.unf.edu/jaxmedia/amanpour.htm.

BOURKE-WHITE, MARGARET
American World War II Photojournalist, b. 1904, d. 1971

A woman in a man's world, Margaret Bourke-White was one of the most influential photojournalists of the twentieth century. A pioneer of the photo-essay, she was in Moscow to record the first bombs falling on Moscow in Operation Barbarossa, the German invasion of the Soviet Union, and later became the first woman photographer with the US Army Air Force. While she was still at the height of her powers, her working life was cut short by the onset of Parkinson's disease.

She was born in New York City, the daughter of an engineer father, Joseph White, and a progressive, demanding mother, Minnie Bourke, who was involved in publications for the blind. As a child she was taken by her father to visit a steel foundry, and images of heavy industry were to remain an inspiration for the rest of her life. Her father, a keen amateur photographer, was also the source of her interest in photography. After graduating from Cornell in 1927, she launched herself as an architectural photographer from a studio in her one-room Cleveland apartment. The money she made by day photographing the homes of the wealthy subsidized her nocturnal and weekend activities recording the working life of steel mills.

By then she had survived a short-lived marriage in the mid-1920s and had reinvented herself as Margaret Bourke-White. In 1929 she became a staff photographer for a new magazine, *Fortune,* launched by Henry R. Luce and focusing on dramatic coverage of US industry. On assignments for *Fortune,* Bourke-White developed the concept of the photo-essay, before embarking on a freelance assignment in the Soviet Union, during which she completed the first comprehensive photographic record of Stalin's Russia. She made a second visit, at the invitation of the Soviet government, in 1931. A third visit, in 1932, to make a documentary film, was a failure.

In 1936, working for Luce's *Life* magazine, Bourke-White toured the American Dust Bowl with the writer Erskine Caldwell. Her pictures for *Life,* accompanied by her own text, saw the photo-essay emerge in full-fledged form. Bourke-White also provided the illustrations for a book with Caldwell on the Depression, *You Have Seen Their Faces* (1937). Two years later she married Caldwell, and during their brief marriage they collaborated on *North of the Danube* (1939) and *Say, Is This the USA?* (1941).

In early 1941, nearly a year before the United States entered World War II, Bourke-White and Caldwell were dispatched by *Life* to the Soviet Union via China to report on how Communism had fared since her first visit in 1930. On June 22, 1941, Hitler launched Operation Barbarossa. As German bombs fell on Moscow on July 20, Bourke-White was the only foreign photographer present to record the scene from the roof of the US embassy, providing *Life* with a major scoop. She also photographed Joseph Stalin in the Kremlin, where she was taken aback by his shortness and nonplussed by his refusal to smile for the camera. However, the Soviet dictator finally cracked a brief, wintry smirk when Bourke-White dropped her flashbulbs, enabling her to capture "the Man of Steel" in an unusually relaxed mood.

After covering the faltering German drive on Moscow, Bourke-White became the first woman photographer attached to the USAAF, in North Africa, where, on January 22, 1943, she also became the first American woman to fly on a combat mission. In 1945 she accompanied General Patton's Third Army into Germany and photographed the liberation of the death camps. She poured her experiences with the Third Army into a vivid book, *Dear Fatherland, Rest Quietly,* which chronicled the sudden and sometimes surreal collapse of the Third Reich. On the road to Frankfurt she encountered a goods train that had been halted by an air attack and which looters were now plundering: "A German *hausfrau* came running down the railroad tracks towards us. Her

arms were so full of pink panties and undershirts that she was scat-
tering a pink trail behind her, and she was laughing and crying at
the same time. 'Germany is *kaput!* Might as well loot!' she
shouted." At the very end of the war she photographed the
corpses of the dead wife and daughter of the assistant mayor of
Leipzig, who had swallowed cyanide rather than accept German
defeat.

Bourke-White later had these reflections on photographing
war victims and scenes of unimaginable horror:

> It is a peculiar thing about pictures of this sort. It is as though a
> protecting screen draws itself across my mind and makes it pos-
> sible to consider focus and light values and the technique of
> photography in as impersonal a way as though I were making an
> abstract camera composition. This blind lasts while I am actually
> operating the camera. Days later, when I develop the negatives,
> I am surprised to find that I cannot bring myself to look at the
> films.

The wartime years were proof of Bourke-White's extraordinary
energy, tenacity, and physical courage. An exceptionally attractive
woman, she was able to focus all her resources of well-bred charm
and journalistic low cunning to get the results she required. Cru-
cially, she possessed an almost supernatural ability to be in the right
place at the right time.

In the immediate postwar years, Bourke-White made long
trips to India, photographing Mahatma Gandhi many times and
taking her last picture of him hours before he was assassinated on
January 30, 1948. In 1950 she rejoined *Life* and in the following
six years covered subjects as diverse as the Korean War and the
gold mines in apartheid South Africa.

It was in Korea, in 1953, that she first felt the symptoms of
Parkinson's disease. She refused to surrender to the condition and
continued to work for *Life,* undergoing a risky operation to the
right side of her brain in 1957. This became the subject of a *Life*
article, written by Bourke-White, with pictures by her colleague

Alfred Eisenstaedt. However, a second operation in 1961 left her able to speak only with great difficulty. She died following a fall. Margaret Bourke-White has been portrayed twice on screen: in *Gandhi* (1982) by Candice Bergen; and in *Double Exposure* (1986) by Farrah Fawcett.

Reference: Margaret Bourke-White: *Portrait of Myself,* 1963; and Vicki Goldberg, *Margaret Bourke-White,* 1986.

DEUELL, PEGGY HULL
Pioneer US War Correspondent, b. 1889, d. 1967

Although the many reports Peggy Hull Deuell filed from the Pacific theater in World War II focused on trivial issues, she had played an important role in an earlier conflict—World War I—in establishing the right of women to send dispatches from the war zone.

Hull Deuell began her career at the age of sixteen as a typesetter for a small-town newspaper in her native Kansas. She gained her first taste of military life, if not action, when in 1916 she traveled to the Texas-Mexico border for the Cleveland *Plain Dealer* to cover the US Army's attempts to deal with the cross-border raids by the Mexican revolutionary Pancho Villa. She went on a fifteen-mile route march with an infantry company and, in her own words, emerged a "hardened veteran." In a contemporary photograph, Deuell posed in a uniform borrowed from the Ohio National Guard, snapping off a salute and looking like an endearingly perky heroine from a Charlie Chaplin movie.

On April 6, 1917, the United States declared war on Germany. The first American troops arrived in London the following August, although it would be many months before they saw any fighting on the Western Front. Nevertheless, Deuell began to press her new employer, the *El Paso Morning Times,* to send her to France as a war correspondent. Her entreaties were initially rejected as being "perfectly ridiculous," principally on the grounds that Deuell was a woman. However, she persisted and in the sum-

mer of 1917 established herself in Paris as a roving reporter, supplying the *Morning Times* with "human interest" on the American
troops in France.

Deuell never made it to the front line, but her lively copy on
conditions in American training camps created something of a sensation and her reports were taken up by the *Chicago Tribune*'s
newspaper for the US troops in Europe, which described her
as a "typical young American woman" full of "grit and energy."
The grit proved an irritant to the male reporters in France, who
ungallantly pointed out that Deuell had not received proper ac-
creditation. She returned to Texas, and mid-1918 found her in
Washington, working for a news syndicate and lobbying hard for
permission to cover the American military expedition that had
been dispatched to Siberia to extract the Czech Legion from the
chaotic aftermath of the Russian Revolution (see **Bochkareva,
Maria,** p. 88) and aid its transfer to the Western Front. Despite the
US War Department's initial reluctance to accede to her request,
Deuell arrived in Siberia in the autumn of 1918 as the first accredited female American war correspondent.

After World War I, she was divorced by her first husband,
journalist George Hull, and settled in Shanghai, where she was
married for a second time, to the English captain of a merchant
ship, John Kinley. The marriage meant that she lost her US citizenship, and her fight to regain it played a part in the reform of the
law affecting citizenship and married women. She was in Shanghai
in January 1932, in the process of divorcing husband number two,
when the Japanese attacked the city, a passage of arms that she reported for the New York *Daily News*. In 1933 she married the
newspaper's editor, Harvey Deuell, who died of a heart attack in
1939.

Deuell's notable pre-1939 career counted for little when in
1943, with America at war with Japan, she went to Washington to
collect her press credentials. She was now in her fifties and was advised that the best place for her to observe World War II was from
a rocking chair on her front porch. Once again Deuell persevered,
and in the winter of 1943 was dispatched to the Pacific. Because of

her age and sex, she was never allowed near the front line, and her reporting duties were confined to military bases and hospitals in Hawaii until the beginning of 1945, when she reported from some of the islands in the Pacific that had been retaken and cleared by the Americans. She conveyed her sense of frustration in a column of August 1944 in which she lamented, "I am a woman and as a woman am not permitted to experience the hazards of war reporting." For her services in World War II, she received a Navy Commendation.

In 1953 Deuell moved to California, where in her declining years she became a devotee of astrology. Her contribution to the history of war reporting was firmly rooted in the "little stories of war," which concentrated on the hopes and fears and daily lives of ordinary soldiers, one of whom wrote to her, "You will never realize what those yarns of yours . . . did to this gang. . . . You made them know they weren't forgotten."

Reference: Wilda M. Smith and Eleanor A. Bogart, *The Wars of Peggy Hull: The Life and Times of a War Correspondent*, 1991.

FRANK, ANNE
German-Jewish Diarist and Holocaust Victim, 1930–45

The author of perhaps the most widely read diary of all time, Anne Frank is also the best-known victim of the Holocaust and, arguably, the one with the most significant impact on posterity.

Anne was born in Germany, but her family escaped to Amsterdam in 1933, when Hitler came to power. In Holland her father, Otto, reestablished his pharmaceuticals business, but in 1940 the Germans invaded and occupied the Netherlands and began to intern Jews. In 1942, as the persecution became more severe, Anne, her parents, and her older sister, Margot, took refuge with four other Jews in a secret apartment in the building that housed Otto Frank's offices. Here they were fed and cared for by some of his former employees.

The fugitives remained in hiding, unable to leave the apartment, until 1944, when they were denounced by an informer. During these years Anne wrote stories and kept a diary in which she rehearsed her hopes, ambitions, and awakening sexuality. She was thirteen when she began the diary, in the form of letters to her imaginary friend "Kitty," and not yet sixteen when she died of typhus at the Bergen-Belsen concentration camp shortly after her deportation.

Her mother and sister perished, too. Only her father, who was in the camp hospital at Auschwitz when it was overrun by the Red Army in January 1945, survived the Holocaust. He was given Anne's papers by Miep Van Santen and Ellie Vossen, two of his former employees and guardians, who had found them in the ransacked secret apartment after they had been tossed aside by the Gestapo. Otto published Anne's diary in the original Dutch in 1947 under the title *Het Achterhuis* (The House Behind). In 1952 it appeared in an American edition as *The Diary of a Young Girl* and was followed by Broadway and Hollywood productions, in 1955 and 1959 respectively, as well as being translated into over thirty languages. The house in which the Frank family sought refuge in Amsterdam has been preserved as a memorial to all the young Jews who suffered and died in World War II.

On February 23, 1944, Anne had not left the cramped apartment since her family slipped into concealment there in 1942. Nevertheless, her luminous and unquenchable spirit shines through in what she wrote that day to "Kitty":

The best remedy for those who are afraid, lonely, or unhappy is to go outside, somewhere where they can be quite alone with the heavens, nature and God. Because only then does one feel that all is as it should be and that God wishes to see people happy, amidst the simple beauty of nature . . . Oh, who knows, perhaps it won't be long before I can share this overwhelming feeling of bliss with someone who feels the way I do about it. Yours, Anne.

Reference: Anne Frank, *Diary of a Young Girl,* 1953.

GELLHORN, MARTHA
US Writer and War Correspondent, b. 1908, d. 1998

A pioneering female war correspondent who covered conflicts from the Spanish Civil War in 1936 to Central America in the 1980s, Gellhorn was also married for four years to the novelist and war groupie Ernest Hemingway, a subject that in later years she was notably reluctant to discuss.

She was born in St. Louis into a liberal, cultured family—her father was a professor of gynecology, and her adored mother was an advocate of women's suffrage and a friend of Eleanor Roosevelt. She attended college at Bryn Mawr but in the late 1920s, at the end of her junior year, she left to pursue a career as a journalist.

In 1930, Gellhorn traveled to Europe. In Paris she wrote her first novel, *What Mad Pursuit* (1934), featuring the first in a long line of fictional journalist heroines, and became active in the pacifist movement. She returned to the United States in 1936 to work as a field reporter for the Federal Emergency Relief Administration (FERA), headed by Harry Hopkins and part of Roosevelt's New Deal. Gellhorn poured this experience into *The Trouble I've Seen* (1936), a novella that combined fact and fiction, established her reputation as a writer, and led to a close relationship with Eleanor Roosevelt.

In 1936, while on holiday in Key West, Florida, Gellhorn met Ernest Hemingway. They were reunited in 1937 in Spain, where Hemingway was reporting on the Civil War for the North Atlantic Newspaper Alliance (NANA) and Gellhorn was working for *Collier's* magazine. Although a novice war reporter, Gellhorn rapidly found a distinctive voice with which to distill her firsthand experience of the effects of the conflict on civilians. Her fiction of the period pointedly stigmatized the failure of the European democracies to face down fascism.

Like the protagonist in her 1940 novel, *A Stricken Field,* Gellhorn recognized the limited influence exerted by the individual writer, commenting "I'm not Joan of Arc, I'm only a journalist."

She was also prey to ambivalent thoughts about the role of women as correspondents in a combat zone, a dilemma reflected in her 1940 short story "Portrait of a Lady," drawn from her experience reporting the Russo-Finnish War for *Collier's*. In the spring of 1940, her unsuccessful attempt to help the writer Max Ohlau, a Communist friend from the Spanish Civil War who had been interned by the French government, provided the background to a pessimistic short story, "Goodwill to Men." Looking back in a 1995 interview with the filmmaker Marcel Ophüls, Gellhorn was at pains to point out the pitfalls that lie in wait for journalists who surrender their objectivity to a passion for a particular cause.

Gellhorn married Hemingway in November 1940 and subsequently traveled with him to the Far East to report the Sino-Japanese War. Their experiences resurfaced in sourly humorous form in the 1978 collection *Travels with Myself and Another,* in which Hemingway appears as "UC" (Unwilling Companion).

The fault lines in their stormy marriage were widened by the time Gellhorn spent with Hemingway in Cuba after completing her own extended tour of the Far East—Hemingway had bailed out after China. After the United States entered World War II, Hemingway's war effort in Cuba consisted of equipping his fishing boat, *Pilar,* to hunt U-boats off the coast of Cuba, an exercise in braggadocio of no military value. The couple spent much time drunk and at loggerheads.

After a stint as a war correspondent in Italy, where she reported on the Allied bombing of Monte Cassino, Gellhorn persuaded Hemingway to join her in Europe. He arrived as a correspondent also writing for *Collier's* as she was, a move calculated to enrage his wife, as female journalists were not accredited to front-line formations.

The rivalry between husband and wife came to a head over Operation Overlord, the Allied landings in Normandy on June 6, 1944. The *Collier's* edition that carried their stories on June 22 concentrated on Hemingway, although the great bombast had never set foot on the invasion beaches. In contrast, Gellhorn arrived in Normandy, on Omaha Beach, just two days after the landings. She had gained an edge on Hemingway by stowing away

on a hospital ship, a feat of initiative that resulted in a brief internment in Britain.

While Hemingway played at running his own private army in
liberated France, Gellhorn covered the closing stages of the war,
with vivid accounts of the Battle of the Bulge, the savage fighting
in the Hürtgen Forest, and the Battle of Berlin. All these were to
provide the material for her 1948 novel *The Wine of Astonishment*.

Gellhorn divorced Hemingway in 1945, and in what she
termed the "honeyed peace" moved restlessly around the world,
reporting from Dutch Indonesia, Israel, Poland, and Germany. In
1954 she married the editor in chief of *Time* magazine, T. S.
Matthews; they were divorced in 1966.

Gellhorn published more fiction drawn from her own life, including *His Own Man* (1958), which was based on the exploits of
her friend, the photographer Robert Capa. She continued to ruf-
fle feathers with hard-hitting reports from the wars in Vietnam,
the Six Day War in the Middle East, and, in the 1980s, the conflicts in Central America. Her last assignment, when she was
eighty-five, was in Brazil. By then she had attracted the admiration
of a younger generation of journalists, including the Australian
John Pilger, and the British Jon Simpson and Kate Adie. She was
always a challenging, cantankerous companion. One of her friends
compared Gellhorn to a rhinoceros "who has no idea that he has
stepped on your foot."

When she was raped in Kenya at the age of eighty, Gellhorn
remained curiously untouched by the experience. The earth only
moved for her, as she suggested to Eleanor Roosevelt, when she
was in the thick of battle, as she had been in the Spanish Civil
War, and could simply "put your body up against what you hate."
In later life Gellhorn refused to be seen merely as a literary adjunct
to Ernest Hemingway, whom she dismissed as a "disgusting
mythomaniac." Although Hemingway was by some distance a
much better novelist, as a war correspondent Gellhorn left the
greater mark.

Reference: Caroline Moorehead, *Martha Gellhorn: A Life,* **2003.**

GILLARS, MILDRED ELIZABETH
"Midge at the Mike," American World War II Propagandist for the Axis, b. 1901, d. 1988

Mildred Gillars sought fame as an actress and, having failed in this ambition, earned lasting notoriety as the Nazi propagandist dubbed "Axis Sally" by GIs in World War II.

She was born a US citizen in Portland, Maine, graduating from high school in Ohio and attending Ohio Wesleyan University, where she studied drama but failed to graduate. A series of dead-end jobs was followed in 1929 by a trip to Europe with her mother in search of an acting career. After studying for six months in France, she returned to the United States and eventually found work in New York as a small-time vaudevillian and musical comedy artiste. However, the breakthrough never came, and in 1933 she returned to France to work as a governess and salesgirl before moving to Berlin in 1935.

In the German capital, Gillars joined Radio Berlin as an announcer and actress. She remained at the station until May 1945 and from December 1941 presented a regular program called *Home Sweet Home,* referring to herself as "Midge at the Mike." The majority of the programs were beamed from Berlin, but some were also transmitted from occupied France and Holland.

Gillars's broadcasts, delivered in sultry, teasing tones, could be heard in Europe, the Mediterranean, North Africa, and the United States. On May 11, 1944, she made her most notorious broadcast, a dramatized prediction of the gory fate that awaited the Allied Expeditionary Force then readying itself to invade northwestern Europe. In other broadcasts, she attempted to interview captured American servicemen while posing as a Red Cross worker, a ploy that was not always successful.

In the immediate aftermath of the war, Gillars remained at large before being arrested in 1947 by the US Army Counter Intelligence Corps. She was held in custody for over a year and in August 1948 was flown to the United States, where she was eventually charged with treason by a federal grand jury. In March 1949 she was found guilty and received a prison sentence of ten to thirty years and a ten-thousand-dollar fine. In 1959 she became eligible for parole but waived the right, apparently preferring prison to the hostile reception that awaited her in the outside world. She was eventually released on parole in June 1961, after which she taught for a while before resuming her studies at Ohio Wesleyan, where she graduated in speech in 1973.

Reference: Williams M. Fuller, *Axis Sally: The Most Listened to Woman of World War II,* 2004.

HANOI HANNAH
Trinh Thi Ngo, North Vietnamese Propagandist, b. 1931

In the tradition of **Tokyo Rose** (see p. 306), Hanoi Hannah was a North Vietnamese radio announcer who broadcast pro-Communist propaganda to South Vietnam with the aim of undermining the morale of the US troops stationed there during the Vietnam War.

Hanoi Hannah broadcast three times daily, reading from lists of killed or captured Americans, playing antiwar songs, and encouraging her audience to question the purpose and morality of the war. Initially she was listened to with a mixture of amusement and contempt, but as the war dragged on, her pointed exaggerations of American casualties, and her reports of antiwar protest back home, undoubtedly prompted some servicemen to question the point of the war. On June 16, 1967, she greeted her listeners in characteristically subversive tones: "How are you, GI Joe? It seems to me that most of you are poorly informed about the going of the war, to say nothing of a correct explanation of your presence over here. Nothing is more confused than to be ordered into a war to die or to be maimed for life without the faintest idea of what's going on."

In her broadcasts, Hanoi Hannah particularly singled out black troops. The aim was to heighten racial tensions within the US Army by convincing blacks that they were being exploited by whites. She had a point. The Vietnam War coincided with the militant stage of the civil rights movement in the United States, which turned the role played by blacks in Vietnam into a major part of an ongoing controversy. Black leaders such as Martin Luther King Jr. argued that young blacks were more likely to be drafted than whites and, once drafted, were more likely to be ordered on dangerous assignments. There was substance to this statement, too. Although blacks made up 13 percent of the US population, in the years up to 1966 they sustained over 20 percent of the combat deaths in Vietnam.

After 1967, both the army and the marine corps made determined efforts to reduce battlefield casualties, and by the end of the Vietnam War, blacks had sustained approximately 5,700 of the 47,200 battlefield casualties—12 percent of the total.

Reference: Peter McInerny, *The Vietnam Experience: A Contagion of War*, 1983.

KIRKPATRICK, HELEN
US War Correspondent, b. 1909, d. 1997

In World War II, Kirkpatrick's dispatches from Europe were a mainstay of the circulation promotion of the *Chicago Daily News*. Posters carrying her stern face informed the city's pedestrians and bus passengers that the best method of keeping abreast of the unfolding events of the war was to read "Our Helen."

Born in Rochester, New York, Kirkpatrick graduated from Smith College in 1931 and then studied international law at the University of Geneva in Switzerland. She turned down a job at the *New York Herald Tribune* in favor of a job in merchandising at Macy's department store.

In 1935 she returned to Geneva, where she wrote for and edited *Research Bulletin,* published by the Foreign Policy Association. At the time, Geneva was the headquarters of the League of Nations and an international news hub, enabling Kirkpatrick to write articles for a number of British newspapers. She acquired a reputation for the assured coverage of great issues of the day and became a stringer for *The Manchester Guardian, The Daily Telegraph,* and the *New York Herald Tribune.*

By 1937 she was acknowledged as a League of Nations insider and was invited to London to work on *Whitehall News,* a weekly newsletter analyzing European current affairs. Here she was perfectly positioned to chronicle the approach of war, in the process ruffling the feathers of the British political establishment with her candid criticism of what she saw as the supine attitude of the British and French when dealing with Mussolini and Hitler.

In 1939 Kirkpatrick became the European correspondent of the *Chicago Daily News* in spite of strong opposition on the paper to the appointment of women as overseas reporters. She recorded an early scoop in the spring of 1940, accurately predicting that Hitler was poised to invade Belgium. In the autumn of that year, she reported on the Blitz on London, writing on September 9, two days after the first heavy Luftwaffe raid, "Fright becomes so mingled with a deep almost uncontrollable anger that it is hard to know when one stops and the other begins. And on top of it all London is smiling even in the districts where the casualties must have been very heavy."

Kirkpatrick later reported from North Africa and Italy, frequently criticizing the often ill-informed and isolationist attitude she encountered among some American officers and men, while also paying tribute to the spirit of cooperation among the Western allies. She was invariably tough and self-sufficient, silencing the oft-voiced criticism that women were too fragile to cope with the rigors of life on the front line without special assistance from the army. When a high-ranking officer voiced the opinion that women reporters should be barred from the Normandy invasion because of the lack of appropriate latrine facilities, one of Kirkpatrick's supporters offered to wager five pounds that "Helen Kirkpatrick can dig a latrine faster than anyone in this room."

Kirkpatrick witnessed the liberation of Paris in August 1944 and was lunching at the Ritz Hotel with fellow war correspondent Ernest Hemingway (see **Gellhorn, Martha,** p. 293) when she announced that she would have to leave to cover the Allied victory celebrations. With characteristic vainglory, Hemingway replied that lunch at the fabled Ritz was far more historic than the story she intended to cover. Kirkpatrick, the better journalist, left to do

her job and was on the spot to record another scoop when a group
of Free French generals came under fire as they entered Notre-
Dame Cathedral:

> The generals' car arrived on the dot of 4:15. As they stepped
> from the car, we stood at salute and at that very moment a re-
> volver shot rang out. It seemed to come from behind one of
> Notre Dame's gargoyles. Within a split second a machine gun
> opened up from a nearby room. It sprayed the pavement at my
> feet. The generals entered the church with 40-odd people
> pressing from behind to find shelter.

After the war, Kirkpatrick worked as European correspondent for
the *New York Post* (1946–49) and then as chief of the information
division of the Economical Corporation Administration (1949–51).
As public affairs adviser for the State Department (1951–53) she
played a part in the implementation of the Marshall Plan.

Reference: Lilya Wagner, *Women War Correspondents of World
War II*, 1989.

K'TUT TANTRI
*"Surabaya Sue," Scots Writer and Propagandist for
Indonesian Nationalism, b. 1898, d. 1997*

In a remarkable career that embraced as many pseudonyms as oc-
cupations, K'tut Tantri was perhaps most celebrated as "Surabaya
Sue," the woman who made propaganda broadcasts for the Indonesian nationalists in their struggle to gain independence from
the Dutch in the years after World War II.

She was born Muriel Stuart Walker in Glasgow and after
World War I made her home in California, where she supported
herself by supplying stories about the movie stars to British newspapers. In 1932 she abandoned her husband and sailed for Bali in
the Dutch East Indies under the name of Mrs. Manx (after the Isle
of Man, birthplace of her parents).

In Bali she became a hotelier, fell in love with the Balinese way of life, and conceived a hatred of Dutch colonial rule. Bespectacled, plump, and barely five feet tall, she now saw herself as more Balinese than European. She dyed her auburn hair black, as the Balinese considered red locks the sign of a witch.

When the Japanese invaded Bali in March 1942, she used her connections with one of the island's rulers, the raja of Bangli, to avoid internment. It was the raja who gave Walker her Balinese name, which roughly translated means "fourth-born child and teller of tales." Then, according to her own highly suspect account, she joined an underground nationalist resistance movement. The likely truth is that she became a collaborator, but this did not save her from imprisonment, in what were undeniably grim conditions, as a suspected spy for the Allies.

In the immediate aftermath of the war, K'tut Tantri joined the nationalist guerrillas in East Java, and broadcast from their headquarters. While the British and the Dutch dubbed her "Surabaya Sue," she worked as an interpreter for the rebel leaders when they were interviewed by Western journalists. She later made broadcasts from Central Java and wrote speeches for Achmed Sukarno, president of Indonesia, who described her as "the one and only foreigner to come openly to our side."

Now it was time for K'tut Tantri to become disenchanted with the Indonesians, and she appears to have offered her services as an informer to the British in Singapore. In the late 1940s, she visited Australia and the United States but her reputation and lack of papers made international travel difficult. Throughout the 1950s she worked as a journalist for the Indonesian Ministry of Information, and in 1960 she published *Revolt in Paradise,* a self-mythologizing account of her life in Indonesia. Truly she was a "teller of tales." Hollywood showed a brief interest, but the project foundered on K'tut Tantri's absolute intransigence when it came to plotting a plausible storyline through her fancifully embroidered memoirs. She died in Australia, a recluse.

Reference: Timothy Lindsey, *The Romance of K'tut Tantri and Indonesia,* 1997.

LYNN, VERA
"The Forces' Sweetheart," British World War II Vocalist, b. 1917

A singer who was equally popular with Britain's servicemen and on the home front, Lynn provided the war generation with a soundtrack to their lives, delivered with unaffected simplicity and sincerity.

A plumber's daughter from East Ham in London, Lynn gave her first public performance in 1924. She subsequently sang with the bandleader Joe Loss, joined Charlie Kunz in 1935, and moved over to Bert Ambrose's orchestra in 1937. In the spring of 1940 she was voted the British Expeditionary Force's favorite singer, ahead of Deanna Durbin, Judy Garland, and Bing Crosby, in a poll run by the *Daily Express*. Her appeal was founded on perfect pitch, simple diction, and homespun good looks. She was the epitome of the girl next door.

In the summer of 1940, at the height of the Battle of Britain, Lynn had a huge hit with "The White Cliffs of Dover," her plangent, haunting delivery overriding the song's sentimentality to paint an idealized picture of Britain at peace and safe from enemy bombs, "where Jimmy will go to sleep in his own little room again." Perhaps her most enduring success, "We'll Meet Again," the song that made Lynn so popular with the forces, had been recorded in the autumn of 1939 and was movingly in step with the feelings of loss, separation, and hope for a better future that characterized the public mood of the war years. Lynn herself believed that its success was due to the fact that the song expressed sentiments that ordinary people felt but were unable adequately to articulate.

From 1941 to 1947, Lynn had her own radio show, *Sincerely Yours,* in which she sang songs requested by men of the armed forces. She recalled, "My songs reminded the boys of what they were really fighting for, for precious personal things rather than ideologies or theories." She also made three wartime films, *We'll Meet Again* (1943), *Rhythm Serenade* (1943), and *One Exciting Night* (1944). In 1944 Lynn visited the troops on the Arakan front in Burma and subsequently led the singing in many of the concerts that marked the end of World War II. After the war, she re-mained a beloved figure in British national life and in the 1990s was closely associated with the campaign to improve pensions for war widows.

Reference: Vera Lynn and Robin Cross, *We'll Meet Again: A Personal History of World War II and Victory in Europe*, 1989.

POLITKOVSKAYA, ANNA
Russian Investigative Journalist, b. 1958, d. 2006

A fearless investigative reporter who exposed the Kremlin's dirty war in Chechnya, Politkovskaya was shot dead by an unknown assailant in the elevator of her Moscow apartment block.

Politkovskaya was born in New York, where her Soviet Ukrainian parents were diplomats at the United Nations. A member of the privileged Soviet *nomenklatura*, she was educated in the Soviet Union and graduated from the journalism faculty of Moscow State University. She worked for the newspaper *Izvestiya* and then the in-house journal of the Soviet state monopoly airline Aeroflot. With the advent of perestroika in the late 1980s, Politkovskaya, unlike many of her contemporaries, did not cash in on her privilege but began to work for the emerging independent press.

During this period, the reforms introduced by Mikhail Gorbachev—perestroika (the introduction of market forces and individual initiative) and glasnost (the promotion of openness in politics and the media)—dissolved the glue that had held the Soviet Union together and broke it into its constituent parts. A series of internal wars erupted, the most savage of which was in Chechnya, on the northern slopes of the Caucasus. In 1992 Chechnya became an autonomous republic. Attempts by the Russian Federation to regain control of Chechnya during the presidency of President Boris Yeltsin ended in a peace deal and troop withdrawal.

In 1999 Yeltsin's successor, Vladimir Putin, invaded the small and war-ravaged region and took deliberate steps to ensure that the brutality of the conflict would not be reported by the Russian

press. Politkovskaya's employer, the biweekly *Novaya Gazeta,*
partly owned by Mikhail Gorbachev, remained one of the few
Russian media outlets to defy Putin. Politkovskaya herself would
eventually become a thorn in the side of the Kremlin and a coura-
geously even-handed reporter of the savagery with which the conflict in Chechnya was prosecuted both by Moscow and the
Chechen rebels.

Politkovskaya's interest in Chechnya had been initially aroused
during the first conflict by the plight of Chechen refugees in Russia, and then by the fate of pensioners stranded in the Chechen
capital, Grozny, by the Russian advance. She traveled to Chechnya, wrote about the Chechens' ordeal under fire, and played a
part in their eventual evacuation. This marked the start of her role
as an intermediary between the Russian military and the Chechen
rebels on behalf of civilians caught in the crossfire. It reached a climax in the Moscow theater siege in 2002, when Politkovskaya
acted as a negotiator. She remained unrepentant that as a journalist
she had become personally involved in the unfolding drama,
claiming that this role gave her insights she could never gain as a
mere observer. Nevertheless, her increasingly proactive role in the
reporting of the conflict in Chechnya gained her many powerful
enemies. In 2004, while flying to Beslan to act as a go-between
in the siege of a school occupied by Chechen terrorists, Politkovskaya was poisoned by the FSB, the Russian security service,
and came close to death.

Politkovskaya had come into her own as a campaigning journalist and war reporter in 1999 at the start of the Second Chechen
War. At that point the relatively moderate wing of the Chechen
resistance, led by former president Aslan Maskhadov, had run out
of money and into the resulting vacuum poured funds from the
coffers of Wahabi Islam, bankrolled by Saudi Arabia. When the attacks on Washington and New York took place on September 11,
2001, they provided Vladimir Putin with a cynical pretext to join
the "war on terror" by stepping up the conflict in Chechnya.
While Politkovskaya was frank about Russia's need to prevent the
establishment of a hostile Islamic state in the northern Caucasus,

she was savagely critical of the means sanctioned by Putin: "It was clear to me it was going to be a total war, whose victims were first and foremost going to be civilians."

From this platform Politkovskaya launched a stream of searing articles and books exposing the atrocities committed in Russia's name. Her first book, *A Dirty War: A Russian Reporter in Chechnya* (2001), chronicles in harrowing detail not only what Russia was doing in Chechnya but also the corrosive effect that this was having on Russia itself. *Putin's Russia* (2004) describes how the new Russian ruling class had acquired its money through a combination of violence and chicanery. Her determination to preserve the embers of democracy at home fueled her repeated expeditions to the cockpit of the northern Caucasus.

She was also contemptuous of Western leaders who, with their desire to exploit Russia's burgeoning markets and their dependence on its oil and natural gas, were careful to remain close to Putin: "It's impossible to talk on the one hand about the monstrous scale of victims in Chechnya and the spawning of terrorism and then lay out the red carpet, embrace Putin and tell him, 'We're with you, you're the best.' " In *Chechnya: Russian Dishonor* (2003), she describes the Putin regime as being even more "morally soiled" than that of Boris Yeltsin. She accused him of confusing chauvinism with patriotism, particularly where it concerned his policy toward the Chechens, which she believed was motivated by racism.

Such outspokenness came at an enormous personal cost. In Chechnya she was arrested by security forces and subjected to a mock execution; her husband left her; and her neighbors in Moscow, cowed by the attentions of the FSB, shunned her. She remained defiant, although she was at pains to point out that she was not particularly brave: "The duty of doctors is to give health to their patients, the duty of the singer is to sing and the duty of the journalist is to write what this journalist sees in reality."

In the last months of her life, Politkovskaya had turned her critical gaze on Ramsan Kadyrov, the Chechen prime minister (son of a former Chechen ex-president, another old foe), who, she claimed, had publicly stated his intention to kill her. Politkovskaya was set to testify against Kadyrov in a case concerning the kidnapping and killing of two Chechen civilians. In her last interview, she announced that she planned to publish in *Novaya Gazeta* the results of a wide-ranging investigation into torture in Chechnya.

She never filed the article, although part of it was published posthumously. In another piece, however, she foresaw her own death:

Some time ago Vladislav Surikov, deputy head of the presidential administration, explained that there were people who were enemies but whom you could talk sense into and there were incorrigible enemies to whom you couldn't and who simply needed to be "cleansed" from the political arena. So they are trying to cleanse it of me and others like me.

Reference: Anna Politkovskaya, *A Small Corner of Hell, Dispatcher from Chechnya,* 2003.

SURABAYA SUE, see K'TUT TANTRI, p. 300.

TOGURI, IKUKO
"Tokyo Rose," Japanese-American World War II Propagandist,
b. 1916, d. 2006

"Hello, boneheads. This is your favorite enemy, Ann. How are all you orphans of the Pacific?" These are the opening words of an October 1944 broadcast, *Zero Hour,* from Radio Tokyo to American troops in the South Pacific. The young broadcaster was known to Allied troops in the Pacific not by her real name but by a nickname they had coined, "Tokyo Rose."

Tokyo Rose was born Ikuko Toguri in Los Angeles in the summer of 1916, a first-generation Japanese-American who attended high school and junior college in Los Angeles. In January 1940, she graduated from the University of California with a degree in zoology. She was known as Iva by her classmates and was athletic, popular, and considered a loyal American.

In July 1941 she sailed for Japan without a US passport, ostensibly to visit a sick relative and to study medicine. While in Japan she applied for a passport to enable her to return to live in California. However, her application was overtaken by the Japanese attack on Pearl Harbor on December 7, 1941.

Toguri decided to remain in Japan for the duration of the war and from mid-1942 worked as a typist in a Tokyo news agency. In August 1943 she obtained a second job as typist for Radio Tokyo, and three months later she began a career as one of the many female English-speaking presenters on the station.

Toguri filled a twenty-nine-minute slot in an hourlong program known as *Zero Hour,* whose presenters and scriptwriters were captured Allied personnel and which was broadcast six days a week. She introduced herself as "Orphan Ann" and mixed dance-band music with teasing comments about the inadequacies of the US Navy and the infidelities of navy wives back at home. It was crude psychological warfare and earned her, and other female Japanese broadcasters, the mock-affectionate nickname bestowed by US service personnel in the Pacific. Toguri was unique in that she was the only American-born broadcaster dubbed "Tokyo Rose." Her real loyalties remained ambiguous, and it seems that, at some personal risk, she smuggled food, medicine, and blankets to the Allied POWs who had been coerced under threat of execution into producing *Zero Hour.*

In April 1945, Toguri married Felipe D'Aquino, a Portuguese citizen of Japanese descent. After the marriage she did not renounce her US citizenship and, in spite of her husband's misgivings, continued to appear on *Zero Hour* until the Japanese surrender on August 15, 1945.

In the immediate aftermath of the war she was tracked down by American journalists and rashly agreed to give an interview, signing the contract as "Tokyo Rose." The interview notes were later handed to the US Army Counter Intelligence Corps and Toguri, now D'Aquino, was arrested, imprisoned, and released in 1946. She was rearrested by the US Army in September 1948 and brought under military escort to San Francisco, where the Federal Bureau of Investigation was waiting with a warrant for her trial for treason.

The trial opened at the beginning of July 1949 and lasted sixty-one days. Tokyo Rose was found guilty of only one of the charges brought against her: "that on a day during October 1944, the exact date being to the Grand Jurors unknown, said defendant at Tokyo, Japan, in a broadcasting studio of the Broadcasting Corporation of Japan, did speak into a microphone concerning the loss of ships." She was sentenced to ten years in prison, becoming the seventh person to be convicted of treason in the history of the United States, at an estimated cost to the US government of $750,000. The trial judge, Michael Roche, disallowed much of the mitigating evidence in her favor and later admitted that he was prejudiced against her, as his son had served in the Pacific.

D'Aquino was released in January 1956 after serving six years as a model prisoner at the Federal Reformatory for Women at Alderson, West Virginia. She successfully resisted attempts by the US government to deport her, and in January 1977 she obtained a pardon from President Gerald Ford. Her marriage to D'Aquino was dissolved in 1980. He could not live in the United States, as he had been deemed an undesirable alien after testifying for his wife during his trial.

Reference: Masayo Duus, *Tokyo Rose, Orphan of the Pacific,* 1979.

WALKER, MURIEL, see **K'TUT TANTRI,** p. 300.

10

VALKYRIES, FURIES, AND FIENDS

—∞∞—

Ruthless Opportunists, Sadists,
and Psychopaths Unleashed and
Empowered by War

As bonny a girl as one could ever wish to meet.

—SS concentration camp guard Irma Grese, as seen by British hangman
Albert Pierrepoint, who executed her in 1945

For CENTURIES, the myth has persisted that men make war to protect and defend women, and that the only task of the female of the species is to keep the home fires burning, and to encourage "our boys." World War II Hollywood films like *Mrs. Miniver* (1942) and *Since You Went Away* (1944) embody these archetypes, with Greer Garson and Claudette Colbert, respectively, portraying women as the gentle sex, passive but warmhearted and conformist guardians of hearth and home.

Women have not always conformed to this saccharine stereotype. When they did go to war, accounts of their activities stress their valor, nobility, and self-sacrifice: **Joan of Arc** and **Florence Nightingale** are the archetypes here (see pp. 75 and 264). Otherwise, men went to war and if women came along, they were seen as nonparticipants, trailing behind, "following the flag." Military "experts" are particularly prone to insist that women only enter the annals of warfare as hapless bystanders, or as the spoils of war.

Yet many women have been drawn to war both for its excitement and for the chance it offered of escaping the female role (see chapter 3, "Runaways and Roaring Girls"). Of these, a fearsome few sought or found in war the opportunities for a level of cruelty and sadism rarely acknowledged as part of the female psyche. Societies everywhere normally experience violence as the problem, preoccupation, and even recreation of the male, but not all the horror and violence in human nature can be blamed on men. Numbers of women in war have demonstrated that they can be as capable of cruelty as men, when, like men, they are given the power to inflict it.

This dark side of female nature is well recognized in myth and legend, from the Celtic Great Goddess of war and death, the Morrighan, to the Hindu goddess Kali Ma, "the Black Mother," with her girdle of venomous snakes and her necklace of men's skulls. Many tribal societies empowered their women to take revenge on a defeated enemy, and some developed refined rituals of sadism in which the women tortured prisoners to death (see **Tribal Revenge,** p. 330).

These were particularly significant in warrior societies like Afghanistan, where women's low status denied them any other role of importance in the tribe. In North America, the Cherokee, Iroquois, Omaha, and Dakota tribes also followed this tradition, with the aim of adding the pain of humiliation to their victims' physical agonies. In the immediate aftermath of the Battle of the Little Bighorn (1876), which saw the annihilation by the Sioux and Cheyenne of a contingent of the US Seventh Cavalry commanded by General George Armstrong Custer, Native American women roamed the battlefield, pounding the faces of dead and dying cavalrymen to a bloody pulp. And as late as the 1930s, British aircrew flying air control missions over Afghanistan carried a so-called blood chit, a piece of paper promising to ransom any captured servicemen, but only if they were returned with their full complement of testicles, penises, fingers, toes, and eyes.

Nazi Germany, too, provides support for the dispiriting observation that when authorized to do so, women can behave as badly as men. The Hitler regime was initially reluctant to mobilize women for the war effort, stressing that their contribution was essentially reproductive and domestic. But the SS, the most powerful administrative arm of the Third Reich, had a special role to play. With the encouragement of its chief, Heinrich Himmler, it found a niche for a few thousand females in the one industry at which it excelled, the industry of death, in whose execution its personnel, both male and female, were given almost unlimited power.

Some women have undoubtedly found it easier to liberate their capacity for cruelty when acting in groups. But power, not gender, is the key to behavior that transgresses all the norms. The women who were enrolled to serve as guards in the Nazi death camps were accorded a limited and grotesquely negative form of empowerment. In them, the ideological obsessions of this intensely chauvinist society were responsible for producing some arch-sadists of the female sex. Nazi theories of racial purity and Aryan superiority created the concentration and death camps of the Third Reich and with them a climate that made it possible for a number of women to be appointed to positions where they could exercise arbitrary power—the power of life and death— over the female inmates (see **Braunsteiner, Hermine,** p. 314, and **Grese, Irma,** p. 316).

The women invested with this power in war had made no previous mark on peacetime society. They had lived anonymous and often frustrated lives, with one at least, Irma Grese, experiencing the violence she was later to inflict: the first time she presented herself at home in her SS uniform, her father beat her up. In this sea of apparently motiveless malignity, it is also noteworthy that some of the SS women met the classic psychological profile of the "true believer." In common with many a cult follower, they found in the rituals and paraphernalia of their new calling an escape route from the humdrum world of nonentity they had previously inhabited. Perhaps most remarkable of all, one of the worst of these women, Braunsteiner, who initially escaped justice after World War II, quietly sank back into drab suburban anonymity as if nothing had happened, and remained undetected for many years after the war.

In recent years in the Middle East, a complex web of social and political factors has given rise to a new phenomenon, the female **suicide bomber** (see p. 327). These women and girls form a far more varied group than the SS women of the death camps. They range from bright young lawyers to the unemployed, the uneducated, and even the elderly. There is no template for the woman who loads herself with bombs and goes out to kill, without even the promise of eternal sexual delight in paradise that is offered to her Islamic male colleagues.

Perhaps a more accurate comparison can be made between the SS women and the female US service personnel at the heart of the 2003 scandal at the Abu Ghraib prison in Iraq. Official sanction there was given to a regime in which Iraqi prisoners were treated with a contempt that recalls some of the racial persecution of World War II. Images of the grinning figure of **Lynndie England** (see p. 315) straddling naked and cowed Iraqi men, or the use of snarling attack dogs to exert "control" over them, conjures up the pictures of laughing Nazi troops viciously tugging the beards of terrified Jews in occupied Poland. In a link to the female role in tribal revenge, being stripped naked and tormented by a woman would immeasurably add to the humiliation of devout Islamic men. Like their SS forbears, at least some of the perpetrators of the outrages at Abu Ghraib had to answer for the lawlessness that prevailed there. But those who devised such policy and authorized its implementation have not been brought to justice.

AFGHANISTAN, WOMEN OF, see **TRIBAL REVENGE,** p. 330.

AMMASH, DR. HUDA SALIH MAHDI
"Mrs. Anthrax," Iraqi Scientist, b. 1953

Ammash was one of the few women in the inner circle of the Iraqi dictator Saddam Hussein, and the only female to feature in the

United States' list of fifty-five most wanted Iraqis catalogued by the Pentagon on a deck of playing cards issued to US troops during the 2003 invasion of Iraq. Saddam was the ace of spades; Ammash was the five of hearts.

The chairperson of the Baath Party's Youth and Trade Bureau, Ammash sat on the eighteen-member Iraq Command that ran the party and was also a party regional commander. However, the US-educated microbiologist was better known to Americans for her involvement with Saddam's program for weapons of mass destruction. US intelligence dubbed her "Mrs. Anthrax" and accused Ammash of masterminding the rebuilding of Iraq's biological-warfare inventory after the 1991 Persian Gulf War.

After gaining a master of science degree from Texas Woman's University and a doctorate in microbiology from the University of Missouri—Columbia, Ammash returned to Iraq in 1983 to train under Nassir al-Hindawi, the father of Iraq's biological-weapons program. In 1996 she became the head of Iraq's Microbiology Society, a front for research into the military uses of anthrax and smallpox. In the 1990s she also reputedly conducted research into the illnesses that may have been caused by the use of depleted uranium expended by Allied forces in the 1991 Gulf War, which resulted in her developing breast cancer.

The mother of four and a fluent English-speaker, the busy Ammash also served as Saddam's unofficial ambassador to Jordan, Yemen, and Lebanon, and as the dean of the University of Baghdad. She was the only woman pictured at a meeting of Saddam and eight of his most senior officials in Iraqi television footage shot in March 2003 shortly after the launching of the US-led invasion. After the collapse of Saddam's regime at the beginning of May 2003, Ammash disappeared and was initially thought to have escaped to Syria. However, shortly afterward she was found in hiding in Baghdad by US troops and taken into custody. She was released in December 2005 along with Dr. Rihab Taha, who had led Iraq's biological weapons program until 1995.

Reference: Charles Duelfer, *Comprehensive Report of the Special Advisor to the DCI on Iraq's WMD,* 2005.

APACHE, WOMEN OF, see **TRIBAL REVENGE,** p. 330.

BRAUNSTEINER, HERMINE
"The Stamping Mare," German SS Auxiliary and War Criminal, b. 1919, d. 1999

The daughter of prosperous Viennese parents, Braunsteiner failed to realize her early dream of becoming a nurse and was equally unsuccessful when she tried to enter domestic service in England.

Her life changed in 1939 when she was plucked from a job at a Berlin aircraft plant and sent for training as a guard at the nearby Ravensbrück concentration camp for women. It was here that she was dubbed "the Stamping Mare" after trampling a number of old women to death with steel-studded jackboots.

In October 1942, she was transferred to Maidanek, a labor camp near the Polish city of Lublin that in early 1942 had been converted into an extermination center. Promoted to the rank of assistant wardress (*Aufsehirin*), Braunsteiner was able to give free rein to her sadistic impulses. She was involved in the selection of women and children for the gas chamber and also subjected them to random homicidal whipping and stomping.

In March 1944, with the Red Army poised to drive through Poland, Maidanek was evacuated. Braunsteiner was ordered back to Ravensbrück and promoted first to head a work detail and then to the post of supervising wardress at a satellite camp.

In May 1945, with Germany in ruins, Braunsteiner became one of millions of displaced persons fleeing the Red Army. She found refuge briefly in Vienna before being arrested by Austrian officials in May 1946 and imprisoned until April 1947. In April 1948 she was rearrested for crimes committed at Ravensbrück; she was released in November 1949.

Braunsteiner received an amnesty from the Austrian government and thereafter supported herself by working in hotels and restaurants. She became engaged to an American soldier, Russell Ryan, and in 1959 married him. The couple settled in Queens, New York, and Braunsteiner became a US citizen in January

1963. However, time was running out for the Stamping Mare. She was tracked down and exposed by a *New York Times* reporter, Joseph Lelyveld, who had been tipped off by the Nazi-hunter Simon Wiesenthal. When Lelyveld confronted Braunsteiner on her Queens doorstep, she greeted his arrival with weary resignation.

In March 1973 Braunsteiner became the first Nazi war criminal to be extradited from the United States to Germany. She stood trial, with fifteen other SS men and women, for crimes committed at Maidanek. In 1971 she had been stripped of her US citizenship, and in May 1980 she was given a life sentence. Suffering from diabetes, she was released from prison in 1996, and she died three years later.

Reference: Daniel Patrick Brown, *The Camp Women: The Female Auxiliaries Who Assisted the SS in Running the Concentration Camp System,* 2002.

ENGLAND, LYNNDIE
US Army Private and Antiheroine of the Iraq War, b. 1982

Lynndie England was a bit player who came to symbolize a horror story of American misconduct and mismanagement in the aftermath of the war against Iraq.

The daughter of a railroad worker, England grew up in a trailer park in Fort Ashby, West Virginia. She joined the army reserve in 2001, when she was in high school, to earn money to go to college and train as a meteorologist. After an unsuccessful marriage, she was posted to Iraq to serve as a specialist with 372nd Military Police Company.

England reportedly expected a desk job in Iraq. Instead she found herself guarding hundreds of Iraqi prisoners in Baghdad's Abu Ghraib jail. She was thrust into the center of a media storm when she was identified as one of the US soldiers abusing Iraqi prisoners. In one shocking image, England was pictured pointing at the genitals of naked prisoners; in another she held a prone prisoner by a leash fastened around his neck; in a third she posed grinning and giving the thumbs-up sign with her boyfriend, Specialist Charles Graner, behind a pyramid of naked Iraqis.

In May 2004, before formal charges were brought against England, who was pregnant by Graner, she was transferred to Fort Bragg, North Carolina, and assigned to light duties. After a mistrial, England was retried in September 2005 and convicted on one count of conspiracy, four counts of maltreating detainees, and one count of performing an indecent act. She was given a dishonorable discharge and received a three-year prison sentence. Graner, the alleged ringleader of the abuse at Abu Ghraib, was convicted separately and given a sentence of ten years.

England's mother, Terrie, defended her, protesting that her daughter was just doing "kid things, stupid pranks." Terrie England was more accurate in her observation that her daughter was a scapegoat for failings higher up the army's chain of command and in the Department of Defense.

The revulsion felt by many at England's conduct stemmed partly from the fact that during the Iraq War the Pentagon was happy to portray women as potential victims of enemy violence and sexual assault (see **Lynch, Jessica,** p. 229) and reluctant to admit that they could also be active players in sordid games of power and cruelty. Nevertheless, it must be said that the Bush administration, requiring a scapegoat for its colossal strategic misjudgment in Iraq, attempted to use England and her colleagues to bear the moral burden for its war.

Reference: Janis Karpinski, Steven Strasser, and Bernadette Dunne, *One Woman's Army: The Commanding General of Abu Ghraib Tells Her Story,* 2005.

GRESE, IRMA
German SS Auxiliary and War Criminal, b. 1923, d. 1945

Irma Grese lived an unremarkable life before World War II, when Nazi preferment gave her the power of life and death over the inmates of the concentration and death camps in which she served as a wardress *(Aufseherin).*

Grese came from a farming family in Mecklenburg. She left school in 1938 and after a series of dead-end jobs was taken on as an apprentice nurse at the sinister SS sanatorium at Hohenlychen run by Dr. Karl Gebhardt, a distinguished surgeon and die-hard Nazi who in 1948 was executed as a war criminal. Grese did not qualify as a nurse, but Gebhardt found her a place in the training program for female warders at the Ravensbrück concentration camp. The failed nurse was an archetypal adolescent "true believer," mesmerized by the rituals and paraphernalia of the SS, the organization that employed her at Ravensbrück from the summer of 1942 and gave her an escape route from the tedium of her early life.

In March 1943, Grese was transferred to Auschwitz-Birkenau, in southern Poland, where she participated in the selection of inmates for the gas chamber. At Auschwitz she was promoted to the rank of *Oberaufseherin* (senior SS warder) and had a brief affair with the camp's senior doctor, Josef Mengele. Prompted, no doubt, by her failed attempt to become a nurse under the tutelage of Karl Gebhardt, Grese was also an active observer at the grotesque medical experiments undertaken at the camp hospital by Mengele and his assistants.

In breach of camp regulations, Grese had numerous homosexual liaisons with inmates, later consigning them to the gas chamber. Her immaculate uniforms were tailored by inmates who had in previous lives been seamstresses. In March 1945, after another period at Ravensbrück, Grese was transferred as labor-control officer to Bergen-Belsen, a camp on Lüneburg Heath near Hanover, whose senior SS officer, Josef Kramer, had previously been in charge at Auschwitz and was thought to have been another of Grese's lovers. Bergen-Belsen was a camp for invalids transferred from other parts of Germany; by the end of the war, the malevolent neglect by Kramer and his subordinates had ensured that it was hideously overcrowded and swept by waves of typhus and spotted fever. When Bergen-Belsen was overrun by the British on April 15, 1945, some thirteen thousand corpses lay strewn around the camp and the remaining inmates were barely alive. Far from fleeing the scene of her crimes when the British arrived, Grese re-

mained on the site and physically attacked a senior British officer
when he tried to enter a camp hut.

The survivors at Bergen-Belsen attested to Grese's brutality,
her beatings and arbitrary shootings and the savaging of prisoners
by her half-starved dogs. She habitually wore heavy boots and carried a silver-plated pistol. She beat many women to death, using a
plaited cellophane whip, rubber truncheon, and "whipping stick."
In a chilling photograph taken by her captors, Grese glares at
the camera, her handsome features twisted by a scowl of barely
contained violence. Her homely sweater and skirt are disturbingly
offset by black knee-length boots. The British military police
nicknamed Grese "Jut Jaw."

At her trial she showed not a flicker of remorse for the horrors
for which she had been responsible, weeping uncontrollably only
when her sister appeared as a character witness. Grese, camp commandant Josef Kramer, and eleven others were sentenced to death
and were hanged on December 13, 1945, by the British execu-
tioner Albert Pierrepoint, who, apparently without irony, recalled
that Grese "was as bonny a girl as one could ever wish to meet."
Grese's last word as she stood on the gallows, a white hood pulled
over her head, was *"Schnell"* (quick).

Reference: Daniel Patrick Brown, *The Beautiful Beast: The Life and
Crimes of SS Aufseherin Irma Grese,* 1996.

KHALED, LEILA
*Palestinian Terrorist Hijacker and Popular Front for the Liberation of
Palestine Fighter, b. 1944*

In the 1970s, Khaled rivaled Che Guevara as a modish poster
pinup. With her head scarf, a Kalashnikov slung over her shoulder,
her black bob, and her burning eyes, she was the epitome of revolutionary chic, inspiring a character in the British TV science-
fiction series *Doctor Who* and a love song, "Leila Khaled Said," by
the 1980s band the Teardrop Explodes.

She was born in Haifa, which was then part of the British
mandate in Palestine. When in 1947 Palestine's Arab population

rejected the United Nations' plan to partition Palestine, fighting broke out between Arabs and Jews, and in 1948 Khaled's family moved to Lebanon, leaving behind her father, who was a fighter with the fedayeen, the armed Palestinian militias.

At fifteen, Khaled joined the radical Arab nationalist movement, which had been founded in the late 1940s by George Habbash, a medical student at the American University of Beirut. In 1967, following the Six Day War, the Palestinian faction of this movement became the Popular Front for the Liberation of Palestine (PFLP).

On August 29, 1969, Khaled was part of the team that hijacked TWA flight 840 as it flew from Rome to Athens, on the mistaken assumption that Yitzhak Rabin, the Israeli ambassador to the United States, was on board. The hijackers diverted the Boeing 707 to Damascus after flying over Haifa to allow Khaled to see her birthplace. The aircraft was blown up in Damascus, but none of the passengers was injured.

After the hijacking, Khaled underwent the first of several plastic surgery operations to change her appearance. On September 6, 1970, in the company of Nicaraguan Patrick Arguello, she attempted the hijack of El Al flight 219 from Amsterdam to New York, one of a series of simultaneous hijackings carried out by the PFLP. However, Israeli sky marshals on the flight killed Arguello after he shot one of the crew, and overpowered Khaled, who was carrying two hand grenades. The aircraft was diverted to London, where Khaled was taken into custody and a month later released as part of a prisoner exchange. Khaled had failed in her mission of September 6, but on that day the PFLP successfully hijacked a Swissair and a TWA jet, which were flown to Dawson's Field in Jordan, where along with a BOAC VC-10 hijacked on September 9, they were blown up three days later. A year later the PFLP abandoned hijacking, although terrorist groups that it spawned continued the tactic, notably in the Entebbe incident of 1976.

Khaled later admitted that she had found her incarceration in London sufficiently agreeable to prompt a correspondence with the two policewomen responsible for her there and a number of return visits to the United Kingdom to address supporters. Still a handsome woman in late middle age, Khaled has announced that she no longer considers hijacking a legitimate tactic, although she remains highly critical of the "peace process" aimed at improving relations between the Israelis and Palestinians. She is a member of the Palestinian National Council and appears regularly at the World Social Forum, a talking shop for members of the anti-globalization movement.

Reference: Leila Khaled, *My People Shall Live*, 1973.

LAKWENA, ALICE
Ugandan Prophetess and Insurgent, 1956–2007

A self-proclaimed prophetess and spirit medium, Lakwena inspired a long-running and bloody insurgency in northern Uganda against the government forces of President Yoweri Museveni.

Born Alice Auma, she was an Acholi, the predominant ethnic group in northern Uganda, which formed the core of the Ugandan army. She was rumored to have worked as a prostitute, although some sources describe her as a fisherwoman. At some point she converted to Roman Catholicism. She was married twice but had no children.

The origins of the insurgency led by Lakwena date back to the overthrow by Museveni of the regime headed by General Tito Okello, a former sergeant and a member of the Acholi tribe. The downfall of Okello traumatized the Acholi, and their leaders formed the rebel Ugandan People's Democratic Party (UPDA) in an attempt to drive Museveni's forces from the north and regain their former status.

In 1985 Auma claimed that she had been possessed by the spirit of a dead Italian army officer called Lakwena, who ordered her to create a Holy Spirit Movement to liberate the world from sin and bring an end to the bloodshed in Uganda. She consulted witches about her mission, but they remained cautiously noncommittal. The animals in the Paraa National Park proved more communicative, and after forty days Lakwena, as she was now to be called, emerged to become one of the many spirit mediums prophesying and practicing healing near the town of Gulu.

As Uganda descended into chaos, Lakwena instructed Auma to redirect her work for the Holy Spirit Movement, which aimed to bring about the Second Coming of Christ and the inauguration of an earthly paradise. She gathered a group of followers and persuaded the UPDA leaders to place some of their troops under her control. In December 1986, acting under the command of His Holiness Lakwena, the Holy Spirit Movement achieved two unexpected victories over government forces. After a recruiting drive, the movement was able to put some ten thousand fighters into the field.

They fought as a regular army, although they relied more heavily on magic than on conventional hardware. Lakwena urged her followers to smear themselves with nut oil and ingest potions that would make them invulnerable to bullets. The formations of the Holy Spirit Movement had their own spiritual commissars who attended Lakwena when she was possessed by spirits, and who blessed stones that they claimed would explode like grenades. Units marched into battle in cross-shaped formations bawling hymns. After an engagement in July 1987, rebel survivors were reported to be wandering around in a trance, and the battlefield was littered with wire models of helicopters and grenades, slaughtered cats, live chameleons, and Bibles. Government troops also found an altar decked with flowers and a "trench dug to resemble a river."

Magic proved no match for modern weaponry, and in subsequent engagements automatic weapons mowed down the hymn-chanting rebels. Nevertheless, they advanced to within one hundred miles of Kampala, the Ugandan capital, before they were cut to pieces by machine guns and artillery bombardment at Jinja in August 1987.

The Holy Spirit Movement splintered into a number of small groupings, many of which were little more than bandit gangs. Some regrouped to form the sinister and ultra-violent Lord's Resistance Army, which continues to operate in Uganda.

In the aftermath of the defeat of the Holy Spirit Movement,

Lakwena was accused of being a witch, and deserted by her Italian spirit guide, she fled to a refugee camp in Kenya. From there, seated on a throne, she continued to command a few faithful followers and vowed to dedicate the rest of her life to finding a cure for AIDS, a fantasy she pursued until her death.

Reference: Heiki Behrend, *Alice Lakwena and the Holy Spirits: War in Northern Uganda, 1985–1997,* 2000.

MBANDI, JINGA
Angolan Queen, b. ca. 1580, d. 1663

Described by the Dutch leader of her bodyguard as a "cunning virago," Jinga Mbandi led her forces in an ultimately unsuccessful war against a European power with designs on her kingdom. In the twenty-first century, she remains a popular heroine in Angola and a symbol of national resistance and of Pan-Africanism, despite keeping "concubators" (male concubines) and rejecting Christianity in favor of cannibalism.

She was born in West Africa at a time when the two most powerful tribes in the region were the Kongo and Ndongo. In all probability, she was the daughter of the *ngola* (king) of the Ndongo, who in the mid-sixteenth century had welcomed Portuguese missionaries. However, it was not the promise of Christian converts but the financial rewards of the slave trade that led the Portuguese to found Loanda (present-day Luanda, capital of Angola) in 1575 and to install a governor.

We first encounter Jinga in the early 1620s, when she negotiated with the Portuguese on behalf of her brother, who had become the *ngola* but had been exiled to an offshore island by the governor. The *ngola* had become entangled in the murky politics of the slave trade, which in the early seventeenth century was booming. A Portuguese official boasted that the teeming population of the African interior would supply slaves "to the end of the world" to work in the Brazilian plantations and mines. Local chiefs became an integral part of the trade, raiding rival tribes for valuable human cargo. Naturally enough, the Africans wanted to control the trade on their own terms, but the Portuguese begged to differ. The *ngola* had become a casualty of this brutal jostling.

Jinga's task was to secure the return of her brother and enlist the help of the Portuguese in expelling a rival tribe from Ndongo territory. To curry favor, Jinga shrewdly allowed Portuguese missionaries to baptize her and her two sisters, acquiring in the process the name Anna de Sousa. Her siblings became Lady Grace and Lady Barbara. Her encounter with the governor was, if the legend is to be believed, an indication of her composure and sense of style. When he insisted that she remain standing while he was comfortably seated, Jinga summoned a slave, ordered her to go on all fours, and settled on her back. Some versions have Jinga killing the slave after the meeting, explaining that a queen never uses the same chair twice.

Jinga's brother died in 1624, possibly at her hands. She is also credited with the death of a nephew, whose heart she devoured, in the style of Hannibal Lecter or Idi Amin. She was now ready to abandon her hastily acquired Christianity and take power. This prompted reprisals from the Portuguese, who appointed a puppet chief to supplant Jinga and drove her into exile.

Jinga's response was twofold. First she struck an alliance with a neighboring tribe, which closed the slave routes to the Portuguese. She then led her own people to the kingdom of Matamba. Here she overcame the cannibalistic Jaga tribe and adopted wholesale their grisly rituals, which included infanticide as a means of promoting tribal strength.

Jinga's military strength stemmed from a Dutch mercenary, who led her bodyguard and left a detailed record of her remarkable rule. He noted that she donned male attire for ritual sacrifice and was festooned fore and aft with animal skins. She carried sword, axe, and bows and arrows and, although well into middle age, was extraordinarily agile. In addition to her ritual clothes and formidable personal armory, she also repeatedly hammered at two iron bells: "When she thinks she has made a show long enough, in a masculine manner, then she takes a broad feather and flicks it through the holes of her Bored Nose for a Sign of War." Jinga was now ready for the first sacrifice. The victim was selected, his head cut off, and the blood gathered in a cup, which she drained in a great gulp.

Jinga may have had a "masculine manner," but like **Catherine the Great** (see p. 32) she had a legendary appetite for men. She kept a harem of male concubines ("concubators"), who could take as many wives as they pleased, provided they dressed as women at all times. There was a sinister edge to this playful role reversal. If a young man failed in his obligations, he would never be seen again.

By shutting down the slave routes at their source, Jinga forced the Portuguese to mount ever longer expeditions into the interior. Seizing the advantage, the Dutch cut the Portuguese supply lines and in 1641 took Loanda, after which they struck a treaty with Jinga, which in turn enabled her to harry rival tribes and the Portuguese. She recorded a string of successes, but in one engagement the Portuguese captured her sister Mukumbu (Lady Barbara). Her other sister, Kifunji (Lady Grace), had long been a prisoner of the Portuguese, who drowned her in October 1647.

In August 1648 the Portuguese recaptured Loanda, forcing Jinga to fall back on her stronghold in Matamba, where she negotiated peace terms with them in 1656, principally to obtain the release of her sister. The price of the deal was the provision by Jinga of 130 slaves and her agreement not to interfere with Portuguese slave trade. She also abandoned ritual sacrifices and allowed Christian missionaries into Matamba. In return the Portuguese pledged military help whenever she needed it. The grizzled old warrior was buried with a bow and arrow in her hand.

Reference: Ronald H. Chilcote, *Portuguese Africa,* 1959.

MUKAKIBIBI, SISTER THEOPHISTER
Roman Catholic Nun and Genocide Perpetrator, n.d.

In November 2006, Theophister Mukakibibi became the first nun to be convicted in Rwanda for participating in the genocide of 1994, when some eight hundred thousand people were butchered. Using her position as a Roman Catholic nurse in the National

University Hospital in the town of Butare, she systematically murdered Tutsi patients, starving some to death, denying others lifesaving drugs, and handing others over to machete-wielding gangs.

As a Hutu, despite her professed religious faith, Mukakibibi enthusiastically embraced the chance to act when her tribe turned on the Tutsis, the minority in Rwanda, in an orgy of killing that spared no one. She played a strategic role in the Hutu massacres, selecting Tutsi patients for murder, with a special emphasis on wiping out children and pregnant women. She disconnected others from drips or medical machinery. In the words of the judge, Jeane Baptiste Ndahumba, presiding over a *gacaca* (village) court, "she controlled the switches of life and death." When these methods proved too slow, she handed patients over to face the machetes of the Interehamwe, the blood-stained militia leading the genocide, either for summary slaughter or more protracted deaths.

Mukakibibi was not acting alone. In 2005, a court in Belgium convicted two other nuns of participating in the genocide, and complicity in the Rwanda holocaust reaches up to her religious superiors and beyond. The majority of Rwanda's 8.5 million people are Roman Catholics, and there is clear evidence that senior figures in the Church aided the genocide or actively participated in mass murder.

In 2006 Mukakibibi, a lowly player among thousands who escaped, was jailed for thirty years by a village court.

Reference: David Blair, "Nun Is Jailed over Rwanda Genocide," *London Daily Telegraph,* **November 12 2006.**

PLAVSIC, BILJANA
Serbian Politician and War Criminal, b. 1930

Dubbed Bosnia's "Iron Lady," Plavsic was sentenced by the International War Crimes Tribunal to eleven years' imprisonment in 2003 for crimes against humanity.

Plavsic entered politics late in life, after a career as a biologist in which she published more than one hundred scholarly papers.

In 1956 she was appointed Professor of Biology at the University of Sarajevo, and subsequently she took up academic posts in Czechoslovakia and the United States.

In the 1992–95 war in Bosnia, Plavsic became deputy to Radovan Karadzic, leader of the Bosnian Serbs, who in 2006 remained at the top of the International War Crimes Tribunal's wanted list for the "ethnic cleansing" of tens of thousands of Bosnian Muslims and Croats. Even in the company of men whose hands were dripping with blood, Plavsic was seen as a radical. She once observed, "There are twelve million Serbs, and even if six million perish on the field of battle, there will be six million to reap the fruits of the struggle."

Her frequent outbursts led the president of the Federal Republic of Yugoslavia, Slobodan Milosevic, to question her mental health, while his wife, Mirjana Markovic, called her a "female Mengele," in reference to the infamous Nazi doctor who operated on women and children in the Holocaust. In 1992 a widely circulated photograph showed Plavsic stepping over the body of a dead Muslim to kiss the notorious Serb warlord Zejko Raznatovic (aka Arkan). Nevertheless, Plavsic backed the 1995 Dayton peace accord for Bosnia, which accepted the separate existence of Bosnia and Croatia in return for the lifting of US sanctions.

In 1996, Plavsic was elected president of the Bosnian Serb republic and was welcomed in the West as a "moderate" who condemned Communism for subjecting the Serbs to slavery. She also drove the Bosnian Serbs' wartime commander, Ratko Mladic, into retirement and secured the dismissal of his chief lieutenants.

She then formed her own breakaway faction, the Serbian Popular Alliance, but in the summer of 2000 began to withdraw from politics after suffering a setback in local elections. She resigned her seat in the Bosnian Serb parliament the following December. In January 2001 she turned herself in to the International War Crimes Tribunal, having learned that there was a sealed indictment against her.

Plavsic initially rejected the war-crimes and genocide charges brought against her, but as the trial deadline approached, she shifted her position. She pleaded guilty to crimes against humanity, and in return the prosecution dropped the charges of genocide. In her statement accepting responsibility for the killings and deportations, Plavsic named Slobodan Milosevic as the mastermind behind the ethnic-cleansing campaign. The court also took into consideration the testimony by former secretary of state Madeleine Albright and others that Plavsic had played an important role in the negotiations at Dayton. In 2003 she received a sentence of eleven years in prison, less the 245 days she had spent in jail since her surrender. Milosevic died in The Hague in March 2006 during his trial for war crimes.

Reference: Colonel Bob Stewart, *Broken Lives: A Personal View of the Bosnian Conflict,* 1993.

SUICIDE BOMBERS (1985–2006)

The phenomenon of the female suicide bomber, most commonly associated in the West with the conflict in the Middle East between Israel and Palestine, evokes a series of disturbing images and prompts uneasy reflection. Nevertheless, it is as well to remember that the notion of female martyrs is a thread that also runs through Western cultural and military history, from the host of martyred saints celebrated by the Catholic Church, of whom **Joan of Arc** (see p. 75) is one of the most notable, to SOE women such as **Noor Inayat Khan** (see p. 351) who died at the hands of the Nazis in World War II. On the darker side of the coin, postwar Europe and the United States have seen women terrorists fighting with Italy's Red Brigades, Germany's Baader-Meinhof gang, and the American Weathermen.

Nor are the activities of the female suicide bomber confined to the Middle East. In 1991 a female Sri Lankan separatist, Thenmuli Rajaratnam (aka Dhanu), a member of the Liberation Tigers of Tamil Elam (LTTE), succeeded in killing herself and former Indian prime minister Rajiv Gandhi. Since then similar bombings have occurred in Turkey, Pakistan, Uzbekistan, and Iraq, as well as Israel. In Russia, the separatist Chechen cause has attracted female suicide bombers, including those who were part of the multiethnic group that launched the seizure in September 2004 of a school in Beslan in the Caucasus, which resulted in the killing of more than 330 hostages, 172 of them children. A month earlier two Daghestani women of the al-Islambouli Brigade of al-Qaeda, blew up in midair one of two Russian airliners that were downed in a synchronized terrorist attack. This atrocity occurred only days after a female suicide bomber killed ten people outside a Moscow subway station.

In the Middle East, one of the first women to become a suicide bomber, or *istishhadiya,* was nineteen-year-old Loula Aboud, a Lebanese Christian who blew herself up in 1985 as Israeli troops occupied the town of Aoun in southern Lebanon. The first Palestinian would-be suicide bomber was Atef Eleyan, a Palestinian Islamic Jihad (PIJ) activist, who planned to carry out a suicide attack with a car bomb in Jerusalem in 1987 and was sentenced to ten years' imprisonment by the Israeli authorities.

The role of the female suicide bomber has inevitably become entangled with the region's violent political and religious crosscurrents. Tight Israeli border-security measures made it all but impossible for unmarried men under forty to obtain legitimate permits to cross into Israel and obliged militant groups to consider the use of female suicide bombers. In addition, the antagonism of conservative Islamic clerics discouraged women from playing an active role in society and in the intifada, the struggle against the continuing Israeli occupation of Arab land. By contrast, radical groups such as the al-Aqsa Martyrs Brigade cynically used suicide bombers to break down the frail barriers that in the Middle East continue to draw a distinction between combatants and noncombatants, terrorists and innocent civilians.

In the late 1990s, using reasoning reminiscent of that employed in World War II by the **Special Operations Executive** (see p. 366), the Palestinian Islamic Jihad began to recruit women in the northern part of the West Bank. Calculating that young women would be less likely to arouse suspicion than young men, and would also blend more easily into the Israeli "street," the PIJ recruiters focused attention equally on highly educated and qualified young women and on those with neither education nor career prospects.

They also found Islamic justification for the use of female suicide bombers in the teaching of Sheikh Ahmed Yassin, founder of the militant Islamist organization Hamas, who supported suicide bombers both male and female, provided that they attacked only Israeli military targets. The sheikh was killed in 2004 in an Israeli raid on Gaza. Another supporting voice was that of Sheikh Yusuf al-Qaradawi, whose view of women's martyrdom (suicide) operations was that "when jihad is obligatory, as when an enemy invades a country, the woman is summoned to jihad with the man, side by side. . . . A woman must act, even without the permission of her husband."

The bombing campaign that followed threw into sharp relief the PIJ modus operandi. On May 19, 2003, Hiba Daraghmeh, a nineteen-year-old student, detonated an explosive device strapped to her body in front of a shopping mall in Al Afoulah, killing three civilians and injuring eighty-three. On October 4, 2003, Hanadi Jaradat, a trainee lawyer from Jenin, blew herself up in a Haifa restaurant, killing twenty-one people and injuring fifty-one. In June 2003 Jaradat's brother and a cousin, both of whom were PIJ militants, had been killed by the Israeli Defense Forces (IDF). The twenty-seven-year-old Jaradat was unmarried—a stigma in Palestinian society—and was grieving the death of her brother and cousin when she was approached by PIJ, who expertly manipulated her grief and desire for revenge.

Sexual stigma is the leitmotif that runs through the story of Reem Raiyshi, the twenty-two-year-old Palestinian mother of two small children, who in January 2004 became the first female bomber used by Hamas. Raiyshi was compelled to undertake the mission as an atonement for her adultery. Her husband, a member of Hamas, was active in urging her to "purify" herself and restore her family's honor. His wife blew herself up inside a security office at the Erez crossing point into Israel from the Gaza Strip. Four Israelis died in the blast.

The fate of women like Hanadi Jaradat and Reem Raiyshi

prompted the American feminist writer Andrea Dworkin to observe critically that "the female suicide bombers are idealists who
crave committing a pure act, one that will wipe away the stigma of
being female. The Palestinian community is not sacrificing low
women, women of no accomplishment, women with no future.
Instead, the women suicide bombers are the society's best in terms
of human resources, a perverted example of the best and the
brightest."

In November 2005, a Belgian woman became the first European suicide bomber when she died in Iraq in a failed attack on
American troops. Muriel Degauque, from Charleroi, had become
a devout Muslim after marrying a radical Moroccan Islamist and
had adopted the *chador* (Islamic dress that covers women from
head to toe). She later traveled to Iraq through Turkey. A Belgian
passport was found near her body. It has been estimated that between 2001 and 2006 some fifty women carried out suicide attacks
worldwide.

In April 2006, Hamas announced that it intended to abandon
its use of suicide bombers. However, this did not deter Hamas activist Fatma Najar from becoming, at seventy, the world's oldest
female suicide bomber (and the first to be a great-grandmother) in
November 2006 when an explosive device strapped to her body
was activated by a grenade thrown at her by Israeli soldiers as she
advanced toward their position north of Gaza. In a video she made
shortly before she died, Fatma Najar, a mother of nine, declared,
"I offer myself as a sacrifice to God and to the homeland."

Reference: Barbara Victor, *Army of Roses: Inside the World of Palestinian Women Suicide Bombers,* 2003.

TRIBAL REVENGE

For thousands of years, women of many cultures who were
banned from the battlefield were given their chance for revenge
on the enemy when their victorious warriors brought home the
prisoners of war. Fully aware of what they would have suffered at
the hands of the victors if their menfolk had lost, women young

and old sharpened their shells, blades, or knives and set to work. This work was exclusively assigned to the women because of their lowly and despised status in their warrior tribes. Prisoners being tortured to death suffered, in addition to the physical agonies the women were ready to inflict, the overwhelming humiliation of dying at the hands of a woman, something like a cross between an untouchable in India and an *Untermensch* of Nazi race-hatred theory.

These practices are most clearly documented among some of the Native American tribes of North America in the nineteenth century, notably the Apache, Cherokee, Iroquois, Omaha, and Dakota. The women of the Shasta tribe of California accompanied their men to war and had the special task of hobbling the enemy, cutting the hamstrings of the fallen to disable them from fighting again. But the history, myths, and legends of the ancient world all speak of women who haunted battlefields to torture, murder, and pillage the fallen. For the Greeks, the goddess Demeter was the Mother, who took her "children," the dead and dying warriors, to their last home. In Celtic mythology, five goddesses of war—Fea, "the Hateful," Nemon, "the Venomous," Badb, "the Fury," Macha, "Battle," and their leader, Morrígú or Morrighan, "Great Queen"—all served as role models for the flesh-and-blood women who combined business with pleasure as they scoured the fields of the fallen, cutting off a finger to release a ring here, excising an eye or a testicle there, until sated with booty and blood.

For women who were largely powerless and widely abused in the traditional society of tribes, these rituals of rapine and revenge were an opportunity to assert themselves in ways that their men could neither prevent nor control. This may account for their extraordinary cruelty and viciousness, which drew this dark verse from the poet and chronicler of the British Empire, Rudyard Kipling:

> *If you're wounded and left out on Afghanistan's plains*
> *And the women come out to cut up what remains,*
> *Just roll to your rifle and blow out your brains*
> *And go to your Gawd like a soldier.*

As late as the mid-twentieth century, the women of Afghanistan retained their fearsome reputation for the sadistic mutilation of prisoners. Pilots and crew flying air-control missions over the North-West Frontier between India and Afghanistan in the late 1930s always carried a "blood chit," a piece of paper promising to pay the bearer a reward if they handed back any captured servicemen, but only if they were still unmutilated and in full possession of all their organs and appendages.

Afghani and Apache women traditionally enjoyed the reputation of being the cruelest practitioners of this hideous art. But it is found everywhere, challenging once again the belief that men go to war to protect a sex that is inherently softer and weaker than their own. In seventeenth-century colonial Massachusetts, a mob of women tortured two Native American prisoners to death, after overcoming their guards. In the same vein, the women of the Tupinambá of Brazil not only enthusiastically tortured prisoners of war to death but dismembered and ate them, too. And in 1993, in an action that brings the savage man-killing Maenads of ancient Greece right up to the present day, women were active in a Somali mob that dragged the bodies of US soldiers through the streets of Mogadishu, mutilating and dismembering them. In the same year Somali women also took part in the lynching of four foreign journalists.

Reference:

www.opinionjournal.com/editorial/feature.html?id11000491

www.etext.org/Politics/Somalia.News.Update/Volume.2/snu-2

11

ARMIES OF THE SHADOWS

∼∞∞∼

Spies, Agents, and Underground Workers

Without the Resistance, I was nobody. . . . the Resistance gave us wings.
—Female member of ELAS, Greek Resistance movement in World War II

Of all forms of warfare, undercover operations have afforded the greatest opportunities for women to serve in the front line and have witnessed some of their most extraordinary feats of heroism, daring, and endurance.

As spies, women have enjoyed one great social advantage, the routine undervaluing of the female sex that has always been a woman's lot, and the most successful undercover agents turned this to good account. Many men in war missed women's underground activity because they could not conceive that women were capable of it. **Andrée de Jongh** (see p. 347), organizer of one of the most successful escape lines in World War II, was released by the Nazis because they could not believe that a formidable enemy was sitting before them in the person of this demure young woman.

Women are also equipped by nature for subterfuge, as their biological capacity for multitasking enables them to keep a number of different realities alive at the same time. So they could convincingly play their assigned role, no matter how dull (a number of the Cold War spies were no more than modest housewives to external eyes) while relentlessly pursuing their covert ends, making light both of the reality of their situation and of the often elaborate deceptions and charades they devised.

The story begins with the earliest recorded texts. Women spies were active on behalf of the Chinese in the fifth century BCE, when the philosopher Mo-tzu advocated reporting anyone who committed evil deeds to the authorities. Since then the roll call stretches from one of the world's first "honey trap" operatives, Delilah, who ensnared Samson for the Philistines, through the **American Civil War** (see p. 336), on into the Cold War and up to today.

An early mistress of the honey trap, Delilah anticipated by almost two thousand years the techniques employed by **Cheryl Bentov** (see p. 341). Delilah worked for money; the price of trapping Samson was eleven hundred pieces of silver from each of the lords of the Philistines.

Then as now, money was a key factor in procuring intelligence, but women spies and undercover agents in the Bible more often acted out of love or loyalty.

More undercover work for women came when the international power politics of medieval and Renaissance Europe encouraged the growth of intelligence networks, and every ruler had a chief adviser like King Henry VIII's lord chancellor, Cardinal Thomas Wolsey, who in sixteenth-century England sat at the center of a spider's web of spies. Henry's daughter, **Elizabeth I** (see p. 34), similarly understood that mastery of the secret world was more than half the battle, and her choice of the brilliant Francis Walsingham to run her intelligence network was a key factor in maintaining England's international security in a troubled and warlike age.

The role of women as capable, plausible, and sometimes ruthless intelligence agents remained unchanged for centuries. In the American Civil War, outdated notions of male gallantry, and much strong drink, enabled skillful operators such as the Confederate spy Belle Boyd in the **American Civil War** (see p. 336) to ply their trade, gathering useful "overheard" indiscretions from bibulous Union officers. Echoes of this amateur but often effective approach reverberated into twentieth-century warfare, perhaps most notably in the tragicomic espionage career of **Mata Hari** (see p. 137).

In 1940, as in 1588, Britain was fighting for national survival.

That year saw British prime minister Winston Churchill establish the **Special Operations Executive** (SOE, see p. 366), an agency whose purpose was to gather intelligence in occupied Europe and Southeast Asia, to carry out sabotage, and to liaise with Resistance groups. Its American counterpart, the **Office of Strategic Services** (OSS, see p. 355), was formed in 1942. SOE in particular made significant use of female agents in the field and found, in the figure of **Vera Atkins** (see p. 339), a formidable but sometimes fallible spymaster to match Walsingham in the single-minded harrying of the detested enemy.

SOE's chief recruiter in the early years, Selwyn Jepson, was a keen advocate of the use of women in the secret world. In a battle in which moral strength often counted for more than mere physical prowess, he believed that the right kind of woman would always be more ruthless and clinical than her male equivalent. "Men usually want a mate with them," he observed. "Women have a far greater capacity for cool and lonely courage than men." His view was borne out by the phenomenal bravery and resourcefulness of women such as **Pearl Witherington** (see p. 375), and **Virginia Hall** (see p. 348), the latter of whom did not let a trifling thing like an artificial foot, code-named "Cuthbert," stand in the way of a successful career in the field both for SOE and OSS.

In the postwar years, OSS evolved into the Central Intelligence Agency (CIA), and SOE veterans gravitated toward the British equivalent, MI6. In the Cold War they were fighting a new enemy and former World War II ally, the Soviet Union. In the war years, Joseph Stalin devoted almost as much attention to spying on his Western allies as he did to fighting Nazi Germany. This was to pay the Soviets handsome, albeit temporary, dividends in the late 1940s and early 1950s, an era of nuclear paranoia and seemingly endless spy scares, when despite Soviet shortages, there was always enough money to fund intelligence gathering.

But female spies generally follow their lonely and hazardous career out of conviction, not for cash. Among other noteworthy dedicated denizens of the shadows are the Cold War warriors **Ruth Werner,** code-named "Sonya," the German Communist spy dubbed "the most successful female spy in history," and **Jeanne Vertefeuille,** the CIA operative who doggedly uncovered one of the most dangerous Soviet spies in the United States, the traitor **Aldrich Ames** (see pp. 370 and 372).

In the early 1990s, the Soviet Union collapsed and was replaced by a new threat, militant Islam. During this sea change in the 1990s, two British women, **Eliza Manningham-Buller** and **Stella Rimington** (see p. 353 and 358), rose to the top of the intelligence tree. Inconceivable as it would have been to the great killer and casual sexual psychopath 007, Miss Moneypenny had ousted James Bond.

AMERICAN CIVIL WAR

The American Civil War (1861–65) was arguably the first war of the modern era, in which increased firepower (early machine guns, improved artillery, mass-produced rifles) and improved communications (railways, the telegraph, the submarine) changed the technological terms of conflict and massively favored the industrial North over the primarily agrarian South. However, these factors had relatively little effect on both Union and Confederate commanders, many of whom handled their troops in a manner more fitted to the Napoleonic battlefield than the Civil War killing grounds dominated by weaponry whose lethality far outstripped that of Bonaparte's Grande Armée. In similar fashion, the attitude of these commanders to intelligence gathering often displayed naïvéte and a reluctance to move with the times in equal measure, not least when it came to the activities of the Civil War's female spies.

These were many and varied, on both sides of the national divide (for one of the Union's most successful female intelligence agents, see **Harriet Tubman,** p. 117). One of the most famous Confederate spies was **Belle Boyd** (b. 1844, d. 1900) of Martinsburg, West Virginia. Her father's hotel provided the forceful and flirtatious Belle with a ready-made listening post, where she gathered overheard fragments of conversation with amorous and indiscreet Union officers and then conveyed the information to the Confederacy. During the Shenandoah Valley campaign in the spring of

1862, Boyd provided valuable intelligence about the Union forces' intentions to General T. J. "Stonewall" Jackson. The grateful Jackson appointed her a captain and honorary aide-de-camp on his staff, enabling Boyd to attend troop reviews. In July 1862 she was arrested by the Union and detained for a month in Washington before being released in an exchange of prisoners. Belle proved to be a lively prisoner, gaily waving Confederate flags from her window and warbling "Dixie" to admirers below. She communicated with them by means of a rubber ball, which was tossed in and out of her cell and onto which she sewed messages. She was arrested for a second time in June 1863 but contracted typhus and was released. In May 1864 she sailed for England, but her ship was intercepted and she was arrested as a courier for the Confederacy. The resourceful Boyd escaped to Canada with the help of a Union officer, Samuel Hardinge, who then accompanied her to England and married her in August 1864.

While in England, Belle wrote her colorful memoirs, *Belle Boyd in Camp and Prison,* and appeared onstage. Hardinge died in 1865, and the following year Belle returned to the United States, where she continued her stage career, styling herself "the Cleopatra of the Secession" and performing in a Confederate uniform. She acquired two more husbands, the second seventeen years her junior, and died of a heart attack while touring in Wisconsin, broke but unbowed.

Another successful spy, **Rosie O'Neal Greenhow** (b. 1817, d. 1864), was a prominent figure in Washington society and a passionate secessionist. The intelligence she gathered is said to have played a part in the Confederate victories at the Battles of Bull Run. Dubbed "the Wild Rose," she was imprisoned twice by the Union but continued to smuggle messages to the Confederacy and was then exiled to the Confederate states. She was warmly welcomed by their provisional president, Jefferson Davis, who dispatched her to England as a propagandist and fund-raiser for the Confederate cause. Greenhow's memoirs were published while she was in London, where she moved easily in aristocratic circles and met Queen Victoria. In Paris she was granted an audience with Napoléon III.

In 1864 she returned to the United States on the blockade runner *Condor,* which ran aground at the mouth of the Cape Fear River in North Carolina. With a Union gunboat closing on the *Condor,* Greenhow escaped in a rowboat but drowned when it capsized and she was dragged to the bottom by the weight of the gold sewn into her skirts, the royalties from her best-selling memoirs.

She was buried with full military honors in October 1864. Her coffin was draped with the Confederate flag and borne by Confederate troops. The marble cross that marks her grave bears the epitaph "Mrs. Rose O'N. Greenhow, a bearer of dispatches to the Confederate Government."

One of the members of Greenhow's spy ring was **Eugenia Phillips** (b. 1819–d. ?), the Jewish wife of a successful politician and lawyer, Philip Phillips. Eugenia was a Washington socialite whose secret sympathies lay with the Confederacy. Her husband sided with the North and was understandably astonished when in August 1861 federal detectives placed the entire Phillips household under arrest. Phillips secured the release of his wife and daughters by agreeing that they would settle in the South, in Richmond, where Eugenia resumed her spying career. On a visit to Jefferson Davis she handed over military maps and memoranda that she had smuggled out of Washington.

Eugenia and her daughters later moved to New Orleans, which was then occupied by Union troops. Here she was arrested after allegedly showing disrespect at the funeral of Union soldiers by bursting into peals of laughter as the procession passed by. She was arrested under the so-called Women's Order, issued by General Benjamin Butler, which imposed draconian punishments on those who "by gesture, look or word" showed contempt for Union officers and men.

Phillips was imprisoned on the malarial Ship Island in the Gulf of Mexico. The spirited spy had one last shot in her locker as she was escorted to the ship that was to take her into internment. She turned to a triumphant Butler and withered him with the observation that "[Ship Island] has one advantage over the city, sir—you will not be there. It is fortunate that neither the fever nor General Butler is contagious." The release of Phillips and her daughters from Ship Island was secured after some months by her long-suffering husband, but internment had taken a toll on her health. The date of Eugenia's death is not known.

Reference: Belle Boyd, Drew Gilpin Faust, and Sharon Kennedy-Nolle, *Belle Boyd in Camp and Prison*, 1997.

ATKINS, VERA
World War II Intelligence Officer, 1908–2000

A woman of mystery and formidable self-control, Vera Atkins was the assistant to Maurice Buckmaster, head of F (French) Section in the British **Special Operations Executive** (SOE, see p. 366). Many of her contemporaries considered Atkins to be the section's real boss.

She was born in 1908 in Galat (now Galati), Romania, the daughter of a prosperous Jewish timber merchant, Max Rosenberg, and an English-born mother. She was intelligent, multilingual, and had attended a finishing school in Switzerland. In Romania, both father and daughter had informal links with British intelligence. In the mid-1930s Vera's work as a "foreign correspondent" in the strategically important Romanian oil industry, and her friendship with the German ambassador in Bucharest, Friedrich von der Schulenburg, placed her in an ideal position to supply undercover British intelligence agents in the Romanian capital with useful economic and diplomatic information.

Her father died bankrupt in 1932, and in 1937, as anti-Semitism grew in Romania, Vera moved with her mother to London, where she adopted the latter's maiden name of Atkins. In March 1941, she joined the Special Operations Executive, the agency established in July 1940 to gather intelligence in Nazi-occupied Europe, carry out sabotage, and support Resistance movements. Vera Atkins was still a Romanian citizen—she did not become a naturalized Briton until 1944. Thus from June 1941, when Romania joined the war on the German side, Vera Atkins was technically an enemy alien.

At SOE's headquarters on London's Baker Street, Atkins

rapidly rose from her position as a secretary to become a key member of F Section. Her "special confidential work" included the preparation and briefing of agents before their dispatch to occupied France, maintaining contact while they were in the field, their subsequent debriefing on their return, and liaising on a guarded "need-to-know" basis with her charges' next of kin.

Of the four hundred agents dispatched by F Section, some one hundred failed to return after German intelligence successfully penetrated a number of the section's networks. Arguably the most serious setback suffered by F Section in the whole of the war was the disabling of the large Prosper network based in Paris, as a result of the treachery of its field air-transport officer, Henri Déricourt. For reasons never fully understood, Buckmaster stubbornly ignored all the warning signals and carried on as before (see **Noor Inayat Khan,** p. 351).

Although Atkins and Buckmaster worked hand in glove, and the former had the gravest doubts about Déricourt's reliability, she was unable or unwilling to challenge her boss and intervene to limit the damage to the Prosper network. Several factors played a part in this. First, there was a degree of unacknowledged anti-Semitism in SOE, of which Atkins was well aware. Second, her status as an enemy alien would place her in a vulnerable position within the organization, should this awkward fact become well known. Third, it seems likely that, before she joined SOE, Atkins had traveled to Nazi-occupied Belgium on a private mission to negotiate with German intelligence a safe passage to Istanbul for a Jewish cousin, Fritz Rosenberg. For these reasons, she might have been powerless to prevent the fate that overtook the Prosper network.

On March 24, 1944, Atkins was given her certificate of British nationality, and two weeks later she was promoted to F Section intelligence officer. Soon after the end of the war SOE was dissolved, but in January 1946, Atkins was dispatched to liberated Europe with the rank of squadron officer to assist Allied war-crimes investigators. She was armed with a list of fifty-two missing SOE agents, thirteen of whom were women.

Atkins proved a relentless and implacable interrogator of Nazi war criminals, displaying emotion only on the rarest of occasions. The traces left by one agent in particular, Noor Inayat Khan, a victim of the Prosper debacle, proved immensely difficult to follow, prompting Atkins to reach an initial mistaken conclusion that she had died at Natzweiler-Struthof, a small concentration camp in the Vosges Mountains. When Atkins determined that "Madeleine" had died at Dachau, she falsified the records to mask her initial error.

In the postwar years, Atkins became the unofficial guardian of the SOE flame, adviser to movie productions celebrating agents she had handled, such as **Violette Szabo** (see p. 368), and keeper of the agency's many awkward secrets. Pathologically reluctant to admit any error, she deployed a daunting reserve to deter unwelcome questions about SOE, periodically weeding the large collections of wartime files that she retained. Noor Inayat Khan's brother remembered Vera Atkins as "not charming, but remarkable in her own way."

Reference: Sarah Helm, *A Life in Secrets: The Story of Vera Atkins and the Lost Agents of SOE,* 2005.

BENTOV, CHERYL
Israeli "Honey-Trap" Operative and Mossad Agent, b. 1960

In 1986, Bentov sprang the "honey trap," the oldest trick in the armory of a female spy, when she accompanied the smitten Israeli nuclear whistle-blower Mordechai Vanunu to Rome and delivered him into the hands of a Mossad snatch squad.

Born Cheryl Hanin in the United States, she emigrated to Israel in 1977, served in the **Israeli Defense Forces** (see p. 165), and was later recruited by Mossad (Institute for Intelligence and Special Operations). After two years of intensive training, she was chosen to work as a female escort in Mossad's operations worldwide. In 1985 she married Ofer Bentov, an officer in Israeli Army intelligence.

From the early 1960s, Israel has followed a policy of deliberate ambiguity about its nuclear-weapons program. In 1986, however,

its ability to maintain this stance was threatened by Mordechai Vanunu, who between 1976 and 1985 had worked as a technician at
the Dimona nuclear facility in the Negev desert. Vanunu was now
in London, telling *The Sunday Times* all he knew about the top-
secret programs at Dimona. Mossad was alerted when Vanunu,
frustrated by the slow pace at which the *The Sunday Times* was developing his story, approached another newspaper, *The Sunday
Mirror,* with the story. The *Mirror*'s owner, Robert Maxwell, an
old friend of Mossad, tipped off the intelligence agency.

In September 1986, Bentov flew to London under the name of
Cynthia Hanin, her sister-in-law, and joined a Mossad team tasked
with bringing Vanunu back to Israel to stand trial. She engineered
a "chance encounter" with the impressionable Vanunu and, posing
as an American beautician named Cindy, drew him into the trap.
Vanunu was putty in her hands, and she persuaded him to travel
with her to Rome to stay in a vacant apartment belonging to his sister. No sooner had they arrived at the apartment than Vanunu was
rendered unconscious, heavily sedated, and spirited by ship to Israel. He stood trial and received an eighteen-year prison sentence.

In 1988 British journalists traced Bentov to a suburb of Ne-
tanya in Israel, where she still has a home. However, she spends
the greater part of her time with her family in Florida, where she
works as a real estate agent under her maiden name and is a pillar
of Orlando's Jewish community. Mordechai Vanunu was released
from prison in 2004 and has subsequently insisted that Bentov was
an agent of the CIA or the FBI.

Reference: Peter Hounam, *The Woman from Mossad: The Torment of
Mordechai Vanunu,* 2000.

BROUSSE, AMY ELIZABETH
*"Cynthia," American-Born British and US Agent in World War II
Washington, b. 1910, d. 1963*

Amy Elizabeth Brousse was part of a daring operation launched by
the American **Office of Strategic Services** (OSS, see p. 355) to
steal, photograph, and return naval codes held in the Vichy France

embassy in Washington during the run-up to the November 1942 Allied landings in North Africa.

She was born Amy Elizabeth Thorpe in Minneapolis, the daughter of a much-decorated officer in the US Marine Corps and a mother who had studied in the United States and Europe. She herself studied in America and France before marrying, in 1930, Arthur Joseph Pack, a commercial secretary in the British embassy in Washington who was twenty years her senior. They led a globe-trotting life as she accompanied him to postings in Poland, Spain, and Chile, and entered the world of intelligence gathering.

In 1939 she left Pack and adopted her maiden name, Elizabeth Thorpe. After the outbreak of war in Europe, the former Mrs. Pack became an agent for British Security Coordination (BSC), an intelligence-gathering network based in New York and headed by William Stephenson. Stephenson found her an apartment in Washington and instructed her to use her feminine charms to obtain information about codes and ciphers from the Italian embassy. His new agent was well suited to the task; she had auburn hair and eyes "like a dash of green chartreuse in a pool of limpid brandy."

After its formation in 1942, the chief of OSS, General William "Wild Bill" Donovan, was instructed to cooperate with the BSC in a plan to remove and photograph the naval codes from the Vichy embassy. This mission involved a high degree of diplomatic risk, as the Vichy government in the unoccupied part of France was at the time recognized by the United States.

"Cynthia" was given an OSS controller, Colonel Ellery C. Huntington, chief of the agency's security branch and a personal friend of Donovan's, and provided with the services of a safecracker to gain access to the plans. She was in an ideal position to play a central role in the operation, as from May 1941 she had, on orders from the BSC, become the mistress of Charles Emmanuel Brousse, a former French naval pilot who was aide to the Vichy ambassador. With Brousse's help she had already supplied BSC with a stream of diplomatic cable traffic between the Vichy government and its Washington embassy.

The plan went ahead in June 1942. The codes were kept in a safe in the French naval attaché's office, to which Brousse, a married man, gained entry by persuading the embassy's guards to make it available to him as a late-night meeting place for love trysts with his mistress, "Cynthia." Even so, it took three separate attempts to complete the operation—opening the safe undisturbed and removing the code books to have them photographed in a nearby hotel and then returning them within a matter of hours and without detection. On the third attempt, an inquisitive embassy guard had been forced to beat a hasty retreat upon discovering Cynthia and her lover naked in the naval attaché's office. The codes proved particularly helpful to OSS agents embedded in North Africa in the run-up to the Operation Torch landings in North Africa.

"Cynthia" was subsequently posted to the **Special Operations Executive** (SOE, see p. 366), but never went operational again. However, the break-in had a bonus, as it later provided indirect cover for the maintenance of the Ultra secret, the British cracking of the German Enigma code. Information about the Washington break-in was leaked to the Germans to allay suspicions that Enigma was being read.

"Cynthia" subsequently married Brousse, who had been interned in the United States, and retired with him to a hilltop château near his native Perpignan, in France. There she died of cancer at the age of fifty-three.

Reference: Elizabeth P. McIntosh, *Sisterhood of Spies: The Women of the OSS*, 1998.

COHEN, LONA
aka Helen Kroger, American Soviet Master Spy, b. 1913, d. 1992

In the 1940s and the late 1950s, Lona Cohen and her husband, Morris, were among the Soviet Union's most productive intelligence assets, first in the United States and later in the United Kingdom.

Lona was born in Adams, Massachusetts, and in 1939 was recruited into Soviet espionage by her husband. After 1942, when Morris was drafted, Cohen ran a network in the New York area that included engineers and technicians at munitions and aviation plants. Simultaneously she worked at two defense plants. During this period Cohen also acted as a courier, collecting reports from the atomic-bomb project at Los Alamos, New Mexico. Among her contacts at Los Alamos was Theodore Hall, a physicist and spy who provided Soviet intelligence with a detailed description of the plutonium bomb known as "Fat Man," and the process for purifying plutonium.

After the defection in 1945 of Igor Gouzenko, a cypher clerk in the Soviet embassy in Ottawa, the Cohens abruptly severed their contacts with Soviet intelligence. They were resumed in 1949 when they began working with Vilyam Genrikhovich Fisher (aka Rudolf Abel), who had entered the United States as an "illegal" in 1947, and posed as a retired artist while recruiting and controlling new and existing agents. However, after the 1950 arrest in the United Kingdom of the spy Klaus Fuchs, another Soviet agent at the heart of Los Alamos, the Cohens fled to Moscow, where Lona underwent training as a radio operator and cypher clerk. In 1954 the Cohens resurfaced in northwest London under the names Peter and Helen Kroger.

The Krogers' cover was an antiquarian book business. In the basement of their house in the nondescript suburb of Ruislip, near the military airfield at Northolt, they installed a high-speed radio transmitter on which to send Moscow messages of "special importance." With their associate Gordon Lonsdale, a Russian posing as a Canadian businessman who sold jukeboxes, they then infiltrated the Royal Navy's Underwater Weapons Establishment at Portland in Dorset. Lonsdale recruited Harrry Houghton, a civil servant at the weapons establishment, and his girlfriend, Ethel Gee, who worked there as a clerk and had access to classified information.

In 1960 the Central Intelligence Agency (CIA) was informed by a Soviet mole, Michael Goleniewski, that Soviet agents were at work in Portland. The information was passed to MI5, who tailed Houghton and Gee to their regular meetings in London with Lonsdale and monitored Lonsdale's frequent trips to Ruislip to confer with the Krogers.

On January 7, 1961, Houghton, Gee, and Lonsdale were

arrested in London by officers of the Special Branch. In Gee's shopping bag they found quantities of top-secret film and photographs, and details about HMS *Dreadnought,* the Royal Navy's first nuclear submarine. The Krogers were arrested immediately afterward, and their suburban home yielded up a treasure trove of intelligence material, including large sums of money, photographic equipment, code pads, the couple's long-range radio transmitter, and, after further searches, two forged Canadian passports.

Neither the Krogers nor Lonsdale took the stand at their subsequent trial, but in a written statement the plausible Lonsdale took full responsibility for the charges of espionage, claiming that the Krogers were wholly innocent and that he had installed the spying equipment in their house while they were away. However, this did not explain the fake passports, bearing the couple's photographs and ready for a quick getaway.

All the defendants were found guilty. Houghton and Gee were sentenced to fifteen years' imprisonment and married on their release in 1970. Lonsdale was sentenced to twenty-five years and in 1964 was exchanged for the British spy Greville Wynn. The Krogers received sentences of twenty years and in 1969 were exchanged for a British citizen, Gerald Brooke.

The Cohens returned to Moscow, where they were given jobs training Soviet spies. Lona was awarded the Order of the Red Banner and the Order of Friendship of Nations, a decoration in which she evidently saw no irony. In the Soviet intelligence traffic decrypted by the Americans in the so-called Venona Project, Lona Cohen's code name was "Lesley."

In 1964, a downbeat British feature film, *Ring of Spies,* dramatized the Krogers' story. In 1983 the British playwright Hugh Whitemore revisited the tale of the Portland spy ring in *Pack of Lies,* which played in London's West End and starred Judi Dench and Michael Williams. In 1985 the play transferred to Broadway with Rosemary Harris starring as the neighbor whose house was used for surveillance by MI5. In 1987 it became a TV production, concentrating again on the neighbors, with Ellen Burstyn and Alan Bates in the leading roles.

Reference: Rebecca West, *The New Meaning of Treason,* 1964.

DE JONGH, ANDRÉE
"Dédée" or "Little Cyclone," Belgian Resistance Heroine (b. 1916, d. 2007)

In Nazi-occupied Europe the largest and most successful escape line transporting downed Allied airmen, escaped prisoners of war, and Resistance workers to safety was the "Comet" line running from Belgium. The mastermind of the Comet operation was a petite twenty-four-year-old nurse turned commercial artist, Andrée de Jongh, called Dédée or "Little Cyclone" by all who knew her.

The line made its debut in August 1941 when the demure de Jongh, wearing a simple blouse, skirt, and bobby socks, turned up at the British consulate in Bilbao on the northern coast of neutral Spain. She informed the consul that she had brought three fugitives with her from Brussels—two young Belgians and a British soldier who had been stranded after the Dunkirk evacuation in May 1940. She made only a modest request for financial assistance and promised that she would return with more British servicemen.

MI9, the secret British agency established to encourage escape and evasion in occupied Europe, provided financial assistance, but in all other respects de Jongh went her own way. She declined London's offer of radio operators, fearing that their transmissions would compromise security. She also insisted that the escape line be an all-Belgian operation. Furthermore, in contrast to the other escape line running from northern France and Belgium—the "Pat" line led by Albert Guérisse (whose nom de guerre was "Pat O'Leary")— de Jongh was determined to avoid Vichy France and take a more dangerous route to Spain through German-occupied France.

Initially MI9 code-named de Jongh's escape line "Postman," because she referred to her charges as "packages." In 1942, however, the name was changed to Comet after she delivered the crew of a British bomber, downed over Belgium, in less than a week. Eventually the line ran from Brussels through German-occupied France, over the Pyrenees to the British consulate in Madrid, and then to Gibraltar. Security was paramount: the Comet line's safe houses always had two exits and were usually staffed by elderly, childless couples who lived scrupulously quiet lives. The line itself consisted of a series of self-contained boxes. The personnel in each box remained unaware of the identity of their counterparts in the adjacent boxes. As the "packages" passed from box to box, they were left at pickup points to await the arrival of a new courier. The couriers communicated in code from public telephone boxes or by prearranged signals—for example, a potted plant placed in a window to indicate the presence of a German patrol.

In spite of all these precautions, Dédée was arrested on January 15, 1943, on her nineteenth crossing into Spain. The Pat line was broken up a month later and Guérisse arrested. Dédée's father, Paul, went into prison in Paris on June 7, 1943, and was later executed. Many of their colleagues were executed, but in spite of the loss of their leaders, and the grievous damage they had suffered, both lines managed to survive. It was not until early 1944 that traffic along the Comet line was halted, ironically because of the severity of Allied bombing in the buildup to D-Day. To alleviate the situation, MI9 established a new escape route, the Shelburne line, to ferry downed airmen directly to the coast of Brittany and thence to England.

Dédée's German captors could not believe that she had organized Comet and, after a spell in the Fresnes prison, near Paris, she was sent to the Ravensbrück concentration camp, from which she was released by advancing Allied troops in April 1945. Guérisse also survived the war. In all, the Comet line helped some 600 Allied servicemen, of whom 118 were personally accompanied on their journey by Dédée. Andrée de Jongh was awarded the American Medal of Freedom and made a Belgian countess. In the postwar years she worked with lepers in the Belgian Congo and Ethiopia.

Reference: Peter Eisner, *The Freedom Line: The Brave Men and Women Who Rescued Allied Airmen from the Nazis During World War II*, 2004.

GRANVILLE, CHRISTINE, see SKARBEK, KRYSTYNA, p. 364.

HALL, VIRGINIA
American SOE and OSS Agent, b. 1906, d. 1982

Virginia Hall had the rare distinction of serving with both the British intelligence agency **Special Operations Executive** (SOE, see p. 366), and later with its US equivalent, the **Office of Strategic Services** (OSS, see p. 355). On active service in the front line, she never allowed herself to be deterred by her artificial foot, variously described as made of wood or brass, the result of a shooting accident in Turkey in the 1930s.

Hall was educated at Radcliffe College, where she showed a flair for modern languages, and in 1931 she joined the staff of the US embassy in Poland. Appointments followed in Estonia, Austria, and Turkey. She was forced to resign after the accident in Turkey, as the State Department then had a rule barring the employment of anyone with an amputation "of any portion of a limb."

On the outbreak of war in September 1939, Hall was working in France, where she joined an ambulance unit. When Germany launched its blitzkrieg in the West on May 10, 1940, she traveled to London, where she found work in the US embassy. In London, Hall joined the SOE, despite the fact that its rules expressly stipulated that anyone serving in the agency had to have been born British, "a subject of the Crown." In fact there were many exceptions—some of the SOE staff and agents had dual nationality, and many volunteers came from foreign, even enemy, nations (see **Atkins, Vera,** p. 339). Reliability was the watchword, and Hall more than fulfilled this vital requirement.

Hall returned to mainland Europe in the summer of 1941 to operate in Vichy France, the unoccupied two-fifths of the country, whose seat of government was in the spa town of Vichy, some seventy-five miles northwest of Lyons. Hall went under her own name as an accredited correspondent of the *New York Post*. In early 1942 she moved her center of operations to Lyons, where she ran an extensive liaison network until a sudden setback saw her escaping over the Pyrenees with the Gestapo in hot pursuit.

Before she began the journey, Hall had signaled SOE headquarters on London's Baker Street that she hoped "Cuthbert" would not prove a problem. London flashed back, "If Cuthbert troublesome, eliminate him." Baker Street had forgotten that "Cuthbert" was the code name for Hall's prosthetic foot. For her service in France, the British awarded Hall the MBE, the Member of the Order of the British Empire.

Hall returned to France in March 1944, this time code-named "Diane" and working as a wireless operator for the American Office of Strategic Services. After landing by boat on the coast of Brittany, she joined the Resistance in the Haute-Loire region with the cover of a farmworker. She had no training in sabotage, but the teams she recruited, with the help from August 1944 of a joint SOE/OSS three-man unit known as a "Jedburgh," brought down four bridges, severed a key railway line, and derailed a number of freight trains. At the same time Hall and her Jedburgh team provided OSS with daily intelligence on local conditions and the movement of German troops. The Germans, who were well aware of Hall's identity, dubbed her "the lady with the limp." In spite of her disability, which she tried to disguise with a swinging gait, Hall's drive and planning ability were more than equal to these demanding operations.

In 1945 President Truman awarded Hall the Distinguished Service Cross, making her the only female civilian of World War II to receive this military honor, second only to the Medal of Honor. In 1948, after a period of intelligence work in postwar Europe, she settled in New York, where she joined the National Committee for Free Europe, a front organization of the newly formed Central Intelligence Agency and an adjunct to Radio Free Europe. Three years later she joined the Central Intelligence Agency in Washington as an analyst on French political affairs. In 1952 she became one of the first women operations officers in the newly created Office of the Deputy Director of Plans responsible for countries in Western Europe. Here Hall prepared political-action projects, interviewed exiles from behind the Iron Curtain, and planned stay-behind resistance and sabotage networks to be activated in the event of a successful invasion by the Soviet Union.

In 1956 Hall was made a member of the agency's select career staff. A CIA colleague recalled Hall in her early days with the CIA as "a gung-ho lady left over from the OSS days" to whom young female CIA recruits would pay rapt attention. "She was elegant, her dark brown hair coiled on top of her head with a yellow pencil tucked into the bun. She was always jolly when she was around the old boys. She was a presence!" However, with the passage of time Hall became an increasingly isolated figure at the CIA, and in 1966 she retired at the mandatory age of sixty to live on a Maryland farm. In December 2006, her niece, Lorna Catling, was presented with a certificate signed by George VI, which should have accompanied Hall's 1943 MBE. The British government had mislaid it for sixty-three years.

Reference: Elizabeth P. McIntosh, *Sisterhood of Spies: The Women of the OSS,* 1998.

HALLOWES, ODETTE, see **SANSOM, ODETTE, p. 361.**

KHAN, NOOR INAYAT
"Madeleine," Indian Princess and British SOE Agent, 1914–1945

The beautiful and tragic heroine of the **Special Operations Executive**'s (see p. 366) F (French) Section had an unusual and exotic background for a World War II spy. Her father, Hasra Inayat Khan, was descended from "the Tiger of Mysore," the last Mogul emperor of southern India, making his daughter a princess by direct descent. He was also a follower of Sufism, a supremely mystical branch of Islam, and her mother was related to Mary Baker Eddy, founder of Christian Science.

Noor Inayat Khan was born in the Kremlin, in Moscow, where her father was teaching at the Conservatoire. She grew up in Paris, studied child psychology at the Sorbonne, and achieved some fame as a writer of children's stories and as a broadcaster on French radio. The year 1943 found her in London, where she was transferred from the **Women's Auxiliary Air Force** (see p. 209) to the Special Operations Executive to train as a wireless operator.

Petite, lovely, and almost desperately eager to please, Khan was the source of some concern to several of her SOE instructors, one of whom observed, "Tends to give far too much information.

Came here without the foggiest notion what she was being trained for." Another reported that she was "not overburdened with brains [and] it is very doubtful whether she is really suited to work in the field."

Nevertheless, great confidence was placed in Noor Inayat Khan by **Vera Atkins** (see p. 339), and on June 16, 1943, she was landed in France by Lysander aircraft as F Section's first female wireless operator. Her mission was to work with the Cinema circuit, itself a component of the larger Prosper network based in Paris, to maintain Prosper's links with London and to send and receive messages about planned sabotage operations or the Resistance fighters' needs for arms. Her cover was that she was a children's nurse, Jeanne-Marie Renier, and her SOE code name was "Madeleine."

She was not to know that in 1943 the life expectancy of an SOE wireless operator was six weeks. In addition, the security of Prosper had already been fatally compromised by a French double agent, Henri Déricourt, air-movements officer for F Section and the man responsible for the reception and return to England of agents in the field. Déricourt was also working for the Sicherheitsdienst (SD, the security element of the SS). Prosper was soon rolled up by the Germans, although "Madeleine" was allowed to remain at large until October 13, during which time she unwittingly implicated fellow members of Prosper. After her arrest her radio was also used by the Germans to communicate with SOE in London, who remained unsure about her fate, although other reliable agents in France had provided the head of F Section, Maurice Buckmaster, with clear indications that she was in German hands. These he chose to ignore.

Noor Inayat Khan was initially held at the Gestapo headquarters on Paris's Avenue Foch, from which she made two unsuccessful attempts to escape. Thereafter a succession of transfers brought her to the concentration camp at Dachau, where she was raped, appallingly beaten, and then shot. Her last word, faintly audible, was *"Liberté."* Throughout her captivity the beautiful young woman "not overburdened with brains" had shown unflinching courage. After the war, Vera Atkins told Khan's biographer, Jean Overton Fuller, "Her motives were so pure—of such a high spiritual order—it was as if she was from another world."

Reference: Jean Overton Fuller, *Noor-un-nisa Inayat Khan: Madeleine,* 1952.

KROGER, HELEN, see COHEN, LONA, p. 344.

MANNINGHAM-BULLER, ELIZA
Director-General of MI5, b. 1948

In her days as an undergraduate at Oxford University, Manningham-Buller played the fairy godmother in a student production of *Cinderella*. She later became godmother to MI5 and the guardian of some of Britain's most valuable intelligence secrets. In the age of global terrorism, many of these are more nightmare than fairy tale.

She was born the Honourable Elizabeth Lydia Manningham-Buller, the daughter of an attorney-general and lord chancellor under two British Conservative prime ministers, Harold Macmillan and Sir Alec Douglas-Home. She attended the exclusive girls' public school Benenden at the same time as Princess Anne, where she earned the nickname "Bullying Manner."

At Oxford she studied English and, as often happens to very bright and well-bred undergraduates, was approached by MI5. However, after graduating she worked as a teacher at the exclusive Queen's Gate School in London, where the future celebrity chef and journalist Nigella Lawson was one of her pupils.

She joined MI5 in 1974, at the height of the Cold War, and progressed swiftly from typing up transcripts of tapped telephone conversations between Warsaw Pact diplomats to becoming a full-fledged spy catcher. Specializing in counterterrorism rather than counterespionage, she was one of only five people in British intelligence in the early 1980s who knew that Oleg Gordievsky, the deputy head of the KGB at the Soviet embassy in London, was a double agent. Gordievsky's life was literally in Manningham-Buller's hands, as two of her assistants shared an office with Michael Bettaney, a traitor working for the KGB (see **Rimington, Stella**, p. 358). An incautious word in front of Bettaney would have resulted in the KGB yanking Gordievsky straight back to Moscow for a hot date with a firing squad, at best.

Manningham-Buller was heavily involved in the investigation that followed the 1988 bombing of Pan-Am flight 103 in the skies over the Scottish town of Lockerbie. A Libyan, Abdel Baset Ali Mohamed al-Megrahi, was convicted of planting the bomb and sentenced to twenty-seven years in prison. However, many believe that he is a fall guy and that the mastermind behind the operation goes unpunished to this day.

During the Persian Gulf War, Manningham-Buller worked in Washington as a senior intelligence officer liaising with the Americans. In 1992 she was put in charge of the newly created Irish counterterrorism section when MI5 took over responsibility for this work from the Metropolitan Police. She moved steadily to the top, having been promoted to the Management Board of the Security Services in 1993 and then appointed director of surveillance and technical operations. In 1997 she was appointed MI5's deputy director-general and succeeded Stephen Lander in the top job in 2002, becoming the second woman to take on the role (see **Rimington, Stella**, p. 358). A doubtless grateful Oleg Gordievsky said that her appointment was "the best news for the service in a decade." In 2005 she was appointed a Dame Commander of the Order of the Bath.

After taking over as director-general, Manningham-Buller's working life was dominated by the threat from al-Qaeda, which obliged her to adopt a higher profile than her predecessors. In June 2003, at a conference at the Royal United Services Institute (RUSI), she pledged complete backing for the "war on terror" and warned that renegade scientists had provided terror groups with the information needed to create chemical, biological, radiological, and nuclear weapons. She stated that the fight against terrorism "would be with us for a good long time." In November 2006, in a speech at Queen Mary College, London, she announced that MI5 was tracking thirty terror plots and two hundred groupings or networks in the United Kingdom, comprising some sixteen hundred individuals. She repeated her 2003 warning that terrorists would not flinch from using a nuclear weapon.

In contrast, Manningham–Buller has been reluctant to respond to accusations that MI5 is not overscrupulous in acting on information obtained in other countries by torture. In January 2006 she refused to appear before the Joint Committee on Human Rights in the British Parliament to speak about "the extent to which the Service [MI5] is, or could take steps to ensure it is, aware that information it receives from foreign agencies may have been obtained by the use of torture." She also declined to talk to the committee about the use of airports in the United Kingdom in the program of "extraordinary rendition" (see **Rice, Condoleezza**, p. 51).

When not battling al-Qaeda, Manningham–Buller lived in the city of Bath with her husband, a retired lieutenant colonel in the army, who, appropriately perhaps, used to lecture in moral philosophy. Reportedly, Manningham–Buller still found the time to cook for her large family (she has inherited her husband's five children from a previous marriage) a roast lunch on Sunday. In April 2007 she was succeeded as director-general of MI5 by Jonathan Evans.

Reference: Marie Hollingsworth, *Defending the Realm: Inside MI5 and the War on Terrorism,* 2003.

OFFICE OF STRATEGIC SERVICES
OSS, US Intelligence Agency, World War II

The American equivalent of the British **Special Operations Executive** (SOE, see p. 366), the Office of Strategic Services was established in 1942 to support Resistance movements in Axis-occupied countries.

Friction sometimes arose between OSS and SOE, particularly over dealings with the Vichy French authorities in North Africa. This prompted General Eisenhower, the Allied Supreme Commander from 1943, to bring the two agencies together under one roof. This was the Special Forces Headquarters, which formed part of the Operations Division of the Supreme Headquarters Allied Expeditionary Force (SHAEF).

OSS was run by General William "Wild Bill" Donovan, a much-decorated World War I hero and postwar New York lawyer. In its early days, recruitment for OSS was mainly from fashionable and well-connected men and women on America's East Coast, earning the agency the nickname "Oh So Social." Its early structure broke down into seven main branches, all of which employed women in support functions or in operations:

- Research and Analysis (R&A), the amassing of background material to aid the planning of operations
- Secret Intelligence (SI), the obtaining of covert information, principally through agents in the field
- Special Operations (SO), clandestine activities including sabotage and guerrilla warfare
- the Operational Group (OG), which deployed service personnel with foreign-language skills on clandestine activities
- the Maritime Unit (MU), which concentrated on the destruction of enemy shipping
- the Counterintelligence Branch (X-2), which monitored and manipulated enemy intelligence operations and liaised with the British over the latter's penetration of the Enigma code, which the Germans thought unbreakable
- Morale Operations (MO), which included "black propaganda"

Few women took part in SO, OG, or MU operations, and in the somewhat patronizing words of General Donovan, "The great majority of women who worked for America's first organized and integrated intelligence agency spent their war years behind desks and filing cases in Washington, invisible apron strings of an organisation which touched every theatre of war." Nevertheless, in the field of Special Operations there were notable exceptions to the rule (see **Brousse, Amy Elizabeth,** p. 342, and **Hall, Virginia**, p. 348).

One of OSS's most effective morale operations against the Germans in the European theater was the so-called Musac Project, which was launched in July 1944 and run jointly from London with the British Political Warfare Executive. The OSS liaison officer in Washington was a woman, Rhoda K. Hirsch.

The Musac Project took the form of radio broadcasts, supposedly from German stations but actually from London, bringing slanted news and music items to troops on the front line. The British handled the news and the Americans the entertainment. The songs were provided with lyrics written by an OSS operative, Lothar Letzl, and orchestrated by Bertolt Brecht's collaborator, Kurt Weill, whose wife, Lotte Lenya, sang many of them. Another regular performer on the project was Marlene Dietrich, one of the few theatrical participants who was aware of the material's OSS connection—the songs, recorded in a secret New York studio, were a breach of US copyright laws. Not all the songs had a direct propaganda slant, but they were intended to supply mood music to enhance the war weariness felt by many of the Third Reich's service personnel and their disillusionment with the Nazi leadership.

One OSS agent, Canadian-born Betty Lussier, had a distinguished wartime career with X-2 in southwest France. In 1942 she joined the British **Air Transport Auxiliary** (see p. 151) but resigned in 1943 when she was told that female ATA pilots would not be permitted to fly in European combat zones after the Allied cross-Channel invasion secured a foothold in France. She joined OSS in the same year and became one of the first OSS personnel to train in England for counterespionage and code work.

Lussier became one of the select few who were privy to the Ultra secret—the British breaking of the German Enigma code—and joined one of the top-secret Special Liaison Units (SLUs). These were tasked with passing Ultra-derived information to Allied commanders in the field in northwest Europe, while simultaneously preserving the all-important secret itself. Originally based in Algiers, Lussier's SLU followed the Allied advance to Rome

and was then earmarked to operate from Toulon in the wake of
Operation Dragoon, the Allied invasion of southern France.
Lussier, however, remained in Italy, as women were forbidden to
serve near the front line.

In spite of this setback, the resourceful Lussier hitched a ride
with the Army Air Corps, landing in Grenoble and eventually
linking up with an SLU attached to the US Seventh Army in
northeast France. On a visit to liberated Paris, she was formally
reassigned to X-2, and dispatched to Nice to help start a counterintelligence unit.

She was next posted to Perpignan, on the French–Spanish border, where the X-2 chief was a flamboyant Catalan leftist, Ricardo
Sicre, whose nom de guerre was Rick Sickler. With Sicre, Lussier
formed a highly effective partnership, controlling a stable of double agents and exposing collaborators and stay-behind members of
German military intelligence. Lussier was not overly impressed by
her Nazi enemy. After the war, she recalled: "I got this impression
over the years reading their cable traffic. Their messages were
banal, trivial; much of it was about social plans. It never seemed to
occur to them that their agents could be captured and turned.
They had a certain arrogance about them that you couldn't miss."

Reference: Elizabeth P. McIntosh, *Sisterhood of Spies: The Women of
the OSS,* 1998.

RIMINGTON, STELLA
Head of MI5, Cold War, b. 1935

Rimington was the first woman to be appointed to the post of
director-general of MI5, the first MI5 head to be publicly identified, and the first to publish a volume of memoirs in which she described her years in British intelligence. These covered a changing
and challenging era from the late 1960s to the mid-1990s, a period
that saw the queasy certainties of the Cold War give way to the
first alarming intimations of the global "war on terror."

Rimington was born in South London, the daughter of a
draftsman father and a health-worker mother. At Nottingham

High School in the English Midlands, her fourth-year report read, "With consistent effort Stella could do well." After gaining a second-class degree in English from Edinburgh University, Rimington worked for a time as an archivist and in 1963 married John Rimington, a childhood boyfriend and civil servant.

When her husband was posted to the New Delhi High Commission in India, as a first secretary, Rimington became a dutiful diplomatic wife until 1967, when she was recruited to work part-time with the local MI5 station. It was her introduction to a world that was "intensely male, public school, and clubby. They were all men from the same colonial service/military sort of background. In those days the organisation was very closed. I think the arrival of women like me—and people like me—did begin to challenge that." Reflecting on her own lower-middle-class background, she drew this conclusion: "I always felt slightly revolutionary because I was clearly quite different. There were a lot of women like me scattered around but we weren't able to exert much influence. But I've never felt like working for people who I didn't think were as competent as me. You can call it a sort of arrogance, if you like. I suppose it caused me to push to get into more senior, more responsible positions."

When the couple returned to London in 1969, Rimington secured a permanent post with MI5 and went on to work in all three of its main arms—counterespionage, countersubversion, and counterterrorism. In countersubversion, she played a part in government action against the 1984–85 miners' strike, the Greenham Common women's antinuclear protest, and the growth of the far-left Militant Tendency and the Socialist Workers Party. She was also involved in the monitoring of the left-leaning National Council for Civil Liberties at a time when it was run by Patricia Hewitt and Harriet Harman, suspected "pinkos" who by 2005 were senior figures in the United Kingdom's New Labour government.

In 1990 Rimington was appointed one of MI5's two deputy director-generals, in which post she oversaw the agency's move to new headquarters. In December 1991 she led a team to the Soviet Union to establish friendly contact with the KGB, a shadow of its former self and soon to pass into history. In a complex that contained the infamous Lubyanka prison, a chilling symbol of the Cold War, Rimington was presented with a bunch of roses by a KGB man whom she remembered from her days in Delhi. The rest of her dealings with the grizzled veterans of Soviet intelligence were less cordial. Rimington was told in no uncertain terms that in spite of the disintegration of the Soviet Union—a phenomenon that she admitted in her memoirs took her by surprise—normal service would continue uninterrupted in the intelligence game.

In 1992 Rimington became director-general of MI5 and was the first head of the agency to have her photograph published in the British newspapers—a fuzzy long-lens shot of the spy mistress carrying her shopping bags (the government had been unwilling to release her picture). Nevertheless, she had come a long way since her first job as an archivist in the Worcestershire County Records Office, a trajectory that might not have occurred either to Ian Fleming or to John Le Carré.

In 1993 Rimington presided over the publication of a booklet, The Security Service, this time complete with her photograph, as part of a campaign of public transparency about the role of MI5. Unsurprisingly, the booklet contained little or no revealing information beyond the fact that the staff canteen served a particularly appetizing chicken curry. As director-general, Rimington approached the running of MI5 with the tone of a briskly competent suburban housewife. In her memoirs, she recalled with satisfaction that her management style was based on the same principles as she "used on the nannies and au pairs."

Rimington's selective and elliptical autobiography, Open Secret, was published in 2001, five years after she left MI5. It was a move that was strongly opposed by her former MI5 colleague and successor Sir Stephen Lander and the head of MI6, Sir Richard Dearlove, both of whom mounted a campaign to deter her from going into print. The colonel-commandant of the elite Special Air Service, David Lyon, warned Rimington that she could expect a "long period of being persona non grata, both to many she has worked with and with many she has yet to meet in the general public."

A principle was at stake, particularly as during her time as director-general, Rimington herself had threatened employees with the Official Secrets Act. However, her critics need not have worried. When it appeared, the book was blandness itself, in which Rimington painted a self-portrait of a feminist who had long fought prejudice in a male-dominated world. This came as a surprise to former colleagues, who recalled her behavior in a notorious episode of the 1980s, when she ignored explicit warnings about the reliability of an MI5 employee, Michael Bettaney (see **Manningham-Buller, Eliza,** p. 353), an alcoholic controller of agents in Northern Ireland, who had sold secrets to the Soviet Union. After Bettaney was arrested, he continued to supply the Soviets with information while awaiting trial. Rimington managed to avoid censure, an indication perhaps of her political skills, although it has been alleged that she attempted to shift the blame for the debacle onto two junior colleagues, both of them women.

Those who have met her have commented on Rimington's abundant personal charm and puzzling lack of depth. In her retirement she has published two novels as unexceptionable as her memoirs and taken a remunerative directorship with the retailers Marks & Spencer.

Reference: Stella Rimington, *Open Secret,* 2001.

SANSOM, ODETTE
"Lise," French SOE Agent, 1912–1995

Odette Sansom was born Odette Marie Celine Brailly in France and married an Englishman, Roy Sansom, with whom she made her home in England in 1932. The couple had three daughters. On the outbreak of World War II she joined the **First Aid Nursing Yeomanry** (FANY, see p. 161) before being recruited into the **Special Operations Executive**'s F (French) Section, where she trained as a radio operator.

In October 1942, with the code name "Lise," she was landed on the French Riviera by felucca, a small sailing boat, to join Peter Churchill, who acted as the liaison officer between F Section and the Carte network that was based in Antibes, in Vichy France.

Carte was run by an artist, André Girard, who was in touch with senior officers in the Vichy army and promised much but delivered little. Girard's sloppy security, the German occupation of Vichy France in November 1942, and the dissolution of the Vichy army led to the winding up of Carte and the arrest near Annecy in April 1943 of Churchill and his courier, Sansom. They were seized by Sergeant Hugo Bleicher of the Abwehr, the counterintelligence arm of the German high command. Bleicher found them in bed, which led to later accusations by the French Resistance that they were more interested in making love than in fighting the Germans.

Sansom was initially imprisoned at Fresnes, near Paris. The SOE had marked her out in training as a "shrewd cookie," and on her capture Sansom had the presence of mind to call herself "Mrs. Churchill," believing that this entirely fictitious connection with Britain's wartime leader Winston Churchill might help her. At first, however, she received no favors. At Fresnes her toenails were ripped off and her back was burned with an iron bar. Nevertheless, she gave nothing away.

With a number of SOE prisoners, Sansom was sent to a holding prison in Germany at Karlsruhe. After two months she was separated from her comrades, and in July 1944 she was taken to the women's concentration camp at Ravensbrück, where she was placed in solitary confinement and kept alive by the camp's kommandant, Fritz Suhren. He believed the story Sansom had spun on her arrest and, with the war going against Germany, intended to use her as a bargaining chip with the Allies.

In April 1945, with the Red Army approaching Ravensbrück, Suhren personally drove Sansom toward the American lines. He was to be disappointed. Sansom told the Americans precisely who Suhren was and had the satisfaction of watching him being led into captivity and the additional pleasure of retaining his bag, which contained his pajamas, writing case, and pistol. Sansom subsequently made a gift of these trophies to **Vera Atkins** (see p. 339).

On August 20, 1946, Odette Sansom was awarded the George Cross by King George VI and received the Légion d'Honneur from France. After the death of her first husband, she married

Peter Churchill in 1956, and when that marriage was dissolved she married Geoffrey Hallowes, another veteran of the SOE's F Section. In 1994, a year before she died, Sansom made an emotional return to Ravensbrück, which is now a memorial site. *Odette,* a sanitized but successful film celebrating her wartime career and starring Anna Neagle, was released in 1956.

Reference: Jerrard Tickell, *Odette: The Story of a British Agent,* 1952.

SENDLEROWA, IRENA
Polish Resistance Heroine, b. 1910

Until 1995, when a plaque was unveiled near the site of the Jewish ghetto in Warsaw, few of Sendlerowa's fellow Poles were aware of her heroic role in saving 2,500 children from the Nazis in 1942–43.

Sendlerowa, a welfare officer in Warsaw's health administration, was a member of Zegota, a secret organization set up by the Polish government-in-exile in London to rescue Polish Jews. By virtue of her job, she was permitted to enter the ghetto, which had been established by the Germans in the autumn of 1940 and by 1942 contained some 430,000 Jews. Wearing a Star of David, used by the Germans to mark Jews, she handed out money, clothes, and medicines and smuggled children to safety through the sewers or hidden in workmen's bags before placing them with friendly families, convents, or orphanages.

Sendlerowa noted the names of the children on cigarette papers, which she then sealed in glass bottles and buried in a colleague's garden. In the summer of 1943 the Warsaw Ghetto was liquidated, and the following October Sendlerowa was arrested. She was taken to Gestapo headquarters, where she was badly beaten. Her legs and feet were broken, but she refused to betray her comrades. She was driven away to be executed, but Zegota used a sackful of dollars to secure her release. She was left by the roadside, crippled and unconscious.

After the war, the bottles Sendlerowa had buried were dug up and a list of names handed to Jewish representatives. Attempts were made to reunite the children with their families, but most of their relations had perished in the death camps. One of the children saved by Sendlerowa, Elzbieta Foicowska, had been smuggled out of the ghetto in a toolbox on a truck when she was five months old. In 2007 she told journalists, "Irena Sendlerowa is like a third mother to me."

For many years Sendlerowa's story went unremarked both inside and outside Poland, but interest in her was revived when a group of schoolchildren in Kansas wrote a play about her wartime exploits, *Life in a Jar*. In April 2007, Sendlerowa was honored by the Polish parliament for "rescuing the most defenceless victims of Nazi ideology—the Jewish children," and nominated for the Nobel Peace Prize. Sendlerowa, crippled but serene, was insistent that she had done nothing out of the ordinary, observing, "I was brought up to believe that a person must be rescued when drowning, regardless of religion or nationality."

Reference: R. Lukas, *Did the Children Cry? Hitler's War Against Jewish and Polish Children, 1939–1945*, 1994.

SKARBEK, KRYSTYNA
"Christine Granville," Polish SOE Agent, 1915–52

A Polish-born **Special Operations Executive** (SOE, see p. 366) agent of outstanding resource and iron nerve, Countess Krystyna Skarbeck operated under the nom de guerre Christine Granville. She survived a remarkable secret career in World War II only to die at the hands of a disappointed suitor in postwar London.

Her father was Count Jerzy Skarbek, a member of one of Poland's oldest noble families, and her mother, Stefania Goldfeder, was the daughter of a wealthy assimilated Jewish banker. Granville's early childhood was spent under German occupation, which left her with little love for Germany. On the outbreak of World War II, when Germany invaded Poland for a second time, Granville was living in British East Africa with her husband, the writer Jerzy Gizycki. The couple made their way to London, where the British authorities showed little interest in employing Granville until the intervention of friends secured her a mission to Hungary, whose dictator, Admiral Horthy, was not only a German sympathizer but also a distant relation.

Granville had been a keen skier and knew many of the ski instructors on Hungary's mountainous northern border with Poland. Working with a Polish army officer, Andrzej Kowerski, she exfiltrated Polish and Allied personnel and, armed with much intelligence, escaped with Kowerski to Egypt via the Balkans and Turkey. Her mother refused to accompany them and later died in a concentration camp. It was during this episode that Skarbek became Christine Granville, traveling on a British passport bearing a name that was supplied by the British ambassador to Hungary, Sir Owen O' Malley, a personal friend. Kowerski, who was now her lover, traveled under the name Andrew Kennedy.

In Cairo, Granville and Kowerski were unable to convince the Poles in exile that they had not made their escape with the connivance of the enemy. Their passage through Syria, then controlled by Vichy France, excited the Poles' suspicion. Had they known her better, they would have readily understood that it was Granville's remarkable charm and coolness that had extracted visas from a pro–Vichy consul.

After a long hiatus, Granville, who was a fluent French-speaker, joined the F (French) Section of SOE. She was parachuted into the Vercors region of southeastern France on July 6, 1944, to work with the Anglo-Belgian Francis Cammaerts, who ran SOE's Jockey network.

On August 13, two days before the Allied Dragoon landings in southern France, Cammaerts, fellow-SOE agent Xan Fielding, and a French officer were captured at a roadblock by the Gestapo. Granville's reaction was swift and decisive. She called at the prison where Cammaerts and his comrades were held and, armed with three million francs dropped specially for the purpose, secured their release after making a series of decidedly unladylike threats about the fate that awaited the Gestapo men if they chose not to cooperate.

But in 1945, the war and its excitements ended. The British

gave Granville a George Medal, an OBE (Order of the British Empire), one hundred pounds, and a handshake. She was left stateless, penniless, and husbandless after she divorced Gizycki in 1946. She found employment as a stewardess on an ocean liner, and there she met her fate. In 1952 she was stabbed to death in the lobby of a shabby London hotel by George Muldowney, a besotted fellow steward, a tragic end for a woman of such courage, strength, and flair. Granville's wartime companion, Andrzej Kowerski, died in 1988 and is buried alongside her in the Roman Catholic cemetery in Kensal Green. "Christine Granville" lives on in popular fiction in the shape of Vesper Lynd, the beautiful spy created by Ian Fleming in *Casino Royale,* for whom Granville provided the real-life model.

Reference: Madeleine Masson, *Christine: SOE Agent and Churchill's Favourite Spy,* 2005.

SPECIAL OPERATIONS EXECUTIVE
SOE, British Intelligence Agency, World War II

SOE was the brainchild of Britain's wartime premier, Winston Churchill, formed at his behest in July 1940. Its purpose was to gather intelligence, undertake sabotage, and support Resistance movements in the countries of Europe and the Far East occupied by Germany and her allies. By the summer of 1944, SOE employed some fourteen thousand personnel, of whom about 3,200 were women. Of these, about 5,000 were agents in the field or awaiting dispatch.

Although the majority in the field were men, women played a significant role in SOE. The agency's F Section, which was responsible for operations in occupied France, sent 470 agents into the field, 39 of them women. In all, 118 failed to return, among them 13 women. This represented an overall casualty rate in the F Section of one in four, or 25 percent, severe but not unsustainable losses in conditions of world war. In contrast, the British engineers who went ashore at low tide on D-Day to remove mines from the beaches suffered a casualty rate three times greater, at 75 percent.

Until 1943, the man principally responsible for recruiting men and women for fieldwork in SOE was Selwyn Jepson, who in peacetime had been an author. Jepson accorded women a perfect equality with men, although in this he initially encountered stiff opposition within the agency. He later defended his decision:

> In my view women were very much better than men for the work. Women, as you must know, have a far greater capacity for cool and lonely courage than men. Men usually want a mate with them. Men don't work alone; their lives tend to be always in company with other men. There was opposition from most quarters until it went to Churchill, whom I had met before the war. He growled at me "What are you doing?" I told him and he said, "I see you are using women to do this," and I said, "Yes, don't you think it is a very sensible thing to do?" and he said, "Yes, good luck to you." That was my authority!

Equality was also observed in training for field operations. This can best be appreciated by viewing a fascinating documentary film of 1944, *Now It Can Be Told* (later retitled *School for Danger*), depicting the recruitment and some of the training of two real F Section agents, Harry Rée and Jacqueline Nearne. The rigorous program included exercises in physical fitness, raiding tactics, weapons handling and maintenance, sabotage, tradecraft, parachute drops, and radio transmission. The agents also faced tough mock interrogations and learned how to pick locks and break into safes. One SOE heroine, **Violette Szabo** (see p. 368), joked that the agency had equipped her for a wonderful career after the war—as a cat burglar.

In the field an SOE network, or circuit, depended on three figures—a courier, a wireless operator, and an organizer. Most of SOE's female field agents in France worked as couriers, traveling around as messengers and liaison officers. Because they were constantly on the move, couriers ran the highest risk of being stopped and arrested. It was thought that in this situation women would find it easier to invent plausible cover stories and would attract less attention than men, who from early 1942 were liable to be picked up by the Germans from the streets of France and sent to Germany as forced labor.

Women were also less likely to be body-searched and thus

could more easily secrete messages. Other female SOE field agents, such as **Noor Inayat Khan** (see p. 351), worked as wireless operators, maintaining regular contact with London. Some, such as **Pearl Witherington** (see p. 375), rose to the position of organizer, heading an SOE network, recruiting local Resistance fighters, arming and supplying them with air drops from Britain, and identifying targets for sabotage.

Many of the female agents had been drawn from the **First Aid Nursing Yeomanry** (FANY, see p. 161). The commander of the FANY was a personal friend of General Sir Colin Gubbins, who had been appointed SOE's director of operations in November 1940 and who in September 1943 became the agency's executive head. As well as supplying some of SOE's female field agents, members of the FANY staffed SOE holding and wireless stations in the United Kingdom, North Africa, Italy (from 1943), and the Far East, handling communications and in some cases the decryption of encoded enemy radio traffic.

Reference: M. R. D. Foot, *SOE: The Special Operations Executive,* 1984.

SZABO, VIOLETTE
British SOE Agent, b. 1918, d. 1945

The daughter of a French mother and an English father, Szabo grew up in South London. As a teenager, she gained the reputation of being a crack shot in the neighborhood shooting galleries, showing early signs of the unusual and adventurous temperament that was to lead her into the secret world of spies. Her precocious skill with a gun was also to prove invaluable in her underground work when she saved the life of a colleague, though at the cost of her own freedom and, eventually, her life.

After the outbreak of war, she married a young Free French officer, Etienne Szabo, and had a baby girl. When her husband was posted to the Middle East, she joined the **Auxiliary Territorial Service** (ATS, p. 153), serving in a **mixed antiaircraft battery** (see

p. 233) defending the key British port of Liverpool. Later, as a member of the **First Aid Nursing Yeomanry** (FANY, see p. 161), she joined the Special Operations Executive's F Section.

Szabo was now a widow—her husband had been killed in the autumn of 1942—left alone to care for her small daughter. A note in her file, written by a FANY officer, read, "This girl has a young baby. I wonder if she fully realises what she is doing."

In 1943, Szabo was prevented from undertaking her first mission by an ankle injury sustained in parachute training. She had to wait until April 1944, when she was flown to France in a Westland Lysander light aircraft during the buildup to D-Day. Her cover story was that she was Corinne Reine Le Roy (her mother's maiden name). Her primary mission was to establish whether one of SOE's subsidiary networks had been penetrated. Szabo returned to England three weeks later, having successfully ascertained that the operational usefulness of the circuit was at an end.

On June 6, 1944, Szabo was parachuted into France accompanied by Philippe Liewer, who was tasked with the revival of his Salesman network in the area of Limoges. On June 8, while with a Maquis colleague, she was captured by an advance party of the Second SS Panzer Division Das Reich near the village of Oradour-sur-Glane. Szabo had covered the escape of her colleague with a Sten gun, holding off some four hundred SS troops before her ammunition ran out and her suspect ankle gave way. Two days later, in a reprisal raid against the Resistance, one of Das Reich's panzergrenadier battalions surrounded Oradour, herded the entire population—men, women, and children—into the church and neighboring buildings, and set them alight. Those attempting to escape were shot. Some 642 people perished in this atrocity.

After her capture, Szabo was initially held in the Fresnes prison, near Paris, and later in the women's concentration camp at Ravensbrück. On January 26, 1945, she was executed there alongside two fellow SOE agents, Lilian Rolfe and Denise Bloch.

Reference: *The Life That I Have,* Susan Ottoway, 2003. Szabo was played in the 1958 British film *Carve Her Name with Pride* by Virgina McKenna.

VERTEFEUILLE, JEANNE
CIA Counterintelligence Officer, b. ca. 1930

The Central Intelligence Agency, which was founded in 1947, grew out of the wartime **Office of Strategic Services** (OSS, see p. 355). Its first director was an old OSS hand, Allen Dulles. The agency's principal function was to obtain and analyze information about foreign governments and to disseminate this material into all branches of US government. The agency's methods and remit, including those for the mounting of clandestine operations, were in general terms roughly equivalent to those of the similar British secret agency, MI6.

By the mid-1990s, 41 percent of the agency's employees were female. One of them was Jeanne Vertefeuille, who had joined the agency in 1954, working in Africa and Europe before finding a niche in counterintelligence as head of the CIA's Soviet Research Section. In the mid-1980s she became the station chief in Libreville, the capital of Gabon. At the same time Aldrich Ames was assigned to Vertefeuille's former office in counterintelligence at the CIA's headquarters in Langley, Virginia.

In June 1985, Ames began to pass large amounts of secret material to Sergei Chuvakhin, first secretary in the Soviet embassy in Washington. Over the course of the following nine years, Chuvakhin handed over some three million dollars to Ames. In return Ames betrayed dozens of agents recruited by the CIA, and revealed up to one hundred of the agency's clandestine operations. One of the men betrayed by Ames was Colonel Oleg Gordievsky, deputy head of the KGB at the Soviet embassy in London (see **Eliza Manningham-Buller**, p. 353), whom the British managed to extract from the Soviet Union.

In 1986 the CIA became aware that something was gravely amiss when twenty agents in the Soviet Union disappeared off their radar (at least ten were later executed). Back from her African tour, Vertefeuille was assigned to a small team, consisting of two women and two retired male CIA officers, which was tasked with closing the breach in security.

Worryingly for Vertefeuille, the CIA appeared most reluctant to countenance the possibility that the culprit came from within the agency. The agency's willful blindness to the threat stemmed in large part from the savaging it had received over the Iran-contra scandal that had broken in 1987, and the chaos caused in the 1970s by the brilliant but paranoid CIA employee James Jesus Angleton, who had become convinced that the organization had been penetrated at every level by Soviet double agents. A significant number of careers had been wrecked by Angleton's obsession.

One of the women on Vertefeuille's team, Sandy Grimes, had known Ames, with whom she had carpooled when they both lived in Reston, Virginia. At the time she had found him slobbish and disagreeable. Now he was elegantly clothed and coiffed and drove to work in a white Jaguar from his expensive home in Arlington. Ames attributed the change in his fortunes to money left to his second wife, the Colombian-born Maria del Rosario Casas Dupuy, whom he had met while working in Mexico City. More detective work indicated that the "legacy" story could not be true.

The net began to close around Ames when Vertefeuille pressed the CIA to examine Ames's bank accounts and credit card records. The trawl revealed that Ames had systematically banked several hundred thousand dollars. Grimes then succeeded in correlating the dates of the deposits with regular lunches Ames had enjoyed with Chuvakhin, ostensibly to recruit him to the CIA.

The FBI was called in. The Ameses' house was bugged, their phone calls were monitored, and files were downloaded from Ames's computer. In February 1994 Ames was arrested by the FBI, on the day before he was scheduled to visit Moscow on agency business and, in all probability, defect.

At the meetings in which Ames was debriefed by the FBI, Vertefeuille represented the CIA. There she learned that Soviet intelligence had gotten cold feet in 1985–86, after they had arrested the agents betrayed by Ames. They were concerned that the CIA would draw the obvious conclusion that a mole was in their midst, and suggested to Ames that he give them the name of another CIA officer whom they could implicate. Ames obliged. As his chosen fall guy, Vertefeuille was only mildly surprised to hear that Ames had nominated none other than herself.

At his trial Ames received a life sentence; his wife received five years. He subsequently confessed that the reasons for his treachery were "personal, banal and amounted really to a kind of greed and folly."

Reference: Mark Riebling, *Wedge: The Secret War Between the FBI and the CIA,* 1994. Aldrich Ames was the subject of a 1998 TV movie, *Aldrich Ames: The Traitor Within.* Timothy Hutton starred in the title role, and Jeanne Vertefeuille was played by Joan Plowright. In the credits Ames is listed as a "technical adviser." He also appears as a character in *Icon,* a 1997 novel by Frederick Forsyth.

WERNER, RUTH
"Sonya," German Communist Spy, 1907–2000

Dubbed "the most successful female spy in history" and code-named "Sonya," Ruth Werner always denied that she was a spy. Until the end of her long life she insisted that she was no more than "a member of the Red Army, in the reconnaissance service."

She was born Ursula Ruth Kuczynski in Berlin, the daughter of Polish Jews who were supporters of the German Communist Party, and joined the Communist Youth League when she was seventeen. In 1929 she married her first husband, Rolf Hamburger, an architect and Soviet agent, and went with him to Shanghai, where he had taken a job with the British-administered municipal council.

In China, she was shocked by the extremes of wealth and poverty and was soon moving in revolutionary and Communist circles. She met the American journalist and triple agent Agnes Smedley and her lover and collaborator, the German journalist and Soviet spy Richard Sorge, who ran a network of agents in Japan and was privy to many international secrets. Sorge persuaded Werner to work for the GRU (Soviet military intelligence) and gave her the code name "Sonya." She later described this as "one of the most decisive events of my life."

At Sorge's suggestion, Sonya traveled to Moscow, where she underwent training in espionage and radio communications at the

GRU's headquarters. She traveled widely as a GRU agent before returning to China, where she worked with revolutionary forces fighting the Japanese on the Manchurian border. In 1937 Sonya returned to Moscow for promotion to the rank of GRU major, advanced training, and the award of the Order of the Red Banner, the highest honor then available to a non-Soviet citizen.

In 1938 Sonya settled her children in England, where her father and brother Jürgen had been living since the mid-1930s, and was then ordered by the GRU to Switzerland. In the late 1930s and wartime years the neutral state was a happy hunting ground for espionage networks, among them the Soviet-controlled Rote Kapelle (Red Orchestra) and the so-called Lucy network, also controlled by Moscow, which in the war years was used by British intelligence to channel discreetly laundered information about German military intentions to the Soviet Union.

In Switzerland, Sonya met Allan Foote, a British member of the Lucy network, who in turn introduced her to her second husband, Len Beurton, an English veteran of the International Brigade who had fought in the Spanish Civil War. The GRU had ordered Sonya to divorce Rolf to marry Beurton, a move that conferred a British passport. She married Beurton in February 1940 and received a British passport in May.

In England, Sonya and her family moved into a large house in the village of Great Rollright, near Oxford. From 1941, this provided her with an ideal location for working as a courier with the German émigré scientist and atom spy Klaus Fuchs, a naturalized Briton, who was then employed at the atomic research establishment at Harwell. Sonya had been put in touch with the scientist by her brother Jürgen, who had known Fuchs in his Communist past. Jürgen was to finish the war as an officer with the American Office of Strategic Services (OSS), the forerunner of the CIA. In the war years, Jürgen's antifascist credentials and Communist sympathies proved no bar to working for US intelligence, indeed would have been considered an advantage.

After a series of meetings with Fuchs in Banbury, Sonya passed a stream of information on the British atomic program either to her Soviet controllers in London or directly by radio to Moscow.

In late 1943, Fuchs joined the Manhattan Project in the United States and thereafter passed into the hands of other controllers.

At the end of the war, Sonya's brother, now a lieutenant colonel in the US Army, supplied her with details of the results of the Strategic Bombing Survey, the American assessment of the air campaign against the Third Reich.

In 1946 Moscow mysteriously and abruptly broke off all contact with Sonya. Within a year both her own and her husband's cover had been exposed by Foote, and she was paid a visit by British Special Branch officers. Sonya later recalled, "They left us calmly and politely but empty-handed." Sonya and her husband kept their nerve, and British intelligence did not return.

In 1950 Sonya and two of her children left Britain for East Germany on the day before Fuchs stood trial for betraying the West's atomic secrets to the Soviet Union. In her autobiography she reflected, "Either it was complete stupidity on the part of MI5 never to have connected me to Klaus, or they may have let me get away with it, since every further discovery would have increased their disgrace."

Subsequently suspicion fell on Roger Hollis, then head of MI5's F Division and responsible for the surveillance of Soviet agents. In the late 1920s Hollis had worked as a journalist in Shanghai and may have met Sonya at this early stage in their careers. He was later to become director-general of MI5. It has never been conclusively demonstrated that Hollis was a Soviet agent.

In 1969 Sonya received her second Order of the Red Banner. She lived long enough to see the Berlin Wall come down, a small white-haired woman with a prominent nose, peering intently through heavy spectacles. In an interview shortly before her death, she fondly remembered England and English friends but had no regrets about her fight against fascism and few reservations about Stalinism. Her pen-name was Werner and in her autobiography she observed, "I had not worked those 20 years with Stalin in mind. We wanted to help the people of the Soviet Union in their efforts to prevent war, and when war broke out against German fascism, to win it." She dismissed German reunification, referring to it as an "annexation." She was one of the last of the generation who had dedicated their lives to Communism in the belief that they were striving for a more just and humane society.

Reference: Ruth Werner, *Sonya's Report: The Fascinating Autobiography of One of Russia's Most Remarkable Secret Agents,* 1991.

WITHERINGTON, PEARL
"Marie" and "Pauline," British SOE Agent, b. 1914

Witherington was born in Paris, the eldest of four daughters of an expatriate British couple. In 1940, during the Battle of France, she was working as a shorthand typist in the British embassy. In 1941 she made her way to England, where she found a job in the Air Ministry before joining the **Special Operations Executive** (SOE, see p. 366).

Code-named "Marie," but subsequently known to the French as "Pauline," Witherington was parachuted into occupied France on September 22, 1943. There was no one to meet her, and she spent the night on top of twenty tons of ammunition disguised as a haystack. Witherington subsequently joined the Stationer network, run by Maurice Southgate and covering a substantial part of central France, and for the next eight months worked as his courier.

In April 1944, Stationer brought the Dunlop tire factory at Montluçon to a halt with two pounds of well-placed explosive. Shortly afterward Southgate was captured and Stationer split into two new circuits, Wrestler and Shipwright, which were run respectively by Witherington and Southgate's principal wireless operator.

As the head of Wrestler, Witherington now controlled a private army of two thousand Resistance fighters in the Valençay-Issoudun-Châteauroux triangle of France. One of their primary achievements was to ensure that the main railway line from Paris to Bordeaux was almost permanently cut in the run-up to D-Day. The Germans were so infuriated by Witherington's activities that they placed a bounty of a million francs on her head. Later she admitted to being terrified on occasion but insisted that the worst part of her time with SOE was grueling journeys in unheated trains during the harsh winter of 1943–44. In October 1944, Witherington married a Resistance colleague, Henri Cornioley.

At the end of the war Witherington was recommended for the Military Cross but was offered only a civilian MBE, as women were not eligible for the former decoration. She returned the MBE with the observation that during the war she had done nothing civil, shaming the authorities into giving her a military MBE. It took a little longer for Witherington to receive her parachute wings, but her persistence paid off. She finally received them in the spring of 2006 at the age of ninety-two.

Reference: Pearl Witherington, with Herve Laroque, *Pauline,* 1997.

AFTERWORD

We conclude our work on women and war with a sense of infinite regret. Pressure of space meant that we have not been able to do justice to all the women who have suffered, fought, and died in the world's endless conflicts: Nothing but a work of far vaster scope could contain all the names we wanted to include. For every individual or group who has made their way into these pages, there are countless others with an equal right to be present and to receive the honor that is their due.

We also wish to pay tribute to the female victims of war. Their contribution to its annals has not been merely to perish, often in unimaginable horror or pain, and to end their lives in some forgotten grave. We are conscious that there is much more to be said on this subject, but that must be for another book.

We acknowledge, too, the constant support and interest that this project has aroused from colleagues and contacts, friends and family, fighting men and women, and the veterans of former wars. In particular, the editorial team at Crown Publishing has had faith in the book from the start. We thank you all, and hope the result is in some way worthy of you and of our extraordinary subjects.

Despite all our efforts and those of our tireless editors, this book must contain omissions and errors that we would be only too pleased to correct. Any communication will be gratefully received at reader@rosalind.net, and we thank readers in advance for their participation.

We hope to have stirred readers' interest in these outstanding women, and the citations at the end of each entry indicate our suggestions for further reading on these varied topics.

Finally we are left to contemplate the futility and the grandeur, the unthinkable horror, and the inevitability, of war itself. As long as war remains a fact of life, may women take their part in it, for better and for worse. A growing female participation both in the worlds' armies and in the governments that send their fighting forces to war, may be our only hope of reducing, if not ending, the calamitous conflicts that mark the history of the human race.

—Rosalind Miles and Robin Cross

INDEX